DIVERSION AND DECEPTION

DIVERSION AND DECEPTION

DUDLEY CLARKE'S "A" FORCE AND ALLIED OPERATIONS IN WORLD WAR II

Whitney T. Bendeck

UNIVERSITY OF OKLAHOMA PRESS : NORMAN

This book is published with the generous assistance of the McCasland Foundation, Duncan, Oklahoma.

Library of Congress Cataloging-in-Publication Data
Names: Bendeck, Whitney T., author.
Title: Diversion and deception : Dudley Clarke's "A" Force and Allied operations in
    World War II / Whitney T. Bendeck.
Other titles: Dudley Clarke's "A" Force and Allied operations in World War II
Description: Norman : University of Oklahoma Press, [2021] | Includes bibliographical
    references and index. | Summary: "Explores how Britain's "A" Force, under the
    leadership of Dudley Clarke, orchestrated both strategic and tactical deception plans
    to create notional threats across the southern perimeter of Europe, with the chief
    objective of keeping the Germans pinned down across the Mediterranean during
    World War II"—Provided by publisher.
Identifiers: LCCN 2020032974 | ISBN 978-0-8061-6846-3 (hardcover)
Subjects: LCSH: Allied Forces. Headquarters. "A" Force—History. | World War,
    1939–1945—Deception. | Deception (Military science)—History—20th century. |
    World War, 1939–1945—Military intelligence—Great Britain. | World War,
    1939–1945—Campaigns—Mediterranean Region. | Operation Overlord. |
    Operation Bodyguard. | Clarke, Dudley, 1899–1974.
Classification: LCC D810.S7 B386 2021 | DDC 940.54/8641—dc23
LC record available at https://lccn.loc.gov/2020032974

The paper in this book meets the guidelines for permanence and durability of the Committee on Production Guidelines for Book Longevity of the Council on Library Resources, Inc. ∞

CONTENTS

PREFACE

In 2019, many Western nations commemorated the seventy-fifth anniversary of D-day. There was considerable media coverage of the event, and along with a look back at the military campaign and the men who served, there was also coverage focused on the use of deception. What was missing from most of the stories on Plan Bodyguard, the deception devised to cover Operation Overlord, was a discussion of events in the Mediterranean theater of operations. Bodyguard consisted of multiple plans: Fortitude North, Fortitude South, Graffham and Royal Flush (diplomatic deceptions targeting the neutral countries), and Zeppelin. Plan Zeppelin could be broken down further as it contained two large subsidiary campaigns—Plans Vendetta and Turpitude. While Fortitude South, the effort to play up the threat to the Pas de Calais and divert Adolf Hitler's attention away from Normandy, is the best known of the deception plans, Zeppelin was the largest and most complex of the Bodyguard plans. It was also a resounding success. Zeppelin, in conjunction with the Mediterranean Strategy—which served as a diversion to keep the Germans engaged across their entire southern flank and as far away from northwestern France as possible—succeeded in pinning down sixty German divisions from southern France to the Balkans in time for D-day. In the absence of diversion and deception in the Mediterranean, to include the genuine campaign in Italy, most of those sixty divisions would have been divided between the eastern and western fronts.

This book tells the story of the UK's only military deception organization tasked with carrying out both strategic and tactical deception in World War II. Formed in 1941, it developed the strategic and tactical deception model used by the Western Allies throughout the war, and was responsible for Plan Zeppelin—the largest of the D-day deception campaigns. That organization was "A" Force.

ACKNOWLEDGMENTS

Writing a book is never truly a one-person feat. While there may be a single author, there is a whole team of people who deserve credit for the final product.

I must begin by thanking my parents, Del and Alice Talley. My parents have always been my greatest supporters. They have been a constant source of encouragement, and both have generously sacrificed so much of their own time and resources to see me succeed. When I headed to London to begin this project, I had a monumental task before me and limited time to accomplish it. My original intent was to go alone, but one evening my mom called to tell me that she was going with me to help. If only she knew what she was getting herself into! My poor mother spent an entire week in London doing nothing but taking photographs of documents—more than two thousand of them. Her fingerprints (and literally photographs of her index finger) are all over this project. I was in over my head and could not have done this without her. I am forever grateful.

Being a woman in academia, and at the same time a full-time wife and mother, has its challenges. For that, I am so thankful for my husband, Oscar, who has been a steady source of support. Without his assistance and willingness to make sacrifices, I could never have even dreamed of taking on this project.

I also want to thank Lee Metcalf from Florida State University for her continued support throughout this process, and express my deep appreciation for the research travel grant provided by the International Affairs' General Development Fund (FSU). Finally, I offer a special thanks to M. Sheddan, R. Berry, Zach Reddick, and so many others – friends, family, and colleagues – who offered their assistance, support, and/or encouragement.

Writing a book is one thing; getting it published is another altogether. I had the privilege of working with two amazing acquisition editors, Adam Kane and Kent Calder. There is also a team of professionals at the University of Oklahoma Press, or affiliated with the Press, who have been instrumental in putting this work into print. Those individuals include Amy Hernandez (marketing), Stephanie Evans (project editor), Robert Fullilove (copy editor), Erin Greb (cartographer), and so many others. I must also thank my dear friend and colleague, Christopher Griffin (indexer), for his contribution to the final product.

I am likewise grateful for the two anonymous reviewers who offered excellent feedback and insight after reviewing my manuscript. I appreciate the time and effort that went into their reviews, as well as the very constructive and thorough comments they provided.

Last but not least, I must also mention the incredibly helpful and professional staff at both the British National Archives (Kew, UK) and the Imperial War Museum (London). Conducting research at both organizations was, as always, a pleasure.

TERMS AND ACRONYMS

AA	antiaircraft
AAI	Allied Armies in Italy
Abwehr	German military intelligence organization
AFHQ	Allied Force Headquarters
BEF	British Expeditionary Force
B1A	Double-Cross subsection of MI5
CBI	China-Burma-India theater of operations
CCS	Combined Chiefs of Staff
CIGS	Chief of the Imperial General Staff
COS	Chiefs of Staff (UK)
COSSAC	Chief of Staff to the Supreme Allied Commander
EAM	National Liberation Front (Greece)
G(CAM)	Camouflage Organization under Allied Headquarters
GHQ	General Headquarters
GIS	German Intelligence Service

ISSB	Inter-Services Security Board
JCS	Joint Chiefs of Staff (US)
JSC	Joint Security Control (US)
LCS	London Controlling Section
LCT	landing craft, tank
LST	landing ship, tank
L of C	lines of communication
MAAF	Mediterranean Allied Air Forces
MI5	British Security Service
MI6	British Secret Intelligence Service
MI9	Escape and Evasion
OKW	Oberkommando der Wehrmacht (German High Command)
Ops B	SHAEF deception organization
OSINT	open source intelligence
OSS	Office of Strategic Services (US)
PR	photographic reconnaissance
PWB	Psychological Warfare Board
RTR	Royal Tank Regiment
SACMED	Supreme Allied Commander, Mediterranean
SAEC	South African Engineering Corps
SAS	Special Air Service
SHAEF	Supreme Headquarters Allied Expeditionary Force
SIME	Security Intelligence Middle East
SOE	Special Operations Executive
Tac HQ	Tactical Headquarters "A" Force
USAAF	United States Army Air Force
USSR	Union of Soviet Socialist Republics
VCIGS	Vice Chief of the Imperial General Staff
XX	Double Cross, operated by the Twenty Committee
X2	OSS Counter-Espionage Branch

INTRODUCTION

On the morning of June 12, 1944, British officer Major R. B. Booth left Cairo for Ankara, Turkey. After two and a half days of traveling, including an uncomfortable six-hour delay in Aleppo, Booth's train finally entered Turkey. With a half-emptied bottle of brandy sitting on the bedside table, Booth was sleeping in his private compartment when the Turkish customs official and a sleeping-car attendant entered to inspect his luggage. When the customs official asked Booth if he had any money to declare, the drunk, half-asleep, and clearly annoyed British officer handed over his wallet with obvious impatience. In addition to his own money and Syrian currency, Booth happened to be carrying two £5 notes of British administration currency—one for Greece and the other for Bulgaria. The official recorded the money, and Booth signed the declaration form, for which he was provided a duplicate copy for receipt.

The next morning, a clearer-headed Booth frantically sought out the sleeping-car attendant and demanded the original copy of the declaration form. He was informed that the customs official had already exited the train, with the form in his possession. Booth explained, in confidence, that he had made a terrible mistake and that it was imperative that the Germans not learn that British administration currency was "readily available" to the Allies. The attendant reassured Booth that he was pro-British and promised to keep the information to himself.

Given that he had committed an egregious security error, Booth then sought out the British military attaché in Ankara, General Allan Arnold, to explain his mistake. Arnold reprimanded Booth and promptly arranged for his return to Cairo. Arnold then initiated a series of damage-control measures. Among other actions, he contacted the Turkish secretary-general, whom he spoke to as an ally under the condition of "strictest confidence." He urgently requested that any information about the currency be suppressed and that the original monetary declaration form be returned or destroyed. Arnold went one step further to request that London dispatch a military accounts expert to Ankara, and the necessary administrative measures were taken immediately. On June 21, Booth was sent back to Cairo on a flight from Adana.

Major Booth was a camouflage officer of G(CAM), and the entire "Booth affair" was a ruse concocted by Lieutenant-Colonel Michael Crichton of "A" Force, Security Intelligence Middle East (SIME), and General Arnold in Ankara. It was part of Plan Turpitude, a subcomponent of Plan Zeppelin, to convince the Germans that the Allies intended to attack Greece through Turkey. The goal was to reveal to the Germans that advanced planning was underway, evidenced by the fact that the British had already issued special administration currency for Allied personnel to use in Greece and Bulgaria. The British expected the train attendant to sell the information to the Germans, and further hoped that information regarding General Arnold's efforts to suppress the whole affair would be duly leaked to the Germans.[1]

The Booth affair was typical of "A" Force deceptions. It represented one piece of a very large puzzle that the deceptionists planted from many different sources to allow the enemy to put the puzzle together himself. By mid-1944, the deceptionists at "A" Force were highly skilled and accomplished in the art of deception. They had crafted a deception machine responsible for the most elaborate, extensive, and successful deceptions ever seen in warfare. Through its skillful implementation of deception and diversionary tactics, "A" Force played a significant role in the Allied success in World War II.

World War II witnessed the greatest use of deception in the history of warfare. Deception itself, however, was by no means new to warfare. Deception has ancient roots, and it is not difficult to find examples of clever ruses and hoaxes throughout history. The average person has certainly heard of the famous Trojan Horse, and military enthusiasts are well aware of China's ancient strategist Sun Tzu and his bold proclamations on utilizing deception in warfare. Yet, while such examples of military deception abound, it was not until World War II that deception, both strategic and tactical, was practiced on a global scale. A report by the London Controlling Section (LCS), the British organization responsible for developing the Allies' global strategic deception policy, noted that deception had been "practised individually in the past," but was "developed on scientific and all-embracing lines" in World War II.[2]

World War II represented the apex of total war, backed by an advanced military-industrial complex and energetic push for innovation, so it is not surprising that the deception machinery expanded alongside traditional military and modern technological developments. Due to its tremendous contribution to the war effort, deception can therefore be seen as a vital component of total war. At the same time, deception was one of the safest and most cost-effective resources available to the Allied powers. The same report concluded that "of the many diverse methods of warfare pursued to bring about the defeat of Germany, few can have cost less in manpower and money."[3]

For all of the creativity and detailed work dealing with both operations and intelligence that deception entailed, there is one thing it should not be mistaken for: espionage. Espionage is the act of covertly gathering intelligence. The deceptionists were not spies or secret agents of any variety; nor were they saboteurs. Their job was to deceive by creating a false narrative, supported by a steady flow of disinformation and deceptive evidence, to mislead the enemy. The direction of the false narrative could vary quite significantly depending on the needs of the military situation and the specific plans developed to support the military, but the goal was always the same: to induce the enemy to draw the wrong conclusions, thereby encouraging him to make a move—or perhaps fail to make a move—that was ultimately to the Allies' benefit and the enemy's detriment.

Another goal of deception, which was of great importance to Dudley Clarke, the commander of "A" Force, was to reduce the bloodshed of war by shortening battles. Clarke wanted to avoid a repeat of World War I with its horrendous carnage. If deception could aid in achieving surprise, battles could be won more quickly and with fewer casualties on both sides of the battlefield. Reflecting on the work of "A" Force after the war, Clarke wrote that the "secret war was waged rather to conserve than to destroy: the stakes were the lives of the front-line troops."[4] The ability to reduce casualties through deception is still recognized today. Hy Rothstein and Barton

Whaley, in their 2013 work *The Art and Science of Military Deception*, argue that "when properly designed and executed, stratagems reduce the horrific costs of war."[5]

The British were the master practitioners of deception in World War II. They beat their opponents at the game, went to great lengths to train their Allies (namely the Americans), and implemented deception on an unprecedented scale. British deception, however, developed from a position of weakness—it was the result of desperation born of a seemingly hopeless military situation. After Italy declared war on Britain in June 1940, the British found themselves surrounded and grossly outnumbered on the African continent. They faced many threats, but given Britain's reluctance to rearm in the 1930s and its hasty retreat from France in May–June 1940, the British had little by way of supplies or reinforcements to send to the beleaguered front.[6] After the British evacuation from Dunkirk, for example, Prime Minister Winston Churchill declared that the British "had lost the whole equipment of the Army to which the first fruits of our factories had hitherto been given," and everything produced thereafter was needed to defend the British home islands.[7]

The need to maximize the few resources they had was the genesis of organized and systematic British military deception in World War II. General Archibald Wavell, then commander in chief of the Middle East theater, was the first to employ deception on the theater level.[8] It was also Wavell who recognized the opportunity to utilize deception as a valuable weapon of war. At that time, he was "striving, with pitifully inadequate forces, simultaneously to recover a shattered army from Greece and Crete, to conquer the vast territory of Italian East Africa, to invade Vichy-French Syria, defeat the rebel forces of Iraq, and to launch a counter-offensive against the German-Italian Desert Armies on the Egyptian border."[9] In order to make optimal use of deception, Wavell requested the transfer of Dudley Clarke from London to the Middle East theater to assist in that effort. Wavell saw in Clarke an "original, unorthodox outlook on soldiering."[10] Well after the war, Wavell affirmed that he had made the right decision.[11] His assessment of Clarke had been quite accurate.

Dudley Clarke described his "A" Force organization as unique to the time and theater in which it developed. In other words, outside of the World War II setting, "A" Force may not represent a model that could—or should—be replicated in its entirety, as it developed under very unique circumstances and was shaped by its environment and the specific leadership it was under. Subsequent deception organizations would need to develop their own character and design based on their specific circumstances and needs, not necessarily those faced by "A" Force during World War II. Nonetheless, Clarke identified several universal components necessary for successful deception.

Deceptionists must correctly identify their target. In the case of deception, the target is always the enemy's intelligence staff (and top leadership). Using the intended target as the standard, Clarke clearly distinguished deception from psychological warfare. Psychological warfare seeks to influence a much larger audience, to include the enemy population, but Clarke argued that psychological warfare is unlikely to have a significant effect on the enemy's general staff. If the deceptionists can influence the head of the enemy's intelligence apparatus, they have succeeded in their objective. Clarke wrote: "If they can influence him to accept as true the evidence they have manufactured for his benefit, then they have accomplished their entire aim, since it is only through the Head of the Intelligence that any enemy commander receives the impression of his opponent upon which he has to base his plan of operation."[12] Thus, deceptionists must correctly identify their target audience, and that audience must be very small and have the ability to directly impact operational plans.

Knowing and understanding the enemy is the next component of successful deception, regardless of the structure of the individual deception organization. Clarke asserted that the deceptionists need to have a clear understanding of their enemy's national characteristics and language. But beyond that, they need to know the individuals they are seeking to deceive. They must understand their thought process, the methods and procedures that they use, and their strengths and weaknesses. Clarke once noted that he understood the Germans and their thought process well, which made it easy for him to deceive them; he could put himself in the enemy's place and think like the enemy.[13] He instinctively knew how far he could go, what the enemy was likely to accept, or outright reject.

Also crucial to success is recruiting the right individuals for the role of deceiver. As Clarke viewed it, deception is an art, not a science. Thus, the deceiver takes on the role of an artist. Clarke recognized that this idea was a challenge for many in traditional military circles who held the common view that "average educated" soldiers can be taught the "art of war" regardless of their enthusiasm or aptitude for it. In contrast, deception required a very specific type of mind—one that thinks creatively and is willing to search for new or unorthodox solutions. Clarke recounted the example of two British Army intelligence officers who were appointed to "A" Force, but who utterly failed to comprehend the art of deception. He praised them as exceptional operational officers, but noted that they simply were not cut out for deception and could not be taught to think as a deception officer must think. In his words, they lacked the "sheer ability to create, to make something out of nothing, to conceive their own original notion and then to clothe it with realities until eventually it would appear as a living fact." Clarke concluded that the "art of creation" was a quality the deceptionist must possess. Finally, he warned that expecting an officer who did not possess those creative qualities to produce successful deceptions would "lead to risks beyond that of mere failure."[14]

The last component Clarke identified pertained to the object of deception. Every deception plan had to have a well-defined object. Moreover, the object of deception should always be designed to make the enemy act, as opposed to think, in a certain way. Clarke stated that "it matters nothing what the enemy THINKS, it is only what he DOES that can affect the battle." Commanders may be tempted to want the enemy to think in a given way, but thinking that way does not guarantee the desired action. Therefore, deception should always be designed to induce a specific behavior. It is the general's job to properly relay to the deception commander what he wants the enemy to do. It is the deception controlling officer's job to devise a deception that produces the desired behavior. Once the commander has relayed that information, he should step back and allow the deceptionists to do their job without interference. After all, the deceptionists are the ones trained in the art of deception and have the most experience deceiving the enemy.[15] It was a system that worked exceptionally well for "A" Force in the Middle East and Mediterranean theaters.

As should be obvious from the preceding discussion, deception is complicated and extraordinarily detailed. When thinking of deception, it is natural to conjure up colorful images of fanciful ruses, glorious escapades, double agents, inflatable tanks, and exciting stories of trickery and intrigue. While those images may have a basis in reality, the true experience of World War II deception was not so glamorous or Hollywood-ready as one might expect. Strategic deception, which is designed to deceive the enemy's intelligence and high command, and tactical deception, used to impact the battlefield directly by influencing the enemy commanders, was painstaking and meticulous work. As the saying alludes, the devil is in the details. The deceptionists had to be exceedingly thorough and always follow through on their plans. A notional division, for example, could not be created and then simply forgotten. That division must be continually represented, otherwise it was likely to disappear from the enemy's assessment of the Allied order of battle and, of greater concern, the enemy may suspect that he had been misled. Clarke referred to his two extensive order of battle deception plans, Cascade and Wantage, as the "least spectacular of all the "A" Force plans," but by far the most successful and important of its plans. He added that "for three and a half years they had formed the firm foundation upon which had been built every one of the major Strategic Deceptions."[16] Glamorous they were not, but essential and successful they most certainly were.

In a similar vein of paying attention to detail and providing consistency, dummy vehicles and camouflage efforts had to be meticulously maintained, as well as accompanied by ever vigilant security measures. The deception "story" relayed to the enemy had to be plausible and come from multiple and varied sources. Moreover, that material had to be carefully relayed and layered over a period of weeks and sometimes even months. The enemy had to be able to verify the information he received, or at the very least be unable to disprove it. Deception is like a puzzle with many pieces for the enemy to put together himself. Yet if the enemy discovers one piece to be a fake, the entire puzzle may be compromised. In a real situation, that could mean that sources, secret channels, or other assets could be completely lost, with potentially devastating results. Thus, deceptionists had to be methodical and pay attention to every minute detail as if the entire deception campaign rested on the success of that one tiny element. It was not fanciful work, but, done right, it was successful.

That is not to say that the men at "A" Force, or other deception bodies, never had fun or managed to find distractions. After reading through the thousands of pages found within the "A" Force files, it is easy to get a feel for Clarke and his personality. His statements occasionally betray his obvious amusement and sometimes a mischievous sense of humor. In July 1941, for example, "A" Force arranged for the transport of a regiment of dummy tanks by train through Palestine. After one of the tanks blew right off its truck during transport, Clarke described the situation as "a distressing struggle for Sense of Security over Sense of Humour."[17] He was able to see the humor in mishaps of the sort, assuming no harm was done. The operation of secret channels and double agents provides another example of taking a jocular approach to otherwise serious work. The messages sent through "A" Force's controlled channels had to be carefully thought out and perfectly timed, but the controllers still found ways to have fun with their task. An April 1943 report on the health of some of the Middle East agents began in good-humored form:

> This is the epidemic season and we have had the usual run of childish ailments.
>
> CHEESE had a bad attack of neurasthenia and both he and QUICKSILVER have suffered from inflammation of the money problem.
>
> QUACK has passed away and gone to fields anew and CAPRICORN is slightly moribund.
>
> PESSIMIST is very healthy but we are afraid he may catch the money trouble any minute.[18]

As can be discerned, the many ailments plaguing the agents were designed to extract money from the Germans. While that was in reality a complicated and rather delicate business, it is clear that the controllers enjoyed the game.

There were, for better or worse, distractions as well. The more disruptive distractions seemed to stem mostly from a conflict of personalities. In February 1943, Lieutenant-Colonel David Strangeways formed a new tactical deception headquarters, Tac HQ "A" Force, in Algiers under Allied Force Headquarters (AFHQ). Nöel Wild, then second in command at "A" Force, took a distinct disliking to Strangeways and was prone to write letters to Clarke to complain and express concerns that Strangeways was overstepping his duties. While Wild was clearly the chief culprit of the drama, he was quick to recruit support. He managed to enlist Michael Crichton, the head of "A" Force's Advanced Headquarters, as an accomplice and repeatedly reassured Clarke that Crichton agreed with him in his negative portrayal of Strangeways. Clarke consistently defended Strangeways and did an admirable job of smoothing things over between his deception officers.[19]

Strangeways had his own struggles. He found it occasionally arduous to work with the Americans due to what he saw as an onerous system of command. While he spoke highly of the American deception officers that he trained and worked with on a regular basis, he found the American command structure to be "impossible." He lamented that nothing ever got done because every plan ultimately had to move up the chain of command, going through the executive officer who served as a middleman, wasting precious time. He came to the conclusion that the US military did not trust its officers, a situation he deemed "ridiculous."[20] Certainly the American and British militaries functioned differently, and it was not always easy to reconcile their methods.

Despite any drama or distractions, "A" Force was without question the most extensive, experienced, and successful of the British deception organizations. It possessed a unique degree of independence and high level of trust among Allied commanders. Yet, it had to earn that trust. "A" Force carefully developed its craft over years of fighting against the German and Italian armies in North Africa. By the time of the Second Battle of El Alamein in October 1942, Clarke described "A" Force as a "well-oiled machine."[21] Its ability to deceive the enemy against seemingly insurmountable odds bought it the trust and support of commanders who began to see deception as a crucial asset to all military planning. The London Controlling Section, the body responsible for developing global strategic deception policy and plans, recognized the officers of "A" Force as the experts in military deception. It drew heavily on the experience and knowledge of Clarke and his team at "A"

Force on a regular basis. When the deception planning shifted to provide cover for Operation Overlord (D-day), the LCS turned specifically to "A" Force to draw on its expertise and recruit manpower. There was, in fact, a notable exodus of "A" Force deception officers from the Mediterranean in the months leading up to D-day. Those officers were crucial in implementing the strategic deception (Plan Bodyguard) for D-day, as well as key players in the tactical deception efforts to assist D-day and the subsequent drive to Berlin. Thus, to truly understand the depths of British deception in World War II, one cannot ignore "A" Force.

Diversion and Deception looks at the detailed work of the "A" Force organization in the Mediterranean from 1943 to the end of the war. It picks up where my previous book, *"A" Force: The Origins of British Deception during the Second World War*, left off. *"A" Force* was focused on the early years of deception and primarily covered the war in North Africa. This current project begins as the North African campaign drew to a close and Allied leaders were challenged with deciding how best to capitalize on their success. The "A" Force organization continued to play a direct role in deception, but over time its focus did change. As the war progressed and the Allies began planning for the Normandy invasion, "A" Force was tasked with diverting the Germans' attention to the Mediterranean. "A" Force set out to manufacture threats from the Balkans to southern France, as well as in Italy where genuine operations were underway, in order to convince the enemy to disperse his manpower and resources as far away from the Normandy landing beaches as possible.

As was also the case with my previous work, I bring the military and deception histories together to tell a more complete story than typically found in many published works. The military histories have a tendency to either neglect, or quickly gloss over, the deception efforts that accompanied the military campaigns they describe in such great detail. Deception histories often focus on the deceptions themselves, without providing sufficient background and explanation of the military situation. Combining the two provides context for the deceptions, as well as adds a deeper layer of knowledge regarding the actual military operations, especially in the planning stage. Furthermore, most deception histories of World War II tend to focus on Plan Bodyguard—the elaborate deception coordinated in London to provide cover for the Normandy landings—along with its well-known subplan known as Fortitude, and/or intriguing stories of the double agents operating under the elaborate Double-Cross (XX) system. This work is exclusively focused on the "A" Force organization and will highlight its work in the Mediterranean theater, to include the extensive deception it carried out there as a vital component of

Bodyguard (Plan Zeppelin), and its success. The more narrow focus of this work allows for a deeper exploration of the "A" Force organization—its structure and command, its operations and procedures, its methods, its successes and failures, and the undeniable contribution it made to the Allies' victory in World War II.

Additionally, a point this work seeks to convey is the importance of the Mediterranean as a theater of operations in World War II, as well as its place in Allied grand strategy and connection to the western front. There are some who dismiss the Mediterranean theater as a needless sideshow or an unimportant theater in the overall context of the war. Neither viewpoint is accurate. While one can certainly argue that there were strategic miscalculations and tactical errors in the Allies' approach to Mediterranean operations, and there is little doubt that the Allies misjudged Germany's willingness to fight in Italy—especially with regard to its defense of the southern portion of the peninsula—that does not diminish the overall strategic importance of the Mediterranean to the Allied cause. The war in the Mediterranean kept the threat level to the Germans' southern flank alive. That threat necessitated that the Germans spread themselves thin in order to actively defend every vulnerable point of "Fortress Europe." When Operation Overlord was launched on June 6, 1944, the Germans had 25 divisions tied down fighting the Allies in Italy. Moreover, they had another 25 divisions divided between Greece, the Balkans, and the Dodecanese ready to defend against an invasion that the Allies never intended to launch, as well as an additional 10 divisions positioned to defend southern France.[22] If the Allies had not maintained the Mediterranean as an active theater and created notional threats across the Germans' southern flank, those 60 divisions would have been freed to fight on the eastern front or defend northwestern France. All one has to do is imagine Normandy reinforced by even one-fourth of those divisions to grasp the overwhelming importance that the Mediterranean held as a diversionary theater. Thus, the war in Italy may have been clumsy and considerably more difficult than the Allies anticipated, but it most certainly did its part, along with the rest of the Mediterranean, to tie down hundreds of thousands of enemy forces far away from the northwestern shores of France.

Finally, for those who may argue that operations in the Mediterranean theater delayed the launch of Operation Overlord, the facts simply do not support that assertion. The American leadership, represented most vocally by Gen. George C. Marshall, adamantly desired to launch the cross-Channel invasion as early as 1942. However, multiple leadership conferences made clear that the Allies could not feasibly mobilize the proper level of manpower, landing craft, and resources necessary to mount a successful amphibious assault until 1944. The Allies ultimately made the best use of the interim time period between the North African campaign and D-day by keeping the Germans actively engaged defending the southern expanse of Fortress Europe and maintaining a heightened threat level—through genuine and notional threats—across the Mediterranean. One of the more intriguing aspects of that success was that it was accomplished using both real and entirely fake armies!

For the sake of transparency, I reiterate that this work is designed to present the history of "A" Force and does so through the organization's perspective of events. To that end, I have made the conscious decision to rely heavily on the "A" Force files to present this history. Where possible, I have corroborated the information found within those files in primary and secondary sources. However, because deception was highly secretive and closely guarded using extensive security measures, it is not always possible to find confirmation of its activities in contemporary primary sources, or even later secondary sources. The full story of Allied deception was not revealed until the latter part of the twentieth century and into the twenty-first century. Beyond that, most traditional military histories are not focused on deception, so those histories cannot always be used for confirmation of specific deception policies and practices. As for the Germans, they were not even aware that they had been deceived in such a systematic and organized fashion until many decades after World War II.

As a final point of note, I have chosen to use the language and terminology used by Dudley Clarke and the deceptionists of the day in order to most accurately represent their activities and viewpoints. The same goes for names of organizations. On many occasions the "A" Force files referenced the German Intelligence Service (GIS), for example. This might very well mean the Abwehr, but unless the Abwehr was identified by name, I have provided the titles that "A" Force used.

Chapter 1 begins with a very brief discussion of Dudley Clarke himself. Because he created "A" Force and was the man behind both the organization and its many successes, it is helpful to gain a better sense of the man himself. It follows with a discussion of the design and construction of "A" Force.

Chapter 2 addresses the dilemma the Allies faced after the North African campaign came to an end in May 1943. It was no longer just the British making the decisions, as the Americans had joined them in the war against Germany. Developing a mutual Anglo-American strategy proved quite challenging, but the immediate result was the Mediterranean Strategy. On the deception front, the Allies adopted a strategic deception policy for 1943, and "A" Force expanded and entered a new stage as the war broadened.

Chapter 3 is focused almost exclusively on Plan Barclay, the deception campaign aimed at drawing German attention away from Sicily in the lead-up to Operation Husky. It details the challenges faced in developing and implementing a deception plan to mislead the enemy when Sicily was the most obvious and logical target.

In chapter 4, the focus in on the campaign in Sicily, the decision to follow that campaign with an invasion of the Italian Peninsula, the accompanying deception campaigns, and the obstacles faced once in Italy. The Allies achieved one of their key objectives in that Italy surrendered, but the war in Italy did not go in any way according to plan. The Allies hoped for a quick advance to Rome, but those hopes were dashed after the Germans decided to stand firm and defend southern Italy.

Chapter 5 opens with a discussion of the Allied conferences at the end of 1943 that cemented Allied strategy for 1944. The decision to launch Operation Overlord and cover it with Plan Bodyguard developed out of those conferences. The chapter concludes with a review of the Allied campaign in Italy, the attempt to break the Gustav Line, the landing at Anzio, and the strategic and tactical deceptions that accompanied those efforts.

In chapter 6, the focus is on Plan Zeppelin, the Mediterranean component of Plan Bodyguard, covering the first two stages of the plan that ran from January until April. In order for Zeppelin to succeed and the Mediterranean to achieve its purpose as a diversionary theater, those stages had to be successful.

Chapter 7 explores the last two stages of Zeppelin, with particular emphasis on two major subsidiary plans: Plan Vendetta, the notional threat to southern France; and Plan Turpitude, the threat to the Balkans by way of Turkey. This chapter also discusses Plan Copperhead, the successful effort to create a double for General Bernard Law Montgomery, and Operation Diadem, the Allies' spring offensive to break the Gustav Line and capture Rome before D-day.

The last chapter begins by detailing Plan Ferdinand, the deception plan to cover the genuine invasion of southern France—Operation Dragoon. Next, it looks at the conclusion of the Italian campaign and the supporting deception efforts. Finally, it relates the various stages that "A" Force went through as it began to shut down.

1 DUDLEY CLARKE, "A" FORCE, AND THE DEVELOPMENT OF ALLIED MILITARY DECEPTION

Dudley Clarke is widely known as the master of deception. For those who were either involved in deception, or otherwise aware of its practice during World War II, Clarke's skills were undisputed. Moreover, his successes time again proved that deception was a powerful "secret weapon." "A" Force met with extraordinary success and managed to achieve surprise in some of the most impossible situations, which convinced its detractors of its worth. This book tells the story of "A" Force, but it must start with a short discussion of Dudley Clarke because it is impossible to separate the two. While "A" Force was a "wholly British product," it was Clarke's creation and every aspect of it bore his signature.[1] He served as its commander, or controlling officer, from its inception in early 1941 until its end, and was intimately involved in all aspects of the organization. Thus, it is appropriate to begin with a brief discussion of the man behind the "A" Force organization.

Dudley Clarke.
© Imperial War
Museum (Art.IWM
ART LD 5401).

Clarke was an interesting man, and some might even call him unusual and rather eccentric. He was highly intelligent, but his mind was an enigma to most. In complete contrast to his above average intelligence and eccentric nature, in appearance he was strikingly plain. That, however, worked to his advantage because he never stood out. Given his position, the ability to blend in and not attract attention was a tremendous asset. David Mure, who headed the "A" Force outstation in Beirut and knew Clarke as well as anyone could, described him as "inscrutable" and likened his appearance to "somebody's butler." He recalled: "Beneath his bland rather old world exterior it was impossible to guess what he was thinking, and what he said nearly always came as a surprise. He was certainly the most unusual Intelligence officer of his time, very likely of all time. His mind worked quite differently from anyone else's and far quicker; he looked at the world through the eyes of his opponents."[2] Clarke was certainly unconventional, as was his military career. The journey that brought him to develop "A" Force revealed both his intelligence and his ingenuity, but also displayed a tendency to act outside of traditional military custom.

Clarke was born on April 27, 1899, in Johannesburg, South Africa, during the time of the Boer Wars. His father was working in South Africa at the time and had even played a peripheral role in the ill-fated Jameson Raid of 1896, when the British tried to take over the Transvaal from the Boers. In 1916, at seventeen years of age, Clarke joined the Royal Artillery. He was eager to participate in World War I, but was prevented from doing so due to his age. Not to be deterred, he joined the Royal Flying Corps and served as a pilot in Egypt in 1918. After the war he returned to the Royal Artillery. In the interwar years, he served with the Royal Artillery in Mesopotamia from 1919 to 1920, observed a rebellion against the Spanish in Morocco in 1925 while working as a correspondent for the *Morning Post*, served with the Transjordan Frontier Force from 1930 to 1932, attended the Staff College at Camberley from 1933 to 1934, was posted to Aden in 1935, and finally served in Palestine during the Arab Revolt from 1936 to 1938.[3] It was in the mandate where his superiors took note of his unique and rather unconventional qualities.

Clarke first served under General Sir John Dill in Palestine. He apparently made a positive impression, because General Dill, who later became the Chief of the Imperial General Staff (CIGS), appointed Clarke to serve as one of his military assistants.[4] General Archibald Wavell succeeded Dill in Palestine, and Clarke made a favorable impression on him as well. In the introduction to Clarke's autobiography, *Seven Assignments*, Wavell wrote: "When I commanded in Palestine in 1937–38, I had on my staff two officers in whom I recognised an original, unorthodox outlook on soldiering; and I pigeon-holed their names in my mind for use should I ever command an army in war. One was Orde Wingate, the second was Dudley Clarke." In 1940, Wavell specifically requested Clarke's transfer to Cairo to assist him with special duties—deception. Upon reflection, Wavell noted: "I was right in judging that this was work for which Dudley Clarke's originality, ingenuity, and somewhat impish sense of humour qualified him admirably."[5]

After Palestine, Clarke returned to London, where he worked at the War Office as a deputy assistant military secretary. He was serving in that position when World War II broke out, and was promoted to lieutenant colonel. The onset of war marked the beginning of Clarke's eight wartime assignments. His first assignment took him to Northeast Africa to scout a land supply route from Kenya to Egypt that the British could use in the event that Italy declared war on Britain and closed off the sea routes. For his second and third assignments, from April to May 1940, he served in Norway as a liaison officer. His fourth assignment came at the end of May as the Germans quickly routed the French and the British Expeditionary Force (BEF) in France with their blitzkrieg offensive. Clarke attempted to organize the reinforcement of the beleaguered British 30th Infantry Brigade trapped at Calais, but the German drive through France was too swift and the brigade ultimately surrendered.[6]

While Clarke was still preoccupied with the Calais operation, he was summoned for his fifth assignment. For that, Clarke was sent on a secret mission over a weekend, in full disguise, to "a neutral country" to work out plans in case the Germans attempted a further expansion. The entire experience was shrouded in mystery and felt completely surreal to Clarke. When he returned to London from his mysterious "dreamlike" adventure, he learned that General Dill had become the new CIGS, and Clarke was appointed to serve as his military assistant. That was his sixth assignment, and it came when the British and French forces were evacuating from Dunkirk.[7]

Clarke's seventh assignment, while he was working under Dill, took place between June and December 1940. It was one of his more notable accomplishments—the formation of the British Commandos. The British Army was demoralized after Dunkirk, and Dill sought a way to improve morale and revive its offensive spirit. Clarke began thinking of a solution and looked back upon history for inspiration. In "The Birth of the Commandos," Clarke described how he naturally thought of the Boers in South Africa, given that he spent his first years of life there at a time of conflict, and he grew up hearing stories of the Boer's guerrilla tactics. He wrote:

> I remembered how their main Army had been broken and scattered at the end of 1900 by Roberts and Kitchener. It must have seemed to them then that the Boers could do nothing more than make an unconditional surrender.
>
> But they didn't. Instead they collected small bands of mobile horsemen, who could do without cumbrous supply columns, and who were prepared to win their equipment and their arms from the enemy. These were the Boer Commandos, and with them Smuts and his colleagues had managed to fight on for two more years against a highly organized army some ten times their own strength.
>
> Well, if the Boers could do this, why shouldn't the British Army follow their example against the Germans? Why shouldn't we have British Commandos to work the same mosquito tactics—"Hit sharp and quick—then run to fight another day"?

To replicate the Boer Commandos, the British needed speed and mobility. Britain's strength was traditionally not on land with horses, but at sea. Thus, Clarke envisioned the British Commandos as an amphibious strike force. Dill embraced Clarke's idea and the plan moved forward.[8]

In spite of Dill's support, there were obstacles that had to be overcome. In an ironic twist, the War Office took issue with their name—the "Commandos"—arguing that it was "scarcely an appropriate term to appear in the formal nomenclature of the Ministry." It took Dill throwing his support behind Clarke for the name to be accepted. But that was only the beginning of Clarke's problems. Clarke was unconventional and did not think like his peers. That is what Dill and Wavell liked about him, but it caused problems with the traditionally minded leadership. If Clarke had his way, the Commandos were not going to be a conventional force. Clarke mentioned that Wavell had once described his ideal infantryman as a "mixture of cat-burglar, poacher and gunman." For the Commandos, Clarke envisioned "a dash of the Elizabethan pirate, the Chicago gangster and the Frontier tribesman, allied to a professional efficiency and standard of discipline of the best Regular soldier." They needed to be independent, free-thinking, and capable of immense flexibility, something he thought would be a challenge for traditional soldiers taught to conform to an established order.[9]

Not surprisingly, the Commandos' training was also highly unconventional. They were encouraged to avoid following a routine and had to fend for themselves for food, transportation, and housing, as that would be their reality in the field. Clarke explained his logic with this scenario: One evening the Commandos in Southampton could be told to meet in Dover the next morning. The men would find their own transportation, and the only thing that was important was that they arrive at their designated location. Clarke further pointed out that his method would result in "greater secrecy than if it were to arrive with a blare of trumpets in a troop-train or a convoy of army lorries."[10]

Even though the effort took considerable convincing and met a fair amount of pushback from traditional circles, Dill and Clarke finally received permission to begin recruiting. The first Commando, No. 11 Commando, began its training and trial runs. The first Commando raid took place on June 24, 1940. Clarke requested permission to participate. He was allowed to go on one of the boats, but not permitted to accompany the Commando on land. No. 11 Commando set out for the French coast in four boats. While all four teams went ashore, only one group engaged the enemy, resulting in the death of two Germans. Nonetheless, the raid was viewed as a success in that it demonstrated the fighting spirit of the British.[11] Clarke was pleased and stated that "their birth was so secret that the first time the enemy even knew of their existence was when an unseen hand struck down two of

Hitler's sentries on a still night." He took pleasure in knowing that from that night forward, the Germans could never feel safe during their night patrols because the "men with blackened faces, who made no sound on their approach and who struck like lightening" could be lurking around any corner.[12]

In the months that followed, Clarke devoted himself to the Commandos' development and found himself repeatedly having to negotiate with the War Office to maintain its support of the unconventional force. He fully intended to continue his work with the Commandos, but that all changed when Wavell, then commander in chief of the Middle East, sent a letter to London requesting that Clarke join him immediately in Cairo for "special duties." On December 18, 1940, Clarke, promoted to colonel, arrived in Cairo to begin his eighth assignment; he noted that his last assignment was the "longest and infinitely the most gratifying assignment of them all."[13]

Dudley Clarke's task with his eighth assignment was to develop and implement deception. He was, perhaps, an interesting choice for the position. He had never served on an intelligence staff and had no experience with military deception. He admitted that he found himself suddenly in Cairo in December 1940 unsure of where to start, so he consulted military manuals on deception, though he found little on the subject.[14] Fortunately, Clarke was a quick learner and, as hindsight shows, a natural fit for the task. So even though Clarke's previous military experience did not specifically prepare him for deception, his intelligence, creativity, and tendency to resort to the unconventional did. By the end of March 1941, Clarke had formed the "A" Force deception organization—Britain's only military deception organization tasked with devising and implementing tactical and strategic deception plans—to which he served as its controlling officer.

In terms of Dudley Clarke's personal life, he was the consummate bachelor. He had two relationships that were important to him, but both ended in disappointment. The first was with a Russian woman named Nina, who succeeded in deceiving the deceiver. After she conned him out of money, she disappeared from his life. The second relationship was important enough for Clarke to propose marriage, but his love interest rejected his proposal. After the two misadventures, Clarke never expressed an interest in a serious relationship again. He did not swear off women, though. He was known to appreciate beautiful women and enjoyed their company.[15]

All of that makes his Madrid escapade all the more interesting, yet in truth much less controversial than some saw it at the time. In October 1941, Clarke was arrested in Madrid dressed as a woman. True to form, Clarke had taken every detail into consideration. He was caught in makeup wearing a dress, stockings, and high heels complemented by a ladies' turban cap, jewelry, long gloves, and purse. He gave a false name and claimed to work for the London-based newspaper the *Times*. It was never completely clear what Clarke was up to, but there is no evidence to suggest that he was a cross-dresser or homosexual as some have suggested. It is far more likely that he was either on an intelligence-gathering mission, which was entirely plausible given that Spain was a hotbed of intelligence as a German-friendly "neutral" country, or simply donned a disguise, albeit an eccentric choice, to travel incognito as he was known to do. Either way, it was a one-off incident. It did cause quite the stir back in London, which resulted in Clarke being interviewed by Lord Gort to ensure that he was of sound mind. Once he was deemed stable, he was allowed to return to Cairo.[16] Soon the affair was forgotten, and there were no further incidences. Aside from that one controversy, Clarke maintained a clean record and made a name for himself for his exceptional work at "A" Force.

Dudley Clarke played a central role in the development of British military deception in World War II. Under his direct command, "A" Force was the only British organization to receive a war establishment during World War II for the exclusive purpose of conducting military deception, and under its direction deception was practiced on a scale unseen in previous wars.[17]

"A" Force was unique in its design and construction. It functioned like a private army, with Clarke as its commander, and enjoyed an unusual degree of independence. It operated under the immediate command of the commander in chief of the Middle East theater. In the early days of British deception, Clarke took his orders directly from the commander in chief. For the sake of security, which was practiced to the extreme at that time, Clarke only met with the commander in chief, his chief of staff, and the directors of Operations and Intelligence. As the war developed and security measures were ever so slightly relaxed, Clarke met with the commanding generals and/or their staff during the planning stage of any operation within their theater—they relayed their objectives, and Clarke devised a deception plan to support their efforts.[18] In this way, Clarke had direct access to the commanding generals in theater and was included in the planning phase of Allied operations.[19]

Before "A" Force came into being, the only British organization to conduct deception was the Inter-Services Security Board (ISSB), an administrative body composed of representatives from the army, navy, air force, MI5, and MI6. ISSB was established in 1940 as the British and French contemplated intervening action in support of Finland. Its responsibilities, according to Michael Howard, were to prevent leaks of critical information to the enemy and to prepare and execute "action in connection with measures designed to deceive the enemy as to our plans and intentions."[20] Yet, ISSB's efforts were largely restricted to the strategic realm and were therefore limited. Howard clarifies that "its deceptive activities, such as they were, were confined to the protection of convoys or the movement of troops overseas, and it met only *ad hoc* to consider them. . . . It was responsible neither for formulating nor implementing any overall deception 'policy."[21] ISSB was thus primarily focused on providing cover and security for British operations. F. H. Hinsley states that ISSB assisted the London Controlling Section "in the preparation of schemes to deceive the enemy," but adds that "in practice its work was limited to its security function."[22]

According to the official LCS papers, by the summer of 1941 "A" Force stood alone as "virtually the only Deception organization in existence."[23] Moreover, its responsibilities were far-reaching. It conducted both strategic and tactical deception, worked closely with the armed services, and simultaneously developed and implemented all deception policy for the Middle East and Mediterranean theaters of operation.[24] "A" Force perfected its techniques over the long and hard-fought years of desert warfare in North Africa, and its early experience can best be described as one of trial and error.[25] By the time of the Second Battle of El Alamein, however, "A" Force had perfected its techniques and matured into "an effective and well-oiled machine," in Clarke's assessment.[26] As Howard remarks, from "December 1940 onwards "A" Force had proved its worth, growing from a body concerned purely with tactical deception in the Western Desert to one masterminding strategic deception throughout the Middle East."[27]

A point of particular interest is that as Britain's first official military deception organization, there was no model or existing manual for "A" Force to follow. Instead, it was "A" Force that developed the blueprint for deception during the early years of the desert campaign that the British used for the remainder of the war—to include Plan Bodyguard, the deception campaign to cover the invasion of Normandy in 1944.[28]

An early challenge that "A" Force had to overcome was the lack of overall centralized control of deception. In the beginning, Clarke developed deception operations for the Western Desert Campaign without any guidance from London; yet, there was real danger that any one of his efforts could unwittingly compromise genuine operations or strategic policies in other theaters. For that reason, both Clarke and Wavell urged London to establish an organization committed to the centralized control of global deception. Clarke observed: "The time had arrived when the need of a central guiding hand was beginning to be felt, in order to ensure that Deception policy over the whole British war area was related to one main theme. Failing that, there was a grave risk of "A" Force in the MEDITERRANEAN, knowing nothing of plans outside it, innocently compromising the intentions of another command."[29] The result was the creation of the London Controlling Section.

The British Chiefs of Staff (COS) approved the formation of the London Controlling Section on October 9, 1941, after meeting with Clarke in London to better understand how "A" Force was organized and operated.[30] The LCS charter called for the new organization to coordinate global strategic deception and oversee its implementation. To avoid confusion, the COS provided that the new organization should plan and arrange for the "execution of cover plans for major operations, while leaving the cover for small operations and the sailing of convoys within the sphere of the Inter-Services Security Board."[31] The COS appointed a controlling officer for deception, Colonel Oliver Stanley, to direct its activities. Stanley was a distinguished veteran of World War I, as well as an accomplished politician who had served in Neville Chamberlain's administration. He was, therefore, a seemingly logical choice for the position.

The task awaiting Stanley was monumental and paved with obstacles, especially when it came to bureaucracy. As the controlling officer for deception, he was expected to maintain close contact with the "Planning Staff, Joint Intelligence Committee, Directors of Intelligence, Political Warfare Executive, Special Operations Executive and with the Press through Service representatives."[32] His success in coordinating global strategic deception was largely dependent on the cooperation of these multiple entities; thus, it was unfortunate that his cover title as head of the Future Operational Planning Section of the Joint Planning Staff and vaguely defined responsibilities failed to convey the importance of his task. Unsurprisingly, the armed services proved reluctant to work with him or his organization. To make matters worse, any potential for success was further eroded by the fact that Stanley was never appropriately briefed on the deception machinery at Britain's disposal, which severely limited his effectiveness as a deception officer. Ultimately, there was little Stanley could do under such circumstances.[33] The result was a rather underwhelming and ineffective debut for the London Controlling Section.

The failure to provide the type of strategic deception policy and central guidance that "A" Force needed frustrated both Wavell and Clarke. On May 21, 1942, Wavell telegraphed Prime Minister Winston Churchill directly to reemphasize the importance of centralized control and long-term planning. Fortunately, his pleas fell on sympathetic ears, and on June 21, the LCS was officially reorganized.[34] The organization's purview of responsibility was expanded and a new controlling officer, Lieutenant-Colonel John Bevan, was appointed following Stanley's resignation.[35]

Bevan had extensive experience in military and operational intelligence, making him well suited for the position. While his responsibilities were better defined than Stanley's had been, Bevan also understood that the only way he would have the support of the armed services was to emphasize the operational, as opposed to intelligence, aspects of his duties. In this he was successful.[36] Bevan was able to maintain extensive relations with the Chiefs of Staff, Joint Planning Staff, service ministries, Foreign Office, and secret services. Moreover, the Americans were encouraged to create a similar deception organization to work with the British in devising Allied deception.[37] From that point forward, London provided ever more-effective centralized control over deception, which in turn allowed for remarkable growth in the deception machinery.

The acceptance of both organized and formalized deception on such a grand scale reveals its importance to the British war planners, but that had not always been the case. Clarke and his team at "A" Force had to convince the military brass of the usefulness of deception. Many looked down on deception, as it clearly fell outside of traditional military thinking and operational procedure. In a lecture draft on the state of deception dating back to February 1942, Clarke frankly noted that "the British Army does not take very kindly to deceptive measures and if, in doing your deception, you were to prove a nuisance, people would get fed up and you would not get what you wanted."[38] It took years of successful deception for the military leaders to fully appreciate the value of deception and accept it as an essential component of military planning. Clarke reported that by 1944, "A" Force "was meeting with the fullest possible support from all three Services, British and American, in regard to the physical measures required to back up a Deception 'Story.'"[39] That was particularly important because "A" Force could implement strategic deception measures using its own resources, but it was often dependent on the military to provide the physical support to serve as visual evidence; for example, troop movements, training operations, beach reconnaissance, aerial photographic reconnaissance, bombing raids, naval exercises, staged leadership conferences, and so much more were all crucial to add realism to the deception stories being fed to the enemy through secret channels and other strategic means.

Due to "A" Force's many successes over the years, deception was increasingly recognized as instrumental to the British war effort and its victory over the Axis powers by not only the prime minister, but the Chiefs of Staff and the military leadership as well. In a revealing report contained in the LCS papers, British leadership acknowledged deception must be "organised as effectively and as widely as our real resources," thus putting deception planning on par with military planning.[40]

The report continues: "If we could gain surprise, if we could cause the enemy to dispose his forces in positions unfavourable to himself but favourable to ourselves, if we could confuse his mind as to the precise objective or timing of our projected operations, we might be able to influence very materially the successful outcome not only of battles and campaigns, but of the war itself."[41] That was the overall objective of deception: to influence the successful outcome of battles, campaigns, and ultimately the war. "A" Force proved it was possible in the Western Desert Campaign. The challenge in 1943 was to restructure the deception machinery to keep pace with the expanding war and subsequent shift to the European continent.

2 EUROPE BOUND

STRATEGIC PLANNING FOR 1943

The German surrender in North Africa in May 1943 represented the Anglo-American forces' first campaign victory against the Axis. Yet, the swift advance to Tunisia and ultimate victory brought new challenges. First and foremost was one of organization and logistics. Beyond that, it brought serious questions regarding what strategy the Allies should pursue to capitalize on the German defeat.

The Germans' western retreat and the arrival of the Americans in North Africa, both in November 1942, necessitated changes to the existing military organization and command structure. To accommodate the combined Anglo-American effort following Operation Torch, British military headquarters was transferred from Cairo to Algiers. At the Casablanca Conference in January 1943, Prime Minister Winston Churchill and President Franklin D. Roosevelt agreed upon crucial changes to the military command. Gen. Dwight D. Eisenhower was appointed as the Supreme Allied Commander; General Harold Alexander, previously serving as the

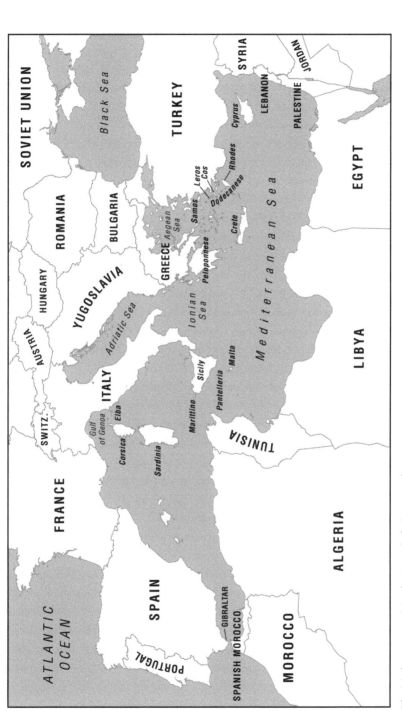

The Mediterranean. Map by Erin Greb Cartography.

commander in chief of the Middle East, took over as Eisenhower's deputy supreme commander and was allocated responsibility for planning, preparing, and executing land operations.[1] Eisenhower's Allied Force Headquarters and Alexander's newly formed 18th Army Group headquarters were both established in Algiers.[2]

The greatest challenge facing "A" Force was one of logistics. "A" Force headquarters sat in Cairo, yet the success of the Battle of El Alamein led to an Axis retreat that ended approximately 1,700 miles away in Tunis. Further, the establishment of AFHQ in Algiers placed the military headquarters more than 2,000 miles away from "A" Force headquarters, an unfavorable separation given the need for close cooperation between the two. At the War Office in London, the same concern was noted. The Vice Chief of the Imperial General Staff (VCIGS) sent a telegraph to Alexander with the following message: "British Chiefs of Staff place utmost importance on cover plans . . . no doubt you will therefore include the excellent deception team now in CAIRO in any staff you transfer to ALGIERS."[3] While the request was gratifying for "A" Force, given that it revealed London's overt support for deception as an instrumental component of British military efforts, it simultaneously posed a challenge. Clarke recognized the need for "A" Force to be represented in Algiers, but he was not at all interested in relocating to Algiers himself. Instead of moving, he reorganized "A" Force.

Because Clarke preferred to remain centrally located to coordinate deception operations throughout the Middle East and Mediterranean theaters, the main headquarters stayed in Cairo. A new body was provisionally formed, Tactical Headquarters "A" Force (Tac HQ), which was located in Algiers alongside AFHQ. It officially became operational on February 17, 1943. Tac HQ was placed under the command of Lieutenant-Colonel David Strangeways and accompanied Alexander's armies for the remainder of the war in the Mediterranean. It was staffed at that time with a total of five officers and six other ranks.[4]

Eight days later, on February 25, 1943, the provisional reorganization became permanent after the unit received a new comprehensive war establishment, approved by AFHQ, London, and "A" Force itself. The changes were designed to allow for further expansion of "A" Force and it operations. Simultaneously, all of the individuals involved in deception and MI9 (escape and evasion) activities were brought together under the singular authority of "A" Force. The areas affected by this reorganization applied to "A" Force's "triangle of territory" that stretched from Gibraltar to Tehran to Cape Town.[5] Compared to the original version first approved by the COS in 1941, these changes, which went into effect on March 15, represented a dramatic shift in both organization and responsibilities.

The clarification of responsibilities and lines of authority was especially necessary given that the Americans brought their own security staff and deception officers with them to North Africa. The American organization, along with its representative Lt. Col. Carl Goldbranson, became operational in Algiers on January 23, 1943.[6] The London Controlling Section initially intended for the Americans to take responsibility for deception in the western Mediterranean, leaving the eastern Mediterranean to "A" Force.[7] That meant that as of November 1942, between the time the US military arrived in North Africa to late January 1943, the responsibility for planning and conducting deception in the western Mediterranean was ambiguous at best, and highly problematic. As Clarke lamented, the Americans were "entirely inexperienced."[8] More importantly, their delay in establishing a headquarters in Africa until late January meant lost time for the development and implementation of deception plans in the Mediterranean. If there was a lesson to be learned, Clarke declared it was the "need for a single unified control of Deception throughout any one theatre." He observed that "had it been possible to foresee this, and to provide for it before the TORCH forces landed in NORTH AFRICA, there is little doubt that Strategic Deception could have played a greater part than it did in the MEDITERRANEAN during the Winter of 1942/43."[9]

The solution was to unite the British and Americans under one single deception command. On February 5, Goldbranson flew to Cairo and there he and Clarke decided to incorporate the American deception apparatus into "A" Force. "A" Force was therefore given control over deception for the entire Mediterranean, and it made sense to keep it under Clarke's authority as he had the expertise and advantage of two years' worth of experience deceiving the Axis powers in his role as commander of "A" Force. From February 1943 forward, the Americans worked under "A" Force as an "inter-Allied" body with representatives from the army, navy, and air services on both the British and American sides. Although the British described "A" Force as "inter-Allied," it did remain under British leadership and retained its unique British character and personality throughout the war.[10]

The growth of "A" Force from its inception in 1941 was impressive. What began as a tiny deception organization run by only one man, Dudley Clarke, had blossomed into an expansive organization with four separate headquarters: Main HQ "A" Force in Cairo; Advanced HQ "A" Force in Algiers; Tac HQ "A" Force at Alexander's 18th Army Group HQ, at that time located in Algiers; and Rear HQ "A" Force in Nairobi. Each of the headquarters had a Control section (command and administration), "G" section (deception), and "N" section (MI9). The new establishment also allowed for the staffing of eight outstations located in Oran–Casablanca, Tunis, Malta,

Cyprus, Smyrna, Beirut, Baghdad, and Tehran. Finally, subsections of "A" Force, specifically the Technical Unit, Special Correspondents Section, and the 74th Armoured Brigade—which produced dummy equipment under the command of Colonel Victor Jones—were granted war establishments of their own. All told, there were 596 individuals working under the "A" Force umbrella—94 officers and 502 other ranks.[11]

The growth of the organization was undeniably necessary given the expansion of the war effort. With the Axis defeat in May 1943, the Allies controlled the entirety of North Africa. Moreover, the war's center of gravity was soon to shift to Europe. As had been the case since its formation, wherever the British forces went, so too went "A" Force. It was up to the Combined Chiefs of Staff (CCS) to determine where the Allies were headed next, and up to the LCS to devise the overall deception strategy to complement the military plans. As for "A" Force, it was now ideally reorganized to both accompany the Allied armies in southern Europe and maintain its operational base of command in Cairo, where it could continue to plan and implement deception efforts across the Middle East and Mediterranean theaters.

After Allied leaders met at the Casablanca Conference in January 1943 and agreed upon the overall grand strategy for 1943 (discussed below), the LCS formulated its global deception strategy. On February 27, 1943, "A" Force received the "Deception Policy 1943 (Germany and Italy)," drafted by Lieutenant-Colonel John Bevan and approved by the Chiefs of Staff. The overall strategic goal of deception in the Mediterranean was to force the Axis powers "to give first priority to the maintenance and reinforcement of his forces in the south of France and the Balkans." Concurrently, the plan was to "lower Italian morale and will to exist" and "retard" the enemy's reinforcement of Sicily.[12] Having received the LCS central directive on global deception, which Clarke identified as "the first of its kind," "A" Force was able to begin formulating comprehensive deception plans in support of the Allies' strategic military goals.[13]

In the military realm, the British were facing a completely different scenario from years past. Aside from the brief campaign in France and the Battle of Britain, World War II for the British was fought mostly across the deserts of North and East Africa. At times, the British war effort teetered upon disaster. In the Western Desert Campaign, where the British first fought the Italians and then the combined weight of the German and Italian armies single-handedly from June 1940 until November 1942, the British occasionally found themselves facing what seemed to be imminent defeat.[14] As 1942 gave way to 1943, however, the British and Allied war effort as a whole gained momentum and dealt a series of devastating defeats to German forces on multiple fronts.

In August 1942, the Germans attacked Stalingrad in the battle for Russia. Joseph Stalin, it became clear, was determined to defend his namesake city. A Red Army counterattack in November enveloped General Friedrich Paulus's German Sixth Army. Cut off from supplies and reinforcements that never arrived, Paulus's men grew increasingly desperate as the weeks turned to months and winter literally froze the German war effort. On February 2, Paulus, newly promoted to field marshal, surrendered the battered remnants of the Sixth Army to the Soviets.[15] Not only was the Battle of Stalingrad over, so too was Germany's forward momentum on the eastern front. The defeat, as Churchill aptly observed, "ended Hitler's prodigious effort to conquer Russia by force and destroy Communism by an equally odious form of totalitarian tyranny."[16] Though far from over, the eastern front campaign had reached its turning point. The significance for the British war effort was profound. With the offensive capabilities of the German Wehrmacht severely degraded, the risk of Germany penetrating the Middle East, or even Turkey for that matter, was greatly reduced. In turn, it relieved substantial pressure from the British in the Middle East theater and allowed them to focus on other fronts.

The eastern front was just one of the areas where the German military effort faltered in 1943. In May, the Allies finally neutralized the German U-boat menace in the Atlantic as well. From the onset of the war through mid-1943, the German navy aggressively exploited Britain's greatest vulnerability—its extreme reliance on imports of food, resources, and equipment—in the Battle of the Atlantic. All told, the Germans employed 1,170 U-boats and sank over 14 million tons of Allied merchant shipping. Despite the losses, it was ultimately Allied innovation and ingenuity that won the day. To combat the U-boat wolf packs, the Allies reverted to a convoy system accompanied by heavy escort and air cover. New technology, such as the invention of an undetectable short-wave radio, high-frequency radio detectors known as "Huff-Duff," and improved depth charges gave the Allies the advantage. Of equal importance, in May 1941 the British captured a German submarine, U-110, with its cipher machine and codebook intact. The work of the code breakers at Bletchley Park deciphering German naval messages provided precise information regarding the location of the wolf packs, enabling the Allied convoys to avoid them altogether. Ingenuity, combined with the Allies' industrial ability to produce ships in great quantities, ultimately tipped the balance in the Allies' favor.[17] Moreover, to add to the Germans' growing troubles, they also faced increased pressure from guerrilla-based resistance movements across German-occupied territories.[18]

Finally, 1943 saw the end of the Axis effort in North Africa. In October 1942, the British Eighth Army, commanded by General Bernard Law Montgomery, launched Operation Lightfoot, beginning the Second Battle of El Alamein. The success of that offensive forced the Axis armies into a retreat that ultimately signaled their defeat in Africa. The Axis fate was further sealed with Operation Torch, the British and American amphibious invasion of northwest Africa. Pressed on two sides by the Allied armies, the Germans capitulated in May 1943.[19] On May 13, Alexander signaled Churchill with the victory message: "Sir: It is my duty to report that the Tunisian campaign is over. All enemy resistance has ceased. We are masters of the North African shores."[20] After years of fighting, the British could finally claim victory, and British morale soared. As for the prime minister, his relief and excitement was palpable. He remarked that nobody "could doubt the magnitude of the victory of Tunis. It held its own with Stalingrad."[21] From Britain's perspective, especially in light of the significance of an Axis defeat following the long and protracted desert campaign, Churchill's statement rang true.

Despite the monumental Allied victories of early 1943, final triumph over the Axis powers remained elusive. In fact, one might observe that the war had simply changed course. It quickly became obvious that Europe would become the new center of gravity, but the specific target of future Allied action was uncertain. Allied options in 1943 included a cross-Channel invasion into northwestern France, an assault against either southern France or the Balkans, or a campaign to neutralize Italy.[22] Hindsight, history, and geography might combine to make the Allies' decision to focus on Italy by way of Sicily appear straightforward, if not obvious, but that was far from obvious to war planners, British and American alike.

By late 1942, the Combined Chiefs of Staff—comprising the British Chiefs of Staff and American Joint Chiefs of Staff—were working concertedly on their grand strategy for 1943. After years of planning and fighting a largely defensive war, planners were encouraged by the fact that Allied forces had seized the initiative from the Germans. In 1943, Allied strategic planning entered a new phase. According to Maurice Matloff, the official historian for the United States Army, the "power to call the turn on strategy and to choose the time and place to do battle passed to the Allies."[23] The long-awaited luxury of offensive strategic planning, however, brought many challenges and hurdles that had to be overcome. The most immediate and overwhelming question revolved around the appropriate course of action to capitalize on the anticipated Axis defeat in North Africa. It soon became clear that there was a marked difference of opinion between British and American leaders, as well as within the leadership of both countries.

In Britain, the chief divide lay between the prime minister and the Chiefs of Staff. Churchill initially favored Operation Roundup, the cross-Channel invasion of northwestern France. He assumed that the success of Operations Torch and Lightfoot in North Africa would render the cross-Channel invasion possible. Churchill was so convinced of this, in fact, that he gave Stalin "virtual assurance" that he could expect the invasion of France in 1943. The news no doubt pleased Stalin, who was insistent that the Allies open a second front to relieve the Soviet Union as soon as possible. But the British COS adamantly disagreed with the prime minister. They argued that the Allies did not possess the numerical strength to launch a cross-Channel offensive in 1943. In the words of Foreign Secretary Anthony Eden:

> There were still more German divisions in France than we could land there and they would have local air superiority. We could not land sufficient forces to remain in France and would be driven out without the Germans having to withdraw anything from the eastern front. To collect the shipping necessary to land fifteen to twenty divisions would be an almost insuperable task and would imperil our position in the Middle East.[24]

Given the unfavorable conditions for a cross-Channel offensive and the improbability that such action would relieve the Soviets, the Chiefs of Staff argued that Allied strategy should instead focus on exploiting and furthering the success in the Mediterranean.[25] As the COS argued, the Allies needed to "wear down the German war machine." To do so, "'Torch' should be exploited in such a way as to turn the whole Mediterranean into a heavy liability to Germany."[26]

The Chiefs of Staff plan, to which Churchill reluctantly acquiesced, became known as the Mediterranean Strategy. The strategy focused on coaxing Italy out of the war, thereby forcing Germany to spread itself thin in an effort to defend the peninsula and replace the Italian divisions at that time stationed in the Balkans.[27] From there, the Allies could focus on the Balkans with the aim of cutting Germany's supply routes and lines of communication, as well as using the area as an access point to strike the Romanian oil fields. Additionally, it was hoped that Turkey would then enter the war on the Allies' side. Churchill was particularly interested in Turkey, as it would give the Allies the strategic advantage by allowing them to pressure the Germans on the eastern front if needed, as well as cut Germany off from critical resources such as oil, chrome, and copper.[28] To coincide with the Mediterranean Strategy, the Allies committed themselves to tightening the economic blockade and intensifying the strategic bombing campaign over Germany in order to lower civilian morale. A cross-Channel invasion would not take place, they agreed, until the German military was weakened and civilian morale reduced.[29] On December 29, 1942, the Defense Committee of the Cabinet accepted the COS plan. From there it was sent to the JCS in Washington for American approval.[30]

On the American side, the situation was less conclusive. There were bitter differences of opinion within the armed services, between the services and the president, and consequently between the United States and Britain.[31] Because Britain had been at war with Germany since 1939, it had ample time to work through the many administrative and military territorial battles that the United States began facing in late 1941. Referring to the United States, Michael Howard similarly comments that "between Army, Navy and the civilian agencies there did not even exist the harmonious co-operation which had been established in London by the various committees of the War Cabinet and the Chiefs of Staff Committee."[32]

In terms of interallied cooperation, the primary differences between the United States and Britain revolved around each country's respective national interests. While neither country can be blamed for pursuing its own national interests, the divergence of views complicated negotiations. Moreover, in the United States there was notable distrust of Britain's long-term objectives, and many suspicions were voiced that the British sought to manipulate the United States into another world war in order to help bolster the British Empire, a political objective that held no appeal in the United States.[33] Britain's focus on North Africa, the Mediterranean, the Balkans, and the peripheral approach to warfare in general appeared to many US military leaders as serving only British imperial interests. They did not view the strategy as one conducive to fighting a global war.

The American discussion of Allied global strategy was often contentious. Going back to May 1941, before the United States entered the war as a belligerent, American leadership had agreed to ABC-1, otherwise known as the Germany-first (or Europe-first) approach. That agreement saw the United States fighting alongside the British to defeat the Axis in Europe, but it had its critics. Many in the military disagreed with Britain's "indirect approach" and wanted nothing to do with the North African campaign or continued operations in the Mediterranean, as the British ultimately proposed. After the Japanese attack on Pearl Harbor on December 7, 1941, the American military and public naturally viewed Japan as the primary enemy. As a result, a Pacific-first strategy gained traction in the United States.[34]

Among the US military leadership, the question ultimately boiled down to Germany or Japan. If the British were willing to strike the Germans directly by way of a cross-Channel invasion in 1942, most were amenable to continue with the Germany-first approach—but the British refused. From Britain's point of view, such an offensive was "suicidal" given existing German strength in northwest Europe, nor would it divert German forces away from the Soviet Union.[35] As such, the British were not willing to consider it; they preferred to expand operations in North Africa, ideally with American help, to defeat the Axis forces there. The reaction in the United States was to completely redirect focus to the Pacific. Churchill, dismayed by the American shift in opinion, remarked: "Just because the Americans can't have a massacre in France this year, they want to sulk and bathe in the Pacific."[36]

Even though many US military leaders believed the best approach to win the global war was to focus on Japan in the Pacific, with the benefit that it would enable them to aid China and possibly the Soviets through Siberia, Roosevelt vetoed the plan in July 1942. The president suspected that the Pacific-first strategy was nothing more than a bluff intended to frighten the British into accepting the American military leaders' cross-Channel approach. Roosevelt was convinced that the Pacific-first strategy was "strategically unsound," would do little to win the war in the near future, and would ultimately work to Germany's advantage while failing to aid the USSR. As such, he agreed with the British Chiefs of Staff that the Mediterranean Strategy was more likely to meet with success and offered the greatest opportunities to accomplish the Allies' goals.[37] The decision was made, and plans began for the United States to assist with Operation Torch in North Africa.

The decision to launch Operation Torch was a step forward in interallied cooperation, but what would follow Torch? That was the question at the end of 1942 as leaders from both Britain and the United States worked to develop a combined strategy for 1943. Not surprisingly, the same arguments made throughout 1942 were voiced yet again. Gen. George C. Marshall, the United States Army Chief of Staff and Roosevelt's foremost military adviser, strongly advocated for the cross-Channel attack. In fact, he had been greatly disappointed with Roosevelt's decision to participate in Operation Torch, which he saw as "periphery-pecking" in a theater that was Britain's strategic responsibility, not that of the United States.[38] He was supported by others who had argued in favor of the cross-Channel invasion in 1942 and were doing so again with 1943 in mind. Increasingly, however, Marshall's view lost traction. At the end of 1942, American army planners came to the same conclusion as the COS—namely that the Allies were understrength, rendering a cross-Channel operation infeasible.[39] The only viable options remaining were to stay in the Mediterranean and seek to exploit German vulnerability there, or shift focus to the Pacific. The final decision was to be made by Churchill and Roosevelt, along with the CCS and representatives from the Joint Planning Staff, War Cabinet Secretariat, and Joint Staff Mission, in Morocco during the Casablanca Conference of January 1943.[40]

Given the sheer number of high-ranking officials leaving London for Casablanca, a cover story was necessary to prevent the enemy from learning of the conference. The plan was code-named Symbol. A War Cabinet report reveals that planners believed it was impossible to hide the fact that a conference was taking place, so they indicated that it was merely a meeting of low-level officials in Cairo. The reports states: "our endeavor should be to indicate that the conference is on a lower level than is in fact the case and with this in view it is proposed to provide separate cover for the four Chiefs of Staff."[41] It was of the utmost importance to conceal information regarding the absence of the Chiefs of Staff from the UK, as that would indicate a major meeting. To that end, the vice chiefs of staff effectively assumed the role of the chiefs, even in name, without indicating in any manner that the chiefs were unavailable. Family members were provided false stories to explain their absence from home, though all were led to believe that the chiefs remained in Britain. Finally, the War Cabinet prepared plausible explanations, complete with alternate destinations, for the flight of one Clipper and one Liberator transporting London's highest-ranking officials to Casablanca.[42] The London Controlling Section implemented the cover plan.

The Casablanca Conference began on January 14, 1943. Going into Casablanca, the British participants' strategic objective was clear and united. They wanted to concentrate on Germany with only minimal resources earmarked to contain Japan, defeat the U-boat menace in the Atlantic, expand the Allies' bomber offensive over Germany, maintain the supply of the Soviet Union, knock Italy out of the war, bring Turkey into the war, and maintain constant pressure on the Axis forces. Unlike the British, the Americans were not united in their objectives, and stark disagreements remained between the armed services, as well as between the military and the president.[43] Accordingly, the ongoing arguments persisted: some wanted to see a shift away from the Mediterranean to focus on northwest Europe, others advocated that greater importance be placed on defeating Japan, while yet others recognized the merits of the Mediterranean Strategy.

Given the disagreements, a compromise policy was put forth that held broader appeal. The "Memorandum on the Conduct of the War in 1943," which was approved by the CCS on January 19, allowed for the Germany-first approach but did not block the transfer of resources to the Pacific. It also stipulated that the full weight of the Allied war effort would fall on Japan following Germany's defeat. In the meantime, the bomber offensive against Germany was to continue. The Allies also agreed to continue the concentration of forces in the United Kingdom (Operation Bolero) to enable the Allies to launch the cross-Channel offensive as soon as it was practicable.[44]

Since the cross-Channel invasion of France was effectively ruled out for 1943, the Germany-first approach entailed remaining in the Mediterranean. Marshall, still not content with the plan, sought reassurance that the Mediterranean Strategy was sufficient to bring about progress in the war against Germany. For that, Alan Brooke (after the war known as Lord Alanbrooke), the head of the British Chiefs of Staff and Chief of the Imperial General Staff (CIGS), reiterated the argument that operations in the Mediterranean would force Germany to spread thin its forces in Europe in order to bolster Italy, likely result in Italy's withdrawal from the war, force Germany to transfer resources away from the eastern front, and potentially entice Turkey into the war against Germany. The argument was that the Germans, "with 44 divisions in France, could deal with any threat the Allies could bring against them from the United Kingdom without withdrawing any forces from Russia. Instead therefore the United Nations should force Italy out of the war, which would compel Germany not only to occupy the Italian peninsula but to replace the Italian forces in the Balkans as well." Furthermore, an attack on Sicily would require Germany to further disperse its forces to protect Sicily, Sardinia, Greece, and the Dodecanese, resulting "in a far greater diversion of resources from the Russian front than any that could be provided by any cross-Channel operation that could be contemplated in 1943."[45] It was also noted at the conference that Germany could move seven divisions from the Soviet Union to France in less than two weeks if needed. Yet, in order to reinforce Italy or the Balkans, Germany could move only one division at a time across the Alps. Only in the Mediterranean would the Germans be fighting at such a disadvantage.[46]

Brooke's defense of the Mediterranean Strategy was persuasive and hard to counter. Moreover, the fact that the Allies were understrength and unprepared to cross the English Channel in 1943 was undeniable. At the same time, all parties agreed that a cross-Channel invasion must remain a priority. It was therefore agreed that the Allies would launch the cross-Channel offensive in 1944.[47] After the long and laborious meetings, Brooke commented that the Americans "are difficult though charming people to work with." From his daily diary entries, however, it is clear that he was less enchanted with Marshall, whom he described as "having no strategic vision. . . . his part has been that of somewhat clumsy criticism of the plans we put forward."[48]

Despite the early disagreements over strategy, the British and Americans came together to adopt the Mediterranean Strategy. Certainly, this was a great victory for the British strategic vision, but it had not solved every issue. The Allies still had to decide where to strike first in the Mediterranean: Sardinia or Sicily. Proponents of Operation Brimstone (Sardinia), namely the Joint Planners along with Lord Louis Mountbatten, pointed out that it could be launched three months sooner with fewer resources and at lower cost than Operation Husky (Sicily), all while achieving similar objectives as invading Sicily. Importantly, Sardinia was ideally situated to serve as a key base for air attacks against Italy's northern industrial sites. On the opposite end, however, it did not provide the same degree of protection for shipping as a successful Operation Husky could.[49] Swayed by the need to keep the Mediterranean open to Allied shipping, all parties opted for Sicily. The CCS chose Sicily because it was the "greater political and military prize." The Americans preferred it because it opened the Mediterranean; Churchill liked it because it presented a more legitimate second front to offer Stalin than did Sardinia.[50] The operation was initially set to commence during the full moon in July 1943.

General Eisenhower, chosen as the supreme commander for the Allied forces at Casablanca, was given overall command for the upcoming operations in the Mediterranean, to include Husky. Yet, Eisenhower lacked operational command experience. It was to the Allies' advantage that the land, air, and sea operational commanders under his direct authority, all British, were each highly experienced. Alexander, head of the 18th Army Group, was named deputy commander and given control of planning and executing the Allies' land operations. Air Chief Marshal Arthur Tedder and Admiral Andrew Cunningham commanded the Allied air and sea forces, respectively.[51] Fortunately, Eisenhower proved to be a skilled and level-headed coalition commander, capable of bringing about unity and consensus in an environment where personalities, egos, and visions often clashed.[52]

While Eisenhower was coordinating the ongoing military effort against the Axis in North Africa, Alexander was expected to begin the planning and preparations for Husky. The seemingly insurmountable challenge was that every commander responsible for ensuring the success of Husky was at that time fully occupied with the battle for North Africa and "only in their spare time could they think spasmodically about the shape of things to come." The official historian further comments that it was remarkable that a plan was ever agreed upon, and that it turned out to be a good plan at that.[53] Nonetheless, the necessity of devoting undivided attention to the ongoing battle in North Africa made planning for the upcoming battle all the more difficult and disorganized.

Although the Mediterranean Strategy could not commence in full until the fighting in North Africa concluded, the Casablanca Conference proved successful in formulating Allied grand strategy for 1943. In the meantime, one aspect of the Mediterranean Strategy that Churchill viewed as particularly crucial was immediately implemented: the effort to entice Turkey into the war. While Turkey was a recurring theme at Casablanca, and the desire for its involvement in the war was clearly laid out as an objective of the Mediterranean Strategy, it can also be claimed that Churchill was its most enthusiastic supporter. In fact, there were many in the British government who saw little use for Turkey. Eden did not expect to see any positive results from "that stubborn quarter," a view that was shared by the War Cabinet and Clement Atlee.[54] Neither the United States nor the Soviets were overly enamored with Turkey either.[55] Churchill, however, saw Turkey as a great strategic prize, a prize that was consistently part of his political agenda.[56]

After parting ways with Roosevelt at Casablanca, Churchill made his way to Cairo, en route to Turkey. On January 30, 1943, Churchill, along with Brooke, Sir Alexander Cadogan of the Foreign Office, and select military leaders, arrived in Adana, Turkey, to meet with Turkish leaders, including President Ismet Inönü. The objectives of the meeting were to demonstrate British goodwill, impress upon the Turks that the Allies had seized the initiative in the war, and induce them to abandon their neutrality. Churchill assured Inönü that the situation was favorable for Turkey's entrance, but time was of the essence. According to the prime minister:

> The danger to Turkey on her Northern flank has been removed for the time being by the shattering victories of the Russians over the Germans, and on her Southern flank by the fact that Generals Alexander and Montgomery have chased Rommel 1600 miles away from Cairo. . . . There remains however the Germans' need of oil and of the "Drang nach osten," and they may in the Summer try to force their way through the centre. Turkey must be in the best possible condition to resist any such act of aggression by force of arms. We have come here to find out how we can best help our Ally at this serious but at the same time hopeful juncture.[57]

In order to assist the Turks, the British offered armor, aircraft, and additional supplies of British and US military equipment to amounts previously agreed upon, some of which was already in transit.[58] They also offered direct military support by way of anti-tank units, antiaircraft (AA) units, and the readiness of divisions of the Ninth Army, located in Syria, to assist Turkey.[59]

Despite the friendly negotiations and offers of military aid, the Turks refused to enter the war. Their concerns were many. For one, the Turks feared that an Allied victory could potentially prove ominous. Historically, the Turks viewed Russia as an enemy, and an Allied victory would result in a strengthened Soviet Union. They were also worried, as Churchill referenced, that Germany's failure to seize the Caucasus oil fields might induce the Wehrmacht to instead seek access to the Romanian oil fields by way of Turkey. Joining the Allies, or even granting them access to Turkish air bases in order to bomb the Romanian oil fields, would only invite a German attack.[60] German desperation on the eastern front could also prompt an attack. As it turns out, Turkey's fears may have been justified to a degree. After Adana, the Nazi foreign minister, Joachim von Ribbentrop, began advocating for an attack on Turkey as a Turkish campaign could assist in relieving the pressure on the encircled German Sixth Army at Stalingrad. He likewise believed it would impede Turkey's "mischief-making."[61]

The overriding concern for the Turks was ensuring their security and uncompromised sovereignty. As a young and fairly weak country, Turkey had good reason to pursue a self-serving foreign policy. While Turkish leaders leaned marginally toward the Allies, they could not risk Turkey's security by joining the war. Nor, from their perspective, did they stand to gain from what they viewed as a war of Europe's own making.[62] As such, the Turks were not to be persuaded at Adana to abandon their neutrality.

But the Adana Conference was not a complete failure. To the contrary, it produced favorable results in the strategic realm. While Turkey was the focus of British diplomatic efforts, it was simultaneously the object of British deception efforts. "A" Force was operating two strategic deception plans in early 1943, Warehouse and Withstand, both of which capitalized on Turkey's unique position and strategic importance to the Axis and Allied powers alike.

Plan Warehouse was developed in November 1942, just prior to the Torch landings. After meeting with Alexander in Cairo, Clarke created Warehouse with the objective of minimizing the number of enemy reinforcements sent to North Africa to combat the Allied armies in that theater. To achieve that goal, "A" Force set out to simulate a threat to the Balkans. The plan was approved on November 18 and implemented by way of "A" Force's established intelligence channels. The deception story claimed that the Allies intended to invade Crete in the opening weeks of 1943. Crete, the story held, was merely a conduit to the real objective—Greece. Warehouse was kept alive utilizing a proven technique—the notional postponement—and remained operational until March 1943.[63] As it developed, it incorporated the likelihood of Turkey entering the war as part of the deception story.

In January 1943, "A" Force developed another strategic deception plan that ran parallel to Warehouse: Plan Withstand, which focused on Turkey specifically and echoed the prime minister's conviction that Turkey was of vital strategic importance for the Allies. The inspiration for Withstand came after Axis agents in Turkey observed the presence of British missions helping Turkey improve its air defenses and extend its airfields. In the meantime, those agents also observed the flow of British tanks and aircraft into Turkey from Syria. Major-General Allan Arnold, the British military attaché in Ankara, noted there were "great arguments in the Axis camp as to the meaning of these tanks,—and we have evidently got them guessing." Clarke, never one to let an opportunity pass, recorded: "It seemed to be a moment for Deception to step in and make them guess wrong."[64] Since the British leadership was planning to meet with the Turks later in January, the circumstances were ideal for "A" Force to provide a false interpretation of the observed military assistance, all the while using the leadership conference as its mouthpiece.

Like the other neutral powers of World War II, Turkey was overrun with enemy agents. Yet, Turkey was a unique case for "A" Force. Turkey's vital geographic and strategic position rendered it the "espionage centre" of the Middle East.[65] Instead of that hindering the work of "A" Force, it presented the organization with ample opportunity to pass misleading information to Axis agents. The "A" Force Narrative War Diary states: "There was no country in all the MEDITERRANEAN in which "A" Force was in a better position to influence the thoughts of secret intelligence organisations than TURKEY."[66] It was in that vein that Plan Withstand was devised on January 15, 1943.

Withstand was particularly interesting, and equally complex, in that the goal was not to deceive the Turks. While the British certainly hoped to influence the Turks to enter the war, it was the Germans who were the intended target of the ruse. The deception story, however, was to be funneled through the Turks because the British assumed "that information passed to the Turks will be known to the Axis and vice versa."[67] Because it would be incredibly difficult to pass one story to the Turks and a completely different story to the Germans, Clarke had to devise a single story that would, in his words, "make the Turks themselves more amenable to our political approaches, even to the point of entering the War on our side, and would also offer opportunities for deceiving the enemy as to our strategic intentions."[68] If successful, the Turks would join the Allies and the Germans would reinforce the Balkans instead of North Africa.

Plan Withstand was devised on the premise that Turkey intended to join the war when it was clear which side would emerge victorious; naturally, the Turks hoped to profit from any postwar peace talks. The plan, therefore, was to play up Allied gains and the prospects of peace. At the same time, the British sought to increase Turkish fears of a possible German threat to Turkey, with the hope that Turkey would seek increased Allied support for its defense. Meanwhile, to add support to Plan Warehouse, the story stated that Britain intended to drive the Germans out of the Balkans. The emphasis on the Balkans was advantageous as it could be used to influence the Turks as well. The British sought to play on Turkish fears of Soviet imperialist aims in the Balkans, especially with regard to Bulgaria, and accordingly argued that the British needed Turkey's help to access the Balkans before the Soviets could get there.[69]

The "A" Force "Strategic Plans 1943" file lays out the deception story that was passed to the enemy and lists the following critical elements that were to be relayed at the Adana Conference:

a. We are extremely apprehensive of an Axis invasion of TURKEY.

b. That, while wishing to do all we can to help TURKEY resist it, we have no intention of infringing Turkish neutrality until the Turks invite us to do so.

c. That we are very much afraid that the Turks will delay this invitation until it is too late for us to give effective help along a very indifferent land L of C.

d. We are therefore insuring [sic] against an Axis Blitz over-running TURKEY by concentrating on an adequate defence of the Syrian-Iraq border.

e. We have got to get into the BALKANS somehow to forestall the Russians. If the Turks will not give us a free passage through TURKEY, we shall take advantage of the Axis concentrations against TURKEY (and against the Russian interference on their left flank) to capture CRETE and the PELOPONESE.[70]

Clarke hoped that the Turks would respond by inviting Britain to increase its commitment to the defense of Turkey, allow the British "free passage of troops" to the Balkans, and enter the war on the Allies' side. As for the Germans—the target of the deception—they ideally would take countermeasures against Britain's passage through Turkey and reinforce both Crete and the Peloponnese.[71] The inherent difficulty and time-consuming process of transferring forces to the Balkans would place considerable strain on an already overstretched system, and profoundly impact the Germans' ability to reinforce North Africa—or the eastern front for that matter.

"A" Force passed the Withstand deception story mostly through its intelligence channels, specifically double agents, as well as rumors, leaks, diplomatic indiscretions, and more. As alluded to above, it was also poignantly conveyed through the language and arguments made at the Adana Conference itself. To that end, Cadogan of the Foreign Office was briefed in Cairo on the deception story prior to his departure for Turkey. Finally, physical deception was implemented as well. The Ninth Army in Syria relocated troops to Aleppo and conducted training exercises near the Turkish border, where they were certain to be observed. Moreover, when British and Turkish patrols met, the British leaked bits of the Withstand story. In an effort to simulate strength, the 102 RTR (Royal Tank Regiment), a notional armored force under the command of Colonel Jones of "A" Force, was positioned in Aleppo to provide visual confirmation of tank formations along the border. Finally, camouflage units created the illusion of strengthened defensive works.[72]

Because of the overlapping focus of the two strategic deceptions, Withstand was eventually merged into Warehouse. Moreover, Warehouse was reinvigorated after the Casablanca Conference and the decision made there to pursue Operation Husky over Operation Brimstone. Once Clarke was informed that Sicily was the next military target, he was able to modify Warehouse accordingly. The revised plan, Warehouse (1943), was approved in March. In accordance with the "Deception Policy 1943 (Germany and Italy)," it continued to pose a notional threat to the Balkans. The plan stated that the Allies intended to invade the Balkans from the Middle East in the summer of 1943. Beginning with an attack on western Crete and the Peloponnese, the ultimate objective was to relieve Greece and establish a foothold in Europe. The story continued that the Allies were optimistic that Turkey would then declare war, allowing Britain to transfer air and armored forces to Thrace.[73] The deceptionists also suggested that the Allies intended to bypass the enemy's strongholds of Rhodes and Crete proper. This was a crucial component of the story; if the Germans believed that Crete and Rhodes were genuinely threatened, they very well could go on the offensive to protect the islands.[74] The British wanted the Germans to reinforce the Balkans, thus diverting forces away from genuine areas of engagement, not open another front there.

In order to reinforce the perception of Britain's ability to carry out such extensive operations, "A" Force created a new, albeit fake, army—the Twelfth Army. The Twelfth Army added strength to an already extensive false order of battle. It was notionally stationed in Cairo.[75] Warehouse (1943) was passed through the use of double agents, rumors, display of dummy landing craft and aircraft, the notional buildup of the Twelfth Army, training of Greek troops, aerial reconnaissance, administrative efforts, and other means.[76] According to the "A" Force Narrative War Diary, other measures taken were to "call for the return of linguists in Greek, Turkish, Bulgarian and Roumanian; and to secure a well-advertised increase in the normal awards offered to Service personnel qualifying as Interpreters in those languages."[77]

Together, Warehouse and Withstand were collectively considered to be a success. The "A" Force files contain captured German documents from the *Heeresarchiv* files revealing that the German High Command anticipated attacks in Turkey, launched from Aleppo, as well as in Crete and the Peloponnese. They expected the British to use four and one-half divisions for each of the two offensives. The German assessment included a note stating that the objective of the attacks was to bring Turkey into the war. Furthermore, an order signed by Field Marshal Wilhelm Keitel on March 29, 1943, called for the continuation of secret arrangements with Bulgaria to resist an "Anglo-American-Turkish" invasion. According to Clarke, this "marked the first effects of our long sustained efforts to contain German forces in the BALKANS as a whole by means of Deception—efforts which continued until the Summer of 1944."[78] In fact, "A" Force's primary role became one of deception for the purpose of diversion. "A" Force was to redirect German attention to the Balkans, always a sensitive area to the German High Command and Adolf Hitler, and away from genuine targets—whether that be in the Mediterranean or Normandy—for the remainder of the war.

Warehouse (1943) had a relatively short life. As the Allies prepared for the amphibious invasion of Sicily, the deceptionists also began to focus their craft on the Sicilian campaign. Their main task was to divert German attention, resources, and reinforcements as far away from Sicily as possible. To accomplish that, they had to provide the enemy with other "likely" targets, but the target had to be chosen carefully and "must be so vulnerable and so important that the enemy must move troops to its defence."[79] Given Germany's ongoing preoccupation with the Balkans, it presented itself as the perfect diversion.

Just as Withstand was merged into Warehouse, Warehouse was merged into the broader strategic deception plan covering the whole of the Mediterranean in the spring of 1943. All focus shifted to Plan Barclay, the deception effort to cover Operation Husky.

3 THE DILEMMA OF SICILY

At the Casablanca Conference in January 1943, Allied leaders had finally settled on the invasion of Sicily as the most practical follow-on to the North African campaign. Located just ninety miles off the coast of Tunisia, Sicily offered the Allies a solid base from which they could continue operations in the Mediterranean. It likewise provided vital air bases within striking distance of Axis targets and great prospects for reopening the Mediterranean Sea to safe passage of naval and merchant vessels. But the decision was fraught with obstacles. Every commander slated for Operation Husky, specifically Generals Dwight D. Eisenhower, Harold Alexander, Bernard Law Montgomery, and George S. Patton, were all preoccupied with the ongoing battle for North Africa. Consequently, planning and preparations for Sicily were delayed, sporadic, and disorganized at best. Another obstacle was that the offensive would be the first combined Anglo-American operation in Europe against Axis home territory, a reality that merely underscored the likelihood of stiff resistance. Moreover, the fact that Sicily's geographic location made it such an obvious target increased the odds that the Axis command would reinforce the island in anticipation of an attack. To add to the challenges, the invasion of Sicily, by nature of it being an island, required a large-scale amphibious landing. The Allies' only combined experience with such an operation, however, was the fairly soft invasion of northwest Africa during Operation Torch. Finally, the terrain on the triangular-shaped island was treacherously rugged and mountainous. This worked to the advantage of the defense but posed grave obstacles to an invading mechanized force.

Consensus, something the Allies struggled to achieve, also proved a major challenge leading up to the invasion of Sicily. The Mediterranean Strategy, which came to fruition with the Sicilian campaign, remained unpopular within some American circles. The British and Americans differed in their approaches to the war, and the Mediterranean Strategy brought those disagreements to the forefront. The Americans preferred a direct approach, which for many meant targeting Germany itself with a cross-Channel invasion of France. Prime Minister Winston Churchill bemoaned that the Americans possessed an "undue liking for logical clear-cut decisions."[1] In contrast, the British seemed opportunistic in their strategy, overtly favoring an indirect approach. The indirect approach, so despised by American military planners, was consistent with Britain's historical approach to warfare. As a formidable sea power, but weak land power, Britain traditionally allied itself with a strong continental power while the Royal Navy implemented economic blockades and exploited the enemy's weakness by sea.[2] In many ways, the Mediterranean Strategy was a continuation of Britain's tendency to exploit its enemy's vulnerabilities on the periphery, while avoiding a direct confrontation that was not to Britain's advantage.

Though the British and Americans came together to agree on Sicily, they had difficulty in determining what should follow the Sicilian campaign. Predictably, the Americans rejected any idea that would prolong operations in the Mediterranean, and especially those with the potential to expand into the Balkans. Their focus was on preparing for the cross-Channel invasion without delay. The British, preferring to seize opportunities as they arose, favored knocking Italy out of the war altogether, even if that meant following Sicily with land operations on the peninsula. In May 1943, Allied leaders met in Washington, D.C., to hammer out future strategy. Churchill dubbed the meeting the "Trident" conference.[3]

Allied leaders reaffirmed that a cross-Channel invasion would be launched in 1944, but they encountered greater difficulty in determining what course of action should be pursued in the interim period between Sicily and the invasion of France. The Americans proposed an attack on Sardinia, while the British advocated maintaining the offensive momentum in Italy. Churchill was clearly frustrated and later recorded:

> I knew that the American Staff's mind had been turned to Sardinia. They thought that this should be the sole remaining objective for the mighty forces which were gathered in the Mediterranean during the whole of the rest of 1943. On every ground, military and political, I deplored this prospect. The Russians were fighting every day on their enormous front, and their blood flowed in a torrent. Were we then to keep over a million and a half fine troops, and all their terrific air and naval power, idle for nearly a year?[4]

Despite his pleas, Churchill was unable to garner American support for an Italian campaign during Trident. As a result, Eisenhower was given vague instructions to seek Italy's elimination from the war. The final decision, however, would be determined by the course of the Sicilian campaign and Eisenhower's recommendations to the Combined Chiefs of Staff thereafter.[5]

Once the Tunisian campaign concluded in May, Anglo-American attention shifted exclusively to planning and preparing for Operation Husky. The invasion was organized around two task forces. The Cairo-based Eastern Mediterranean Task Force, also known as Force 545, was led by Montgomery and comprised the British Eighth Army. The Western Mediterranean Task Force, or Force 343, was commanded by Patton and located in Rabat; once the invasion commenced, Force 343 became the US Seventh Army.[6] In addition to the two task forces, Alexander's headquarters—referred to as Force 141, but shortly thereafter renamed the 15th Army Group—was based out of Algiers.[7]

The planning for Husky, further complicated by the fact that it had to be coordinated among planning centers in London, Washington, D.C., Algiers, and Cairo, went through multiple stages and revisions. The original plan envisioned by the British Joint Planning Staff called for multiple landings over a broad stretch of coast from Palermo in the northwest to Catania on the eastern coast. Because Sicily's ports were too heavily defended for a frontal assault, the Allies planned to bypass them in favor of beach landings. Once ashore, the primary objective was first to seize the enemy airfields in order to guarantee air superiority, followed by the capture of Sicily's main ports, excluding Messina.[8] The plan received heavy criticism from Montgomery. In a telegram to Alexander in early March, he complained that the "operation as planned in London . . . breaks every commonsense rule of practical battle-fighting and is completely theoretical. It has no hope of success and should be completely recast."[9] On April 24, Montgomery sent another telegram to Alexander that betrayed his anxiety over the lack of time for proper preparation and what he saw as persistent faulty planning: "Time is pressing. If we delay while the toss is being argued in London and Washington, the operation will never be launched in July. All planning is suffering because everyone is trying to make something of a plan which they know can never succeed."[10] Montgomery preferred a concentrated landing to ensure the successful capture of the beachhead before redirecting focus to the airfields. Admiral Cunningham and Air Chief Marshal Tedder adamantly disagreed. They argued that the army could not succeed without proper supplies, and the navy would be unable to deliver those supplies or reinforcements if the enemy controlled the skies and ports—nor could the navy provide adequate fire support if it came under aerial attack. Both men wanted to see greater emphasis placed on the capture of Sicilian airfields and ports in the initial stages of the assault.[11]

The final version of the plan eventually adopted in May was a victory for Montgomery. On his suggestion, the American landing at Palermo was abandoned altogether. Instead, the US Seventh Army would land at Gela in the southeast, although this relegated Patton's Seventh Army to act as a supporting arm for the British Eighth Army. Few were happy with the plan, and Cunningham and Tedder continued to protest that the Allies were not doing enough to protect the landings or ensure air superiority. Moreover, many viewed Husky as quickly becoming an Eighth Army affair with Montgomery dictating the battle plan; regardless of the disagreements or damaged egos, Eisenhower ultimately approved Montgomery's plan.[12]

Settling on a battle plan was but one hurdle; Allied planners faced many additional challenges with the potential to impact negatively the success of the operation. For one, the scale of the amphibious operation was unprecedented from a logistical standpoint. The memory of the disastrous raid on the French port at Dieppe on August 19, 1942—essentially a trial run by mostly Canadian troops to test the Allies' ability to carry out an amphibious operation against enemy-held territory—did little to inspire confidence.[13] Furthermore, Sicily's location only ninety miles away from Tunisia made it the most logical target, almost guaranteeing that it would be heavily defended by Italian and German forces alike. And even though the Allies held a low opinion of the Italians' fighting ability, they did expect the Italians to put up stiff resistance to protect Italian soil. If the island was heavily reinforced by additional German troops as well, the Allies knew they would have a tough fight ahead of them. For all of those reasons, it was imperative to mislead the enemy regarding Allied intentions to the greatest extent possible; thus, deception planning proved to be a critical component of the overall operational planning for Husky.

Plan Barclay, the deception campaign to provide cover for Husky, was developed and implemented by "A" Force. Early planning for Barclay began in March, at which time Warehouse (1943) was merged into the new and more comprehensive deception plan. Eisenhower approved Barclay on April 10. From there it went to Churchill, who also gave approval with only one warning: "Be careful not to alarm TURKEY."[14] From its inception in March 1943, however, Barclay was a "highly complicated business" riddled with obstacles. It was an enormous plan unprecedented in its challenges, especially in that it had to provide cover for a combined Anglo-American force divided into two separate task forces staging multiple landings against Italian home territory. Moreover, the detailed planning was hampered by the fact that the military commanders were unable to work out the details of the operation until May, and even then Husky underwent subsequent revisions. For Clarke, the complicated chain of command and multiple revisions of Husky "necessitated frequent hurried journeys between ORAN, ALGIERS, TUNIS, MALTA and CAIRO to concert its machinations with all the Commanders concerned."[15]

When it came to providing cover for Husky, the sheer obviousness of Sicily presented the greatest of difficulties for the deception planners. As "A" Force began hammering out its preliminary plan, it recognized that the enemy was certain to conclude that the Allies intended to attack somewhere along the southern European coast, most likely either southern France, Italy, or the Balkans; Sicily figured prominently as a stepping-stone target regardless of the final aim. Clarke labeled it a "painful realisation" that "the enemy could scarcely avoid the one conclusion that an attack on SICILY must be General EISENHOWER's next move, no matter what his ultimate strategic intentions might be." To further complicate matters for the deception staff, the observable buildup of invasion forces across North Africa, increased activity on Malta, and unfortunate capture of Allied beach reconnaissance teams in Sicily only reinforced the island as the Allies' intended target. Even more disastrous for the deception team was Eisenhower's decision to take the island of Pantelleria on June 11 as a concession to Cunningham and Tedder. Operation Corkscrew, Clarke lamented, "killed the chances of surprise in SICILY to an extent from which 'BARCLAY' was never able to recover. It virtually nullified the first strategic aim of the plan, for from that day onwards the enemy knew for certain that, at some time and in some fashion, we were going to land in SICILY."[16] If nothing else, the capture of Pantelleria—located midway between Tunisia and Sicily—made the deceptionists' task of diverting the enemy's attention away from Sicily that much more difficult.

Because it was impossible to hide the fact that invasion preparations were underway, the goal was to render the German High Command unable to rule out any particular target during its most critical phase of reorganization following the cessation of conflict in North Africa. It was expected that the Germans would evaluate all potential threats and try to determine the Allies' most likely course of action following the Tunisian campaign. In the absence of information pointing firmly to one target over another, the Germans would have little choice but to disperse their forces along a massive stretch of territory spanning from France to the Balkans to avoid leaving any point along their southern flank exposed and vulnerable to attack. "A" Force's primary objective, therefore, was to increase the enemy's fears of attacks across the Mediterranean and keep him guessing as long as possible. Clarke remarked that if "the enemy was to be induced to make dispositions to meet the several aims of 'BARCLAY,' it was necessary that he should be persuaded to build up in his mind an elaborate and intricate version of the future intentions of the United Nations."[17] As such, the deception story passed in piecemeal fashion to the enemy suggested threats against southern France, Sardinia, Corsica, Sicily, the Balkans/Greece, and various islands in between.

The stated objectives of the Barclay plan were to contain Axis forces in southern France and the Balkans; to prevent the reinforcement of Sicily, especially by German troops; to minimize enemy naval and air attacks against the Husky convoys; and to contain the Italian navy in the seas east of the peninsula. According to the Barclay files, the objectives were divided between the eastern and western Mediterranean as follows:

A. EASTERN MEDITERRANEAN
    i.   To contain enemy forces in the BALKANS.
    ii. To weaken enemy garrisons in the DODECANESE and AEGEAN.
    iii. To cover the passage of the HUSKY Eastern Task Force.
    iv. To contain the Italian Fleet in the IONIAN and ADRIATIC.

B. WESTERN MEDITERRANEAN
    i.   To contain enemy forces in SOUTHERN FRANCE.
    ii. To weaken the enemy garrison in SICILY.
    iii. To cover the passage of the HUSKY Western Task Force.
    iv. To keep the Italian Fleet out of the WESTERN MEDITERRANEAN.[18]

Although the Barclay deception was directed by "A" Force, it was operationally divided between two theaters of military command: the Middle East theater of operations and AFHQ. The Middle East command, based out of Cairo and under Commander in Chief Henry Maitland "Jumbo" Wilson, was responsible for all activity in the eastern Mediterranean. From Cairo, "A" Force contrived to simulate a threat to the Balkans, by way of the Peloponnese, with the aim of also implying that Turkey would soon enter the war. The fictitious Twelfth Army, stationed in Cairo, was built up in the enemy's estimation as the intended invasion force. While Plan Barclay simulated multiple threats of invasion across the Mediterranean, one clear object was to keep the Italian navy in the east. In order to accomplish that, the deceptionists worked to convince the enemy that operations in the eastern Mediterranean would precede those in the west.[19] Clarke and his staff acknowledged that it might very well be impossible to prevent the Italian navy from sailing west to meet the bogus threats manufactured by "A" Force. While they hoped to avoid such a reality, they had little choice but to accept it as a possibility.[20]

Operations in the western Mediterranean came under the authority of Eisenhower and AFHQ. The British Chiefs of Staff directed the Supreme Allied Commander to "put in hand at once preparations to indicate that Allied Forces in the ALGERIAN/MOROCCAN area are being prepared for attacks against SOUTHERN FRANCE. The forces preparing for HUSKY in this area will be included in this plan and the mobilisation of General GIRAUD's French forces will assist this deception."[21] "A" Force hoped to convince the enemy that American forces under Patton, then Force 343, were slated to invade Sardinia and Corsica from Tunisia and Algiers. Alexander's Force 141, the story claimed, was preparing to land in southern France; once a bridgehead was established, Alexander would be joined by the Eighth Army and French forces stationed in North Africa.[22] Clarke clarified that the inclusion of the Eighth Army and French forces into the deception was to provide a believable destination for the British units included in the Western Task Force and the ten French divisions under General Henri Giraud that were at that time being "equipped with brand-new American equipment."[23]

The story was reinforced by messages sent through "A" Force's double agents—both genuine and fictitious—under the direction of the "40" Committee in Algiers.[24] On April 21, for example, the agent code-named Whiskers reported: "The 2nd Front offensive in some weeks. Objective will be SOUTH of FRANCE and re-equipped French troops will be used. SARDINIA and CORSICA will also be occupied. American and British troops to play major part. Embarkation ports will be Algerian, Moroccan and Gibraltar. There is no threat to SPAIN." On May 10,

Jewel reported: "Large amount of material from U.S. landed at CASABLANCA for the French. Great air activity in ORAN area. MARAKESH is large grouping centre for British and U.S. a/c. [aircraft]." On the following day, Oliver added: "French being trained as paratroops at FEZ. French say they will soon be taking NICE from Italians. N.C.O. arrested for talking about training on terrain similar to that of SARDINIA."[25] The agents' alleged observations and reports of rumors gave life to the deception story and pointed the enemy's eyes toward the deception targets. Each channel provided a small piece of the deception puzzle; it was up to the Germans to put the pieces together.

If the story passed to the Germans neglected Sicily and Italy altogether, the Germans were likely to become suspicious. Thus, the story also provided for minor operations against Sicily and southern Italy, as well as identifying Malta and Tunisia as the training ground for those assaults. It was important, however, that the enemy believe the Allies intended to bypass Italy and focus on either southern France or the Balkans as their main target. The cover story for Italy, carefully disseminated to the Germans, claimed:

> "The Allies intend to by-pass ITALY and reduce its resistance by heavy and sustained bombing. For this reason they intend to build up large air forces in NORTH AFRICA, with which they consider they can neutralize the SICILIAN airfields and thus cover passage of convoys for the East through the MEDITERRANEAN." (This was an endeavor to give a false explanation for the heavy concentrations of aircraft building up on TUNISIAN and MALTESE airfields.) "This plan has the further advantage of saving the Allies a long frontal advance through ITALY, a costly occupation of hostile territory, and finally a difficult campaign to force the ALPINE barrier."[26]

Having opted to bypass Italy, the official story held, the Twelfth Army would instead strike first toward the Peloponnese and western Crete in order to advance into the Balkans and establish a foothold in Europe; the story further claimed that the Allies expected Turkey to enter the war at that point. The Balkans thrust offered an additional advantage in that it would allow the Allies to aid the Soviets on the eastern front. In the meantime, Patton would lead his forces against Sardinia and Corsica as a prelude to the invasion of southern France. Finally, the deception story claimed that once the Germans were sufficiently bogged down in Greece, Alexander would spearhead the invasion of southern France. With the bridgehead secured, he would then be joined by Montgomery's Eighth Army and a French army to advance up the Rhône Valley. If at any point the enemy became aware of the Allies' actual movement toward Sicily, the deception story could be modified to suggest that the Allies intended to feint toward Sicily in order to draw the enemy away from their genuine targets.[27]

Because it was highly probable that the Germans would begin to redistribute their forces immediately after the fall of Tunis on May 11, the deceptionists sought to heighten the enemy's fear of an imminent threat to the Balkans and southern France in order to forestall reinforcement of Sicily. Accordingly, the date for the first notional landings was slated for the end of May. The challenge was to keep the deception alive after the notional D-days came and went. For that, the deceptionists used one of their most successful, albeit challenging, tactics—the notional postponement.

The notional plans and postponements had to be carefully synchronized with the Allies' genuine plans. The Allies intended to invade Sicily on July 10, at the crescent moon period, which offered adequate moonlight for the planned airborne drops yet sufficient cover of darkness for the approaching convoys. The trick was to convince the enemy that the Allies intended to strike under the cover of darkness during the new moon period. In this way, it would "encourage him to increase vigilance during the moonless period rather than moonlight periods. Also we hoped that our repeated cry of 'Wolf' would produce a sharp drop in vigilance just after the second notional D-Day had passed without incident. If this worked we should catch him at his worst when 'HUSKY' went in on the 10th July."[28]

All told, Barclay went through three stages and two notional postponements. A simplistic breakdown of the stages can be seen below:

"STAGE ONE"

May 26–28. Landings in CRETE & PELOPONESE.
June 4–6. Landings in SARDINIA, CORSICA & S. FRANCE.

"STAGE TWO"

May 20. All landings postponed for one month. New dates to be:
June 26–28. CRETE & PELOPONESE.
July 2–4. SARDINIA, CORSICA & FRANCE.

"STAGE THREE"

June 20. Landings again postponed for a month, to following dates:
July 24–26. CRETE & PELOPONESE.
July 31–August 4. SARDINIA, CORSICA & FRANCE.[29]

The first stage ran from April 10 until May 20, with the first notional landing date scheduled for May 26. The explicit objective of the first stage was to induce the Germans to make faulty troop dispositions in the immediate aftermath of the Tunisian campaign. Once the realignment was complete, it would be exceedingly difficult for the Germans to implement significant modifications. Every effort was made, therefore, to maximize the threat to the notional targets during Stage 1. Clarke intended the first notional postponement to go forward on May 10, but delayed it until May 15 to better fit the unfolding military situation. With the fall of Tunis, the deceptionists claimed that the invasion had to be postponed on account of the "premature collapse of Axis resistance in TUNISIA." It was expected that the German High Command would be well informed of the postponement through various channels by May 20. The success of the first stage of Plan Barclay, along with its subsidiary plan Operation Mincemeat (discussed later in this chapter), was confirmed by the transfer of two German divisions to the Peloponnese.[30]

After the military leadership finalized its plans for Husky in May, Barclay was amended to accommodate the new battle plan and entered its second phase. Stage 2 ran from May 20 until June 20, with a notional D-day beginning on June 26. The aim of this stage was to delay German reinforcement of Sicily specifically. Clarke regarded this stage as the most important of the three stages. Up until that point, the Germans had only reinforced the Balkans and southern France; "A" Force made it its mission to keep that trend going. As intelligence reports poured in, Clarke remarked that "widespread confusion still existed everywhere." Then, just when everything appeared to be on track, "A" Force experienced a potentially devastating setback. On June 11, the Allies captured Pantelleria, resulting in wild speculation among the foreign press that Sicily was next. Clarke feared that the military operation may have negated all of "A" Force's efforts.[31]

The final stage of Barclay was in operation from June 20 until the Allies landed on Sicily on July 10. According to Clarke, this period was full of anxiety because the genuine invasion preparations were underway and increasingly difficult to hide in their entirety. "A" Force successfully arranged for preinvasion exercises to take place on moonless nights and in locations that aligned with the deception story. As substantial invasion forces accompanied by landing craft began to concentrate around the Tunisian coastal town of Sousse, with two airborne divisions, gliders, and transport planes close behind in Kairouan, the buildup reached a scale that was impossible to hide. The inability to conceal all activity, combined with the fact that Germany had been lured into making faulty troop dispositions that aligned with the deception plan as opposed to genuine plans, led Clarke to modify the objectives of the last stage. Instead of diverting enemy attention away from Sicily per se, all efforts concentrated on concealing the timing of the offensive by notionally postponing operations until the moonless period at the end of July.[32] If successful, the enemy would be caught by surprise on July 10 whether he suspected Sicily or not.

An additional difficulty that "A" Force faced during the final stage arose when Alexander transferred his headquarters from Algiers to Tunis—an impractical location if his forces were indeed slated for southern France as the deception story claimed. Given the short distance between Tunis and Sicily, the location left little room for doubt that Alexander's Force 141 was headed to Sicily. Inspired by necessity, "A" Force implemented an exhaustive wireless deception plan to make it appear as though the general's headquarters had moved to Oran instead.[33] Double agents played a leading role in passing along bogus sightings and intelligence information. On June 28, Le Petit signaled that "several hundred officers are at a H.Q. being established at ORAN. Landing exercises on large scale in ORAN area. Convoys still arriving with war material." On June 29, Arthur added further proof with his report that "preparations are being made at ORAN to establish a H.Q. for Anglo-American Force 141, under command of General ALEXANDER."[34]

The Barclay deception story was extremely complex and detailed. As with any deception, it could not be passed to the enemy in its entirety, but instead in small pieces for the enemy to assemble. Furthermore, Clarke relates that he had only three months to convey the entire story "bit by bit" to the enemy's intelligence service for it to "construct in jig-saw fashion before June was out."[35] Despite its many challenges, deception was an invaluable tool in that it allowed the Allies to redirect the Germans' focus to what they wanted the enemy to see, as well as provide alternate explanations for the concentration and disposition of invasion forces. This was of paramount importance given that the sheer scale of the buildup made the invasion preparations impossible to hide. The deceptionists successfully converted a weakness into a strength by incorporating the genuine preparations into the deception story to present the enemy with a completely false narrative for the preinvasion activity.

The methods utilized to pass Barclay were varied and complex, but by 1943 "A" Force was thoroughly experienced at deception, having spent years mastering its craft in North Africa. The official files list a total of six methods of transmission. The first was by way of "most secret intelligence methods." "A" Force was exclusively responsible for the dissemination of false information on the strategic level. As referenced in the LCS papers, "A" Force received the following order: "The "A" Force organisation will arrange to plant the STORY in piecemeal fashion upon the enemy's Secret Service in the area bounded roughly by the triangle GIBRALTAR–TEHERAN–CAPETOWN. "A" Force will also be responsible for arranging with the LONDON Controlling Section for items to be planted anywhere outside the area as required."[36] To fulfill this requirement, "A" Force utilized its secret agents and controlled channels, as well as orchestrated rumors, leaks, press speculation, and diplomatic indiscretions.

As a neutral hub of intelligence activity and a focus of the Barclay deception itself, "A" Force made full use of Turkey. One creative ruse involved a London newspaper and its correspondent stationed in Istanbul. With the cooperation of the press itself, "A" Force arranged for the correspondent to receive a telegram from England urging him to leave Turkey by the end of June. The timing coincided with the moonless period and the bogus invasion of the Balkans. The correspondent then began to "indulge in deceptive speculations" within press circles that "produced a very considerable display of interest."[37] In order to help pass the notional postponement, the correspondent received a second telegram from London informing him to put off his departure for one month, inciting yet another round of open speculation. According to Clarke, it was "a valuable aid in getting over the idea of a 'postponement' of the notional invasion dates at one of the busiest focal points for Axis agents."[38] Altogether, "A" Force planted deceptive information in tiny bits and pieces across both Allied and neutral territory.

The second method of transmission was the "implementation by the movement and operations of real forces," which included air actions, raids and ground reconnaissance, troop movements, and wireless deception. Since it was common to attempt to neutralize targets from the air prior to attack, heavy bombardment of Sicily was likely to attract undue attention to the island. To direct the enemy's attention to the cover targets instead, Clarke envisioned the dispersal of air attacks to include those locations as well. Unfortunately for the deception efforts, Allied airpower did not possess the resources to conduct such extensive bombing raids on the scale Clarke desired, especially as the proposed targets lacked genuine military value. But all was not lost. The deception story emphasized that Sicily would be neutralized by air as an alternative to invasion. The preinvasion bombardment, therefore, supported the story that was being diligently fed to the enemy. Still, Clarke was disappointed at the lack of air support, especially in the western Mediterranean. He attributed it not only to a shortage of resources, but to a failure on the part of the military to appreciate the importance of deception in general. He recalled:

> It is very probable that the real importance of cover-bombing had not yet been demonstrated sufficiently by the early part of 1943, for it was sometimes very difficult to convince commanders and staffs of the solid results which could be obtained from a reasonable diversion of the air effort. Too often it was looked upon as "wasted," but the Deception

staffs found more and more as time went on how much the attainment of surprise came to depend on it. . . . It was a problem which was never solved to the whole satisfaction of the rival claimants.[39]

Reconnaissance efforts met with greater success and were conducted by air and on land. In contrast to diversionary bombing, aerial photographic reconnaissance of the cover targets required fewer planes and resources and was thus carried out to Clarke's satisfaction. Beach reconnaissance teams were also sent out to survey the invasion beaches, both genuine and fake. The deceptive component took on additional importance following the capture of Allied beach reconnaissance teams in Sicily. In order to simulate a threat to the cover beaches, the deceptionists had to provide evidence of reconnaissance at those locations as well. Creating the impression of realism required, in Clarke's words, "very artful stage-management." As an example, a six-man team was landed by submarine off the coast of Greece; they left behind a canoe "artistically holed," but exhibiting signs of a concerted effort to disguise it. The word "Malta" could be faintly deciphered despite "attempts" to paint over the writing and cover it with canvas. It was hoped that the enemy would connect any observable training efforts in Malta with the invasion of Greece. Given the amount of effort that went into the meticulous staging of evidence, Clarke found it was a tool "best used very sparingly."[40] Though not stated in the files, it stands to reason that overuse of this particular tactic could greatly negate its effectiveness. As a result, it was used only twice—once in Sardinia and once in Greece.

The movement of troops was a very basic ruse. It was carried out mainly through the amphibious training of troops in areas where they were likely to be observed, with the hope that their activity would be spotted by, or reported to, enemy agents. Greek troops were trained in the Middle East near Suez, clearly pointing to an assault on Greece, while French troops trained in Algeria, indicating southern France as the intended target.[41]

The final component under the "implementation by the movement and operations of real forces" was the extensive use of wireless deception. "A" Force was still learning the art of wireless deception in 1943, but had already witnessed its success in the weeks leading up to the Second Battle of El Alamein. In 1942, Operation Canwell, an army-operated wireless deception, masterfully masked the movement of the 10th Armoured Corps into its attack positions at the El Alamein front by continuing to simulate wireless activity from its initial staging location.[42] The success of Canwell encouraged "A" Force to incorporate wireless deception into its repertoire of deceptive weapons.[43]

For Barclay specifically, the chief aim was to minimize wireless traffic in Malta and Tunis while simulating traffic in the eastern Mediterranean, especially to give life to the bogus Twelfth Army. Wireless deception was also instrumental in creating the impression that Alexander's headquarters had moved to Oran instead of Tunis. Finally, it was crucial to hide the American wireless link established on Malta that enabled Eisenhower to cable Washington. The LCS papers explain that British wireless transmissions from Malta might be connected to Allied plans to invade Greece, but American traffic would arouse suspicion and likely compromise the deception. All wireless traffic on Malta was therefore disguised as coming from naval wireless stations, using naval "ciphers, procedures and personnel."[44] Clarke viewed the wireless deception as one of the most difficult endeavors, but also one of the most important. He wrote:

> We were only just beginning to recognise it as one of the chief factors on which success or failure hung, but as the War went on it continued to play an ever-increasing part in every plan, and, now that it is ended, it would be impossible to over-emphasise the importance. One discovery at least we had made already, for "BARCLAY" finally convinced us of the value of working throughout each Plan step by step with a Wireless Deception Committee of experts from all three Services. Their contribution towards "HUSKY" had the most far-reaching effect.[45]

Though meticulous work, wireless deception proved to be one of the Allies' greatest tools of deception and became a mainstay of future deceptions.[46] Five primary uses of wireless deception were subsequently identified:

a. To conceal moves of HQs and units by simulating their wireless layout in the old position and keeping the actual troops on wireless silence in the new position until the need for surprise is removed.

b. To give the impression that a unit has moved to a specific place, when in fact it has moved elsewhere or has not moved at all.

c. By control of traffic levels in a static wireless layout to conceal or accentuate activity in a given sector of the line.

d. By the imposition of wireless silence to conceal the arrival of new units in an operational area.

e. By means of a "double bluff," an obviously dummy wireless layout may be used to make the enemy appreciate that a cover plan is in progress. In this way he may be made to believe that a formation has moved when in fact it has not. This is the most difficult to handle of all types of cover plan.[47]

Many of these methods were utilized for Barclay.

Another means of transmission for Plan Barclay was the "implementation by deceptive administrative measures." Due to the degree of bureaucracy involved, such efforts tended to be some of the most tedious and painstaking methods used by Clarke and his team of deceptionists. They were, however, crucial to success, adding a layer of realism to almost any deception plan. While the administrative process may not be the most sensational, it was highly effective and integral to the outcome of Barclay and other deception plans.

To aid in the buildup of the notional Twelfth Army, Montgomery's Force 545 Headquarters was officially redesignated as Twelfth Army HQ by the War Office. The abundance of official Twelfth Army HQ documents in circulation beyond that point had its effect, and the Twelfth Army found its way into the German estimation of Allied strength. Other measures saw the issuance of maps, informative pamphlets, leaflets on enemy troops, and language phrase books, all pointing toward either the Balkans or southern France. Interpreters and native speakers from the cover target locations were solicited as well. "A" Force also arranged for the transfer of foreign bullion to Cairo:

> The Chief Paymaster at G.H.Q. started a heavy buying of Greek drachmae. At the same time L.C.S. sent out by sea from ENGLAND no less than fifty boxes suitably inscribed and alleged to contain Greek bullion. On arrival at SUEZ these were transferred with some ceremony and under a heavily armed guard to the vaults of a Bank building in CAIRO, where they were deposited in the name of the Army's Civil Affairs Branch. L.C.S. also supplied us with small quantities of British £1-notes surcharged "FRANCE" or "GREECE" or "BULGARIA"; and a few of these "A" Force contrived to get "lost" in various different ways in centres such as ALGERIA, TRIPOLITANIA, MALTA, EYGPT and TURKEY.[48]

Additionally, lists were made of local fishermen in North Africa familiar with the cover targets, and officers toured bookshops in search of guidebooks on those same locations. A June 6 report on the progress of Barclay records that "Lt. Col. [Carl] Goldbranson and Major [R. A.] Bromley-Davenport made inquiries in seven book stores in TUNIS for travel guides and/or maps of SARDINIA and Southern

FRANCE, actually making purchases in two of these stores. At the last place visited they were considerably aided by an interested civilian spectator."[49] In Clarke's words, their efforts allowed for the "right kind of speculations and rumours."[50]

Administrative measures were also used to help pass the notional postponements. All efforts were made to create the appearance that a formal decision had been made on June 15 to delay the invasion by one month. At AFHQ, orders had been issued stating that no leave would be granted after June 20; on June 15, however, the order was rescinded. Security Intelligence Middle East (SIME) played an important role here as well. SIME, as was customary before any major operation, agreed to close the borders of the counties in the Middle East theater of operations, as well as cut off all communications beginning on June 16. SIME ensured that both military and civilian agencies, as well as the radio broadcasting station in Syria, were informed of the upcoming closures. This was carried out simply because the enemy had come to expect it before major events. On June 15, the measures were suddenly canceled. The Syrian broadcasting station reported that its programming would no longer be interrupted and that travelers could continue on with their plans in safety. According to the official record, the "net effect of it all was to raise public excitement to its height in the middle of June, and then to drop it with a bump into a stage of complete anti-climax immediately before the movement of the 'HUSKY' forces towards SICILY."[51]

A tried-and-true administrative scheme involved bogus travel plans. For Barclay, Montgomery first visited Force 545 headquarters in Suez, and from there plans were made for him to travel to Jerusalem for a little downtime from July 3 to July 6. All of the necessary administrative arrangements were made with the high commissioner in Jerusalem. Accordingly, the high commissioner received the following request from the commander in chief of the Middle East:

> General MONTGOMERY is taking a few days leave and would like to visit JERUSALEM. Would it be convenient for you to put him up from July 3–6? He does not wish to attend any public functions but would like to visit the Holy places. Most grateful if you could arrange this and would much appreciate early reply.[52]

Even though the visit would have to be canceled, it was planned as if it were genuine, and the majority of those involved in the administrative preparations likewise believed it to be genuine.[53]

A final component of administrative planning for Barclay met an unexpected but rather amusing end. To contribute to the perception that the invasion forces amassing in Tripoli, Libya, were slated for Greece, a scheme was concocted by the area commander, Sir Brian Robertson, to hang street traffic signs and notice boards at the docks in Greek; there were even buildings designated as Greek Medical Service facilities. Finally, roughly six Greek officers were attached to the Husky forces in Tripoli; they were later transferred to Malta to further the impression that Malta was the staging area for the Balkans campaign. The ruse was apparently so successful that, according to the War Diary, one "enterprising Greek with no authority but his own contrived to remain with the British unit to which he was attached and to accompany it into battle. Poor man, he must have been sadly disillusioned when it landed him on the beaches of SICILY instead of his native PELOPONESE!"[54] Humorous as this might be, it clearly reveals a reality of deception—for deception to succeed, the deceptionists were often required to deceive enemy and ally alike, although the enemy was the only designated target of the deception.

"Implementation by displays of dummies" was the fourth method of transmission utilized to convey the Barclay deception. The assignment was to create the impression of air and naval concentrations in the eastern Mediterranean that would exist if the threat to Greece had been genuine. In the meantime, the same concentration of forces in the western Mediterranean, and most specifically those located in Tunisia and Malta, necessitated concealment to avoid the obvious conclusion that Sicily was the target. Concealment proved to be a real challenge. While Plan Barclay called for the use of extensive camouflage and sunshields—devices used to disguise tanks as thin-skinned trucks—the camouflage resources in North Africa under AFHQ were not as developed as those in the Middle East.[55] Because they lacked adequate resources to provide sufficient camouflage cover, they had little choice but to seek creative solutions. "To make the real to appear as the dummy," Clarke explains, "wooden supports, throwing a tell-tale shadow on the ground, were put underneath the wings to represent the props needed to hold up those of a dummy."[56] From the air, the grounded fighter aircraft displaying odd shadows underneath its frame would appear to be a harmless decoy.

In the eastern Mediterranean, the deceptionists needed to create the appearance of two entire divisions. According to the deception story, the 8th Armoured Division was to invade the Peloponnese, while the 4th Airborne Division was earmarked for Greece and Crete. The problem, of course, was that neither division existed. Moreover, both divisions were supposed to be launched from Cyrenaica, but Cyrenaica was "very 'dead' and empty" following the success of the Second Battle of El Alamein that saw the war effort shift west into Tunisia. Clarke lamented that, unfortunately, "German reconnaissance had not moved with it."[57] It was not sufficient to claim through double agents and intelligence channels that forces were stationed near Tobruk in Cyrenaica; the visual evidence of their existence and offensive preparations had to be created for the enemy's benefit. For that, Plan Waterfall (discussed later in this chapter) was developed for the long-term display of dummies.

The fifth method of transmission associated with Barclay was the "implementation by means of rumours and propaganda." Not surprisingly, once the Tunisian campaign came to an end, rumors abounded on both the Allied and Axis sides as many speculated about what would come next. In Clarke's view, many rumors came a little too close to the truth. It was his goal, therefore, to "ensure that at least an equal flow of loose talk indicated the cover story of 'BARCLAY.'" For that, "A" Force, SIME, the London Controlling Section, and AFHQ—assisted by the French—each did its part in utilizing established sources and channels to contribute to the rumor mill. Because the troops themselves were given to speculation, they were also led to believe that the cover targets were their true destination. Interestingly, "A" Force even brought a select group of war correspondents into the fold. Although the press representatives were not directly ordered to lie, they were asked to emphasize anything that might support the deception story. From all appearances, the correspondents carried out their task admirably. Their help was especially appreciated when it came to the seizure of Pantelleria, a real debacle from Clarke's perspective. The correspondents were asked to stress that its capture was an "essential feature in the rounding-off of the TUNISIAN Campaign and the re-opening of our sea route between GIBRALTAR and MALTA."[58]

One such report, which serves as an excellent example of how "A" Force disseminated rumors, was planted in Turkey and circulated among the press in neutral Switzerland. The timing coincided with the second notional postponement of Barclay. It can also be seen as an attempt at damage control following Pantelleria:

> By the middle of JUNE expectations regarding the invasion of SOUTHERN EUROPE had reached their height. After the capture of PANTELLERIA and the great military parade in CAIRO on 14th, there was a general feeling that the stage was set for the next act. All officers on leave were due to return to their regiments on June 15th and everyone expected the first landings to take place before the end of the month. In Cairo most people expected these to be in GREECE, CRETE, and RHODES.
>
> In the next few days there was a complete change of feeling and rumours that something had gone wrong. This started when General

Montgomery failed to appear at the parade. He had been staying at the British Embassy a few days before and everyone thought he had come specially to take part in the parade. On June 14th it was rumoured that he had suddenly flown back to Algiers the day before. The next few days many of the officers who were supposed to have left Cairo on June 15th were still on leave and more had been arriving on leave since then. People say now that the invasion has been put off to the end of July and there is much resentment among the Greeks in particular, who think such delays are unnecessary and a waste of precious weeks.[59]

When it came to outright propaganda, the two most common methods utilized were leaflet dropping and broadcasting messages over the radio, although the Psychological Warfare Board (PWB) at AFHQ also arranged for information to be spread by the British Special Operations Executive (SOE) and American Office of Strategic Services (OSS) inside enemy territory.[60] When the civilian population was the intended audience for the radio broadcasts, the greatest challenge lay in not inciting an uprising. Accordingly, in southern France the people were warned not to be tricked into a premature rising. Because the situation in Greece was considerably more volatile, similar broadcasts there were determined to be too risky.

Propaganda leaflets prepared by the PWB were dropped primarily on the Axis forces themselves in order to weaken their morale.[61] At the same time, the enemy was likely to assume that the Allies' leaflet-dropping campaign was not random, but focused specifically on their intended targets. For that reason, it was necessary to drop leaflets on the cover targets as well. Here again, "A" Force encountered difficulties in co-opting the support of the air force. Clarke records that "it was no easy matter to persuade the Air Forces (who had no love for leaflet-dropping in any case) to divert sufficient aircraft to regions which we had no intention of invading." Clarke adds that the leaflet campaign in the western Mediterranean in particular "gained very little benefit" due to the lack of air support.[62] Clarke's recommendation based on the experience was to find ways to make the deception and air efforts more unified for the future.

"Implementation by the manipulation of security measures" was the sixth and final method of transmitting Barclay. The goal was not to try to convince the enemy that the Allies had no immediate plans beyond North Africa, since that was not believable, but instead to mislead him as to the date and destination of those future plans. For Husky it was agreed to settle on a date—referred to as X day and only later formally fixed at July 24—as the notional day of attack. Everyone in the know understood that X day was exactly two weeks later than the genuine invasion date, which allowed them to plan accordingly with accuracy. In that way, the planners were able to conceal the actual invasion date behind reliable security measures. Those not privy to the ruse were led to believe the deception timetable and could unwittingly contribute to the spread of deceptive information as a result.[63]

Throughout Plan Barclay, the deceptionists utilized any and every means at their disposal to pass the deception story to the enemy in pieces that could be verified and substantiated in circles far and wide. "A" Force excelled at its craft to such a degree that the deceptionists' mountain of disinformation and trickery emanating from varied sources and regions was all mutually reinforcing. The complexity of such an undertaking is hard to overestimate.

In addition to the six methods of transmission, Barclay also included three subsidiary plans, as well as a fourth that was prepared but never implemented. The first of the subsidiary plans, as well as the most sensational and well-known, was Operation Mincemeat.[64] Unlike the other plans, Mincemeat was affiliated with Barclay, but was not an "A" Force plan. Instead, it was carried out by the LCS and the British Admiralty in an effort to assist Barclay. Clarke did play a small role in Mincemeat, however. In March, he met with Lieutenant-Colonel John Bevan in Algiers, and together the two men composed a draft of the crucial Mincemeat document—a bogus letter to Alexander from VCIGS Archie Nye.[65] With the exception of the one meeting in Algiers, planning for Mincemeat took place in London.

Although it was an unusual deception, the goal of Mincemeat was consistent with the overall themes of Barclay—to play up the threat to Greece, deceptively referred to as Husky, and Sardinia while diverting attention away from Sicily. The Cabinet files portray it as "brilliantly elaborate in detail, completely successful in operation."[66] While some elements of Mincemeat were rather unconventional, it also employed many classical elements of deception.

Inspired by actual events, the origin of Mincemeat was rather macabre. In 1942, the body of a naval courier carrying Torch documents washed ashore in Spain after a Catalina seaplane crashed off the Spanish coast. The Spaniards recovered the body, as well as the documents carried by the courier, and promptly handed the papers over to the Germans.[67] The British noted that the incident "suggested that the Spanish could be relied on to pass on what they found, and that this unneutral habit might be turned to account."[68] It was Flight Lieutenant Charles Cholmondeley of MI5's B1A (Double-Cross) subsection who first suggested to the Twenty Committee (XX) that the British replicate history and stage a crash in order deliberately to plant false information on the enemy. Cholmondeley dubbed his plan Operation Trojan

Horse. While the idea did not seem practical in late 1942, only months later it proved fertile. Lieutenant Commander Ewen Montagu, a lawyer in peacetime known for his masterful organizational skills, was serving on the Twenty Committee representing naval intelligence. He would develop Cholmondeley's idea, morbidly renamed Mincemeat by ISSB, into one of the most unusual deception plans attempted in World War II.

As the idea of planting a body off the coast of Spain began to take shape, the planners faced many hurdles. The most obvious and urgent was procuring a suitable body. The condition of the body had to be consistent with a plane crash and subsequent death from drowning. Montagu enlisted the assistance of a coroner, Bentley Purchase, who agreed to help. Purchase identified a body that met Montagu's specifications and made provisions to store the corpse until it was required. On January 28, the body of a "labourer of no fixed abode," Glyndwr Michael, was brought to the coroner's office. Michael, who was only thirty-four years of age, died after taking a lethal dose of rat poison. The coroner noted that the poison would likely go unnoticed in a postmortem examination as it would only appear as trace evidence in the liver. The British were optimistic that the corpse would pass inspection, especially as they held Spain's forensic pathology in low esteem. The official report on Operation Mincemeat includes the observation that "Spaniards were bad pathologists: as Roman Catholics they had a dislike of post mortems."[69] The corpse was kept under refrigeration until Montagu was ready to use it. Glyndwr Michael, undistinguished in life, was about to become the legendary Major Martin of the Royal Marines.

Finding a suitable body turned out to be one of the easier tasks. A more daunting challenge was to create a believable identity and story that would explain the deceased's possession of highly sensitive documents. The plan initially called for the body to be that of an army officer since they customarily traveled in battle dress. Conveniently, they did not travel with visual identification, which removed the necessity of providing a photograph of the deceased. Furthermore, it was not uncommon for an army officer to carry sensitive documents on his person. For administrative reasons, however, it was determined to be too risky. If the corpse was in fact portrayed as an officer of the army, his death would be reported to the War Office and the military attaché in Madrid would have to be informed of the plan. This would include too many people and raise too many questions. Instead, it was decided that he could be an officer of the Royal Marines. Though it would require a picture identification, it was not unusual for officers of the Royal Marines to wear their battle dress while serving on special duties. With the decision made, the appropriate clothing, badges, flashes, and government-issued briefcase—complete with the Royal Cypher—were obtained. The deception team also furnished such items as a "watch, money, matches, cigarettes, pencil, keys (including that of the bag), wallet, etc." Additionally, the Cabinet files record that three officers provided photographs from which identification cards were made so that "when the body was removed from the refrigerator for final packing for its journey, the one that was most like it could be used."[70]

The identity given to the corpse was Major William Martin of the Royal Marines on the Combined Operations staff. There was, in fact, a W. H. G. Martin in the Royal Marines, so his existence could be reasonably verified if the Germans chose to investigate that far. The fictitious Martin was a Roman Catholic, which the British hoped would further deter the Spanish from performing a postmortem examination. Personal effects carried on his body revealed that he was a member of multiple clubs, owed money to Lloyds Bank, and had recently become engaged to a woman named Pam, whose picture he carried in his wallet. A ticket stub showed that Major Martin and Pam attended the Prince of Wales Theatre on April 22. He also carried letters from Pam, written in reality by a woman on staff with MI5, as well as a letter from his father.[71]

While the personal effects were vital to give Martin's identity realism and depth, the documents carried in the briefcase, which was attached to his body by chain, were crucial in passing along the key aspects of the deception story. The case contained some pamphlets and photographs, but the critical documents came in the form of letters. One, fictitiously written to Admiral Cunningham by Lord Louis Mountbatten, chief of Combined Operations, explained that Martin's expertise was in landing craft and thus he could offer assistance with the training efforts for the upcoming seaborne operation:

> Dear Admiral of the Fleet,
>
> I promised V.C.I.G.S. that Major Martin would arrange with you for the onward transmission of a letter he has with him for General Alexander. It is very urgent and very "hot" and as there are some remarks in it that could not be seen by others in the War Office, it could not go by signal. I feel sure you will see that it goes on safely and without delay.
>
> I think you will find Martin the man you want. He is quiet and shy at first, but he really knows his stuff. He was more accurate than some of us about the probable run of events at Dieppe and he has been

well in on the experiments with the latest barges and equipment which took place up in Scotland.

Let me have him back, please, as soon as the assault is over. He might bring some sardines with him—they are "on points" here!

Yours sincerely,
Louis Mountbatten.[72]

The final statement was a thinly veiled reference to Sardinia; the writers expected the Germans to get the joke.

The letter to Alexander from the VCIGS, referenced in the Mountbatten correspondence, was the most crucial deception document. Montagu worked with Bevan and Clarke to draft the notional letter that contained revealing information regarding upcoming British operations. "My dear Alex," began the final draft of the letter planted on Major Martin,

> I am taking advantage of sending you a personal letter by hand of one of Mountbatten's officers, to give you the inside history of our recent exchange of cables about Mediterranean operations and their attendant cover plans. You may have felt our decisions were somewhat arbitrary, but I can assure you in fact that the C.O.S. Committee gave the most careful consideration both to your recommendation and to Jumbo's.
>
> We have had recent information that the Bosche have been reinforcing and strengthening their defences in Greece and Crete and C.I.G.S. felt that our forces for the assault were insufficient. It was agreed by the Chiefs of Staff that the 5th Division should be reinforced by one Brigade Group for the assault on the beach south of CAPE ARAXOS and that similar reinforcement should be made for the 56th Division at KALAMATA. We are earmarking the necessary forces and shipping.
>
> Jumbo Wilson had proposed to select SICILY as cover target for "HUSKY," but we have already chosen it as cover for operations "BRIMSTONE." The C.O.S. Committee went into the whole question exhaustively again and came to the conclusion that in view of the preparations in Algeria, the amphibious training which will be taking place on the Tunisian coast and the heavy air bombardment which will be put down to neutralize the Sicilian airfields, we should stick to our plan of making it cover for "BRIMSTONE"—indeed we stand a very good chance of making him think we will go for Sicily—it is an

obvious objective and one about which he must be nervous. On the other hand they felt there wasn't much hope of persuading the Bosche that the extensive preparations in the Eastern Mediterranean were also directed at Sicily. For this reason they have told Wilson his cover plan should be something nearer to the spot, e.g. the Dodecanese. Since our relations with Turkey are now so obviously closer the Italians must be pretty apprehensive about these islands.

I imagine you will agree with these arguments. I know you will have your hands more than full at the moment, and you haven't much chance of discussing future operations with Eisenhower. But if by any chance you do want to support Wilson's proposal, I hope you will let us know soon, because we can't delay much longer.

I am very sorry we weren't able to meet your wishes about the new commander of the Guards Brigade. Your own nominee was down with a bad attack of 'flu and not likely to be really fit for another few weeks. No doubt, however, you know Forster personally; he has done extremely well in command of a brigade at home, and is, I think, the best fellow available.

You must be about as fed up as we are with the whole question of war medals and "Purple Hearts." We all agree with you that we don't want to offend our American friends, but there is a good deal more to it than that. If our troops who happen to be serving in one particular theatre are to get extra decorations merely because Americans happen to be serving there too, we will be faced with a good deal of discontent among those troops fighting elsewhere perhaps just as bitterly, or more so. My own feeling is that we should thank the Americans for their kind offer but say firmly that it would cause too many anomalies and we are sorry we can't accept. But it is on the agenda for the next Military Members meeting and I hope you will have a decision very soon.

Best of luck,

Yours ever,
ARCHIE NYE[73]

The deception letter was well thought-out and meticulously crafted. Crucial details of the deception were interwoven in a fashion that suggested previous discussions and avoided being too direct. The personal tone along with the inclusion of completely unrelated matters of discussion added authenticity.

The deception's success hinged on disposing of the body in such a way as to increase its chances of being found—and found in a timely manner. It was decided to transport the corpse by submarine, the HMS *Seraph*, which allowed the body to be launched reasonably close to shore. At 4:30 A.M. on April 30, 1943, the body dubbed Major Martin was released into the sea near Huelva, Spain. Later that same day, a local fisherman spotted the body floating in the water. The corpse was transported to shore and a postmortem was performed, which confirmed death by drowning. The body was subsequently buried at Huelva on May 2. The Spanish informed the British naval attaché in Madrid that they had recovered Major Martin's body on May 1.[74] There was no mention of the briefcase or any documents at that time.

On May 24, a tombstone was erected at the graveside that read: "William Martin, born 29th March, 1907, died 24th April, 1943, beloved son of John Glyndwr Martin and the late Antonia Martin, of Cardiff, Wales. Dulce et decorum est pro patria mori. R.I.P." A wreath was also placed at the grave with a card from "Father and Pam."[75] Montagu even arranged for Major Martin's death to be announced in the June 4 issue of the *Times*.[76] Montagu later reflected:

> In the Graveyard of the Spanish town of Huelva there lies a British subject. As he died, alone, in the foggy damp of England in the late autumn of 1942, he little thought that he would lie forever under the sunny skies of Spain after a funeral with full military honours, nor that he would, after death, render a service to the Allies that saved many hundreds of British and American lives. In life he had done little for his country; but in death he did more than most could achieve by a lifetime of service.[77]

The emphasis on saving lives was a constant theme and the desired objective of British deception in World War II.

The steps taken by the British after the release of the body reveal an important lesson of deception: the operation is not over until the enemy has had time to absorb and verify the information being fed to him. Naturally suspicious and wary of deceptive traps, the Germans were looking for ways to either confirm or discount the information they had received. Had the Mincemeat deception concluded with the body's release, the Germans may have determined it to be a trap. Because the British responded exactly as they should have had the incident been genuine, it was, at the very least, impossible to disregard as a hoax.

After the British "learned" of the death of Major Martin, they initiated a flurry of activity to discover the location of the briefcase. British authorities informed the naval attaché in Madrid that Martin was carrying secret documents in a black briefcase. It was, they implored, of paramount importance to locate the briefcase and ensure that its contents did not fall into the wrong hands. They asked him to be discreet, but to search diligently for the missing case. As communications continued, the tone from London became more urgent, providing the impression that the British authorities were becoming increasingly concerned over the security of the information contained in the briefcase. Finally, on May 8 the naval attaché learned that the Spanish had recovered the briefcase, which was handed over to him three days later. Though the British could not immediately discern from visual inspection if the letters had been opened or not, subsequent intelligence reports confirmed beyond all doubt that they had. The letters were, in fact, handed over to the Germans in Madrid, who then relayed the contents to Berlin. A May 15 German intelligence report stated: "After being reproduced, all documents were returned to their original condition by the Spanish General Staff and definitely give the impression—as I was able to see for myself—that they had not been opened. They will be returned to the English to-day through the Spanish Foreign Office."[78] Intelligence reports also revealed that after careful inspection, the Germans determined the letters to be genuine.[79] A German intelligence appreciation dated May 14 was drafted for Admiral Doenitz and included strict orders that it was to be "circulated personally." It began by stating that the "genuineness of the captured documents is above suspicion."[80]

There is a bit of irony in the course of events surrounding the recovered letters. It appears that the Spanish unwittingly deceived the Germans as well, or at the very least lured them into a false sense of security. The Germans were naturally concerned that the British might in some way alter their plans if they suspected that the Germans had gotten hold of the revealing letters. The Spanish, however, demonstrated such expertise in resealing the letters that the Germans felt confident they would pass as unopened.[81] Little did the Germans know that British code breakers at Bletchley Park were deciphering their secret messages on a regular basis.

All the evidence suggests that the Germans bought Operation Mincemeat in its entirety. A German appreciation of Allied intentions in the Mediterranean read as follows:

1. A landing in the eastern and western Mediterranean on a fairly large scale is anticipated.
   (a) Target of the operation in the Eastern Mediterranean under General Wilson is the coast near Kalamata and the stretch of coast south of Cape

Araxos (both on the West coast of the Peloponnese). The reinforced 56th Infantry Division is detailed for the landing at Kalamata and the reinforced 5th Infantry Division at Cape Araxos. . . . Code-name for the landing on the Peloponnese is "HUSKY." The Anglo-American General Staff has proposed a simultaneous cover operation against the Dodecanese to General Wilson. Wilson's decision thereon was not yet taken on 23.4.43.

(b) Target for the operation under General Alexander in the Western Mediterranean is not mentioned. A joking reference in the letter points to Sardinia. Code-name for this operation is "BRIMSTONE." The proposed cover target for operation "BRIMSTONE" is Sicily.

2. Maintenance of completest secrecy over this discovery and utmost limitation of circulation of this information is essential.[82]

Further support that the deception was accepted at the highest levels is found in Admiral Doenitz's diary. Doenitz, who had just met with Mussolini, recorded that "the Fuehrer does not agree with the Duce that the most likely invasion point is Sicily. Furthermore, he believes that the discovered Anglo-Saxon order confirms the assumption that the planned attack will be directed mainly against Sardinia and the Peloponnesus."[83]

Doenitz's comments reveal an important point of deception: for strategic deception to succeed, the deceivers must correctly identify the target of their efforts. It was not necessary to deceive everyone, just those who made the final decisions. In the end, it did not matter that the Italians remained unconvinced, or even that some German generals—such as Albrecht Kesselring, who commanded Germany's forces in Sicily—still harbored much anxiety over Sicily. Hitler and the German High Command made the crucial decisions on military matters, so they were the targets of Allied strategic deception. Clarke states that in discussing deception with the generals, he "used the trick of asking them to imagine I had a direct telephone line to Hitler himself, and that he would do anything I told him to do."[84] Clarke recognized that the key to successful strategic deception was in deceiving Hitler; everyone else was secondary.

Clarke's creed for deception was always to determine what the military command wanted the enemy to do, not what it wanted him to think.[85] In this case, German action was exactly what the Allies hoped for. Among other measures taken, the Germans transferred two entire divisions to the Peloponnese immediately after the Mincemeat deception.[86] Sicily, by contrast, was not reinforced at that time.

Interestingly, the Germans did make adjustments in Sicily based on the Mincemeat letters, but they all proved disadvantageous to the Germans. Montagu writes:

> The Germans had switched the effort that they had put into preparing the defences of Sicily, away from the south (where we in fact landed) to the western angle of the triangle and the northern side, which would have been the danger-points if we had been making a diversionary assault during an invasion of Sardinia, or an assault after Sardinia had been captured. Not only were most of the later minefields, demolitions and defences built in the north of Sicily, but the total of defences and reinforcements in the island was less than had been expected and surprisingly deficient in the south and east.[87]

Mincemeat was a resounding success. Moreover, it came at the decisive moment when the Germans had to restructure and reposition their forces following the end of the campaign in North Africa. Through deception, the Allies ensured that the realignment was to the Allies' advantage.

Mincemeat took place during the first stage of Plan Barclay and played a crucial role in its success. Another deception that went into operation during Stage 1 was Plan Waterfall. Waterfall was an "A" Force strategic display of dummies plan that ran throughout all three stages of Barclay. While it was important to conceal the genuine invasion forces in Tunisia given that a buildup there would inevitably point toward an invasion of Sicily, it was of equal importance to provide visual proof of the invasion forces slated for Greece, supposedly based in Tobruk. Clarke stated that "the Story of 'BARCLAY' could have been exploded by a single strip of photographs showing the emptiness of TOBRUK. At once it would have turned attention away from CRETE and GREECE, and most probably directed it immediately towards SICILY."[88] The challenge for the deceptionists was to manufacture the presence of two entire divisions in Cyrenaica: the 8th Armoured Division and the 4th Airborne Division, both notional. The 8th Armoured Division was allegedly slated to lead the attack on the Peloponnese, while the 4th Airborne was earmarked for the attack on Crete and Greece.[89]

Although the deception story claimed that the two divisions were located in Cyrenaica, the reality was that Cyrenaica was "dead" in terms of military activity. The task ahead of the deceptionists was monumental. For a period of three months, as many as seven hundred men worked to create the illusion of preinvasion activity. Clarke recalled:

In the empty desert we had to show a force of more than 20,000 men, with their tentage, their guns, tanks and transport. Landing-craft had to be represented in the harbours as concentrating in a strength to lift the Armoured Division, and behind them the gliders to carry the Airborne Division. Then there was the question of "fighter-cover," without which these divisions could hardly be expected to embark upon their notional operation. CYRENAICA was the only area close enough to bring the targets within fighter range; and so we had to simulate as well a dozen fighter squadrons arriving on the empty airfields and displaying all the associated activities.[90]

As Clarke's description makes clear, it was not enough to display dummies on the ground; the deceptionists had to generate all of the activity that would normally accompany authentic invasion forces, to include dumps, genuine signs of human life and movement, tire tracks and dust, tents, fires, wireless traffic, and workshops. Ironically, this also included antiaircraft fire directed at the enemy's reconnaissance planes. If the concentration had been genuine, the military commanders would have been eager to prevent the enemy from photographing their positions. The 17th AA Brigade was duly posted to Cyrenaica to add credibility to the display.[91] The air command also made arrangements for "fighter interception" in order to imitate genuine military security measures, but also to prevent the enemy from inspecting the dummies too thoroughly.[92] In terms of fighter aircraft, only nine planes were available to simulate the activity of hundreds spread across seven airfields. Clarke added that anytime a "Hun" appeared, the nine aircraft took to the skies. He states that it "was surprising how much activity those nine could create for the few minutes of the day in which it was required, and their contribution towards 'WATERFALL' was of vital importance."[93]

The commanders responsible for seeing Waterfall to fruition were Colonel Victor Jones of the "A" Force Depot and Major E. Southron, the assistant director of camouflage at GHQ Middle East. During the first stage of Barclay, Jones moved his bogus 74th Armoured Brigade headquarters to Tobruk, along with the notional 101 RTR. He was assisted by both the 2nd and 85th Camouflage Companies. Together they displayed 70 landing craft and eleven fighter squadrons by May 10. Jones's 102 RTR soon arrived to simulate tanks and transport vehicles to the scale of an entire armored brigade. After the number of landing craft reached 114, the invasion forces were dispersed in order to convey the first postponement of Barclay.

The enemy conducted two reconnaissance missions over the notional staging area during that initial phase.[94]

As Stage 2 went into effect in early June, the deception teams simulated another concentration of invasion forces to climax on June 16. The landing craft were made visible, along with concentrations of fighter squadrons and twenty-eight Horsa gliders at El Adem. The deceptionists manufactured the presence of a divisional headquarters and two brigades of the 8th Armoured Division. Immediately prior to the second postponement, the intensity of the notional preinvasion activity escalated as tanks and transport moved down to the harbor where landing craft waited in their embarkation positions. On June 17, the forces were again suddenly dispersed to represent the second postponement. The "A" Force Narrative War Diary explains that the tanks returned to their training positions, while the landing craft were "anchored in sheltered coves under deliberately bad camouflage." During that time, the enemy conducted several reconnaissance flights, but their most important efforts to gather intelligence occurred throughout the week preceding Husky. On four different days, German aircraft could be seen over the port of Cyrenaica to photograph a "scene which should by then have given every indication of temporary inaction."[95]

The deception teams were just as diligent throughout the third stage, though enemy reconnaissance was sporadic. While Clarke was disappointed, it did not alter the necessity to continue the facade as "insurance" as the "risk always remained that a successful visit from a single P.R.U. [photographic reconnaissance unit] aircraft on a single day might well have vitiated the whole of the rest of the Deception effort."[96] For Clarke, taking shortcuts on deception was never an option. He recognized the risks of complacency and knew that every effort must be made to achieve maximum realism. Anything short of that could expose the deception as a hoax. Even though efforts on the scale of Waterfall required tremendous resources, manpower, and long-term commitment, they were seen as necessary for success.

For Clarke, deception efforts did not end when the invasion commenced. To the contrary, he continued his deceptive operations beyond the launch of Husky in order to keep the enemy guessing and pinned down in the wrong sectors. Waterfall, for example, continued until July 27 and aimed to keep the threat to the eastern Mediterranean alive. Waterfall was considered a success, "the first of its type ever to be attempted." Clarke himself noted, "Dummy tanks had been employed in the WESTERN DESERT with very marked success during the CYRENAICAN Campaign, but nothing in the form of combined operations had ever previously been attempted."[97] Waterfall, it seems, broke new ground in the realm of combined operations as they applied to deceptive maneuvers.

Another deception operation, Plan Derrick, was approved on June 27. Derrick, a tactical deception affiliated with Barclay, was operated by Lieutenant-Colonel David Strangeways of Tac HQ "A" Force. The idea for Derrick was born after the military command decided to concentrate the Husky landings along the southeast coast of Sicily. Alexander directed "A" Force to "contain enemy forces in the Western portion of SICILY as long after D-Day as possible, and in any case until first light on D plus 3."[98] On July 11, one day after Husky commenced, Derrick went into operation.

The goal of Derrick was to keep the Germans tied down on the western coast of Sicily in anticipation of an attack at Marsala. The Tac HQ files reveal that the planners expected the enemy to appreciate that Sicily was the intended target, as opposed to a diversion, the day after the invasion began (D + 1). It conceded that the enemy would not "be certain on D + 1 that the assaults thus far made are the only ones planned and that we shall not follow them up by assaults in other areas of the Island."[99] Given that the enemy consistently overestimated Allied strength, it stood to reason that the Allies had ample forces remaining to carry out subsequent attacks.

In order to draw the enemy's attention to the west, especially after the genuine invasion began, the deceptionists simulated preinvasion activity at Bizerte from July 9 to 12, arranged for deceptive information to be passed through "A" Force's secret channels, and organized coordinated air and naval action at Marsala to take place on the night of July 11–12. Unfortunately for the success of Derrick, the display of dummies at Bizerte to simulate the concentration of invasion forces met with great difficulty and failed to provide an adequate visual display of force. The US 84th Engineer Camouflage Battalion was tasked with improvising the display; incidentally, it was the first time the battalion worked with dummy landing craft. Clarke considered the effort to be a failure, but not due to the inexperience of the Americans. He attributed it to the lack of preparation time, unsuitability of the equipment, material malfunctions, and strong winds that tossed the dummies about.[100]

Additional components of Derrick met with greater success. The navy, for example, played a vital role in intensifying the threat against Marsala in what was code-named Operation Fracture. On D + 1, the navy diverted follow-up convoys in a northeasterly direction that put them on a route heading toward Marsala. Once night fell, they resumed their normal course. The Royal Navy's 3rd Division of the 12th Cruiser Squadron then unleashed a barrage of firepower on the port of Marsala on D + 1/D + 2 "with the purpose of silencing its Coast Defence Batteries, as though covering a landing effort."[101] The island of Marittimo was bombarded as well by battleships of the 1st Battle Squadron in order to provide adequate "cover" for the invasion forces. Concurrent to the "cover" action at Marittimo, American coastal forces employed sonic devices and laid smoke and gunfire off the coast of Marsala to create the impression of an attack.[102] The Royal Air Force contributed to Derrick as well by bombing the ports and beaches at Marsala and Trapani on D + 1. Simultaneously, Dakota C-47 transport aircraft of 267 Squadron flew behind the beaches to drop decoy fireworks devices, dummy parachutists, and pintails—devices that fired when they made contact with the ground, simultaneously releasing Verey lights into the air to create the impression that additional parachutists had already landed and were signaling their location to others.[103]

Derrick ultimately achieved its objectives. German forces in Sicily's western sector remained in the west. In fact, they did not move east until the British and Americans had firmly established a foothold on the island. An odd, albeit amusing, aspect of Derrick can be found in the German response. On July 12, German radio reported that "landing attempts made by British and American troops near MARSALA had failed in the face of stubborn resistance and the attackers were annihilated."[104] While the report clearly revealed that the Germans took the threats seriously, the claim that the attackers were annihilated was interesting since no troops landed at Marsala, or anywhere near the west coast for that matter.

A final plan associated with Barclay, though not implemented, was the False Armistice Project. The Allies expected the Germans to fight with determination but hoped to minimize Italian resistance. The idea originated with Bevan, who remembered that the Italians had been tricked during the Battle of Caporetto in 1917 into believing that an armistice had been signed. The idea was to draft an armistice proclamation, supposedly issued by King Victor Emmanuel III himself. Back in London, the Political Warfare Executive prepared a draft that was sent to the "A" Force Technical Unit for production.[105] The Technical Unit, under Major E. Titterington, set out to produce a leaflet bearing the armistice proclamation in Italian, complete with the royal coat of arms and the king's signature. Producing the forgery was fairly straightforward, with the exception of obtaining the signature. The deceptionists had a very difficult time in finding anything signed by the king. After an exhaustive search that ended in Cairo, ""A" Force was compelled to buy a six-volume tome in Italian of ITALY's effort in World War I, which had inside it one small reproduction of a signed portrait of the King."[106] With the signature procured and duly forged, the leaflet was sent to Algiers for approval. After both Eisenhower and Alexander gave their approval, plans were made to drop the leaflets on the night of July 9; the PWB intended to simultaneously broadcast the news of the armistice. Despite the efforts, the False Armistice Project did not go forward because London rejected it.[107]

No official explanation for London's decision made it into the official record. Clarke, however, saw the dismissal of the False Armistice plan as rather unfortunate. He pointed out that "subsequent events in SICILY showed that already the Italian Army had little will to resist." He concluded: "The 'False Armistice Project' was admittedly a dirty trick, but it might have worked, and perhaps saved lives by accelerating the whole process of ITALY's collapse."[108] Clarke's assessment reaffirms his personal motivation for using deception—to save lives. If his deceptions were successful and battles were shortened, then lives would be saved.

Plan Barclay was an enormous deception operation. It combined strategic and tactical operations, with coordinated efforts between Britain and the United States, the military services, the commanding generals, political leadership, and Allied deception organizations. All told, it operated for more than three months, over which time Barclay and three of the four subsidiary plans went into effect. It was an organizational feat, to say the least.

Barclay, along with its associated plans, was also a remarkable success. The primary objective was to divert the enemy's attention away from Sicily by manufacturing threats to Greece, Sardinia, and southern France. Despite the odds stacked against it, Barclay succeeded beyond measure. In March 1943, there were eight German divisions in the Balkans—one each in Greece and Crete, with the remaining six in Yugoslavia. By the time Husky commenced in July, the Germans had reinforced the Balkans with an additional ten divisions. Notably, the number of divisions in Greece alone increased from one to nine. Moreover, it appeared that the threat to Greece resonated with Hitler and the German High Command more than any other threat. Montagu records that "on the 23rd July, nearly a fortnight after the Allied landing in Sicily, Hitler *still* believed that the main operation was going to be an invasion of Greece, and appointed his favourite general, General Rommel, to command the forces that were being assembled there."[109] Furthermore, five of the original eight divisions stationed in the Balkans were upgraded from garrison to light or panzer grenadier division status. Finally, southern France saw an increase of between two to three divisions, while Sardinia and Corsica were both reinforced by one division.[110]

Sicily, the genuine target of military operations, was defended by the Italian Sixth Army. Although it numbered approximately 200,000 men, it was weak, poorly trained, and ill-equipped for battle. The deplorable state of the Italian garrison prompted Hitler to reinforce Sicily with the Hermann Goering Division, or what was left of it after its evacuation from Tunisia. Between May and June, additional German units were sent to Sicily to help reconstitute the decimated 15th Panzer

Grenadier Division. Both German divisions were hastily thrown together and understrength, suggesting that the German High Command underestimated the threat to Sicily.[111] Moreover, neither division was positioned on the southeastern corner of the island where the Husky forces landed. In fact, the 15th Panzer Grenadier Division was stationed in western Sicily, and it remained there for forty-eight hours after the invasion had begun, undoubtedly the result of Plan Derrick.[112]

A secondary objective was to mislead the enemy as to the timing of the invasion. Again, "A" Force could count this as a success. Enemy reports show that the Germans and Italians both expected the attack to commence during the moonless period, so they were caught off guard when the invasion began on a moonlit night. An Italian prisoner of war stated of Husky: "We thought it was just a sabotage raid . . . and we sent word through to ROME. My General thought the Allies would not invade in moonlight, and proceeded to take steps to deal with some paratroops. But suddenly everything went poof!"[113]

In spite of the many difficulties encountered, including the sheer obviousness of Sicily as the next target and the assault on Pantelleria, which the deceptionists feared would expose the real operation, Barclay succeeded. Clarke described Barclay as a classical deception that both demonstrated the "possibilities and limitations of large-scale Deception" and "illustrated more clearly than most the principal lessons both of planning and of implementation." Barclay was also used to initiate the Americans into the world of military deception, and Clarke was satisfied that the effort "put deception on the map" for the US military leadership. Clarke viewed Barclay as a model of deception and concluded his report thus: "If a newcomer to Deception were to seek a short road towards initiation into its secrets of success and failure, the Author, with all humility, would recommend him to study the story of the 'BARCLAY' Plan."[114]

Over the course of three months, the deceptionists worked diligently to convey the Barclay story to the enemy bit by bit. They had used every tool in their arsenal, tools that had been sharpened over the previous years of fighting in the desert. After giving it their best, there was nothing left to do but watch and wait to see how the offensive would play out. Operation Husky began on July 10, 1943. As a testament to the effectiveness of deception as a weapon of war, the enemy was caught by surprise and the landings went almost entirely uncontested.

4 ROUNDING OUT 1943 IN ITALY

During the opening hours of July 10, 1943, the British Eighth Army and US Seventh Army—the two armies then comprising General Harold Alexander's 15th Army Group—began their assault on Sicily. Despite the delayed and often chaotic military planning, the Allies amassed an impressive invasion force. Between the Eastern and Western Mediterranean Task Forces, represented by the British and US armies, respectively, the Allies landed over 180,000 men, 400 medium tanks, and 540 artillery pieces. Moreover, the Allies deployed 3,462 aircraft and an invasion fleet of 2,590 vessels for the initial attack alone. By comparison, Sicily was defended by the Italian Sixth Army of roughly 200,000 men, under the command of General d'Armata Guzzoni. Despite its size, the army was poorly trained, inadequately equipped, and overwhelmingly inexperienced; in fact, only one division had ever seen combat.[1] As for the Germans, Adolf Hitler discounted the threat to Sicily but, at the urging of Field Marshal Albrecht Kesselring, commander in chief of Germany's southern forces, had belatedly agreed to reinforce the island with the

Hermann Goering Panzer Division and 15th Panzer Grenadier Division. Both divisions were "improvised" and understrength.[2]

By sheer preponderance of force, the Allies possessed the advantage. They had furthered their advantage through the extensive Barclay deception plan. The evidence of that success lay in the lack of sufficient battle-ready forces stationed on Sicily. Moreover, while Sicily was defended only by the one unprepared Italian army and two understrength German panzer divisions, the Germans had diligently reinforced the Balkans, Corsica, and Sardinia in expectation of Allied attacks. The disposition of the German divisions on Sicily further indicated the success of the deception efforts. Instead of establishing a strong defensive line along Sicily's southern and southeastern coast, where the Allies landed on July 10, neither panzer division was even in the region. The Hermann Goering Division was situated in the east within easy reach of Messina, while the 15th Panzer Grenadier Division was the farthest away—positioned on the western coast to meet a possible Allied diversionary attack on the assumption that Sardinia was the Allies' chosen objective.[3]

On the whole, the Axis forces were poorly prepared to defend the Italian islands. Kesselring became painfully aware of the inadequacies after touring Italy's island defenses prior to the assault. He lamented in his memoirs:

> On the maps everything was in order. Their plans cleverly thought out, in some respects too cleverly by half. But the only construction work done was mere eyewash. There were no prepared positions on the islands, which were inadequately defended, and had unguarded tank obstacles more likely to hamper the defenders than to check the enemy—all so much gingerbread. . . . The coastal divisions I inspected were on par with the fortifications. With such troops in these defences it was hopeless to offer resistance.

As the protector of Germany's southern flank, Kesselring was unable to discount the attractiveness of Sicily. He oversaw efforts to strengthen the island's defenses and lobbied for reinforcements, which had resulted in the transfer of the two "improvised" panzer divisions. By early July, after the transfer was complete, the commander observed that "the islands had a defence which, though it ruled out a *coup de main*, was hardly powerful enough to withstand a large-scale planned invasion." Since he knew the Axis forces were not strong enough to defeat the Allied armies on Sicily, his plan was to fight a protracted defense making optimal use of the island's terrain to wear the Allies down, followed by a strategic evacuation across the Strait of Messina.[4]

When the Anglo-American assault began on the night of July 9–10, under the crescent moon, the Allies encountered only light resistance. In his memoirs, General Bernard Law Montgomery recorded that the "first waves of our assault achieved complete tactical surprise and the enemy's confusion and disorganization were such that he was unable to offer any co-ordinated opposition."[5] In fact, Kesselring had dispersed his German divisions across the island, so they were unable to respond to the initial attack, while the Italian coastal divisions disintegrated.[6] The Axis was thus unable to repel the invasion. Montgomery's Eighth Army staged multiple landings in the area of Syracuse along the southeastern tip of the island, while the Seventh Army under Gen. George S. Patton landed at Gela on Sicily's southern coast. The amphibious forces were supported by concentrated naval gunfire and the landing of airborne troops. Moreover, during the month leading up to the invasion, Allied air forces flew 42,227 sorties, along with 1,092 sorties on the day of the attack. Although Axis airpower remained active, the Allies had effectively established air superiority.[7]

The landings themselves went largely unopposed, but the Americans bore the brunt of the first German counterattack. Kesselring worked to "repair an oversight" and ordered the Hermann Goering Division to prepare for "immediate action." He sent the division south hoping to intercept the Americans before they could advance inland.[8] On July 11, Patton's forces came under a concentrated counterattack, but the Seventh Army was ultimately able to break the attack with the assistance of naval support fire.

Despite having entered the battle with numerical superiority aided by the element of surprise, the Allies quickly squandered their advantage. Instead of combining their efforts once on land, the two Allied armies fought as completely independent entities. The Eighth Army was regarded as the primary strike force, while the Seventh Army found itself relegated to the position of a flanking guard for the British. It did not take long for the shortcomings in Allied planning to become painfully clear. In fact, what became most apparent was that the Allies had focused their planning exclusively on the amphibious assault, leaving little thought to the campaign beyond the beachhead. The lack of planning and coordination, as well as the failure on the part of the Allied commanders to hammer out a combined strategy for the inland campaign, seriously hampered its conduct.[9]

One further issue revolved around General Alexander's distrust of the American forces. Alexander recalled their poor performance in North Africa, specifically at the Battle of Kasserine Pass, and thus held the Americans' fighting ability in very low esteem. He failed to realize that the American learning curve was advanced,

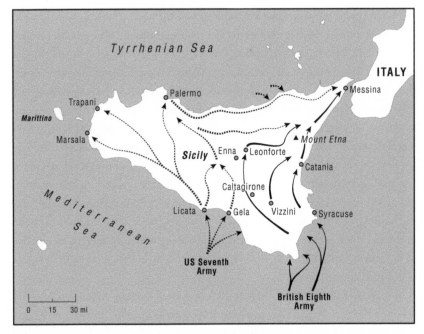

The Sicilian Campaign. Map by Erin Greb Cartography.

and that the American forces in Sicily were a far cry from those at Kasserine Pass.[10] Because of his lack of confidence in the Americans, Alexander was quick to agree that Montgomery should play the lead role in Sicily.[11]

The issue between the British and American commands hit a head only days after the landings. The original plan, albeit vague, called for the British to steadily proceed up the eastern coast toward Messina; the Seventh Army was to drive north to sever the island in half and hold off the German forces positioned in western Sicily. On July 13, Montgomery suddenly reassessed his options and made a costly blunder that would slow the Allied advance: he altered the battle plan so that the Eighth Army would shift west before driving north to Enna, located in the very center of Sicily. Alexander approved Montgomery's revised plan and instructed that "operations for the immediate future will be for Eighth Army to advance on two axes. One to capture the Port of Catania and the group of airfields there, and the other to secure the network of road communications within the area Leonforte-Enna."[12] In retrospect, the "fool change of plan," as Patton called it, was irresponsible as it caused an unnecessary delay and effectively split one army into two forces, while leaving another army to sit idle.[13]

The result of the changed battle plan was that the Allies lost precious time and momentum, while relations between Montgomery and Patton deteriorated.[14] That fateful decision also removed the immediate pressure from the German defenders, allowing them time to regroup, receive reinforcements, and establish a defensive perimeter. By July 18, the Germans had reinforced Sicily with General Hans Hube's XIV Panzer Corps Headquarters and units of the 29th Panzer Grenadier Division. The Germans proceeded to form the Etna Line, a solid defensive line surrounding Mount Etna, which forced the Allies to fight a protracted battle in rugged mountainous terrain instead of following the coastal roads to Messina.[15] Kesselring observed that "for all its mishaps, the Axis Command was mighty lucky, helped above all as it was by the methodical procedure of the Allies." He added:

> Furthermore, the Allied conception of operations offered many chances. The absence of any large-scale encirclement of the island or of a thrust up the coastline of Calabria gave us long weeks to organise the defence with really very weak resources. The slow advance of the main attack and the remarkable dissipation of their other forces over the island allowed the Axis Command to bring sufficient reinforcements into the defence areas as they were threatened.[16]

Kesselring's reference to the dissipation of the Allies' "other" forces referred to the actions of the Americans. Patton, tired of sitting idle and exasperated with Montgomery's insistence that the Americans play a subsidiary role in the campaign, ordered the Seventh Army west toward Palermo on July 17. In only five days Patton had taken the Port of Palermo and cleared western Sicily, but the move held little strategic value. The Seventh Army still had to turn its attention east to the now reinforced German line around Mount Etna. In the meantime, Montgomery's decision to take Mount Etna by flanking the Germans using a left hook along the western portion of the line forced the Allies to fight in incredibly steep and rugged mountain terrain, ground completely unsuitable for mechanized forces. Moreover, it further separated the Allied forces from crucial naval support. After a treacherous fight across mountains and ridges, the Seventh and Eighth Armies were finally in position to advance toward Messina by early August. On August 17, the Americans entered Messina, followed shortly by the British. Incidentally, the Allies did not have to fight to take Messina; the enemy had already withdrawn and evacuated Sicily altogether.[17]

The capture of Messina on August 17 represented Allied victory on Sicily, yet it was a tempered victory. Again, the Allies had made a costly mistake, specifically in that they failed to block the enemy's escape route. The Germans organized a calculated and meticulously staged evacuation of Sicily across the Strait of Messina from August 11 to 17. Instead of focusing on efforts to block the Axis evacuation from Sicily utilizing naval and air operations, the Allies allowed at least 50,000 Germans and 60,000 Italians to escape with 10,000 vehicles, 47 tanks, 94 guns, and approximately 17,000 tons of ammunition, fuel, and other stores. As a result, multiple battle-hardened veteran divisions, along with a German Corps Headquarters, remained fit to continue the fight from a new defensive position on the Italian Peninsula.[18] The German leadership was dismayed by the Allies' failure to cut off their escape route. Kesselring noted that the "enemy failure to exploit the last chance of hindering the German forces crossing the Straits of Messina, by continuous and strongly co-ordinated attacks from the sea and the air, was almost a greater boon to the German Command than their failure immediately to push their pursuit across the straits on 17 August."[19] Had the Germans not escaped with their veteran forces intact in southern Italy, one can question whether Hitler would have ultimately given the order to defend the southern half of the peninsula.

Although the battle for Sicily was successful in the end, it was unnecessarily sloppy in its strategic and tactical execution. The Allies entered the campaign without a clearly defined strategy for the campaign. Omar Bradley, then a lieutenant general commanding the US II Corps, wrote: "Astonishingly as it seems in retrospect, there was no master plan for the conquest of Sicily. Nothing had been worked out beyond the limited beachhead objectives." He further stated that "seldom in war has a major operation been undertaken in such a fog of indecision, confusion and conflicting plans."[20] The Allies' failure to develop a plan to prevent the Axis forces from evacuating was shortsighted and yet another strategic flaw. And even the decision on Italy—which the Allied leaders failed adequately to address at the Trident conference in Washington—was to be decided based on the progress in Sicily, again leaving little time for strategic planning. For their part, the Germans fought with tactical superiority, made excellent use of the terrain to prolong the battle, and staged a carefully thought-out retreat and evacuation. The Allies were fortunate to possess the material advantage and the element of surprise provided by Plan Barclay.

While the Allies committed many mistakes during the Sicilian campaign, the effort can be viewed broadly as a success. One of the main objectives of the Mediterranean Strategy was to draw German forces away from France and the eastern front. In that regard, it succeeded. The Allied invasion of Sicily, along with the increased threat that it presented to the Italian mainland, forced Hitler to focus his attention on Italy at the expense of France and the Soviet Union.[21] As Hitler lost all confidence in Italy's reliability as an ally and became increasingly concerned that its capitulation was near, he had little choice but to transfer additional German forces to reinforce the peninsula.[22] Another Allied objective was to bring about Italy's surrender, and the Sicilian campaign brought the Allies one step closer to achieving that goal. On July 25, upon Victor Emmanuel III's orders, Benito Mussolini was arrested and removed from power. He was replaced by the former chief of staff of Italy's armed forces, Marshal Pietro Badoglio, and the path toward negotiated surrender began.[23] The campaign also gave the Allies additional experience in staging an amphibious invasion, knowledge that would be put to excellent use the following year with Operation Overlord. Finally, the campaign saw the British and American armies mature. The British made great strides in their understanding and execution of combined operations; in the words of the official historian, Sicily represented the "coming-of-age of British combined operations."[24] American troops proved to be a formidable fighting force that not only could hold its own on the battlefield, but had learned from mistakes committed during the North African campaign.

An aspect of the Sicilian campaign that was an undisputed success was the deception effort that preceded it. Even though Sicily appeared to be the most obvious target, the deceptionists succeeded in focusing the German High Command's attention on diversionary targets, thus reducing its concern over Sicily. That the initial landings met with only minor opposition, the German divisions were positioned on the wrong sides of the island, and the 15th Panzer Grenadier Division was slow to respond were major outcomes of Plan Barclay and a true testament to its success. Official records of the London Controlling Section provide additional evidence to support the deception's success:

> Report by Italian Divisional Commander in the SOUTH EAST on assault as "sabotage raid by paratroopers," and that he had not expected attack till the dark period of the moon at the end of the month. Statements of prisoners as to surprise. Standing down of enemy troops in SOUTH EAST till the end of the month, sending of troops from SICILY to SARDINIA and CORSICA. Statements of two captured Italian General[s] as to belief in assault on SARDINIA and CORSICA, and up to 12/13th July that main attack was coming on West Coast, and assault of 9th July was a feint.[25]

While the deception was a success, the Sicilian campaign was also reminiscent of familiar patterns from North Africa. Time and again, "A" Force managed to secure the element of surprise, but the gains were often squandered on the battlefield as a result of poor execution, leadership decisions beyond the opening of the offensive, and German tenacity in mobilizing defenses. Even though the Allies ultimately prevailed on Sicily, which was not always the case in the desert battles, the similarity to the North African experience was undeniable. The deception had successfully rendered the enemy unprepared for the attack, yet the battle still bogged down as a result of questionable decision making and tactical errors committed during the battle, thus providing the Germans time to rally.[26] In the specific case of Sicily, those mistakes permitted the enemy to reinforce the island—exactly what the deceptionists had worked so hard to prevent him from doing prior to July 10. Unfortunately for the deceptionists, they had little to no control over the conduct of operations once the campaign began. The greatest contribution of deception almost always occurred during the period of planning and preparation prior to a campaign; it was, conversely, inherently limited in its ability to influence the enemy once those campaigns were underway.

Although Allied leaders agreed to target Sicily as the first stage of the Mediterranean Strategy following North Africa, the precise details of that strategy were never clarified or firmly agreed to. Gen. George C. Marshall and the US Army planners disapproved of operations in the Mediterranean, and it can be argued that their insistence on challenging the strategy resulted in a rather ambiguous conclusion to the Trident conference in May 1943. Allied leaders had finally arrived at a consensus on Husky, but they failed to develop a clear strategic plan to follow it. The decision on Italy, therefore, remained unresolved. Gen. Dwight D. Eisenhower noted that the final agreement "left exploitation of the Sicilian operation to my judgment," but he was left with the impression that he was to "take advantage of any favorable opportunity to rush into Italy."[27] At the same time, Eisenhower understood that he could not expect reinforcements for future campaigns in the Mediterranean as strategic planning was increasingly focused on the anticipated cross-Channel campaign; in fact, Allied leadership agreed at Trident that seven divisions and most of the landing craft would depart from the Mediterranean for the United Kingdom in November 1943 to begin preparing for Overlord. The Allies had thus far compromised on the question of continued Mediterranean operations, but both sides agreed that the cross-Channel invasion of France must be the priority in 1944.[28] That relegated the Mediterranean's status to that of a diversionary theater intended only to contain German forces.

As the campaign in Sicily drew to a close, Allied leaders met in Quebec for the Quadrant conference—the sixth Allied conference of the war. The delegations arrived between August 9 and 17, with the conference officially commencing on August 17—the same day the Allies claimed victory in Sicily. The main focus of the conference was to reaffirm Allied commitment to Operation Overlord with a tentative launch date of May 1, 1944. All parties agreed, and Lieutenant-General Sir Frederick Morgan, Chief of Staff to the Supreme Allied Commander (COSSAC), was given the go-ahead to begin making preparations for Overlord. The British did, however, insist that German strength must be reduced before Allied forces crossed the English Channel. To that end, the Mediterranean retained its appeal as a diversionary theater as it clearly offered the best opportunity to pin down German divisions in southern Europe. Allied leaders accordingly agreed to a limited campaign in Italy with three main objectives identified: induce Italy's surrender, establish air bases in Rome and northern Italy from which to continue the strategic bombing campaign against Germany, and contain German forces as far away from northwestern France as possible. Allied leaders also agreed to target Sardinia and Corsica, as well as to plan an operation against southern France—largely utilizing reconstituted French units—to serve as a diversion during Overlord. Turkey and the Balkans were both ruled out as potential areas of military operation. While no genuine operations were planned, the deceptionists made abundant use of the Balkans—capitalizing on Hitler's ongoing concerns over the region—for their purposes. Finally, Churchill and Roosevelt agreed to appoint an American general as Supreme Allied Commander for Overlord, though they had yet to identify precisely which commander.[29]

Aside from American fears that the Mediterranean would consume too many resources and potentially divert Allied attention away from Overlord, and British concerns that Mediterranean options would be so limited that they would fail to divert sufficient German forces away from France, the Allies were largely in agreement. In fact, of all the Allied conferences to date, the British and Americans were the most united in strategy and purpose at Quebec. With the crucial decisions made, it fell to the commanders to begin planning for the campaigns in Italy and France.

Although Eisenhower understood that operations in Italy were likely to follow the Sicilian campaign, he held off on making the final decision to invade the Italian Peninsula until July 18. Because his attention was primarily focused on Husky at that time, the details of the invasion were not hammered out until August 16—less than three weeks prior to the campaign's launch.[30] The final plan called for multiple landings. The first, Operation Baytown, envisioned a landing at Calabria on the "toe" of the Italian "boot," directly across the Strait of Messina, by Montgomery's Eighth Army. Baytown was planned for the opening days of September, and in fact went forward on September 3. It was to be followed by Operation Slapstick, a small-scale landing at Taranto on the "heel." Operation Avalanche, an amphibious landing at Salerno, was the most difficult of the three assaults. Lt. Gen. Mark Clark, who had yet to see battle in World War II, was chosen to lead the American Fifth Army, accompanied by the British 10th Corps, into Salerno on September 9. The key objective of Avalanche was to seize the port at Naples before troops moved north toward Rome.[31]

In the meantime, Clarke and his team at "A" Force were scrambling to develop a strategic deception plan to assist the Italian campaign on short notice. Not unlike Barclay, Plan Boardman had to be tweaked and modified as the commanders reassessed and revised the invasion plans. Boardman was originally intended to serve as a continuation of the Allies' strategic objectives to utilize the Mediterranean as a diversion to keep the Germans pinned down in southern Europe. Clarke began working on Boardman as soon as Operation Husky began and the Barclay deception campaign drew to a close. However, when Eisenhower decided to invade the Italian mainland, Clarke had to modify Boardman to accommodate the new invasion plans. Eisenhower signed off on the deception plan on July 22.[32]

Boardman's first objective remained a continuation of Barclay and the overall "Deception Policy 1943 (Germany and Italy)." It called for "A" Force to continue its focus on containing German forces in the Balkans, ideally in Greece, as well as to maintain the threat to Sardinia, Corsica, and southern France. Its second objective, to weaken enemy forces in central and southern Italy, pertained specifically to the upcoming Italian campaign. The story, however, proved challenging. The goal in the early stages of planning, which occurred at the same time as the campaign in Sicily, was to prevent German reinforcement of southern Italy from the north. The situation changed after the German and Italian defenders of Sicily retreated across the Strait of Messina. With seasoned German divisions then situated in southern Italy, "A" Force needed to divert enemy attention away from the two primary invasion targets—Calabria (Baytown) and Salerno (Avalanche)—by manufacturing a false invasion target. To that end, the deceptionists engineered a threat to the heel of Italy near Taranto. The challenge facing the deceptionists was that while the threat was designed to divert German focus and resources to the heel, it ran the risk of encouraging further German reinforcement of southern Italy in general.[33]

Boardman faced one additional obstacle, in this case pertaining to Sardinia. During Barclay the deceptionists played up the threat to Sardinia to draw German forces away from Sicily. Boardman also included a threat to Sardinia, but Clarke became concerned that the Germans were more likely to evacuate the island than reinforce it if the threat level increased too significantly. After conveying that concern to AFHQ, the decision was made to place a heavier emphasis on Corsica rather than Sardinia to prevent the enemy from abandoning Sardinia altogether at a time when the Allies still needed to utilize it for diversionary purposes.[34]

In the final version of Boardman, the story claimed that the Allies planned to attack Sardinia and Corsica on September 5, the heel of Italy on the 10th, and the Peloponnese by the end of September. The attacks on the heel and the Peloponnese were portrayed as a coordinated effort on the part of the Twelfth Army to gain full control over the entrance to the Adriatic Sea, with the Balkans identified as the Twelfth Army's primary objective.[35] After taking Corsica, the US Fifth Army and British 5th Corps would attack either southern France or northwest Italy. The ambiguity of the latter was intended to keep the enemy guessing on Allied objectives. Clarke explained that this "unusual procedure (which did *not* give very good results) was adopted in order to reconcile the conflicting requirements of the Chiefs of Staff's overall policy and the local strategic needs of the theatre."[36] In hindsight, Clarke acknowledged that "success in the latter direction would have produced more concrete results than the rather hypothetical advantages to RUSSIA" and the deception "would have worked much better had it been possible to concentrate the whole of this one threat against the more important of the two targets."[37]

"A" Force implemented Boardman using the same trusted methods of deception developed in North Africa and carried out with precision during the preceding Barclay operation. Of particular importance, the bogus order of battle efforts continued to pay dividends. The fictitious Twelfth Army, represented by the Air Defense Headquarters in Egypt following the departure of Force 545 (Eighth Army) for Sicily, remained in Cairo and continued to play the leading role in any threat to the eastern Mediterranean. Moreover, Colonel Victor Jones again transferred his 8th Armoured Division to Cyrenaica, where it displayed two hundred landing craft, one hundred Mosquito fighter-bomber aircraft, and thirty Waco gliders—all dummies—in order to simulate a threat against the Peloponnese.[38]

Propaganda was yet another method used to influence the enemy. The PWB at AFHQ worked to implement a psychological warfare campaign dubbed Plan Douglas. The PWB used both radio and leaflets to convey the message that the war was lost. Allied leaders anticipated Italy's surrender, thus they no longer viewed the Italians as a serious threat. The main target of the psychological campaign, therefore, was the average German soldier whose morale was assumed to still be high. A leaflet directive identified the chief message to be conveyed as follows: "The war is lost. From now on you are fighting, not for yourselves or for Germany, but to gain a few months' grace for Hitler and the Nazi leaders. Do not let yourselves be driven to death, do not allow Germany to be driven to destruction and chaos by a suicidal maniac." Leaflets designed to influence German officers read: "You are responsible for your men and their families—do not send them to certain, senseless death." In the meantime, the propaganda experts also sought to reassure the Germans that they would be well provided for and treated fairly in prisoner of war camps. To emphasize that point, the propagandists drafted leaflets containing POW camp menus and ration allotments. The PWB leaflet directive on Plan Douglas did, however, caution the propagandists against going too far and offending the Germans' "soldierly pride."[39]

The main challenge Douglas faced was to meet the needs of the deception staff, specifically insofar as it sought to mislead the enemy as to when and where the Allies intended to strike, while simultaneously seeking to undermine the Germans and lower Italian morale to its breaking point in order to hasten Italy's surrender. As it turned out, the propaganda campaign proved rather ineffective in passing along the deception, but not because of any flaw in its own methods. As the "A" Force Narrative War Diary asserts, the PWB efforts were "rudely upset" by British and American politicians who were "unaware of the Deception element in the propaganda" and boasted of the upcoming Allied invasion of Italy. On July 27, for example, the British prime minister was quoted announcing that the Allies were planning to make war in every quarter of Italy: "North and south and from the sea and from the air and by amphibious descents we shall also endeavor to bring the utmost rigor of war increasingly upon them." Statements of the sort were not helpful to Clarke and his team, who were earnestly trying to discourage the Germans from reinforcing Italy—especially the south.[40]

By that point in the war, double agents were regularly employed to pass deceptive information to the enemy as they were considered among the most reliable channels through which the British could relay information to Germany's High Command. Boardman was no exception, yet it also contained a rare example of triple cross. The case revolved around a team of saboteurs of Spanish and Sardinian nationality who were working for the British. Collectively referred to as Moselle, they were sent to Sardinia and provided a wireless set so they could communicate with their controlling operator. The effort went awry, and the team was captured immediately upon their arrival on the island. The Italians proved to be savvy deceptionists themselves and recognized the opportunity to use the captured wireless set to gather information from the British. Yet, it soon became apparent to the British that the Italians were operating Moselle's wireless set in a clever attempt at double cross.

Although the capture of the agents was unfortunate, the opportunity to exploit the situation for the purpose of deception was invaluable. The channel was thus handed over to "A" Force in May 1943. From that point forward, all messages to Moselle were prepared by the "40" Committee in Algiers. The main theme of the messages to Moselle pertained to the Allies' intent to invade Sardinia. On September 6, with the genuine invasion of Salerno only days away, the British sent one final message:

> Assure potential friends in event Allied landing property and traditions would be respected as in SICILY. Explain that Allies would arrive as liberators and not conquerors. The unpopular but well-armed Germans must be annihilated wherever they are to be found. We are not at liberty to discuss future allied military moves. Essential thing is that you be ready for action as soon as possible.[41]

One of the main challenges of running the Moselle channel as a triple cross was to prevent the Italians from realizing that the British suspected their channel was compromised. To that end, after it took over the Moselle channel in May, "A" Force organized an airdrop of money, arms, and stores in order to demonstrate the Allies' continued confidence in Moselle for the benefit of their Italian controllers. All of this proved highly successful, and the British learned after the war, through the interrogation of Sergeant-Major Silvestri of the Italian Secret Service, that the Italians believed they had thoroughly duped the British.[42]

In addition to the typical intelligence methods and displays of dummies, Boardman also employed physical deception. The tactical plan, Boothby, took on added importance after the German and Italian defenders of Sicily crossed the Strait of Messina to occupy southern Italy. Previously, "A" Force's goal was to prevent the Germans from reinforcing southern Italy altogether. After the Axis evacuation of Sicily and the movement of German forces from northern Italy to the south, focus shifted to influencing the disposition of the German forces in southern Italy. That task fell primarily to Tac HQ "A" Force under the command of Lieutenant-Colonel David Strangeways.

The specific aim of Boothby was to draw German forces away from Salerno. To accomplish that, it was emphasized that the British Eighth Army planned to land in the area of Crotone, while the British 3rd Corps was to stage a landing along the heel near Taranto. While Main HQ "A" Force in Cairo passed the story through its agents and established channels, Tac HQ organized the physical measures in conjunction with assistance from the armed services. Similar to Waterfall, one of the subsidiary Barclay plans, the cooperation of the services allowed for combined operations within the deception apparatus. Accordingly, plans were made for the navy to assist with the bombardment of coastal defenses around Crotone and the heel, naval activity around Taranto, and submarine activity around target beaches. The navy also laid guide buoys off selected beaches beginning five days prior to Avalanche. On land, a Special Air Service (SAS) regiment was sent to conduct reconnaissance of selected beaches, while another was to carry out a raid against the coastal defenses of a designated inland target on the night of D –6/D –5. The air force was asked to participate by conducting photographic reconnaissance (PR) of target beaches, bombing Taranto, and bombing aerodromes located along the heel. Tac HQ also coordinated a signals deception to simulate communication and operational traffic between Alexander's 15th Army Group Headquarters and the British 3rd Corps of the Twelfth Army.[43]

An additional component of Boothby sought to convince the enemy that the Allies had dropped operatives and saboteurs on the heel of Italy. On D –10, they dropped pintails and dummy paratroopers, complete with harnesses and chutes. On D –5, they dropped ammunition and stores supposedly intended for their agents on the ground. It was hoped that the enemy would find evidence of this activity, along with the ammunition and stores that were "missed" by the saboteurs.[44] Finally, to build on the illusion of active Allied agents along the heel, Tac HQ carried out a rather creative ruse on September 4 to drop carrier pigeons over a German headquarters located on the toe. The pigeons carried messages supposedly from the operatives providing beach reports and the location of guide lights that would be visible beginning at midnight on September 10. The pigeons were in reality untrained and thus expected to land in German territory. While clever and indicative of the British willingness to use any means possible for deception, there is no evidence to suggest that the Germans ever discovered the pigeons or their messages.[45]

In his final assessment of Boardman, along with the accompanying Plan Boothby, Clarke declared the results "not dramatic, but by no means unsatisfactory." Given the short amount of preparation time, there was only so much "A" Force could do. Cover plans take time to devise and implement. In the case of Boardman, all Clarke and his team could hope for was to alter the disposition of German troops in southern Italy and divert the enemy's attention to false targets. Satisfactorily, each of the locations targeted by deceptive efforts showed signs of German activity, from a "lively nervousness" in the Balkans to a high alert issued for southern France, as well as reports of imminent invasion pertaining to Sardinia and Corsica. In Italy the results could be measured by the amount of opposition met by the invading Allied armies. On September 3, Montgomery's Eighth Army crossed the Strait of

Messina and made a largely unopposed landing at Calabria; only three days later, the Germans began to pull back.[46]

The Allies had not expected major resistance along the toe, but they were rightfully concerned about the landings at Salerno. The port at Naples and the highway leading to Rome were rather obvious targets for the Allies, and the Germans responded accordingly by sending reinforcements to meet the anticipated threat. The battle-hardened 16th Panzer Division was positioned in full strength to defend Salerno, while the Hermann Goering and 15th Panzer Grenadier Divisions were in close striking range. The "A" Force planners knew that the Germans lacked sufficient time to send additional reinforcements from the north, so they increased their efforts to simulate a threat against the heel in order to alter the disposition of the existing eight German divisions in the south, specifically those in position to oppose Avalanche. Boardman and Boothby paid minor dividends as one parachute division began to move toward the heel at the exact same time as the Avalanche forces were loading onto their convoys, and the invading forces at Salerno were initially opposed by only one German division.[47] Moreover, the British 1st Airborne Division landed unopposed at Taranto, on the heel of Italy, while the German parachute division was still a considerable distance away from the landing point. With the landings executed and the battle for the European mainland underway, Plan Boardman came to a close.[48]

"A" Force's role and the nature of deception began to change once the war shifted to European soil. With the notable exception of Operation Overlord, it was difficult to plan and maintain long-term strategic cover and deception plans. More often than not, strategic efforts were smaller in scope and had to be modified regularly to meet the needs of a rapidly changing military situation. With regard to the Italian campaign, "A" Force began developing strategic deceptions on short notice to support the tactical plans developed at Tac HQ, and tactical deception took on a much larger and consistent role than it had previously.

After reorganizing in Tunisia during the month of July, Tac HQ transferred to Sicily and rejoined the 15th Army Group in Syracuse on August 3. From that point forward, Tac HQ accompanied Alexander and developed small-scale tactical plans to assist battlefield operations. These plans were developed and executed quickly with the goal of softening the enemy and weakening its response to Allied operations. They were not designed or expected to serve as a knockout punch, but instead to knock the enemy off-balance at crucial times during individual battles. The tactical efforts were enhanced by the addition of a dummy unit. Colonel Jones's dummy 74th Armoured Brigade had been used primarily to lend visual evidence to strategic deceptions. However, the new opportunities for tactical deception in Italy necessitated greater means to bolster the ruses with physical support. Accordingly, a "Special Camouflage Company" was formed on September 7, and the 101 RTR, comprising twenty-six vehicles, was attached to it.[49] It was equipped with "Baxter equipment"—inflatable tanks and vehicles produced in the United States. The equipment was named after Major F. G. Baxter of "A" Force, who traveled to Washington, D.C. in order to enlist American aid in producing the dummy equipment.[50] The Americans developed three types of dummy vehicles, of which the British preferred the balloon inflatables. Official documents call the inflatables a "resounding success" and point out that the American model became the standard for not only tanks and vehicles, but also guns and landing craft.[51] Under the command of Captain R. C. Gifford, the "Special Camouflage Company" remained with Tac HQ and the 15th Army Group until April 1945.[52]

The implementation of ad hoc tactical plans, which represented a modification of the standard deception machinery developed by "A" Force over the previous years, revealed the evolving nature of military deception and the versatility of the "A" Force organization as a whole. "A" Force underwent repeated modifications throughout the war, and its ability to reinvent itself to meet the changing needs and circumstances of war was vital to its strength and continued success.

After taking Messina, Allied military planning naturally zeroed in on the Italian Peninsula. Even though an immediate exploitation of the enemy retreat from Sicily would have been to the Allies' advantage, Allied leadership was not prepared to pursue the German and Italian forces onto the mainland. The Allied failure to maintain the pressure on the Axis surprised the German leadership.[53] It also gave the enemy time to recuperate. The delay was without doubt a missed opportunity and a direct by-product of the Allies' inability to reach a clear consensus at Trident on the long-term strategic objectives of the Sicilian campaign, as well as American reluctance to commit to follow-on operations on the Italian mainland. In the Allies' defense, however, an invasion of the Italian mainland required considerable planning, especially with regard to the allocation of men, matériel, landing craft, and support from the various services. That was made all the more difficult considering that those same resources would be required for the cross-Channel invasion. Finally, it can be argued that the Allies' approach to war was methodical; they were not inclined toward hasty maneuvers, thus they paused to plan the next stage. In any case, instead of blocking the Axis evacuation of Sicily, or pursuing the retreating enemy troops onto the peninsula, the halt allowed the enemy to withdraw and reorganize while the Allies made preparations to enter the mainland at a time and place of their choosing.

Although the Germans earned a temporary reprieve, they were under no illusions regarding Allied intentions to bring the war to Italy. The overwhelming concern for the German High Command was the reliability of Italy as an ally. The Germans were aware that Italy was weak and its commitment to the war was faltering. And even before the Duce's removal from power in July, the Germans had recognized that his power was waning rapidly. In May 1943, after learning that the Italian government was planning Mussolini's removal, the Germans devised a contingency plan. Unwilling to let Italy go, "Alarich" called for a German takeover of Italy upon its surrender. The Germans accepted that they would have to neutralize and disarm the Italians to prevent them from joining the Allies in the war against Germany. To accomplish "Alarich," the Germans intended to divert seven divisions from the eastern front and an additional six divisions from France. General Erwin Rommel, who was put in charge of northern Italy as the commander of Army Group B in August, was tasked with overseeing "Alarich." An additional plan, "Konstantin," required the Germans to replace the Italian forces stationed in the Balkans. Hitler's concern over the strategic value of the Balkans never abated, and he remained concerned that the British would seek any opportunity to exploit vulnerabilities in the region. "Alarich" and "Konstantin" were eventually combined into a single plan dubbed "Axis." Upon Italy's surrender, the Germans were prepared to seize control of Rome and activate "Axis" without delay.[54] In the words of one scholar, "Axis" was a "murderous and bloody assault on an erstwhile ally in which the casualties would run into the tens of thousands."[55]

As the Germans made contingency plans for Italy's surrender, they divided their interests between two commands. Rommel was given command of Army Group B extending from Rome to Italy's northern border in mid-August 1943. By that time, the Germans had transferred eight divisions to Army Group B from France, Holland, and Denmark, along with one SS panzer division from the eastern front—though German losses at the Battle of Kursk prevented further reinforcement from the east as originally envisioned by "Alarich." Kesselring was responsible for protecting southern Italy as Germany's commander in chief of the South. His authority extended only to the eight divisions of the Tenth Army commanded by General Heinrich von Vietinghoff. Because the south was the only active Italian theater for the Germans at that time, it would stand to reason that Kesselring held the dominant position over Rommel in Italy; to the contrary, however, Hitler viewed southern Italy as less important than the north. Kesselring's orders in the event of an Allied invasion were to fight a delaying action with the ultimate aim of linking up with Rommel's Army Group B.[56]

In the meantime, the Allies were engaged in surrender negotiations with the Italians. After Mussolini's arrest, the Badoglio government pledged its continued support for the Axis war effort, yet the public commitment was a front. Eisenhower remarked that "it was clear that this statement was made merely in the hope of placating the Germans and giving the Italians a chance to escape punishment from their arrogant ally."[57] Behind the scenes, the Italians entered into talks with the Allies regarding surrender. Tentative at first, the talks ultimately proved successful. In the opening days of September, the Italians agreed to surrender terms. On September 8, 1943, the Italians and Allies officially announced Italy's surrender. With that announcement, Germany's "Axis" plan went forward. The Germans, and Kesselring in particular, responded quickly and brutally against the Italians they now viewed as traitors. It is estimated that between 7,000 and 12,000 Italians were killed, with another 600,000 interned—most of whom were used as slave laborers in Germany's armaments industries. The Germans simultaneously moved to take Rome, neutralize Italy's garrisons, and seize Italian weaponry.[58] Italy's withdrawal from the war was a significant victory for the Allies, and it achieved one of the key objectives of the Mediterranean Strategy. While the Allies could revel in that victory, they still had to contend with the Germans, who had every intention of fighting to maintain control of Italy. Given Italy's location, it was seen as vital for the defense of Germany and thus was too strategic to abandon.

Through Ultra intercepts, the Allies were aware of German strength and strategy. While they knew that Kesselring was under orders to withdraw to the north instead of mounting a protracted defense of southern Italy, they likewise recognized that the Tenth Army was strong enough to repel their forces in the south. They also knew that it would be nearly impossible to achieve surprise. After studying the map of Italy, the Allies had chosen Salerno and the toe as the two most feasible invasion points. Rome may have been ideal, but it would be heavily defended by the Germans and beyond the reach of Allied airpower. Salerno and the toe offered the best chances to get on land with maximum air support, though they were also the most obvious choices. In Eisenhower's words:

> The greatest disadvantage of this plan was that its logic was obvious to the enemy as well as to us. Most of our pursuit planes were still handicapped by short range and Salerno Bay lay at about the extreme limit of their effective support for the landings. Besides, between the

bay and the toe of the boot there were no other particularly favorable landing beaches, so we went into the operation with no illusions of surprising the opposition.[59]

Without surprise, the Allies would have to overwhelm the Germans with force. Time was of the essence as every day the Allies waited was another day for the Germans to prepare and strengthen. To the Allies' advantage, Hitler refused to further reinforce the south. Kesselring expressed dismay in his memoirs at the führer's unwillingness to release any of the northern divisions under Rommel's command. He reasoned that "Rommel's idea that we should evacuate the whole of southern and central Italy and defend only the north had apparently taken such firm root in Hitler's mind that he turned a deaf ear to even the most self-evident tactical demands."[60]

On September 3, the Allies launched Baytown. Montgomery's Eighth Army crossed the Strait of Messina virtually unopposed. Although the Germans fought a delaying action and destroyed the roads and bridges along the way, the Eighth Army was nonetheless able to advance without great difficulty. By September 10, the Germans had pulled back allowing the British to advance one hundred miles north, but the Eighth Army then halted in order to allow the supply lines to catch up.[61] Kesselring viewed Montgomery's slow advance as advantageous as it permitted the 29th Panzer Grenadier Division and 26th Panzer Division to head north to join the fight by then underway at Salerno. They were in battle position by September 11.[62]

Operation Avalanche commenced as planned on September 9. The evening before, the Italian surrender was announced. While Italy's official surrender was beneficial to the Allies, the announcement came too late to allow for Italy's participation in Avalanche. As a result, the Anglo-American forces could not expect help from the Italians.

As the 450 warships and transport vessels that made up the Avalanche convoys approached Salerno on September 8, any faint hope of achieving surprise disappeared—just as Eisenhower feared. Lieutenant General Clark later reflected:

> In view of the fact that NAPLES was the only port large enough to supply large forces and the only suitable beaches for landing within fighter air support available to the Allies were in the vicinity of that city, deception as to the general location of the assault was impracticable. Deception as to timing was almost impossible due to the availability of reconnaissance aviation by the enemy who could follow the movements of the Allied naval convoy.[63]

In fact, not only did the Germans expect the attack at Salerno, but Luftwaffe reconnaissance spotted the invasion convoys on the 8th. The 16th Panzer Division, which was reconstituted after its destruction at Stalingrad and was Germany's only fully equipped division in southern Italy, stood ready and on high alert.[64]

Salerno was a tough target as it was "ringed" by mountains. That worked to the enemy's advantage as the seasoned 16th Panzer Division held the high ground. Just to the north of Salerno sat the Hermann Goering and 15th Panzer Grenadier Divisions recuperating from Sicily; though understrength, both were battle hardened and well acquainted with the Anglo-Americans. Thus, when Lieutenant General Clark's Fifth Army and the British 10th Corps went ashore on September 9, along with British Commandos and US Army Rangers, they faced a determined and ready resistance. Moreover, despite intelligence reports that suggested the Germans might retreat to a more tenable line to the north, Kesselring and Vietinghoff opted to stand and fight. Accordingly, reinforcements were rushed to Salerno, which enabled the Germans to mount a ferocious defense. In the days following the landing, the Germans were able to rally six divisions to defend Salerno.[65]

The fighting at Salerno was brutal, and anything but an assured victory for the Allies. The inexperienced Americans came up against a well-trained and experienced German defense that was determined to repel the Americans back into the sea. The Germans employed their proven methods of "rapid response, lightening maneuver, concentric attack" with practiced precision.[66] The counterattack struck with such force on the 13th that Lieutenant General Clark considered withdrawing from Salerno completely.[67] Despite the commander's concerns, Alexander forbade a withdrawal. While Alexander's leadership may have been questionable during the Sicilian campaign, his decision to maintain the offensive at Salerno revealed true determination. At the same time, the decision to push forward required the Allies to increase substantially their military effort. Again, the Allies showed maturity in their execution of combined operations as the services rallied to support the landed forces. Allied bombers were called in to blanket the German lines with saturation bombing; naval gunfire—which included calling up two British battleships equipped with 15-inch guns—was increased; and Alexander arranged for the immediate transfer of reinforcements from North Africa. Those reinforcements included the seasoned British 7th Armoured Division and the American 82nd Airborne Division.[68]

In addition to the military efforts employed to salvage the Salerno operation, Tac HQ "A" Force stepped up in an attempt to mislead and misdirect the Germans in the crucial days after the landings. The overriding theme of the deceptive efforts was to simulate a concentration of force at Salerno and Taranto in order to increase

The Italian Campaign, 1943. Map by Erin Greb Cartography.

the appearance of Allied strength and convince the Germans that a determined resistance was "useless" with their existing limited strength. Major R. A. Bromley-Davenport was tasked with executing Plan Carnegie, a simple force-maximizing ruse. On September 9, the British 1st Airborne Division had landed at Taranto, the objective of Operation Slapstick.[69] Bromley-Davenport's goal was to convince the Germans that a brigade of the 1st Infantry Division had landed alongside the 1st Airborne Division, and that it would be followed by the remainder of the 1st Infantry Division and entire 34th Infantry Division. The deception was passed using wireless deception and the display of unit insignia on uniforms and vehicles in the region. In a letter dated September 7, Strangeways instructed Bromley-Davenport to "obtain a number of the 1 Divisional signs for wearing on uniforms. You will arrange for these to be worn by suitable persons, for example, signal D.Rs., your own wireless operators, yourself and particularly spare officers." Bromley-Davenport was even advised to purchase white paint and a paintbrush to paint the divisional sign on vehicles and buildings.[70] At Salerno similar efforts were made to convey the transfer of an armored brigade to the British 10th Corps and a British airborne division to accompany the American 82nd Airborne Division—all utilizing the same methods employed at Taranto.[71]

Running concurrent with Carnegie, Plan Colfax was also put into operation by Tac HQ "A" Force. Colfax was an attempt to simulate a threat to the Gulf of Gaeta, to the north of Salerno, in the hopes of keeping the Hermann Goering and 15th Panzer Grenadier Divisions pinned down as far away from the Salerno beachhead as possible. "A" Force used its intelligence networks and double agents, most notably the French agent Gilbert, to leak rumors of a planned landing there.[72] However, the battle outpaced the deception. Alexander ordered "A" Force to begin preparing the notional threat to the Gulf of Gaeta on September 10, but 15th Army Group HQ did not approve the plan until four days later. By then, the two German divisions were already headed south. As the battle raged, time was consistently working against the deceptionists; in fact, Strangeways acknowledged that the lack of time was a negative factor in the deception efforts just one day into the planning of Colfax.[73] Colfax, therefore, came to an end without making any impact on the course of the battle. Carnegie remained active as Strangeways and Tac HQ continued their efforts to simulate strength at Salerno, but that too came to an end when the Germans began to withdraw from Salerno on September 17.[74]

It is impossible to determine if the force-maximizing efforts had any tangible effect on the Germans or played any role in their decision to withdraw when they did, though it is doubtful. Overall, the ad hoc tactical efforts met with minimal success, if any at all, and revealed the challenges of trying to implement spur-of-the-moment deceptions when the battle was rapidly changing. In the case of Salerno, Allied success came not as the result of creativity or trickery, but as a result of the concentration of men, matériel, and overwhelming firepower at the battlefront. It was, therefore, the strength of Allied firepower that won the day.

On the German side of the fight, it can be said that even though the German counterattack on September 13 met with noticeable success, the Germans were ultimately unable to withstand the tremendous display of force the Allied military-industrial complex could supply.[75] The Germans had proven the masters of blitzkrieg early in the war, but they lacked an effective counter to overwhelming Allied firepower.[76] Moreover, the Tenth Army was hamstrung as Hitler stubbornly refused to send reinforcements to the south. Kesselring was dumbfounded at Hitler's refusal and later wrote: "It still defeats me why Hitler chose to write off eight first-class German divisions (six in the south of Italy and two near Rome) and an overstrength flak arm instead of sending me one or two of the divisions already assembled in the north." He remarked that with only two of Rommel's divisions he could have repelled the Allies at Salerno. Without the reinforcements, Kesselring and Vietinghoff had little choice but to retreat. On September 17, the Germans began to fall back to a new defensive position, the Viktor Line, along the Volturno and Bifurno Rivers. On October 1, the Germans withdrew from Naples.[77]

When the Germans withdrew, they retreated north, which was exactly what the Allies expected based on intercepted intelligence reports, but they did not go far. The Germans' strategy had changed, and their decision to hold a defensive line in the south not only surprised the Allies, it completely upended their entire strategy of a quick and steady drive to Rome. Kesselring felt confident that the Tenth Army could hold off the Allies—at least for a while. Instead of overseeing a steady retreat to join up with Rommel, he preferred to force the Allies to fight for every inch of land they gained. He argued, persuasively it would seem, that the Germans were strong enough to block the Allied advance and force them to fight a long and costly war in Italy. To that end, he began to fortify two additional defensive lines, the Reinhard and Gustav Lines. He had full confidence in his ability to use the terrain as a natural defense and, as he said of the Gustav Line, the "British and Americans would break their teeth on it."[78] Kesselring was under no illusions about the ultimate outcome. He knew his men were going to fight a prolonged retreat, but he was determined to draw it out and consume as many Allied resources as possible in the process. In the face of the German commander's staunch resolve, the Allied strategic vision of a quick drive to Rome evaporated. Thus, contrary to what the Allies originally expected, they were in for a long and excruciating contest for every mountain, valley, ridge, river, road, and bridge across the entire length of the peninsula. It is perhaps interesting, in that regard, that both sides viewed the campaign in Italy as an opportunity to wear the other side down, as well as divert his resources to a theater of secondary importance.

In a bid to turn the tide of war to the Allies' advantage, "A" Force began making preparations to assist the ongoing war effort. Tac HQ, which relocated to Bari in southern Italy in October, worked to aid the 15th Army Group with small-scale tactical deceptions as called upon. In the meantime, "A" Force also began working on a new strategic deception to succeed Boardman.

The ill-fated Plan Fairlands was developed with the familiar goal of containing German troops in the Mediterranean and Balkans. Beyond that, it added components pertaining specifically to the eastern and western Mediterranean. In the western Mediterranean sector, the goal was to prevent Rommel's Army Group B from reinforcing Kesselring in southern Italy. The objective in the eastern Mediterranean was to convince the Germans to evacuate Rhodes and Crete. While the latter goal might seem ambitious, the Germans evacuated both Sardinia and Corsica in the wake of the Italian surrender, which occurred at the exact same time as the Fairlands plan was being drafted.[79]

Plan Fairlands was plagued by troubles, especially in light of the rapidly changing military situation. Strategic deceptions typically take time to implement, and they work best when the military situation is stable. In mid-September, when "A" Force began working on Fairlands, the Anglo-American armies had just taken Salerno and were advancing in Italy. In the Aegean, British forces under Middle East Command seized the opportunity to take advantage of Italy's surrender and took the Italian-held islands of Kos, Leros, and Samos in September. Additionally, plans were being developed to take Rhodes, generally considered the most important of the Dodecanese islands.[80] On the whole, there was considerable chaos across the Mediterranean due to Italy's capitulation: Italy was divided politically as Germany controlled the north and the Italian monarchy controlled the south, Italian forces were trying to reorganize (many to fight officially alongside the Allies after the monarchy declared war on Germany on October 13, and others as partisans), while the Germans worked diligently to disarm the Italians and seize control of Italian-held territory across the Mediterranean.[81] Clarke called the situation "fluid" and remarked that "there had seldom been a time when it was more difficult to determine how Deception could best further the various operations of the Allied forces."[82]

It stands to reason that the fluidity of the situation made it difficult for the deceptionists to read clearly the situation and anticipate the needs of Allied field commanders with confidence. As a result, Fairlands was written up as a short-term strategic plan. More often than not, strategic deceptions relay long-term goals, but there was no way for Clarke to know if the war was going to bog down in southern Italy, or if the Allies were on the brink of a breakthrough that would take them to Rome and beyond. The one thing Clarke could be certain of was that it would be detrimental to the Allied war effort in Italy if Rommel released any of his northern divisions to reinforce Kesselring in the south. Thus, Clarke focused the western Mediterranean component of Fairlands on keeping Rommel's divisions in the north.

There was yet another reason for targeting Rommel. Considerable rivalry existed between Rommel and Kesselring dating back to the North African campaign when Kesselring served under Rommel's command. Owing to this history, Clarke recognized an opportunity to exploit the tensions between the two generals. Moreover, given that the German High Command had divided Italy into two commands, there would naturally be a competition for resources, reinforcements, and security measures. Clarke summarized:

> We guessed that there would be a lively tug-of-war between KESSEL-RING's demands for reinforcements at the front and ROMMEL's needs in holding down a much disturbed countryside and in guarding 300 miles of beaches from a possible Allied descent—now appearing to be more probable than ever with jumping-off places available in CORSICA and SARDINIA.

Accordingly, the goal was to manufacture a threat to Rommel's sector along the western coast of Italy.[83]

The target area chosen was Leghorn–Pisa. According to the deception story, Patton's Seventh Army in Sicily and a French corps in Corsica were planning to stage a landing on November 5. The invading forces would be followed by an additional four divisions of Anglo-French forces from North Africa. The total threat amounted to twelve divisions. The deception was passed through various methods. One plan was for Colonel Jones to display dummy fighter aircraft in Corsica that would appear to be fighter cover for the upcoming landings; however, a shortage of shipping and the lack of security on the island nullified that option.[84] Since the ability to utilize physical means was limited, "A" Force relied mostly on wireless deception and special means. Specifically, double agents played a key role in passing the information along. Agents controlled by "A" Force—Gilbert, Le Duc, Jewel, Le Petit, El Gitano, Arthur, and Guinea—were specifically chosen to send various messages telling of increased French activity on Corsica, the further mobilization of French forces in North Africa, plans for Patton's Seventh Army, and specific threats against northwest Italy. Le Petit, for example, sent a message on October 4 making it abundantly clear that the Allies intended to land on Italy's western coast in order to prevent the reinforcement of southern Italy.[85]

Another deceptive element was the use of pamphlets. For Fairlands, the pamphlets were written in French and English to instruct troops about ancient monuments and works of art in the region of Leghorn–Pisa. A pamphlet titled "THINGS

WORTH SAVING AND WHAT TO DO ABOUT THEM" was distributed to forces earmarked for the notional invasion.[86]

Another aspect of Fairlands worth discussing was its integration of Americans. In fact, Fairlands provides a good example of interallied deception. When the Americans arrived in North Africa in November 1942, they brought their own deception organization with them, which was part of Joint Security Control (JSC). JSC was formed by the US Joint Chiefs of Staff on August 26, 1942; thus, it was a young and inexperienced organization. It was also extremely limited in its scope and powers. In the view of Newman Smith, who served as the chief of JSC, American leadership misunderstood and underestimated the usefulness of deception. Consequently, they limited its functions primarily to security and saw cover and deception as of "primary concern to field commanders." They apparently did not yet appreciate the importance of global strategic deception, which the British and their London Controlling Section were so adept at. London, however, clearly saw the usefulness of incorporating the Americans into their plans. When the LCS devised its "Deception Policy 1943 (Germany and Italy)," it designated specific roles to JSC. As Smith relates, it was through that process that JSC began to develop as a deception organization:

> when detailed plans were completed, the London Controlling Section called upon Joint Security Control for certain assistance in implementing them. This assistance mainly consisted of "Special Means" implementation, which for reasons of plausibility had to be originated within the United States. These missions gave impetus to the development of "Special Means" channels by Joint Security Control. Although initially sporadic in character, the "Special Means" implementation done on London's request developed in continuity and gave purpose to the nascent Deception Section of Joint Security Control.[87]

Moreover, after deception officers of JSC arrived in North Africa, Clarke and "A" Force worked to indoctrinate them into the art of military deception. Clarke specifically used the Barclay deception to educate his American counterparts.

When AFHQ was established in Algiers with Advanced HQ "A" Force headquarters attached to it, American officers were assigned to "A" Force. Smith relates that "while the Combined Staff Section was headed by a British Officer and largely retained its British character, U.S. officers quickly grasped the principles of theater and world-wide cover and deception."[88] By the time the British were working on Plan Fairlands, the Americans had made great strides in their understanding and implementation of deception.

The American component of Fairlands pertained specifically to Patton's Seventh Army. The Seventh Army had remained inactive after Sicily, being replaced by the Fifth Army under Alexander's 15th Army Group Headquarters.[89] The Germans, however, expected Patton to participate in the Italian campaign. In order to play up the alleged role of the Seventh Army, "A" Force needed the Americans' assistance. While the Seventh Army was technically still in Sicily, it existed only in skeleton form. Clarke stated that in order to assist the deception, the American leadership would need to make every effort to keep all appearances of activity alive. To that end, General Marshall went so far as to instruct Eisenhower to send Patton and his staff over to Corsica for a visit, which Clarke felt "probably did more than anything else to focus attention towards the LEGHORN-PISA coast." In the end, it was the inactivity of the Seventh Army that caused the most insecurity for the Germans.[90]

In the eastern Mediterranean the primary goal of Fairlands was to assist in the capture of Rhodes and Crete, yet circumstances in that theater required a substantial revision to the plan. After the British took Kos, Leros, and Samos, the importance of Rhodes and Crete as diversionary targets diminished. As a result, "A" Force replaced the two islands with a notional threat to western Greece. It was proposed that the British 3rd Corps, 16th Corps, and multiple divisions of the Twelfth Army were to participate in the invasion. The entire operation was turned on its head on October 3 when the Germans landed in Kos, taking control of the island within days. The Germans next landed on Leros on November 12, which prompted the British to evacuate the island after suffering extensive casualties. Samos fell to the Germans on November 20.[91] While this undoubtedly represented a military reversal in the Aegean, it threatened to expose the deception completely. As Clarke recorded, the "failure to react strongly to this counter-stroke suggested a general weakness in the MIDDLE EAST which hardly conformed to our story of major preparations to invade WESTERN GREECE." As a result, the eastern Mediterranean component of Fairlands was reduced to a state of inactivity.[92]

On the whole, Fairlands failed to achieve its goals. The threat posed to Rommel's coastal flank did not appear to impact the disposition of German forces, and the eastern Mediterranean component had to be called off. Clarke did not seem surprised by its failure. He commented that after the "many vicissitudes" the plan went through, "it was hardly expected that it would succeed in exerting any great effect upon the dispositions of the enemy."[93] Only one aspect of Fairlands seemed to meet with success—the ongoing threat to the Balkans. However, it succeeded in a most unusual way. Swedish and German reports were intercepted that expressed concern over the Balkans, but both reports identified Patton's Seventh Army as the intended invasion force. The Reuters Stockholm report, based on intelligence provided by a correspondent from Budapest, held that "the United States Seventh Army and other completely fresh troops, are concentrated along the Italian Adriatic Coast, ready for invasion of the Balkans. They were said to be stationed along the coast from Bari to Foggia with half dozen excellent airfields at their disposal." The German report also mentioned an army being assembled on the eastern Italian coast to invade the Balkans. It stated that it "should be recalled in this connection that the U. S. Seventh Army, which has disappeared since the Sicilian campaign, has still not put in its appearance anywhere."[94] "A" Force had certainly played up the threat of the Seventh Army, but never in relation to the Balkans. The enemy might have come to the wrong conclusion about the intended use of the Seventh Army, but it nonetheless revealed the high level of anxiety the Germans still held over the Balkans and Patton's absence from the battlefield—both of which would be exploited by the deceptionists in preparation for Operation Overlord.

Although unrelated to the outcome of the deception, Clarke was not physically present for the majority of Fairlands. He was summoned to London to assist in the early planning for Plan Bodyguard; he departed from North Africa on September 25. His second-in-command at "A" Force, Colonel Nöel Wild, stepped up to oversee Fairlands. Wild was accustomed to taking over for Clarke and cannot be blamed for the plan's shortcomings. The plan simply faced too many obstacles, the military situation was too fluid, and it was unavoidably too rushed in its implementation. Fairlands drew to a close at the end of October 1943.[95] Although the plan had not achieved any great results, it did serve as a bridge between the larger strategic plans of Barclay/Boardman and Fairland's successor, Plan Oakfield. If it made any noticeable contribution, it was in keeping the threat to the Balkans alive. That was, however, quite significant. As the Allies began making preparations for Operation Overlord, the Balkans was to play a central, albeit diversionary, role. Hitler's concerns over the security of the Balkans was acute. Because of that, "A" Force put every effort into playing up the threat against the Balkans in order to coerce the Germans into diverting substantial resources and reinforcements to the target area.

By the end of 1943, the Allies had fought numerous treacherous battles in Italy. The US Fifth Army and British Eighth Amy crossed the Volturno and Bifurno Rivers, respectively, by mid-October. By the end of November, the Eighth Army crossed the Sangro River. Finally, on December 17, the Allies broke the Bernhardt (Reinhard) Line. The battles were hard-fought and took a tremendous toll on the

Allies. Instead of a rapid drive to Rome, however, winter set in and the war in Italy bogged down at the Gustav Line.[96]

As 1943 drew to a close, many changes were underway. The time had finally come to put every effort into planning Operation Overlord. Not surprisingly, the long-awaited invasion of France took precedence over all other operations. The Mediterranean experienced a drainage of manpower and supplies as both men and matériel were transferred to the UK. Allied leaders agreed at Trident to transfer seven divisions, which in reality became eight, and the majority of the landing craft from the Mediterranean to the UK to assist with the military buildup for Overlord. To meet the specific needs of the cross-Channel invasion, the Allies needed seasoned divisions, and, most importantly, divisions experienced at amphibious landings.

There was similarly a near exodus of commanders who left the Mediterranean for Britain. Eisenhower was chosen to serve as the Supreme Allied Commander for Overlord. He was informed of the decision when he met with President Roosevelt in Tunis in early December, following the Tehran Conference (code-named Eureka)— the first of the Big Three meetings between Churchill, Roosevelt, and Stalin. The president minced no words as he informed the commander: "Well, Ike, you are going to command Overlord."[97] With that, Eisenhower's involvement in the Italian campaign drew to a swift close. He was replaced by General Henry Maitland Wilson as the new commander in chief of the Mediterranean. Montgomery, the general who was loved by his men yet often disliked by his peers, was similarly summoned to Britain. Although he had made his reputation as the tireless commander of the Eighth Army, British leaders determined that it was time for Montgomery to leave the Eighth Army in order to lead the British effort in western Europe. He was duly appointed commander of the British 21st Army Group. The Eighth Army passed to the hands of one of Montgomery's most trusted commanders, General Sir Oliver Leese.[98] Of the top army brass in the Mediterranean, Alexander was the only one to remain in Italy.

The air and naval branches also faced leadership changes. In October, Admiral Andrew Cunningham, who was chosen to succeed First Sea Lord Dudley Pound, was recalled to London upon Pound's declining health. His cousin, Admiral John Cunningham, took over as the new commander in chief of the Mediterranean Fleet. In December, in an effort to create a more unified and cohesive command to meet the challenges of an evolving war, the Levant command was abolished and Cunningham's theater responsibilities were expanded to cover the entire Mediterranean, consisting of four subcommands located at Gibraltar, Algiers (covering the western Mediterranean), Malta (serving the central Mediterranean), and Cairo (representing the eastern portion of the sea). As for Allied air command, Air Chief Marshal Arthur Tedder was selected to serve as the deputy supreme commander for Overlord; thus, he was also recalled to London. Lieutenant-General Ira C. Eaker assumed command of the Mediterranean Allied Air Forces (MAAF).[99]

A similar transfer of leadership occurred within "A" Force as well. If Allied leadership had learned any lesson from the previous years of warfare, it was that deception was crucial to victory. It therefore became an indispensable component of Allied war planning. As the leadership began planning for D-day, the London Controlling Section was called on to appoint an "entirely new" body of deceivers to assist the supreme commander at SHAEF (Supreme Headquarters Allied Expeditionary Force).[100] As a new entity, Ops B would be completely inexperienced unless seasoned deceptionists could be recruited to man its ranks in London. The official record states that "L.C.S. was therefore compelled to draw heavily on the experienced officers of "A" Force"; as a result, a "noticeable exodus of "A" Force officers from the MEDITERRANEAN to the UNITED KINGDOM" ensued.[101] Given his extensive experience and instinctive ability to turn deception into a highly successful weapon, Clarke was the obvious choice to command Ops B. In fact, Eisenhower requested Clarke specifically. Clarke, however, preferred to remain with "A" Force in Cairo, so he sent his second-in-command in his place.[102] On December 17, Nöel Wild arrived in London. He recalled: "I found myself appointed the 'Head' of a scarcely existent organisation at SHAEF charged with planning and executing a cover and deception plan in support of the forthcoming Normandy landings timed to take place in June."[103] Lieutenant-Colonel Michael Crichton took Wild's place in Cairo. David Strangeways was another key "A" Force officer to leave Italy. He arrived in London on December 11 to head a new tactical deception unit embedded within Montgomery's 21st Army Group. In the months that followed, Strangeways was joined by Major Chandos Temple, Captain P. W. Laycock, and Lieutenant-Colonel S. B. D. Hood, all from Tac HQ "A" Force. "A" Force also lost Commander Alec Finter to London.[104] Consequently, the deception campaign developed in London to assist Operation Overlord not only was built upon "A" Force's many years of experience, but was overwhelmingly directed by former "A" Force men.

As the focus of the war shifted and the leadership was reshaped, so too was the deception machinery. The latter half of 1943 brought many changes to "A" Force, specifically to its organization and mode of operation. When the war shifted to the Italian Peninsula, deception began to change. On the one hand, there was little time for long-term planning, so deception had to be developed and implemented quickly to keep up with the rapidly changing battle requirements. That resulted in a greater role for Tac HQ "A" Force, which remained embedded with Alexander's 15th Army Group. Strategic deception continued to operate, but was increasingly focused on the upcoming invasion of France. Finally, "A" Force saw itself transition from the primary deception organization in the field to playing the crucial role of diversionary deception in what had become a secondary theater.

In a now familiar pattern, "A" Force was reorganized to meet the changing focus of the war. In stark comparison to previous reorganizations, however, "A" Force was downsized. The reduction was carried out to free "A" Force from control over regions that had diminished in importance to the war effort. The explanation contained in the LCS report states: "After STALINGRAD the German threat in the Caucasus, and therefore the importance of PAIC [Persia and Iraq Command], vanished, while the opening of the Mediterranean to Allied shipping meant that the territories overlooking the sea route from the Cape to Suez had little further importance in our supply situation." Those domains were removed from "A" Force's responsibility to allow it to "concentrate all its attentions" on carrying out deception in southern Europe. "A" Force had peaked at a size of 600 personnel earlier in 1943, but the smaller organization of only 186, with its concentrated focus on southern Europe, allowed "A" Force to devote its attention solely toward aiding Overlord by manufacturing threats to Germany's southern flank.[105] The reorganization likewise provided for two advanced headquarters: Advanced HQ (East) oversaw deception in the Middle East, while Advanced HQ (West) was based in Algiers to cover North Africa and Italy. Interestingly, Advanced HQ (West) was placed under an American military intelligence officer—Lt. Col. George Train. Working with him was Maj. E. J. Sweeney, an American army ordnance officer, who took over for Train in mid-1944. Clarke stated that "all progressed in the most satisfactory possible manner with the American personnel playing the major share in Deception in the WESTERN MEDITERRANEAN."[106] Main HQ "A" Force continued to operate from Cairo. Tac HQ in Italy became Tac HQ (West). There was a provision for the formation of a Tac HQ (East), but the need never arose. On December 19, Clarke was promoted to the rank of brigadier general.[107]

With the reorganization of "A" Force and the Allied leaders' focus on Overlord as the primary military objective of 1944, the stage was set. "A" Force was prepared to focus its strategic efforts exclusively on the campaign in western Europe. Meanwhile, Tac HQ (West) continued to assist Alexander's 15th Army Group as it maintained the fight against Germany in Italy.

Incidentally, the Allies were not the only ones to make adjustments to their command structure. The Germans made changes to their leadership in late 1943 as well.

Kesselring had repeatedly urged the German High Command to approve a single, unified command for Italy. Hitler had previously preferred Rommel's commitment to defend northern Italy, but finally seemed swayed by Kesselring's bolder strategy of the protracted defense. Kesselring insisted that the Allies would not advance beyond the range of their airpower, so it made the most sense to defend the south and form a formidable line of defense in the "waist" of Italy where the distance from east to west coast was the shortest. There the Germans could employ fewer divisions, estimated at nine, with maximum defense. After the defeats at Stalingrad and Kursk on the eastern front, Hitler seemed relieved to have at least one general insisting his army stand and fight instead of retreat. Finally, Kesselring's wish was granted.[108] Hitler accepted his commander's strategy of fighting a prolonged defense in southern Italy instead of abandoning the south in order to join up with Rommel in the north. On November 21, Kesselring was appointed commander in chief of the Southwest, Army Group C, giving him full command over the entire Italian campaign.[109] The forces under Rommel's Army Group B were redesignated and placed under Kesselring. As for Rommel, he was transferred to northwestern France to oversee the construction of the Atlantic Wall. Ironically, by the end of 1943 old rivals from the North African campaign—Montgomery and Rommel—were once again positioned opposite one another in preparation for yet another decisive showdown.

As 1943 drew to a close, the war had not only planted itself firmly on European soil, but Allied planning was increasingly focused on the upcoming cross-Channel invasion of France. All efforts—military and deception—zeroed in on the long-anticipated campaign. At the same time, it presented daunting challenges. The Allies could not go at it half-heartedly. If Operation Overlord was to be successful, it would require the largest concentration of men, matériel, shipping, airpower, and resources yet amassed by the British and Americans. Moreover, the various Allied deception organizations would have to utilize every weapon in their arsenal. The Allies had spent years making mistakes and learning the lessons of modern warfare. They had fine-tuned their battlefield tactics, learned how to successfully utilize combined operations, and perfected the deception machinery into an indispensable weapon of war. While some may criticize the Allies' decision to fight in the Mediterranean, the battles there—and especially the amphibious landings—provided invaluable experience that would be applied to the planning for Overlord. As the Allies applied that knowledge forward, they began preparing to launch the greatest amphibious assault known to history.

5 TACTICAL MANEUVERING AND STRATEGIC PLANNING IN 1944

In the early years of World War II, Britain fought battle to battle, at times only one loss away from devastating defeat. The year 1943 brought many changes to the war and how it was fought. The Anglo-American armies gained the advantage against the Germans and finally enjoyed the luxury of offensive strategic planning. That planning allowed the Allies to exploit the success of North Africa by way of the Mediterranean Strategy, in many ways designed to keep the momentum of the war going until the Allies could stage a landing in France. Over the second half of 1943, that strategy brought both success and failure. The Allies took Sicily, Corsica, and Sardinia; prompted Italy's surrender; and began a drive up the Italian Peninsula. Yet, the Italian campaign proved a great disappointment to Allied leaders. Instead of mounting a hasty retreat north, the Germans fought a protracted defensive war and prevented the Allies from conquering their chief objective: Rome. Moreover, the Allies faced opportunities in the Aegean that ended instead in loss, namely with the German conquest of Kos, Leros, and Samos. To Winston Churchill's great disappointment, Rhodes remained beyond Allied reach and the prime minister's goal of coaxing Turkey into the war had thus far failed. As 1943 drew to a close, the Allies were at a stalemate in Italy, the Mediterranean Strategy was again being challenged by the Americans, and the strategic focus and planning had shifted decisively to Operation Overlord, lessening support for continued operations in the Mediterranean.

At years end, the British and American leadership agreed that the time had come to prepare to launch the cross-Channel invasion of France. There was even reason to be optimistic that they could liberate Europe by the end of 1944. At the same time, the alliance still had many internal differences of opinion and needed to reach consensus on the exact focus of strategic planning for 1944. One additional factor, unique to that stage of the war, was the need to coordinate with the Soviets. Two conferences held at the end of 1943, Sextant (Cairo) and Eureka (Tehran), served to clarify the Allies' objectives and put them on a united course for the upcoming year.

Sextant began on November 22, 1943. Attended by Prime Minister Winston Churchill, President Franklin D. Roosevelt, Generalissimo Chiang Kai-shek, and their respective staffs, the Cairo conference was broad in scope. The chief objective was to develop Allied strategy as it applied to the European and China-Burma-India (CBI) theaters for 1944.[1] A significant challenge was to address the competing theater demands for resources and manpower—most notably, the allocation of landing craft. Each theater required landing craft to mount amphibious operations, but the cross-Channel invasion of France took precedence over all other needs and it called for an unparalleled concentration of landing craft. For the British and Americans, all decision making had Operation Overlord at the center in one way or another.

The Anglo-American leadership had already determined at the Trident and Quadrant conferences that the cross-Channel invasion of France would be the main objective for 1944, but with 1944 fast approaching, it was necessary to reaffirm that commitment and hammer out the details. The central question was whether the Allies could launch a successful Overlord *and* maintain operations in the Mediterranean at the same time—and that was where the British and Americans encountered the greatest divergence in views.

US leaders feared that the British intended to expand operations in the Mediterranean, at the expense of Overlord. The Americans, and especially Gen. George C. Marshall, were particularly keen to avoid further action in the Balkans and Aegean as they saw those operations as not only unnecessary, but a great misuse of resources when all attention needed to focus on France.[2] The British, most notably

Churchill, saw the Mediterranean as a strategic theater of operations.[3] The prime minister believed there were opportunities to exploit in the region; he expressed frustration over the setbacks faced in the Aegean in the fall, the stalled progress in Italy, and the failure to better supply resistance forces in the Balkans. Though he was equally committed to Overlord, the prime minister believed that the Germans must be significantly weakened before the cross-Channel attack could be launched, and thus was opposed to a fixed date for Overlord that might rule out opportunities to weaken the Germans on other fronts. The British hoped to come to an agreement that would allow them to continue operations in the Mediterranean, though, to be fair, Churchill was considerably more enthusiastic about operations beyond Italy than the majority of the British planners.[4] The early days of Sextant were spent presenting the various Allied viewpoints, but it was the conference in Tehran that solidified Allied strategy for 1944.

On November 27, Roosevelt and Churchill left Cairo for Tehran, where they met with Joseph Stalin. The Tehran Conference began the following day. After the Americans and British presented their objectives for the coming year, Stalin weighed in with his typical blunt assessment. He gave his full support to Overlord, as well as a closely timed assault on southern France (Anvil). To the Americans' pleasure, he stated that the Mediterranean should only be used as a diversion and that the Allies should maintain a defensive posture in Italy. Stalin outright rejected Churchill's pleas for operations in the eastern Mediterranean. The Allied leaders did agree that sixty-eight landing craft could be held in the Mediterranean until mid-January to allow for one additional amphibious operation (Anzio). The Allies hoped to capture Rome and reach the Pisa–Rimini Line with that drive. After that, the landing craft were to be transferred to Britain for Overlord. As for the Soviets' contribution, Stalin agreed to launch an offensive on the eastern front to coincide with Overlord. He also consented to put pressure on Turkey to enter the war, as well as agreed to declare war on Bulgaria if Bulgaria attacked Turkey. Although operations in the Aegean were not to be considered except under the condition of Turkey's entrance into the war, an agreement was reached to provide the partisans in Yugoslavia with supplies and assist with commando raids. Finally, the leaders concurred that the British and Americans needed to appoint a supreme commander for Overlord immediately.[5]

Eureka proved to be the most decisive of the conferences. As one historian aptly noted: "All was therefore still in the melting pot when, on 28th November, the Western Allies arrived at Teheran. When the Combined Chiefs of Staff left on 1st December, the shape of operations in Europe over the next six months had been settled."[6] In fact, the meeting between the three powers was long overdue. Allied planning for Overlord, regarding both military operations and deception, had been hampered by the lack of coordination with the USSR up until that point. In the early planning for both Overlord and the corresponding deception campaign, Plan Bodyguard, the London Controlling Section was often frustrated and left to make assumptions about the Soviets' role: "At that time the Western Allies were completely ignorant of Russia's intentions, and indeed if she was prepared to co-operate in a grand strategical plan for the final overthrow of Germany, nor was our military mission in Moscow having any success at interchanging information or achieving co-ordination."[7] With the decisions made at Tehran having removed all doubts about the Soviets' involvement, the Western Allies were in a position to continue their discussions at Cairo.

Churchill and Roosevelt left Tehran for Cairo on December 2, and Sextant resumed the following day. Although the strategic objectives had been prioritized, there were still many decisions to be made. The two most important discussions revolved around the availability of landing craft and the future leadership for Overlord and the Mediterranean. The issue of shipping also proved a daunting challenge as leaders had to balance production figures with the desire to launch multiple seaborne operations across multiple theaters. Overlord took precedence in all planning, and after the conference with Stalin, the invasion of southern France was elevated in importance. In addition to those, the British continued to call for operations in the Aegean and a January offensive in Italy. Not to be forgotten, there was also the need to assault Japanese shipping in the Pacific and for operations to aid Chiang Kai-shek and the Chinese against Japan in Burma. In the end, the much discussed assault against Burma through the Bay of Bengal was postponed so that the landing craft could be used in Europe, while operations against Japan in the Pacific were to continue. In line with the discussions that took place in Tehran, no action was to take place in the Aegean unless Turkey entered the war, and AFHQ was allowed to keep sixty-eight landing craft in order to carry out the Anzio operation in January; after that, the craft were to be sent to Britain.[8]

The issue of landing craft in the Mediterranean may appear on the surface to be a technical matter of supply, but that obscures the matter's broader strategic significance. The position of the Mediterranean theater was changing. It was no longer the center of gravity for Allied military operations, yet its importance to the overall war effort and Allied grand strategy remained high. In its new reality, the Mediterranean was to play the essential role of diversion. In fact, it was considered crucial for the success of Overlord. At the time of Sextant and Eureka, there were twenty-one German divisions in Italy and thirty in the Balkans. The British leadership deemed it as "vital" to tie down and destroy as many German divisions as possible in the Mediterranean in order to assist Overlord. The alternative was a "redisposition of German forces" that could potentially "render an assault on Northern France from the U.K. impracticable."[9] And that is where the landing craft factored into the broader discussion. The Germans had to believe that the Allies were capable of carrying out large-scale operations, to include future amphibious operations, in the Mediterranean. The Allies had to continuously present a threat to Germany, its interests and resources, and its satellites for the Germans to maintain such a high level of vigilance and presence across southern Europe. If the enemy perceived that the Allies were no longer interested in the Mediterranean, he would be free to shift his forces to regions of greater significance to the war effort: the eastern front and France. Thus, maintaining an active military presence and ongoing threat in the Mediterranean—both real and perceived—was just as important to Overlord as the preparations underway in the UK. The British referred to this as the "doctrine of 'stretch'"—forcing the Germans to stretch themselves thin defending every vulnerable point along the perimeter of Fortress Europe.[10]

The second major decision settled in the discussions at Cairo pertained to theater command. The British agreed to the appointment of an American commander for Overlord, with the expectation of a British commander for the Mediterranean. Until that point, Roosevelt had intended to appoint Marshall as Supreme Allied Commander. In a last-minute change of heart, Roosevelt decided to keep Marshall in Washington, where the president viewed his services to be indispensable, and instead appointed Gen. Dwight D. Eisenhower to lead Overlord. In Eisenhower's favor, he was skilled at balancing Anglo-American relations, had experience as a theater commander, and had proven himself adept in that role over the previous year. Roosevelt informed Eisenhower of his decision to appoint him Supreme Allied Commander on December 6, prompting Eisenhower's departure from the Mediterranean.[11]

Upon Eisenhower's transfer to London, it was necessary to choose his replacement at AFHQ. However, that decision revealed larger concerns over the current situation of two theater commands—the Mediterranean and Middle East—operating in relative close proximity to one another. The organization as it then existed between the Mediterranean and Middle East Commands was ambiguous and a "clumsy mechanism" for coordinating a war.[12] The chief dilemma was with the two headquarters and their overlapping, and in some cases contradictory, objectives.[13] The Mediterranean fell under AFHQ, based in Algiers. Under the leadership of Eisenhower (prior to his transfer), it was responsible for all operations in the western and central portions of the Mediterranean, which included Italy. Middle East Command, an all-British structure, was under General Henry Maitland Wilson. From its base in Cairo, it oversaw operations in the eastern Mediterranean, the Balkans, and Turkey. The time had come to unify the two organizations into a more malleable and sensible command structure. On December 10, the CCS decided to unite the two under AFHQ. The British, however, forcefully argued against placing the newly unified command under the control of the European Supreme Allied Commander; thus, Wilson was appointed as commander in chief effective January 8, 1944. In March, Wilson took the title of SACMED (Supreme Allied Commander, Mediterranean).[14] With that, both Europe and the Mediterranean possessed the proper command structure to carry out the tasks assigned to them for 1944. Eisenhower was tasked with overseeing the preparations for, and execution of, the largest seaborne invasion ever attempted; Wilson was set to command a theater that served as a diversion too attractive for Adolf Hitler to ignore, resulting in the stationing of dozens of German divisions in the wrong place to counter the Allies on D-day.

The clarification of leadership was vitally necessary in order for the Allies to proceed with their strategic plans for 1944. The clarification allowed for the acceleration of operational planning, although planning for Overlord had a long history that predated the Sextant and Eureka conferences. Dating back to April 1942, British and American leaders had already concluded that a cross-Channel invasion would be necessary in order to defeat the Germans. At the Casablanca Conference in January 1943, the CCS gave the go-ahead to begin strategic planning for the future campaign. At that time, Lieutenant-General Frederick Morgan was appointed COSSAC to oversee that planning, although the Supreme Allied Commander had yet to be appointed.[15] By the time the Allied leadership met in Quebec for the Quadrant conference in August 1943, Morgan had already completed his first draft. The leaders approved of his planning and gave him orders to begin making preparations. Yet, Morgan faced a difficult task compounded by considerable uncertainty. Eisenhower commented that Morgan, "Chief of Staff to a Commander who did not exist, had to carry the double burden of anticipating important decisions of his future Commander and of convincing military and political heads of two governments of the soundness of those decisions."[16] Once Eisenhower was appointed Supreme Allied Commander, one of Morgan's burdens was removed and planning could proceed with greater clarity. Morgan later referred to his initial planning as the "first rough black-and-white sketch for the great canvas that eventually bore the signature of the master artist, Eisenhower."[17]

By late December, the Allied leaders and their respective staffs had hammered out their strategic goals, found a way to blend their various objectives into a compromise all parties could support, and appointed the necessary leadership to move forward. At the same time, deception planning was also underway. In December, Eisenhower gave a report to the Combined Chiefs of Staff on the use of deception in the Mediterranean throughout 1943. In his final assessment he recommended that, "due to the extent to which the strategic and tactical cover plans have assisted the attainment of real operations, no major operation be undertaken without planning and executing appropriate deception measures."[18] As the Supreme Allied Commander for Overlord, Eisenhower gave his full support to deception planning. Of even greater significance, after years of warfare and successful deception planning, the Big Three—Churchill, Roosevelt, and Stalin—all recognized the importance of deception as an instrumental component to military planning. Though rarely mentioned in postwar accounts, the three heads of state agreed at Tehran that deception must accompany their respective military planning for 1944. They agreed upon the need to "secure the most favourable enemy dispositions for OVERLORD and to assist real operations in containing enemy forces away from the OVERLORD area," to coordinate their efforts to achieve that aim, and to carefully prepare cover and deception plans in direct consultation with each other.[19] With the political and military leadership decidedly in favor of utilizing deception to the greatest extent possible, the deception efforts received full support and allocation of extensive resources.

The primary responsibility for deception planning in Britain fell to two organizations in particular: the London Controlling Section and SHAEF Ops B. The LCS remained the primary body responsible for all strategic deception planning and oversaw the implementation of global deception. With the appointment of Eisenhower and the subsequent formation of SHAEF (made official in January 1944), the LCS was "invited" to recruit a new cadre of deceptionists to form a new deception body—SHAEF Ops B. Ops B was to assist in the deception planning for Overlord from London. In addition to the need to create a deception team to work with Eisenhower at SHAEF, there was also a need to form a tactical deception body "on the lines of Tac "A" Force" to accompany Montgomery's 21st Army Group onto the mainland. Given the need for men already trained and experienced in the art of deception, Lieutenant-Colonel John Bevan was "compelled to draw heavily on the experienced officers of "A" Force." Colonel Nöel Wild and Colonel David Strangeways, referred to as two "shining lights of Mediterranean deception," were transferred to London. Wild, previously the second-in-command at "A" Force, became head of Ops B, while Strangeways continued to organize tactical deception as the head of "Tac Headquarters" embedded within Montgomery's 21st Army Group.[20]

As far as Overlord was concerned, the LCS developed and coordinated the strategic efforts, while implementation of the tactical plans fell to Ops B. Ops B was technically formed in April 1943 when COSSAC came into being, but its powers were quite limited, as it existed more on paper than in reality at that stage. After the formation of SHAEF under Eisenhower's command, Ops B was greatly expanded. Although the work at Ops B took on a new level of importance, it was a very different organization than "A" Force. As head of "A" Force, Brigadier Dudley Clarke directly advised the theater commander and generals on deception matters. He even had troops under his own command, giving him a position "analogous to the head of any army service." Wild did not possess the same level of independent authority as Clarke, nor did he have operational control over troops earmarked for deception. Ops B never possessed the same degree of autonomy as did "A" Force, but instead came under the direct authority of the Operations Division. Wild also did not have direct access to Eisenhower or his chief of staff. Nonetheless, Ops B played an important role in deception planning and worked to delegate responsibilities to the joint service commanders.[21] Together, the London Controlling Section and Ops B worked with B1A, the Double-Cross subsection of MI5, to employ its double agents and secret channels.[22] The LCS and Ops B coordinated closely with Clarke and his team at "A" Force as well, and that close cooperation was crucial to the ultimate success of Plan Bodyguard in its multiple components.

Beyond interagency cooperation, collaboration between the military services and the deception agencies was of paramount importance for Bodyguard to succeed. Given the need to coordinate deception measures with military planning from the earliest stage possible, Bevan was present in Cairo for the strategic planning conference at the end of 1943. After Eureka produced a clear strategy for 1944, Bevan had the information he needed to start formulating the deception plan to accompany Overlord. The deception was dubbed Bodyguard after the prime minister remarked to Stalin at Tehran that "in wartime, truth is so precious that she should always be attended by a bodyguard of lies."[23] Bevan took the opportunity to meet with Clarke in Cairo to discuss Bodyguard and the diversionary role of the Mediterranean theater before returning to London. The LCS completed the first draft of Bodyguard on December 18, presented it to the British Chiefs of Staff on the 21st, completed revisions based on the COS's suggestions on the 25th, and finally forwarded the British-approved plan to Washington, where it was formally approved by the CCS on January 19. Bevan then traveled to Moscow, accompanied by Col. William "Bill" Baumer of the US Army, to present the plan to the Soviets. The Soviets agreed to Bodyguard without revision on March 6, 1944.[24] Despite the late final approval, the deceptionists began working on Bodyguard as soon as it was first drafted.

In the case of Overlord, the need for deception was inescapable. The challenges faced by the planners of Overlord were many and overwhelming as the sheer scale of preparation dwarfed all previous military campaigns. All the while, the leadership was fully cognizant of the fact that the chances of a successful invasion were precarious at best. They could amass and train a colossal invasion force, allocate the necessary resources, and ensure a rapid rate of supply, yet all would be for naught if the Germans knew when and where the attack was coming and were prepared to defend the French coast. And that was where planners faced some of their greatest challenges. Germany did expect a major attack in 1944, and fully expected it to come somewhere along the French coast.[25] Moreover, an attack on France could only originate from the UK. Planners were particularly concerned that German foreign agents and aerial reconnaissance would observe the unprecedented accumulation of troops, aircraft, and assault shipping, and it was only logical that the enemy would appreciate the significance of those preparations. Thus, in order for Overlord to achieve its maximum potential for success, the Allies had to achieve surprise by deceiving the Germans regarding the exact location and precise timing of the attack.[26] Furthermore, once the invasion began, the Allies needed to keep the Germans guessing and concerned about additional operations in order to minimize reinforcement of Normandy.

Even though many were pessimistic about the ability to achieve surprise given the scale of the entire operation, the deceptionists were encouraged by past successes against seemingly impossible odds. In addition to those, the deceptionists pointed to lapses in German reconnaissance, the tendency of the Germans to overestimate Allied strength, Hitler's insecurity over the Balkans, and the führer's tendency to allow his own fears and assumptions to interfere with military planning. They concluded that the "sole favourable factor therefore seemed to be the necessity for the enemy to safeguard himself at every vulnerable point on the perimeter of his European fortress, and to this extent the continuance of our deception policy of keeping him stretched by threatening the Balkans, Southern France and Norway and Denmark seemed plausible."[27] All told, Bodyguard consisted of three main components: Plan Fortitude (Norway and Pas de Calais), Plans Graffham and Royal Flush (diplomatic efforts targeting key neutral countries), and Plan Zeppelin (Mediterranean).

Plan Fortitude was divided into two parts—Fortitude North and Fortitude South. The story carefully built up around Fortitude North was that the Allies, to include the Soviets, intended to assault Norway in the spring of 1944. The intent was to liberate Norway and then launch an amphibious assault from Britain against Denmark to reach Germany from the north. The Allies hoped, according to the story, that Sweden would allow the Allies to use airbases in southern Sweden, and even possibly join the Allies against Germany.[28] Fortitude South emphasized the Pas de Calais in northwestern France as the intended target of the Allies' summer campaign. The Pas de Calais was the most logical target as its location was the shortest distance across the English Channel from Britain, allowing for adequate air cover and the shortest possible sea route for landing troops, supplies, and reinforcements. For those same reasons, Hitler and some of the German generals expected the Allies to land at the Pas de Calais. That proved a major boon for the deceptionists as they could provide evidence to support Hitler's preconceived notions.[29]

Attempts to utilize diplomatic channels to deceive the Germans via the neutral countries resulted in two plans—Royal Flush and Graffham. Royal Flush specifically targeted Turkey and Spain, while Sweden was the primary object of Graffham. Royal Flush and Graffham turned neutral countries into unwitting pawns in a game of strategic deception. From their years of experience deceiving the Germans, the deceptionists knew that Hitler and the German High Command were particularly sensitive when it came to the neutral countries. If the Germans could be convinced that the neutrals might join the Allied cause, or even simply grant the Allies access to their resources and/or facilities, then that would only intensify the enemy's concerns regarding the security of the German fatherland. The British Foreign Office expressed concern that the Allies would not be able to convince the neutrals to abandon their neutrality, but the deceptionists successfully argued that it was not what the neutrals did or did not do that mattered, but what the Germans thought they intended to do that was important. The deceptionists saw it as a win-win scenario, stating that "action by Germany against a neutral country to anticipate a pro-Allied move on its part could do no harm to us. On the contrary since it would inevitably involve an enemy military commitment away from the OVERLORD area, it would be in our favour."[30] Nonetheless, the neutral countries had to be dealt with delicately, and the British had to be exceedingly cautious not to overstep and precipitate an unwanted diplomatic crisis.

Plan Graffham, focused on Sweden, was directly connected to Fortitude North. Sweden was viewed as particularly strategic given that any shift toward the Allies could pose a threat to Germany's position in Norway, as well as present an urgent threat to northern Germany. Through genuine talks with Sweden, visits by British government representatives, and official inquiries made, it was hoped that the

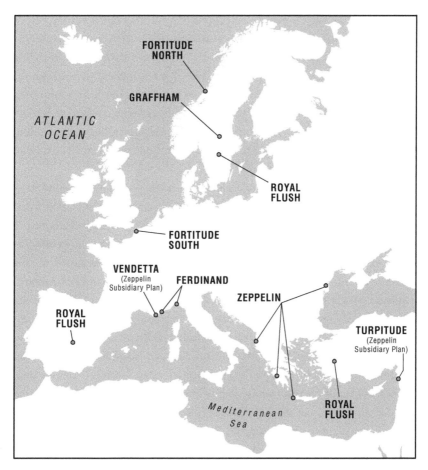

Bodyguard Deception Plans. Map by Erin Greb Cartography.

Germans would deduce that the Allies were planning military operations against Germany's forces in Norway. The objective was to see Germany reinforce Norway in order to protect its interests there.[31] Doing so would ideally draw German forces away from France, or at the very least lessen the number of reserves available to the Germans once D-day commenced.

Unlike Graffham, which drew attention to a diversionary target prior to Overlord, Royal Flush was designed to hold German forces in extraneous locations after the D-day landings took place. A substantial portion of Royal Flush focused on Turkey. One of the moves made by Britain was to station forces on Syria's northern border. The British let it be known that they intended to drive through

Turkey into Thrace in the summer of 1944, whether Turkey opted to cooperate or not. The British also envisioned a scheme whereby the three Allied powers would all issue Turkey an ultimatum two days after Overlord commenced demanding the right to pass through Turkey to the Balkans. It was ultimately decided that the ultimatum plan was too "dangerous" and had to be abandoned. As a substitute, the British hoped that their official contact with Turkey over unrelated issues could be manipulated to look as though the Allies were planning military operations in the Balkans. The British also sought to convince Turkey to break off relations with Germany, which it eventually did.[32]

For the Spanish portion of Royal Flush, which also had to be revised from its more ambitious original form, the American ambassador requested on June 3 that the Spanish government allow the Allies to use facilities located in Barcelona to evacuate Allied casualties from France, as well as allow food supplies to be sent into France via Spain. This was followed two days later by a similar request from the British ambassador. The requests were designed to indicate an upcoming operation in southern France, which supported Plan Vendetta, a subsidiary plan of Plan Zeppelin operated by "A" Force. Sweden was also given a small role in Royal Flush. On June 9, three days after D-day, the British, American, and Russian governments sent a joint demarche requesting that Sweden block German troops from crossing from Finland into Sweden in the event of an Allied attack on Norway.[33] In each case, the Allies expected the neutrals would leak information to the Germans, and that would lead the enemy to conclude that the Allies intended to follow Overlord with military campaigns in other theaters.[34]

The final component of Bodyguard pertained to the Mediterranean theater. Plan Zeppelin, exclusively operated by "A" Force, was designed to create diversions across the Mediterranean stretching from southern France to the Aegean islands and the Balkans. Clarke and his team sought to manufacture as many threats as possible to Germany's vulnerable periphery, in keeping with the doctrine of stretch. The LCS readily recognized that "A" Force was allocated the most challenging assignment of all:

> To "A" Force was assigned the most difficult and intricate task in implementing BODYGUARD. They were directly responsible for three threats, an Anglo-American assault against the Dalmatian coast, a British assault against Greece, and in conjunction with Russia, an amphibious threat by Russia against the Bulgarian and Rumanian coast, together with a British threat through Turkey against the Balkans

either with or without Turkish assistance. Added to this were their commitments in assisting General ALEXANDER's campaign in Italy, and uncertainty as to whether and when a Mediterranean assault was to be made on Southern France.[35]

As Bevan noted, not only did "A" Force have to plan and operate a highly complicated deception campaign laden with uncertainties and an ambiguous timetable, it also had to maintain continual strategic and tactical support for the ongoing war in Italy. Thus, "A" Force was the only deception body responsible for coordinating deception for an active theater while simultaneously providing diversionary cover for Overlord.

Dudley Clarke wrote that "1944 found the MEDITERRANEAN Theatre for the first time in four years surrendering its place as the principle [sic] front in the War with GERMANY," but that did not mean "A" Force was any less active or that the theater was quiet.[36] "A" Force continued to provide strategic cover for ongoing operations in Italy, and Tac HQ "A" Force was actively involved in providing tactical deception on short notice for the 15th Army Group. Meanwhile, even as 1944 dawned, "A" Force was actively coordinating two ongoing plans that had been in operation since late 1943. First, Plan Foynes was designed to hide the exodus of eight divisions from the Mediterranean, many of them seasoned and well known to the enemy, as well as a large-scale transfer of landing craft to the UK.[37] At the same time, it sought to hide the accumulation of Overlord forces in the UK. Second, Plan Oakfield was a strategic deception that went through multiple modifications but was ultimately shaped into a cover plan to assist with the Anzio invasion.

In order to cover the withdrawal of so many divisions and landing craft from the Mediterranean, the London Controlling Section and "A" Force jointly implemented the security plan designated as Foynes. The primary objective of Foynes was to mask, or otherwise explain away, the absence of eight divisions—four British and four American. This was further complicated as some divisions, such as the British 50th, 51st, and 7th Armoured, along with the American 82nd Airborne, were well known to the enemy and their absence was not likely to go unnoticed. Back in the UK, therefore, security measures were taken to prevent public announcements of the divisions' return. Mention of the units' return was strictly forbidden until the Germans became aware of their presence in the UK on their own. Even then, the plan was only to admit, through controlled channels, that "elements" of any given division had been sighted, not necessarily the entire division. At the same time, the deceptionists worked to pass the story that London was implementing a plan to relieve "long service personnel" and replace them with equally experienced soldiers.[38]

"A" Force's channels were instrumental in passing the cover story. In one such instance, for example, Harry, a former French agent operating in Oran, reported that American troops with over eighteen months' service were being sent home on leave, but noted that replacements were "arriving continually."[39] The Germans appeared to have taken note of the transfers and the Foynes story in general. On January 10, Gilbert—a French double agent that "A" Force acquired from the French Deuxième Bureau and who was held in high esteem by the Germans—received an insightful message from his contacts in the German Intelligence Service (GIS). The questions asked suggested that the Germans were eager to update their order of battle on the British, but perhaps were also apprehensive about where the familiar divisions went and what that might indicate:

Which British Divisions have been withdrawn from the ITALIAN front?
Where are these Divisions now?
By whom have they been replaced.?[40]

While the campaign of disinformation sought to provide an alternate explanation for the Allied transfers, it was critical that the enemy not realize the extent of Allied weakening in the Mediterranean. The Mediterranean was subsequently reinforced with three genuine divisions: the 5th Canadian Armoured Division and the American 85th and 88th Infantry Divisions. Because the arrival of three divisions did not alleviate the discrepancy in strength, "A" Force stepped in to create three bogus divisions—the 40th, 42nd, and 57th British Divisions—and bring them to life with the usual display of insignia, reports of sightings by conveniently placed agents, wireless activity, and the necessary trail of paperwork. "A" Force was also able to keep two of the departing divisions alive in the enemy's eyes. The 1st British Airborne Division had in reality left a brigade behind, while the American 82nd Airborne Division left a regimental combat team. Because their insignia were still present and wireless activity continued, all "A" Force had to do was supplement the activity by employing other units to masquerade as the departed airborne divisions.[41]

In addition to the transfer of eight divisions, the deception teams also had to provide explanation and cover for the withdrawal of landing craft from the Mediterranean. Between late January and early February, the Allies intended to transfer sixty-eight LSTs (landing ship, tank), along with smaller landing craft, to the UK. Clarke considered the transfer of landing craft even more significant than the transfer of army divisions as the loss of so many LSTs represented a "crippling reduction in the capacity of the MEDITERRANEAN Theatre for further landings."[42] If the Mediterranean was to serve as a diversionary theater, and the Allies were to sustain a threat level acute enough for Germany to maintain a steady supply of reinforcements to defend its southern flank, the enemy had to believe that the Allies were capable of staging future landings. To mask the weakening and explain the transfer of landing craft to the UK, the story purported that the repair facilities in the Mediterranean were no longer adequate, necessitating that the vessels be sent to the UK for repair before being returned to the Mediterranean. The story also claimed that new and better landing craft were en route from the United States.[43] In this way, the British hoped to disguise the weakening of Allied strength in the Mediterranean and hide the rapid buildup occurring in the UK.

Plan Foynes achieved its objectives, but in some respects only by sheer luck. Most of the plan was passed through secret channels. The deceptionists held out very little hope of being able to conceal the movement of men and landing craft for a long period of time. In particular, they knew that the passage of landing craft through the Strait of Gibraltar was unlikely to go unnoticed. The Germans maintained twelve well-lit observation posts along the strait—seven on the African side and five on the European side. Moreover, it took an average of six to seven hours to cross through the strait. Efforts to hide the ships' passage with fog screens proved impractical, and an attempt to create the illusion of incoming landing craft by erecting dummies on a convoy failed due to a severe storm that brought high winds. In the end, however, the Germans seemed to accept the information passed by the agents and "failed utterly to appreciate the strategic significance" of the transfers of men and landing craft. Clarke referred to Foynes as "one of those pleasant surprises."[44]

While Foynes was underway, "A" Force was at the same time responsible for implementing a strategic cover plan for the Mediterranean. Plan Oakfield began in mid-November, following on the heels of Plan Fairlands. In its original form, Oakfield had two primary goals. The first was designed to help facilitate Eisenhower's goal of breaking through the Gustav Line and reaching Rome before the end of 1943. By threatening northern Italy with simultaneous landings coming from the Adriatic (Rimini) and the Gulf of Genoa (Leghorn–Pisa), "A" Force hoped to induce Field Marshal Albrecht Kesselring to withdraw his forces from Rome, or at the very least, to prevent him from further reinforcing the Gustav Line. Either scenario would greatly assist the 15th Army Group in its effort to break through the formidable line and reach Rome.[45] For this objective, the story read:

i. Landings were to be effected in the PISA Area and on the ADRIATIC Coast N. of RIMINI with the object of isolating and annihilating all German forces in S. ITALY.

ii. The PISA operation to be launched first with the object of cutting communications on the West Coast and establishing advanced fighter landing grounds.

iii. The RIMINI landing would be made with the object of seizing BOLOGNA and thus severing completely all communications with the South.[46]

According to the deception story, the Allies were prodded to launch the campaign by Stalin, who believed the war in Italy was taking too long. He allegedly demanded that the Allies take Italy in 1943. The crux of the information was transmitted by Gilbert. His report on November 18 warned the Germans that Eisenhower "must at all costs, and urgently, make a landing in NORTH ITALY to capture German Army in the South." He credited his information to an American liaison officer.[47]

The second objective of Oakfield, in its original version written in 1943, was directed at the eastern Mediterranean. At that time, the Germans had already taken Kos from the British in October; the British were hoping to prevent the Germans from moving against Leros and Samos by indicating that they had no further objectives in the Aegean, when in fact they were planning an operation against Rhodes. The Germans, however, took Leros and Samos only days later on November 16 and 20, respectively, thereby rendering the second objective moot. In the meantime, the Allied advance in Italy stalled during the winter, thus ending Eisenhower's hopes of capturing Rome before the year was out.[48]

With the two main objectives of Oakfield eliminated, the plan entered a stage of ambiguity. It received new life with talks of an Allied amphibious invasion at Anzio, code-named Operation Shingle, but even that proved challenging as the Allied leadership wavered on a decision throughout the month of December. On December 26, Brig. Gen. Walter Bedell Smith, Eisenhower's chief of staff, informed Clarke that Shingle would in fact take place in January. Clarke then visited the headquarters of General Harold Alexander and Lt. Gen. Mark Clark to determine what shape the deception should take. On January 4, Plan Oakfield was reissued with a new purpose—to do everything possible to achieve surprise when Operation Shingle commenced on January 22, 1944.[49]

The goal of Operation Shingle was to launch a seaborne landing north of the Gustav Line that would both threaten the Germans' vulnerable lines of communication and force Kesselring to withdraw reserves away from the Gustav Line. Clark's Fifth

Army was exhausted after a series of winter campaign frontal assaults against the heavily defended line, and it had become clear that assistance was needed in order to achieve a breakthrough. The Allied leadership hoped the landing at Anzio would offer that assistance by weakening the line. The landing was to be coordinated with an attack by the Fifth Army along the western portion of the line. If successful, the landing would force Kesselring to weaken his defenses, and that would provide the opportunity the Fifth Army needed to break through and link up with the Anzio invasion forces for a drive north to Rome. The Anzio beaches were chosen for their close proximity to both Rome and the Gustav Line (see map 7).[50]

The idea of leap-frogging the German forces with an amphibious assault near Rome played directly into Kesselring's fears. Although he admitted that some credited him with "invasion-phobia," his concerns were merited. He reasoned that given the Allies' dominance in the air and at sea, it was only logical that they would attempt to outflank his forces with an attack in the rear. He later wrote: "I did not believe that Alexander could be satisfied for much longer with the slow and costly way the Allied front was edging forward. Sooner or later he must surely end it by a landing, which taking into account the enemy's systematic methods, could only be expected in the region of Rome." He also accurately predicted that the landings would coincide with a renewed offensive along the Gustav Line. While Kesselring was able to anticipate the Allied course of action, he was frustrated by his lack of precise intelligence. He lamented that the few reports he received were "inaccurate and misleading."[51] Given the campaign of disinformation "A" Force was waging under Plan Oakfield, there can be little doubt that was, at least in part, the work of the deceptionists. It is also highly probable that some of Kesselring's "invasion-phobia" was the product of "A" Force. From its very inception, one of Oakfield's objectives was to plant information on the Germans by way of secret channels alerting them to Allied plans to land in northern Italy. Furthermore, Oakfield followed on previous deceptions that threatened similar amphibious operations.

Despite what appeared to be a fairly straightforward and simple plan, the Anzio operation was plagued with difficulties. For one, the Allies did not have the luxury of time when it came to planning the operation. Whereas they devoted months to planning the invasion of Sicily, and six weeks for Salerno, they had only three weeks to prepare for Anzio. The haste was unfortunate, but its timetable was unavoidably rushed owing to the recall of landing craft as decided at the December leadership conferences. Moreover, the Allies were able to launch the assault with only two divisions, a much smaller invasion force than the generals preferred. Shingle's objectives also seemed overly ambitious for its size. If the invasion force acted aggressively to draw off German reserves and weaken the enemy's defenses along the Gustav Line, it was almost guaranteed that the relatively small invasion force would be destroyed by a powerful German counterattack. If the plan was to secure the beachhead and launch a delayed offensive, it might not offer much assistance to the Fifth Army at all, which was its primary objective, and ran the risk of getting cut off and surrounded by the enemy. To add to the problems, American general and US VI Corps commander Gen. John P. Lucas was chosen to lead the invasion forces. Lucas was known to be a competent commander, but he had no enthusiasm for the task at hand. He viewed Operation Shingle with complete pessimism and seemed to expect the operation to fail. His lack of confidence would ultimately translate into a lackluster and overly cautious approach once on shore.[52]

Under less than ideal circumstances, it was "A" Force's job to help ensure surprise when the invasion forces landed. Beyond that, it was to assist with measures designed to delay the release of key German reserves, then positioned along the eastern portion of the Gustav Line, to the Anzio beachhead. The story presented to the enemy, which built on the original design of Oakfield, was that General Patton's Seventh Army would spearhead a two-pronged amphibious assault against the Leghorn-Pisa region on the western coast and Rimini on the Adriatic on January 17. For Pisa, the Allies claimed that the British 1st and American 3rd Infantry Divisions intended to launch from Naples. They were, in fact, the two divisions chosen to lead the Anzio landings. The Germans would be able to observe those forces congregated at Naples but would expect them to land farther north at Pisa instead of Anzio. The story also claimed that the assault forces at Naples would be assisted by two French divisions coming from Corsica and Sardinia. For the Rimini invasion, "A" Force channels identified a Polish corps from Egypt under General Wladyslaw Anders as the lead force, supported by the American 82nd and British 1st Airborne Divisions, the American 88th Infantry Division, and the British 14th Corps with two divisions (notional) stationed in North Africa. The two assault forces were supposed to link up near Bologna in order to cut the peninsula in half, thereby completely isolating Kesselring's Tenth Army in the south. If the deception succeeded, Kesselring would be hesitant to further reinforce the Gustav Line—which would go a long way toward assisting the American Fifth Army in breaking through the formidable German defenses. Likewise, the Germans' focus would be far north of Anzio, which would aid in the element of surprise when the invasion began.[53]

Oakfield was implemented through traditional means, most of which were a continuation of measures already put in place under the first stage of Oakfield during November and December, as well as through the strategic and rather savvy incorporation of genuine troop movements and other events to add realism. With regard to the latter, the plan gained much credibility when Clarke seized on an opportunity to utilize the movement of a group of aircraft carriers and battleships, along with their escort cruisers and destroyers, through the Mediterranean en route to Ceylon. The timing of their passage was purely coincidental, but Clarke used it to bolster "A" Force's claims of an impending attack in Italy. Plan Dundee, initially an LCS plan intended to deceive the Japanese regarding the destination of those very same capital ships, was refashioned by "A" Force to convince the Germans that the ships were intended for the Mediterranean and were slated to participate in the planned two-pronged attack against northern Italy.[54] The presence of such ships was incredibly advantageous as the Allies lacked the capabilities to reach the projected targets with their available airpower. In fact, the original version of Oakfield was limited because it had to take that into account. The early story had claimed that the initial assault would have to be against Pisa, which would then facilitate the transfer of airpower from Corsica to assist with the subsequent landing at Rimini. Clearly, however, the issue of inadequate air cover would cease to be a concern if the Allies deployed aircraft carriers to the region. Moreover, the inclusion of five battleships certainly represented a significant strengthening of Mediterranean naval power as well.

The chief concern with Dundee was related to timing. The Germans observed the ships pass through the Strait of Gibraltar on January 5. The challenge from that point forward was to ensure that secret agents provided details of the ships' movements and intended destination that fit the deception story and timetable. "A" Force's channels, accordingly, reported that the ships were supposed to join the Rimini assault force located in Egypt. On January 8, agents reported to the Germans that the carrier *Illustrious* needed to dock at Alexandria for repair of an unidentified defect. Because of the repair time, the invasion would have to be delayed until January 22. The Germans were informed on January 15 that *Illustrious* was still not ready, and that meant yet another delay of the invasion timetable, pushing it back to January 27. On January 20, agents reported that *Illustrious* was finally ready and had joined the other battleships in the Gulf of Suez, where they had been waiting in order to minimize the risk of being spotted and attacked by the enemy, but bad weather was keeping the Pisa invasion force tied down in Naples. The new invasion date was identified as January 29. On January 22, only hours before the actual landings at Anzio commenced, agents relayed a final delay of forty-eight hours.[55] In this way, "A" Force was able to take advantage of the movement of ships slated for an entirely different theater, and successfully incorporate their movement into an active and ongoing deception campaign.

"A" Force was also able to capitalize on the genuine movement of Polish forces from Egypt to Italy. As previously outlined, the original Oakfield story had General Anders's Polish corps, allegedly incorporated into Patton's Seventh Army, attacking at Rimini. On January 7, a Polish convoy left Egypt for Naples aboard seven landing craft. Its departure was reported to the Germans and presented as comprising part of the Rimini assault force headed to the Adriatic. The information was passed along with sufficient erroneous information to prevent the Germans from locating and destroying the convoy. On the following day, the Germans were informed that the Polish convoy planned to halt off the coast of southern Italy to wait for escort to take it up to its staging location in the Adriatic. The need to wait for escort was explained as being on account of the prolonged repairs to *Illustrious* that ultimately delayed the planned rendezvous and had resulted in an additional invasion postponement. On January 15, another Polish convoy headed to Italy; the move was duly reported to the enemy.[56]

Taking full advantage of genuine movements, "A" Force was able to craft a tale that painted a picture of imminent invasion. Moreover, by incorporating real activity into the deception, the enemy could verify the information fed to him by "A" Force's channels. Clarke noted that by January 20:

a. In the BAY of NAPLES were the "SHINGLE" forces (described by us as the "PISA Assault Force").
b. At BARI a Polish convoy from EGYPT (described by us as the "RIMINI Assault Force") had just arrived.
c. The capital ships of the naval force (described by us as the Supporting Force for RIMINI) were in the GULF OF SUEZ, actually waiting to continue passage to CEYLON.[57]

This demonstrates the ability to make clever use of genuine activity for the purposes of deception, as well as the importance of providing the enemy with information that he could independently verify. The Germans were fully capable of observing the movements of Allied forces—they could be left to draw their own conclusions regarding the significance of those movements, or the deceptionists could feed them a story that served the Allies' purpose. Clarke always preferred the latter.

An interesting development that went a long way to help make the connection between the Polish corps and General Patton's US Seventh Army came when Patton paid a visit to Egypt in December just prior to Oakfield entering its final stage. On December 12, Patton and eight officers arrived in Cairo. Their journey to Egypt was promptly reported to the Germans by Gilbert, who claimed to have seen them with his own eyes in Tunis on December 11.[58] The presence of the Seventh Army HQ leadership in Cairo was designed to give the impression of ongoing planning conferences to lend support to the deception.[59] For a week Patton participated in activities guaranteed to attract attention and the "keen curiosity of the Cairenes and the Press representatives of half the world." After lecturing British officers in Cairo and paying a visit to the Royal Navy at Alexandria, he inspected the Polish corps located close to Ismailia. The press was conveniently able to capture a few pictures from the troop parade, one of which showed General Patton with General Anders. The deceptionists made it their mission to pay great attention to even the minutest of details, and that proved true for the seemingly fortunate photo opportunity. The photo of the generals, which clearly showed General Anders sporting the unmistakable flash of the Seventh Army on his shoulder, conveniently found its way into a weekly newspaper from Istanbul.[60] Given "A" Force's penchant for passing information through the neutral countries, and especially Turkey, the choice of an Istanbul-based newspaper could hardly have been a coincidence.

The majority of Oakfield was passed through the traditional methods that had become staples of "A" Force's repertoire. They distributed maps of the Pisa and Rimini regions. Pamphlets, written in English, French, and Polish, instructed the troops on the "Preservation of Works of Art," specifically focusing on ancient monuments in the region of Pisa. The information was supported by agent reports, such as one by the agent Harry, who reported to the Germans that a French friend of his had just returned from Corsica and had in his possession a French-English booklet issued to French troops there. He explained that he had seen the booklet and that it contained information on monuments in Tuscany with instructions to "preserve them as far as possible."[61] In addition, "A" Force organized both aerial and beach reconnaissance, and the air force conducted several bombing raids over the notional target areas.

Throughout the duration of Oakfield, considerable effort went into building up Corsica as ground zero for the Pisa assault. During December and January, there was a genuine transfer of French troops, American aircraft, and assault craft to the island. The transfer was supplemented by additional measures intended to add impetus to the ruse, calling attention to the presence of new units and an uptick in activity. "A" Force reports reveal that camps were erected, roads and airfields were either created or extended, phony wireless activity was simulated, and even accommodations for the inevitable casualties were taken into account as seven thousand hospital beds were made ready to receive the wounded. To add to this, two companies of an American camouflage battalion assisted with providing physical evidence by erecting "dummy dumps, vehicles parks, camps, aerodromes and 'hides' for landing-craft" beginning in early December.[62] Agent reports abounded with information to support the story. One agent in particular, Arthur, provided a wealth of information on new hospitals being built, the arrival of French forces, Allied airpower "receiving enormous reinforcements," and extensive work carried out on airfields. Based on the information he claimed to have received from a French captain, he concluded that a "large-scale operation is being planned against Northern Italy for which all the strength available in the MEDITERRANEAN is being concentrated."[63] The notional preinvasion activity caught the Germans' attention, and Tac HQ "A" Force observed an increase in aerial reconnaissance over Corsica. One report noted: "Judging by the increased enemy P.R.U. sorties over CORSICA he is showing great interest in our build up of dumps and assembly of small craft in the Island."[64]

Another important element of Plan Oakfield was to give life to the Seventh Army, which was in reality in "skeleton" form. Here again, Patton readily offered assistance to add authenticity to the efforts. Patton's meager headquarters in Sicily initiated "intensive wireless deception" over a period of weeks to demonstrate increased activity and "operational readiness." To give the impression of training for an airborne operation, gliders were transferred to Sicily and parachute training was organized. It also became necessary to create a new British corps. "A" Force had extensive experience with order of battle deception, so administrative measures were activated to create the 14th Corps, notionally stationed in Algiers. In short order, a headquarters was formed and the newly created corps sign of a wolf's head with lolling red tongue was readily visible on vehicles, Christmas cards, and even invitations to a 14th Corps Christmas party. Clarke related with obvious amusement that some of the invitations "'accidentally' found their way in due course into the oddest hands in centres as remote as SPAIN and TURKEY."[65]

Throughout the deception, "A" Force mobilized its secret channels and oversaw the usual rumors and leaks. Moreover, it closely coordinated its efforts with the Psychological Warfare Board based in Algiers, the Political Warfare Executive, and Security Intelligence Middle East in Cairo to ensure an effective campaign of rumors and propaganda. Clarke noted that special attention was given to the "discreet" reporting of the arrival of air reinforcements, conveyed in a way that clearly connected their arrival in the Mediterranean with the planning of a major amphibious operation.[66]

One of the last elements put into place to assist Oakfield was a tactical deception plan. Administered by Tac HQ "A" Force in Italy, the stated goal of Plan Chettyford was to provide cover for the shuffling of Alexander's 15th Army Group in preparation for Shingle and to create conditions that would discourage the enemy from reinforcing the Anzio region for at least forty-eight hours after the landings began. In addition, as the Allies prepared to go on the offensive, Tac HQ "A" Force set out to keep the Germans ignorant of the genuine targets and preoccupied with notional ones.

The actual plan was for the Fifth Army, in coordination with the landings at Anzio, to stage a concentrated attack against the western sector of the Gustav Line. The Eighth Army was tasked with holding its front and keeping as many Germans as possible tied down in the east, away from the action. Opposite the Eighth Army was the 26th Panzer Division and the formidable 1st Parachute Division; elements of the 3rd and 9th Panzer Grenadier Divisions were stationed within close proximity to the Eighth Army front. To keep those forces stationary and away from the real action, Tac HQ "A" Force sought to manufacture a threat from the British Eighth Army in the east by simulating assault preparations. At the same time, it endeavored to hide the fact that the Fifth Army was preparing another offensive. The deception story claimed that the Fifth Army was weakened after transferring two divisions to Corsica for the Pisa assault; thus, it intended to maintain a defensive posture. The story further claimed that when the invasion forces went ashore at Pisa, the Eighth Army, freshly reinforced with three divisions comprising the 1st Canadian Corps, intended to launch a simultaneous assault northward along the coastal road to link up with the Rimini invasion forces.[67]

Lieutenant-Colonel S. B. D. Hood, Colonel Strangeways's successor at Tac HQ "A" Force in Italy, began to organize physical measures to support the deception story. The most pressing need was to represent the presence of the 1st Canadian Corps. In order to simulate the presence of an entire three-division corps, the Eighth Army's camouflage unit came together with Colonel Victor Jones and his 101 RTR to erect dummy tanks, vehicles, and guns. A tank concentration, representing the 5th Canadian Armoured Division, was simulated using fifty dummy Sherman tanks. The dummy displays were supplemented by the erection of tents and a concentration of genuine vehicles and guns, only partially concealed from enemy eyes. While that was going on, the 5th British Division was transferred from the Eighth Army to the Fifth Army to participate in the offensive along the Gustav Line; thus, Tac HQ "A" Force was also tasked with providing cover for the transfer. Camouflage was used on the Fifth Army front to conceal the arrival of the 5th Division.[68] The deceptionists hoped their physical efforts would lead the enemy to believe that the Eighth Army was reinforced in preparation for an upcoming offensive, while the Fifth Army was weakened to provide forces for the Pisa assault, forcing it to remain in a defensive posture.

In addition to the visual display on the Eighth Army front, the deception was reinforced by way of a vigorous wireless deception campaign. It was well known that the enemy gathered a "large proportion" of its intelligence directly from Allied wireless messages.[69] Thus, it was the ideal medium through which Tac HQ "A" Force could represent the arrival of three divisions. An advance party of the 1st Canadian Corps headquarters moved from Sicily to Italy to begin operating the corps's wireless sets, while those remaining in Sicily resorted to strict wireless silence. The use of the corps's own wireless sets and signals staff was a crucial component of the deception's success. Before his transfer to London, Strangeways had helped to formulate the tactical deception unit's wireless deception policy. He was adamant that the enemy's highly skilled interceptors learned to recognize an operator by his signature. Thus, Strangeways concluded that "it's no good you pretending somebody else is him, you got to use *him*."[70] The transfer of the 1st Canadian Corps' own signals staff lent needed realism to the deception.

Meanwhile, every effort was made to hide the genuine weakening of the Eighth Army resulting from the transfer of two divisions—the 1st British Division earmarked for Shingle and the 5th British Division sent to reinforce the Fifth Army for its coming offensive. Both were notionally kept alive through a dummy wireless campaign designed to simulate the two divisions' presence; even some of their own wireless sets and men were left behind to continue operating the networks. For those who were transferred, they were ordered to remove all identifying insignia to prevent them from being spotted and reported in their new locations; as an additional but necessary measure, both divisions likewise implemented complete wireless silence after their move. Captain P. W. Laycock oversaw the wireless campaign in his position as official liaison for Tac HQ "A" Force with the Eighth Army.[71] Meanwhile, the US VI Corps under the Fifth Army sent a wireless set to Corsica and began operating dummy traffic to represent the transfer of invasion forces to the island. The ruse was reinforced with the issuance of maps and pamphlets with information on Pisa and its history.[72]

In addition to its own efforts, Tac HQ "A" Force was able to organize the assistance of the Royal Navy and RAF as well. The navy participated by sending an assault convoy in the direction of Corsica. From all appearances, Corsica was its destination, though it changed course after dark. The navy also sent a covering force, along with minesweepers, to the island. The minesweepers were to carry out activity in the regions of Corsica and Leghorn. With regard to the RAF, it cooperated by conducting bombing raids over the target areas prior to the Anzio operation. "A" Force also requested that the RAF use dummy wireless and simulate a general movement of aircraft from west to east to lend support to the Rimini threat.[73]

As the launch date for Shingle approached, the deceptionists hoped that the enemy was able to piece together the deception story from multiple angles: genuine agent reports, observations of genuine and cover activity, messages from secret channels, rumors, leaks, propaganda, visual evidence, and bogus wireless chatter. Success, however, would ultimately be measured by the amount of resistance the Fifth Army and Shingle forces met once their respective campaigns began.

The Fifth Army front opened up on the evening of January 17 at Garigliano. The fact that the Germans were caught completely by surprise provides solid evidence that the camouflage and deception efforts succeeded. Kesselring rushed to reinforce the line in fear that his defenses might break. His decision was advantageous for the Shingle forces, as it committed potential reserves into battle along the Gustav Line a safe distance from Anzio. In the predawn hours of January 22, General Lucas's VI Corps made its initial landings, almost entirely unopposed. The only German resistance in the region amounted to two companies of the 29th Panzer Grenadier Division, and they were cautious in their response. The Luftwaffe tried to mount resistance from the air, but Allied air cover dominated, holding the Germans to fifty sorties for the day. By the end of the day, the Allies had 36,000 men ashore, along with 3,200 vehicles. Moreover, the Allies had secured the beachhead and controlled the port at Anzio.[74]

From all appearances, the deception had achieved its goal of complete surprise and the invasion was off to a promising start. The invasion forces were astonished at the soft landing given that they expected stiff resistance. Even Lucas expressed dismay noting that the Allies had achieved "one of the most complete surprises in history."[75] The lack of resistance made it clear that the Germans were not expecting a landing at Anzio. American war correspondent Don Whitehead reported his experience and obvious surprise after landing in the second wave with the troops: "We walked in behind the German lines with hardly a shot being fired in a most sensational amphibious operation. It was so easy and so simply done, and caught the Germans so completely by surprise, that, as I write this despatch six hours after landing, American troops are literally standing with their mouths open and shaking their heads in utter amazement." Additionally, the AFHQ Daily Report for January 22 read:

> It is very evident from the units contacted during the past three days
> on 5 Army front that the enemy had wholly failed to appreciate the
> imminence of a landing in the rear of the GUSTAV or CASSINO

line and had decided to commit all available forces to its defence, presumably in the hope of inflicting very heavy losses on the Allies and thus postponing renewed offensives against the prepared positions. The circumstances of the ANZIO operation confirm this view.[76]

Given the fact that Shingle had been hastily thrown together with little time for adequate military preparations, the unopposed landing came as a pleasant surprise. The very next morning, Bevan congratulated Clarke: "Well, well, well! I suppose it is a bit too early to speak, but first indications are that you have had another roaring success!"[77]

Clarke believed the efforts of Tac HQ "A" Force on the eastern coast had also paid off. As Kesselring began to send reinforcements to the Anzio front, he naturally looked to those not already engaged in combat, thus he ordered the bulk of his forces facing the Eighth Army into action. The majority, including the 26th Panzer Division, left on January 24. If nothing else, the desired forty-eight-hour delay had been achieved. Yet, most of the 1st Parachute Division, one of Kesselring's elite units, remained in its place until February. The 1st Parachute Division was widely regarded as one of the Germans' toughest and most reliable divisions. Case in point, its piecemeal arrival to the Fifth Army front throughout February proved to be decisive for the German defense and was credited with stopping the Allied attack on Cassino in its tracks.[78]

Although the deception planning had gone exceptionally well and met its goals, the ensuing military effort faltered and all momentum was lost. In typical German fashion, Kesselring reacted swiftly and began ordering reserves to surround the Anzio beachhead and block the Allies' path north. The German High Command also transferred to Italy an infantry division from France, another from the Balkans, and several regiments from Germany. Despite the rapid realignment of reserves, Kesselring's greatest vulnerability was the time it would take for those divisions to reach their destination. The earliest he could expect sufficient reinforcements to arrive in Anzio was January 24, and until then the Alban Hills road, and thus the path to Rome, lay open and exposed.[79]

Despite his initial anxiety, Kesselring's concerns quickly turned to relief when he realized that the invasion forces were making no efforts to advance inward in a dash for Rome. General Heinrich von Vietinghoff was already preparing to begin pulling forces off the Gustav Line to counter the invasion force's anticipated thrust north, but Kesselring saw the situation differently. Once he realized that the Allies were not aggressively seeking to mount a major inland advance, he ordered the Gustav Line forces to remain firm.[80] Kesselring then visited the front and noted his "confident feeling that the Allies had missed a uniquely favourable chance of capturing Rome and of opening the door on the Garigliano front. I was certain that time was our ally."[81]

In one final attempt to delay German reinforcement of Anzio and the Gustav Line, Tac HQ "A" Force was called on in late January to simulate an immediate threat from the Eighth Army. This came as there were signs that the 1st Parachute Division was about to move out of the sector to head west. Alexander assigned Hood the task on January 27, and the two men met with General Sir Oliver Leese, commander of the Eighth Army, that afternoon. Their discussions resulted in Plan Clairvale, written and approved that very day, which in most ways was a natural extension to Chettyford. The story was that the significant weakening of German defenses along the Adriatic provided the Eighth Army with the ideal opportunity to advance north. The army intended to send the 1st Canadian Corps up the coastal road toward Pescara. In support of the land thrust, the Allies intended to launch a division from Termoli to land at Pescara, effectively carrying out a "short right-hook."[82] In reality, the Allies simply hoped to keep the 1st Parachute Division out of the fight in the west for as long as possible.

Tac HQ "A" Force quickly began fabricating signs of preinvasion activity. Attention was given to maintaining dummy guns in the Canadian sector, while the air force carried out bombing raids and reconnaissance over Pescara. Most of the work took place at Termoli, where it was imperative to display signs of amphibious preparations. As the work began, all Italian troops and civilians were evacuated from the town and harbor area, a move Hood made sure was reported to the Germans through all available channels. On January 27, the same day that Clairvale was approved and went into action, Hood cabled Lt. Col. George Train, the American deception officer in charge of Advanced HQ (West) in Algiers, for assistance. He specifically asked Train to "counter" all information regarding the evacuation of Italian troops and civilians from Termoli. He further requested that Train "counter" information regarding the building of hides and extension of loading hards after February 3.[83] The term "counter" was code for "spread." The use of such a code was quite crafty since its recipients all understood "counter" to mean "spread," but it would lend support to the deception if the Germans happened to intercept the message as it appeared that the Allies were trying to prevent that information from leaking.[84] As desired, the information found its way into agent reports. During the first week of February, Gilbert reported various observations to his German controllers: "Preparations for a new landing operation are intensified in harbours of BARLETTA and TERMOLI"; "Large landing craft transferred a short time ago from the West coast of ITALY to the East coast"; and "Civilian population evacuated from TERMOLI and district. Officers would seem to say that this is an important decision."[85]

In addition to passing information through strategic channels, Tac HQ "A" Force began a series of physical measures to support the story. It commandeered small boats to be camouflaged as landing craft, built a landing-craft hide, prepared loading hards for landing craft and made them appear to accommodate four as opposed to two craft each, constructed dummy dumps, and displayed embarkation signs. Finally, a wireless deception campaign was activated to represent the arrival of a new infantry division—supposedly the division heading to Pescara. The deception claimed that the Allies would not be able to launch the attack until February 10. The delay was attributed to the British intent to use airborne troops, which meant they had to wait until the moon was just beginning to wane, providing optimal invasion conditions.[86]

Overall, Tac HQ "A" Force had to be content with the results. The 1st Parachute Division began to move out of the area toward Cassino on January 30, which coincided with the time Clairvale reached full operation. Yet, to the Allies' relief, most of the division's battalions were ultimately held back in the Eighth Army sector. From that point, the division departed the area in piecemeal fashion throughout the month of February, the last contingent of which pulled out on February 25. Clarke concluded:

> Thus this very formidable German formation was prevented from intervening in the CASSINO battle of mid-February, a factor which may have made a decisive contribution towards the earlier successes of the Fifth Army against the GUSTAV LINE. It was the 1st Parachute Division which finally stopped the second assault on CASSINO a month later, and it was the one to which General ALEXANDER paid an unusual tribute.

Alexander credited the 1st Parachute Division with success in that later battle, claiming that had it been any other division, the Germans would have lost Cassino.[87] Thus, keeping the 1st Parachute Division out of action for a period of approximately one month was a significant victory for Tac HQ "A" Force.

Between Plan Oakfield and the tactical deception efforts, "A" Force leaders had done everything they deemed practicable in order to aid the Allied military efforts. The deceptionists were called on to help achieve surprise for the Fifth Army offensive and landings at Anzio, to hide the transfer of forces between the armies, and to delay reinforcement of the active fronts. They successfully accomplished each task required of them. As was often the case, the deception efforts helped create optimal conditions for success, but those gains were quickly lost as the military campaigns went awry. Thus, the deception successes were overshadowed by the military disappointments, something over which the deceptionists had no control. Clarke stated that if the "later developments of 'SHINGLE' met with the same success as on its opening day, then 'OAKFIELD' might have gone down as the most successful Deception Plan of the whole MEDITERRANEAN War." Nonetheless, he concluded that the men at "A" Force had "unusual cause to be satisfied with the results."[88]

The Anzio invasion and General Lucas's inertia have garnered much criticism from contemporaries and military scholars alike.[89] The question boils down to the purpose of the invasion. The outlined objective was to cut German communications and assist the Fifth Army by drawing German forces off the Gustav Line, thereby enabling the Fifth Army finally to breach the seemingly impenetrable line and make a dash for Rome. In that it most certainly failed. In retrospect, it appears that any outcome would have ended badly. Because of the Allies' decision to mount such a weak invasion composed of only two divisions, they lacked the strength needed to advance confidently and aggressively beyond the beachhead in the first days of the assault. There can be little doubt that the VI Corps would have been annihilated if it had proceeded toward the Alban Hills and encountered Kesselring's reserves. While such an advance may have forced Kesselring to withdraw forces from the Gustav Line and given the Fifth Army the opportunity it needed to break through, it nonetheless would have resulted in the loss of Lucas's VI Corps.[90] Instead of taking the aggressive approach, Lucas opted to remain conservative by consolidating the ten-mile-deep beachhead, wait for reinforcements, and content himself with minor local attacks before finally going on the offensive on January 30. By that time, however, the German defensive ring around Anzio was solid and no breakthrough was possible. The end result was that the VI Corps remained trapped at Anzio and the Fifth Army's hopes of breaking the Gustav Line, despite some initial successes, ultimately were dashed. Neither achieved the breakthroughs they desired until May 1944.[91]

With Operation Shingle completed and the war in Italy deadlocked in the battle for Cassino, Allied leaders could focus their full attention on Overlord. Military preparations were rapidly underway, and the UK was inundated with the massive accumulation of men, matériel, airpower, and naval power necessary to launch an amphibious assault against the heavily defended French coast. Opposite the

Allies waited the Germans—perhaps weakened by years of war and the losses of 1943—but still a formidable foe. Commanding those forces in Normandy was none other than Field Marshal Erwin Rommel, commander of Army Group B. After being transferred from Italy to France, Hitler charged Rommel with first inspecting, and later overseeing, the construction of the defensive fortifications along Europe's western coast—the Atlantic Wall. The Atlantic Wall was a defensive structure made of concrete, mines, and beach obstacles, all supported by artillery, antiaircraft guns, and panzer divisions. Hitler referred to the wall as "the greatest line of fortifications in history."[92]

In order to breach the Atlantic Wall defenses and establish a beachhead in Normandy, the Allies needed more than military strength—they needed to do everything within their power to weaken the Germans to the greatest extent possible before the attack, and to catch them off guard when it began. That was the task assigned to the deceptionists, who faithfully mobilized every trick of the trade to ensure that Operation Overlord was successful. At the same time as the Allied armed services planned, prepared, and executed the greatest amphibious assault known to history, the London Controlling Section, Ops B, "A" Force, and various other organizations came together to carry out the greatest deception campaign ever employed in warfare.

While the work of those in London is relatively well known, "A" Force operations in the Mediterranean have all too often been glossed over, threaded into a broader discussion, or ignored entirely. However, the exhaustive efforts of "A" Force, along with the knowledge, experience, and leadership it provided London, deserve special attention in any discussion of D-day deception. Moreover, given the value of the Mediterranean as a diversionary theater and one of great importance to the Germans, "A" Force's efforts there paid huge dividends and proved crucial to the success of both the broader deception campaign and the invasion itself.

In 1944 Allied Strategy had one clear aim, and one only—to land an Expeditionary Force on the beaches of Normandy. . . . All other operations were to be subordinate to that one over-riding need: and thus the MEDITERRANEAN Theatre as a whole was set the task of holding away from NORTHERN FRANCE the maximum number of German forces. Within the theatre it became the role of "A" Force to assist in this by the creation of artificial threats to areas where no actual attacks could be launched.

—"A" Force Narrative War Diary, Jan. 1–Dec. 31, 1944

6 DIVERSIONARY DECEPTION

ASSISTING OVERLORD FROM THE MEDITERRANEAN WITH PLAN ZEPPELIN

Plan Zeppelin, the Mediterranean component of Bodyguard, represented the most extensive and exhaustive deception effort undertaken by "A" Force during the entirety of World War II. Moreover, it underscored the Mediterranean's instrumental role as a diversionary theater crucial to the success of Operation Overlord. In order to carry out a diversionary deception campaign on a scale that outpaced all previous deceptions, "A" Force had to commit all of its resources and apply every aspect of knowledge it had gained over the previous years to this one monumental effort.

In the past, "A" Force went to great efforts to preserve the integrity of the organization, its methods, and all individuals and channels involved (which Dudley Clarke collectively refers to as the deception "machinery") for future operations. With the noticeable exception of Tac HQ "A" Force in Italy, where deception operations were expected to continue beyond D-day, the preservation efforts did not apply to

Zeppelin. "A" Force was carefully built up over the years with the singular goal of aiding the Allies toward victory. Allied leaders viewed the Normandy campaign as the most important operation to secure the final defeat of Germany, and for that reason, "A" Force was prepared to employ everything it had. An "A" Force "Special Order of the Day" provided:

> In the past, when nearing the climax of any plan, we have been at pains to conserve our machinery for another day. This time that policy will no longer hold. On this occasion our one aim must be to prolong our work on the current plan for as long as possible AFTER the main landings have taken place. To achieve this the machine will be run to a standstill with no regard for the future.[1]

With that expectation clear, "A" Force mobilized every component of its organization, unencumbered by concerns for maintaining the integrity of the organization for future operations.

Concerted planning for Bodyguard began in December 1943 after the British Chiefs of Staff gave their approval for the 1944 "Overall Deception Policy for the War against Germany" during the Sextant conference in Cairo. Unlike deception policies from years past, this one was singularly designed to support one operation: Overlord. Colonel John Bevan began working on the plan and presented it to "A" Force on January 3, 1944. Bodyguard was made official on January 19 after receiving final approval from the Combined Chiefs of Staff.[2] Bodyguard was a complex plan with numerous intricate components, but its main objectives were to convince the Germans that the Allies could not feasibly launch the cross-Channel operation until late summer 1944 due to a combination of impediments: a shortage of manpower in the UK, the American forces' lack of training, and insufficient numbers of landing craft. All of those obstacles were said to be exacerbated by the "formidable character of German coastal defences" and overall enemy strength across western Europe. The deception story alleged that the Allies would be forced to rely on the strategic air campaign against Germany until late summer; that the campaign to liberate France was to take place only *after* a combined assault by the British, American, and Soviet armies against the Balkans; that the three Allied powers intended to launch a spring assault against Norway—for which they hoped to secure Swedish cooperation and gain access to Swedish air bases to both assist the ongoing strategic bombing campaign against Germany and support a future seaborne assault against Denmark; that the USSR intended to initiate a summer offensive in late June, with the assault against France timed to commence *after* that offensive began and German forces were firmly committed on the eastern front; and finally, that the Allies intended to put pressure on Germany's satellites to reconsider their commitment to Germany. Particular emphasis was placed yet again on trying to induce Turkey to join the Allied cause, or at the very least convince the Turks to allow the Allies to use Turkey as a base for air operations in support of the Balkans campaign.[3]

Another element of the deception story incorporated the Italian campaign. On the one hand, the active front was seen as sufficient to hold German forces in Italy without fear of those divisions being transferred to France. On the other hand, there remained opportunities to exploit the Italian campaign for greater gain. The deceptionists claimed that the Allies intended to launch simultaneous amphibious landings against northwest and northeast Italy in order to bring the Italian campaign to a more expedient end. Once Field Marshal Albrecht Kesselring's forces capitulated, General Harold Alexander's 15th Army Group—temporarily renamed Central Mediterranean Forces—intended to turn east to join the Allied forces earmarked to enter the Balkans by way of Istria.[4] In reality, the Americans adamantly opposed any Allied military operations in the Balkans, so the threat remained exclusively within the deceptive realm. Nonetheless, it served to support the threat to the Balkans, which the Germans perceived as quite real.

One notable benefit of the various deception targets, which should not have been lost on the enemy, was the extensive demand for landing craft. Any assault against Norway, Denmark, the Balkans, and/or northern Italy would require considerable resources, manpower, and most importantly, landing craft. Moreover, the cross-Channel invasion against entrenched German forces would call for the greatest concentration of landing craft that the Allies could possibly muster. The deceptionists capitalized on that point by emphasizing the Allies' shortage of landing craft in the UK and the negative effect on the progress of the planned cross-Channel attack. The deceptionists likewise played up the Allied command's alleged insistence on launching the Norway and Balkans campaigns before opening operations against Germany in France. Those points only reinforced the deception timetable of a late summer offensive against France and the improbability of launching it any sooner.[5]

The London component of Bodyguard saw to the organization of two diversionary campaigns—Fortitude North (Norway) and Fortitude South (Pas de Calais), as well as diplomatic efforts against the neutral countries. "A" Force took the lead in the Mediterranean component of the plan, that which threatened the Balkans and southern France, and played an important role in the diplomatic deception efforts as they related primarily to Turkey.

As soon as Brigadier Dudley Clarke received a copy of Bodyguard, he began working on drafting the Mediterranean component—Plan Zeppelin. He presented the first draft of Zeppelin to AFHQ and GHQ Middle East on January 17. After Clarke received feedback and made modifications, Plan Zeppelin was formally approved by the commander in chief, General Henry Maitland Wilson, on February 4. Clarke was given permission to begin immediate implementation.[6]

Zeppelin was broken down into four stages. During the first three stages, "A" Force played up the threat to the Balkans by emphasizing the Allies' alleged intent to launch an early spring assault against Greece, the Dalmatian coast, and the Bulgarian-Romanian coast. It was of the utmost importance that the Germans anticipated an attack around late March. The deceptionists hoped the Germans would feel the need to strengthen the Balkans against the impending threat and obligingly make adjustments to their force dispositions in the early stages of Zeppelin. Once committed to the false dispositions in the Balkans, it would be exceedingly difficult and time-consuming for the Germans to redirect those forces to France. In order to maintain the threat level beyond March and keep the Germans pinned down in their faulty locations, "A" Force planned to fabricate several postponements. The first notional assault date for the Balkans campaign was March 23, with the Soviet advance from the Black Sea against Varna timed for April 21. The dates coincided with moonless periods with the aim of convincing the Germans that the Allies favored the cover of darkness for any amphibious assault. That was the exact opposite from reality, and Overlord in particular required a full moon to expose the Atlantic Wall's mines and obstacles. When "A" Force enacted its three postponements, the assault dates were pushed back in one-month increments in order to maintain the desired dark-moon stage. In the final postponement, the target date provided for both the Anglo-American and Soviet assaults was June 19, strategically timed to fall after Overlord. In the final stage of Zeppelin, "A" Force intended to intensify its efforts in northern Italy, threaten southern France with invasion, and intensify the threat against the Balkans in one final effort to prevent enemy reinforcement of northwestern France from the Mediterranean and contain the maximum number of German forces far away from Normandy at the time of D-day.[7]

Stage 1 began on somewhat uncertain footing. Clarke referred to it as the "most unpropitious moment" to begin a new large-scale strategic deception campaign, especially given that there was considerable uncertainty regarding crucial components of the plan. For one, when Zeppelin began, the Allies had yet to come to an agreement with the Soviets on their role in the deception, rendering it impossible to include the Soviet threat to the Balkans by way of Bulgaria, until Bevan met with the Soviets and obtained their consent. Soviet support for the deception plan was not secured until March 6; thus, the role allotted to the Soviets could not be implemented until that time. Furthermore, many questions regarding the proposed invasion of southern France loomed large in that early stage of planning. Previous and ongoing deception plans in the Mediterranean had included notional threats to southern France. It was unclear during the early planning for Zeppelin, however, if the genuine campaign (Operation Anvil) was to commence before, during, or after Overlord—or even at all. "A" Force had to tread lightly because it could not simulate deceptive maneuvers that might alert the Germans to a genuine operation, yet it needed to be ready to manufacture a threat when called on to do so. The deception plans relating to Anvil were by necessity postponed until the Allied command determined what role southern France would play in their plans, when, and on what scale.[8]

In addition to the uncertainty over the Soviet Union's role and a potential Allied invasion of southern France, "A" Force had to try to balance the CCS's order to "contain the maximum German forces away from the 'OVERLORD' area" with Wilson and Alexander's needs in Italy. However, those responsibilities often ran counter to each other. Clarke lamented that Zeppelin, which was developed as a subcomponent of Bodyguard designed specifically to assist SHAEF, offered few benefits to the Mediterranean. Rather, it was "always running in direct opposition to the interests of General WILSON's command."[9] Furthermore, the concurrent efforts contended with each other as both required significant manpower and matériel, as well as "A" Force's full attention. Given that SHAEF designated Zeppelin as the overriding priority, the Mediterranean commanders came to resent the Zeppelin deception efforts on some level, viewing the campaign as a "nuisance." Regrettably, it deprived "A" Force of the enthusiasm from the Mediterranean leadership that it had come to rely on over the preceding years. It was an exceedingly frustrating situation for Clarke that was only amplified by the fact that SHAEF retained complete authority for setting the timetable for deception plans in the Mediterranean. That removed control from "A" Force and local commanders, highlighting the new reality that the needs of the Mediterranean—where an active military campaign in Italy continued unabated—were both secondary and subordinate to those of Overlord.[10]

It was during that time of ambiguity that Plan Oakfield concluded, following the Anzio landing, and Zeppelin was born. While it may have been ideal to have a better handle on Allied military plans before moving forward, allowing for a lapse of weeks between deceptions plans was a "sheer impossibility." From Clarke's perspective, "the natural impetus of the monster which had been nourished there all through the past three years was such that it would very soon run wild if left to itself."[11] In that light, it was most expedient to put the first stage of Zeppelin into operation, even if it was a bit tentative, so that the deceptionists could remain in firm control of the extensive deception apparatus they had set in motion.

The Zeppelin story for Stage 1 stated that General Wilson intended to organize an attack against Greece and the Dalmatian coast on March 23. That attack was to be coordinated with General Alexander, who intended to assist by sending American forces to invade Istria at the same time. The final component revived the threat of bringing Turkey into the war, whether by choice or not, by activating the two genuine armored divisions comprising "Saturn Force," then situated on the Syrian border with Turkey. The story purported that Saturn Force and the RAF planned to cross into Turkey in May in order to link up with Allied forces in the Balkans.[12]

The deception story was centered on a fabricated request from Joseph Stalin. When the Allied leaders met in Tehran for Eureka, the deception story alleged, Stalin demanded that the Allies launch a coordinated attack in the Balkans before the Anglo-American forces attempted the cross-Channel assault. The reasoning for the request was threefold: a Balkans operation could force Germany's satellites out of the war, deny Germany essential resources, and assist the Soviet war effort by cutting off Germany's communications with its forces in the Soviet Union, specifically in the south.[13] Those outcomes would greatly benefit the Soviets in their planned summer offensive against the Germans.

While the deception story was beneficial from the standpoint that it helped underscore the Soviet offensive and the threat to the Balkans, as well as made clear that the Balkans campaign was a precursor to the attack on northwestern France, it also gave the Allies the opportunity to explain why Gen. Dwight D. Eisenhower was removed from the Mediterranean. The story held that General Wilson was the better choice between the two men to lead a campaign against the Balkans. He had served as the British commander in Greece in 1941 and then as the commander in chief of the Middle East theater during which time the Balkans fell under his purview of command. Because of his extensive experience with the Balkans, the Allied leadership determined Wilson to be the most qualified commander to lead the upcoming Balkans campaign.[14]

The Zeppelin story further claimed that before Eisenhower departed AFHQ for London, he and Wilson discussed the logistics of the upcoming operation and agreed that the British Twelfth Army should lead the assault against Greece, while the American Seventh Army, which included General Wladyslaw Anders's Polish corps, should be responsible for operations in the Adriatic. The fictitious decisions made by the two commanders were important in playing up the existence of two largely notional armies, as well as capitalizing on Gen. George S. Patton's December 1943 visit to Egypt to meet with General Anders and inspect the Polish troops purported to be incorporated into the Seventh Army.[15]

Despite the fact that the first stage of Zeppelin was viewed as an interim plan, Clarke intuitively realized that it must be extremely detailed in order to lay a solid foundation for the subsequent stages to build on. If the first stage was unsuccessful, and the Germans failed to appreciate a threat to the Balkans and consequently neglected to alter their dispositions to meet that threat, then the diversionary objective of Zeppelin would have been lost. Timing was crucial, and the Allies needed the Germans to commit to faulty troop dispositions as quickly as possible.

As the Zeppelin plan moved forward into operation, it needed to include a balanced combination of genuine and fabricated information—always a delicate task. Given the scale of Zeppelin and need for close coordination across the military services and various involved organizations, Clarke began by requesting assistance. On February 2, 1944, he drafted a directive outlining the aid he required from the services attached to AFHQ. The scale of his requests demonstrates both the immensity of the plan and the necessity for close coordination of all efforts across the Mediterranean and Middle East.

To G-3 (Operations), he requested the following: operations to simulate aggressive intentions against the Dalmatian coast and islands in the Aegean and eastern Ionian Seas; beach reconnaissance operations; the issuance of a directive to SOE and OSS to aid the resistance movements in Crete, the Peloponnese, and Albania throughout February and early March—and to work directly with "A" Force in crafting plans to do so; coordination with "A" Force to issue maps of the Pola region to the US Seventh Army; and finally, Clarke asked that the Allied commander in chief visit Cairo late in February. In order to provide a visual display to support the notion of future operations, Clarke asked the chief engineer to coordinate a large-scale display of dummy LCTs (landing craft, tank) in Bizerte to begin immediately.[16]

Clarke enlisted G-2 (Security/Intelligence) to assist by producing an English-language information pamphlet on Istria and to request that Italian authorities provide names of individuals who could serve as guides in the regions of Pola and Durazzo; further, he requested that G-2 officers at AFHQ compile lists of any Allied personnel with extensive knowledge of Albania or Bulgaria and those who spoke

Albanian, Russian, or Turkish. Furthermore, security forces were informed of "A" Force's efforts to create the impression of increased strength in the Mediterranean; thus, security forces were to avoid actions designed to conceal arrivals to the region, but instead provide cover for any departures that might indicate weakening.[17]

GHQ Middle East played the central role in establishing the threat to the Balkans and eastern Mediterranean islands. Upon Clarke's request, GHQ Middle East was to focus its efforts in February on building up and training Greek troops, to coordinate combined operations exercises for Greek land, air, and naval forces, and allocate specific facilities for well-known Greek "personalities" to observe the exercises. He also requested that GHQ Middle East arrange for visits of key Soviet authorities to the Middle East. Clarke emphasized the necessity of implementing administrative measures that would identify Tobruk as the staging area for an assault on Crete. To that end, GHQ Middle East was instructed to make improvements to the port facilities, roads, and railhead at Tobruk; to repaint red crosses on hospital roofs; to oversee the buildup of one hundred dummy LCTs by March 10; and to provide antiaircraft cover for the growing concentration of landing craft in and around Tobruk. Similar to the task assigned to G-2, GHQ Middle East was asked to issue maps of selected military targets; produce pamphlets on Albania, Crete, Greece, and Turkey; identify individuals with knowledge of Albania and Bulgaria, as well as those who spoke Albanian or Russian; and to collect names of individuals who could serve as guides in the selected target areas. Finally, the headquarters was to carry out a "scheme of calculated insecurity" that would provide ample evidence that the Allies were preparing to establish an Allied administration in Greece.[18]

To effect the greatest degree of authenticity, Clarke required the assistance of the military services. He reached out to the commander in chief of the Mediterranean for assistance in bolstering the naval display at Tobruk and aiding in the Greeks' naval exercises, and requested naval wireless deception measures to simulate an increase in wireless traffic at Tobruk. The commander in chief was also asked to carry out naval operations against shipping in the Aegean and Ionian Seas, with particular attention paid to the passageways to Crete, and to employ American naval equipment to simulate the passage of landing craft convoys through the Strait of Gibraltar into the Mediterranean during night hours.[19]

Requests were likewise made of the air commander in chief. Of primary importance was a demonstration of increased attention to select targets in the Balkans, and especially Crete, as well as assistance to the navy in targeting the Aegean and Ionian Seas' shipping lanes, again with special attention paid to those supplying Crete.

MAAF was asked to fly photographic reconnaissance missions over selected military targets, dispose of gliders—serviceable or not—in Sicily to simulate a growing glider force concentration, refrain from removing any gliders or troop transport aircraft from Sicily, and create a display of five to six dummy fighter squadrons in the region of Lecce, on the heel of the Italian Peninsula, for a period of two months.[20]

In its central coordinating role throughout the execution of the first stage of Zeppelin, "A" Force and its representatives across the Mediterranean theater worked to organize all actions associated with the deception plan. Moreover, certain tasks were allocated specifically to "A" Force. It was directly responsible for the rumor and propaganda component of Zeppelin—in which it was assisted by PWB, the expansion of the false order of battle, and the extensive campaign of disinformation funneled through its secret channels in conjunction with SIME.[21]

Given that the double agents represented one of the most reliable ways to plant information directly on the Germans, "A" Force readily employed its secret channels. All told, more than one hundred separate pieces of information were distributed among the "A" Force agents for dissemination to the Germans during Stage 1. A substantial portion of the information passed at that early stage related to troop movements. The picture created was that of a significant increase in Allied strength across the Mediterranean and Middle East. Some of the movements were genuine, others were completely notional and played into the ongoing order of battle deceptions, while yet others reported on actual movements but provided entirely false explanations for those moves. In one example of the latter, it was reported that a British infantry brigade was being transferred from Gibraltar to Egypt; while the report was accurate, it was not mentioned that it was only going for field training after a long stint of fortress duty. In another example, an agent reported that landing craft had been transferred from India to Egypt. Again, it was true that landing craft were thus sent, but Egypt was merely a stop along their journey to the UK. In that way, the deceptionists were able to relay information on genuine movements that the enemy could independently verify, while providing a false narrative that conformed to the deception story as opposed to the truth.[22]

One of the most important aspects of Plan Zeppelin was that the Germans be led to believe the Allies possessed sufficient strength to follow through on their threats. While the Allies enjoyed numerical superiority in Italy, they did not have sufficient reserves to carry out additional operations in the Mediterranean. In order to convince the Germans that they did, "A" Force set out to substantially expand its order of battle deception plan. The previous plan in operation since 1942, Cascade, was developed by "A" Force to meet the needs of the North African campaign and only sought artificially to enlarge the enemy's estimation of British forces.[23] Clarke replaced Cascade with Plan Wantage on February 6, 1944.[24] Wantage was in essence an expanded version of the original order of battle deception plan, with the notable difference that it took into account the expanding dimensions of the Mediterranean theater and addressed the need to create notional American and French units as well. The order of battle deceptions had become so central to the organization's methods and operations that all strategic deception plans—and most of the tactical plans—were firmly grounded on the Allies' exaggerated strength manufactured under the Cascade and Wantage plans. In reference to Zeppelin specifically, Clarke later noted that it was impossible to divorce the success of Zeppelin from the success of Wantage.[25]

The original objective of Wantage was to exaggerate Allied land strength in the Mediterranean by 33 percent and thereby convince the Germans that the Allies' reserve was sufficient to launch major operations in the eastern and western Mediterranean. In February 1944, genuine Allied strength amounted to 44 complete divisions in the Mediterranean, 23 of which were in Italy. There were also various unallotted units present, thereby technically increasing Allied strength to approximately 52 divisions.[26] The goal was to supplement the unallotted units with bogus ones, thus creating an increase of 18 "complete" divisions; instead of 44 divisions, it would appear as if the Allies possessed 62 divisions. Beyond the needs of Italy, that left 39 divisions (21 real and 18 notional) to parcel out between genuine duties and the threats being manufactured from southern France to the Balkans. Because a minimum of 15 of those divisions were required for garrison duty across the theater, only 24 divisions remained to form the Zeppelin armies.[27]

The two notional armies were the British Twelfth Army stationed in Egypt and General Patton's US Seventh Army based out of Algiers. Both "armies" contained genuine divisions, but were far from army strength.[28] Furthermore, both armies were organized into three notional corps: the Twelfth Army possessed two British and one Polish corps, while the Seventh Army was made up of an American, Polish, and French corps. The Twelfth Army was chosen as the Balkans "invasion" force, whereas the Seventh Army was to be divided in order to threaten Istria on the Adriatic and southern France as part of the various Zeppelin-related deceptive operations. The Seventh Army retained its deceptive role until it was reorganized to spearhead the genuine invasion of southern France on August 15, 1944.[29]

All of the notional units were brought to life in what was by then a fairly routine manner, at least for the British. It began with a request to the British War Office to assign a divisional number, brigade numbers, and specific battalion designations. It had become common practice for the War Office to assign divisional designations and insignia used by World War I divisions. After that, the War Office and deceptionists had to create a unit history and trail of paperwork, while "A" Force saw to the physical display of insignia and establishment of local headquarters. Next was the process of "activation" whereby existing units masqueraded as the bogus divisions. Lt. Col. George Train, the American officer in charge of Advanced HQ "A" Force (West), provided an example of the process of activation in a report dated February 12, 1944:

> the 43 Inf. Bde. stationed in Tunis was "activated" as the 40 Div. The Brigadier commanding 43 Inf. Bde. was authorised to wear Major General's insignai [*sic*], was issued a Major-General's pennant to fly on his car and various members of his staff were correspondingly "upgraded" to higher ranks and authorised to wear insignia thereof. Instructions were issued for all vehicles of the 43 Brigade to display the Division sign and order[s] were given that this sign would be prominently displayed along roads and outside Hqs. In addition, divisional "flashes" . . . were prepared and issued to a large proportion of personnel of the Brigade selected.

Interestingly, Train noted that the British process of establishing and activating bogus units could not be replicated at that time by the Americans. He stated that the procedures used were nonexistent and "unfamiliar" to the American system, specifically the US War Department. The process of creating notional formations would require so many changes in procedure in the United States that it would ultimately expose the entire process as a fraud. He added that the War Department was responsible for activating all new American formations in the United States; thus, it proved impossible at that time to activate local formations on the theater level for the purposes of deception.[30] As a result, when American notional units were utilized in the Mediterranean, they were created by "A" Force and incorporated into the Wantage order of battle deception effort.

The final piece of the order of battle puzzle was to transmit detailed information regarding the bogus units to the enemy by way of "sightings" from the secret channels. It is quite evident from the Germans' response to agent reports and alleged sightings that the secret agents were considered extremely valuable sources of intelligence for the enemy and therefore were instrumental in convincing the Germans of the various units' existence. Over a period of five months, for example,

"A" Force channels Cheese and Savage provided details of the bogus British 15th Motorized Division, reportedly headquartered in Abbassia, Egypt. Over the course of that time period, the Germans sent fifteen messages requesting additional details and clarification regarding the division's exact composition and intended destination. The Germans sent similar queries in reference to the other Cascade and Wantage formations, indicating their confidence in the agents and acceptance of the information provided.[31]

In addition to the false order of battle that greatly exaggerated Allied strength in German estimations, "A" Force had to provide copious visual evidence of the invasion preparations. Much of that effort took place in Cyrenaica under the direction of Colonel Victor Jones, the "A" Force commander in charge of the notional 24th Armoured Brigade, and the 85 Company SAEC (South African Engineering Corps) under his command. The scale of the operation required extensive cooperation between the services. Accordingly, a joint committee, convened by the General Brigadier Staff (Operations) and under the chairmanship of "A" Force, met in January 1944 to begin planning. It consisted of representatives from "A" Force, G(CAM), G (Ops), RAF Middle East HQ, Royal Navy GHQ, and X2 (the OSS counterespionage branch). The general plan was outlined as:

a. LCTs should concentrate at TOBRUK.
b. Aircraft should be displayed on airfields at MERSA MATRUH, BU AMUD, DERNA, and BENINA.
c. Gliders should be displayed at GAMBUT and EL ADEM.
d. 8 Armd Div display should be near TOBRUK.[32]

Jones began his work in Cyrenaica on February 1. He immediately organized a transfer of men and airpower from the Nile Delta to Cyrenaica, as well as landing craft from the port at Alexandria to Tobruk.[33]

Jones's intent was to play up the threat to Crete with the establishment of the 8th Armoured Division (notional) as the amphibious assault force slated to launch from Tobruk. Its headquarters and one brigade of tanks, supplied by the 24th Armoured Brigade, were set up three miles west of Tobruk. As the brigade would have to be transported on landing craft for the invasion, Jones oversaw the erection of landing craft at Tobruk, as well as set up hards and stores dumps. To support the land forces, Jones simulated the arrival of an airborne division (notional) located at nearby airfields in El Adem and Gambut. At Gambut, camouflage teams created the illusion of new runways to support the influx of aircraft. In addition, Jones and his team also had to manufacture a concentration of no fewer than eleven air squadrons to "cover" the invasion. Two hundred dummy Mosquito, Spitfire, and Tomahawk aircraft were used to represent the arrival of nine air squadrons, divided evenly among airfields located at Tokra, Bu Amud, and Derna, respectively. Matruh West showed signs of preparing for the arrival of three squadrons of Lightning aircraft.[34]

To give life to the displays, the deceptionists erected tents, lit fires, and simulated signs of regular activity such as cooking and laundry. Jones organized a steady flow of vehicles in and out of the area in order to replicate realistic motor traffic. The British Army, Royal Navy, and RAF all contributed by simulating extensive wireless activity to provide additional evidence supporting the displays. Moreover, the entire display area in and around Tobruk was protected by a genuine air defense system composed of "a protective smoke-screen, a 24 balloon barrage, 12 searchlights and 50 a.a. guns; while 112 more guns were distributed around the newly 'activated' airfields." Finally, security measures were set up with Tobruk labeled a '"Prohibited Area'" and protected by a security screen.[35]

The total effect was to provide evidence of the land, air, and naval concentrations required for the amphibious assault against Crete. By February 25, Jones and his crew had erected seventy-five landing craft at Tobruk and had the bulk of the land and air dummy concentrations in place. The dummy units and their full accompaniment of activity—both genuine and fake—were on display for the enemy in various states of readiness, determined by the needs of the deception plan, from February 25 until May 10.[36]

After receiving detailed status reports from the military services and "A" Force commanders Train in Algiers and Lieutenant-Colonel Michael Crichton at Main HQ "A" Force in Cairo, Clarke issued a Stage 1 progress report on March 30, 1944. He indicated that almost every one of his requests from the February 2 directive were carried out successfully, although a few, such as the naval wireless campaign at Tobruk, were strategically delayed to occur in Stage 2. The display at Bizerte also had to be postponed due to the belated arrival of canvas supplies and incessant rain. Clarke was satisfied that the rumor campaign and double agents had successfully planted the deception story on the Germans, and noted that there was ample evidence that the enemy accepted the story. He was immensely pleased with the efforts carried out by Allied naval forces, yet somewhat frustrated with the air efforts. Clarke noted that while MAAF carried out PR and some bombing operations over the Balkans, it had not succeeded in notably increasing its efforts targeting the Balkans or Crete as he had requested—actions deemed necessary in order to identify those areas as specific landing targets. MAAF had also failed to

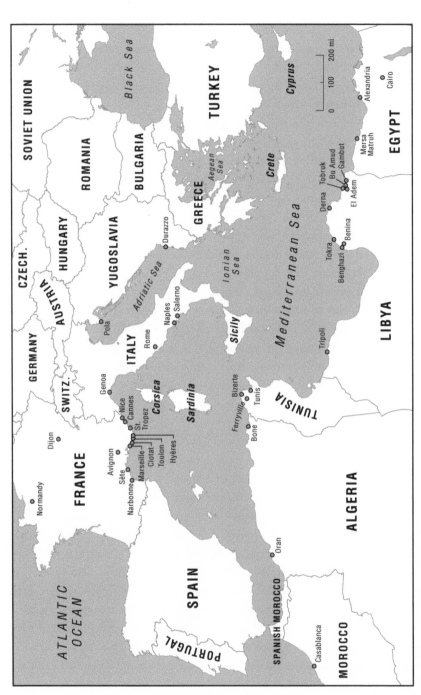

Plan Zeppelin (with Vendetta & Ferdinand). Map by Erin Greb Cartography.

create the dummy fighter display at Lecce and, at the time of the report, had not provided any information on the status of the glider display in Sicily.[37]

Another area that encountered difficulties related to the Greeks. The effort to supply Greek resistance forces was delayed owing to internal disagreements and infighting within the Greek resistance. The discord had to be resolved before Allied support could be resumed. The training of Greek forces in Egypt also proved difficult. Crichton reported: "I can hardly bring myself to write on this subject: They are the most maddening part of this plan and seem to even occupy my dreams." He specifically cited, as among the problems, convoluted political issues and Greek demands that the British make good on previous promises, which Crichton regarded as incomprehensible. In detailing the requested formation of Greek units, Crichton warned Clarke of the likelihood of a Greek mutiny if the British proceeded with plans to create an additional Greek battalion, but expressed complete bewilderment over the cause. He further provided a list of objectives that had not been met due to the problems. Addressing his inability to transfer Greek troops to Cyrenaica, he explained that "if they get anywhere near a railway they will desert to CAIRO and cause a mutiny." Crichton, therefore, had been unable to achieve the required buildup of Greek forces because of ongoing political instability and fears of mutiny.[38]

"A" Force had devoted a tremendous amount of effort to Stage 1 of Zeppelin since the initial stage was viewed as the most crucial. It was in Stage 1 that the Allies had to induce the Germans to make faulty force dispositions and lay the foundation for the subsequent stages to build on. In spite of a few setbacks, the plan had proceeded as intended, and "A" Force viewed the first stage of Zeppelin as a success. In addition to very specific questions the Germans directed to their agents on the ground (in reality "A" Force double agents), intelligence reports on enemy movements and expectations further reinforced confidence in the plan's success. In late February a report emanating from Greece suggested that the Germans expected an attack in the Balkans, likely at Albania, and a partisan report indicated that the Germans were anticipating an assault on Istria. Likewise, German forces in Yugoslavia were expecting an Allied attack along the Dalmatian coast to begin in mid-March. On March 8, Berlin sent an urgent request for its agents in Istanbul to investigate port activity at Benghazi, Derna, and Tobruk, while on the same day a report from Crete stated that the Germans expected the Allies to open an offensive against Crete from Egypt and North Africa, and that they were making "deceptive dispositions" to meet that threat. Furthermore, SIME was able to report that the rumor campaign was successful and the gossip mills in Alexandria abounded with expectations of an Allied assault on Crete.[39] All reports indicated that the objectives laid out for Stage 1 had been met.

Throughout the entirety of Stage 1, which ran from February 4 to March 9, Clarke was absent from the Mediterranean. He was instead in London consulting with SHAEF on Bodyguard while Bevan was in Moscow negotiating the USSR's role in the Allied deception activities. Once Bevan was able to secure Soviet participation in March, "A" Force was clear to move forward with measures to simulate a Soviet threat to the Bulgarian port of Varna. While in London, Clarke hoped to work out a solid plan for Stage 2 in consultation with the London Controlling Section and Ops B/SHAEF; however, continued uncertainty over what role southern France should play in the deception proved an obstacle to the planning. The result, as Clarke phrased it, was an "emasculated version" of Stage 2.[40]

Stage 1 of Zeppelin went a long way toward laying the foundation of success for the remainder of the plan, but there were still setbacks that had to be overcome in the subsequent stages. Stage 2, in fact, encountered its fair share of difficulties. The greatest single obstacle that "A" Force faced in planning the second stage centered again on the role of southern France. SHAEF had yet to determine if the Allies would attack southern France before, after, or simultaneously with the Normandy landings. Nonetheless, as Zeppelin entered its second stage, SHAEF's main desire was to see the Germans held as far away from France as possible. That meant that "A" Force continued to focus all of its efforts on emphasizing the threat to the Balkans. Even so, the ambiguity over southern France continued to plague the planning efforts. It was unclear at that time if "A" Force should be preparing to create a notional threat to southern France or seek to draw German attention away from France altogether, yet "A" Force knew that it would eventually need to mobilize a threat against the southern French coast. Those anxieties overlapped with uncertainty over how the Germans would view the Allies' intentions in France as D-day approached. Clarke described the dilemma:

> It was obvious that a time would come when the enemy would be bound to detect the preparations in ENGLAND for the cross-Channel Invasion, and would then feel an inclination to move reserves into FRANCE. At this point, however, he would be uncertain as to whether both Northern *and* Southern FRANCE were to be invaded and, if so, which invasion would come first. It was obvious, therefore, that

when the moment arrived every effort would need to be devoted to persuading him that Southern FRANCE was to be attacked first.[41]

Once "A" Force determined that its best course of action was to do everything possible to direct German attention away from the entirety of France until the Germans expected an attack, and then play up the threat to southern France alone, the next challenge became one of timing and method.

Insofar as the threat to southern France was concerned, all planning—genuine and deceptive—had to bear in mind SHAEF's objective to keep the Germans far away from any sector of France. If the Allies intended to launch Anvil before the invasion of Normandy, then the genuine buildup of forces in North Africa and Corsica would provide ample visual evidence and tip the Germans off to the impending threat. That would require "A" Force to employ extensive camouflage and cover strategies in order to provide the enemy with an alternate explanation for the buildup, complete with a notional target. If Anvil was to take place after D-day, then "A" Force needed to simulate a threat significant enough to keep German forces pinned down in southern France leading up to the cross-Channel invasion, but that threat could not be manufactured prematurely or it would run counter to SHAEF's overarching goal of keeping the Germans pinned down outside of France until it was impossible to delay any further.

The approach that developed, known as Plan Vendetta, was to activate the threat to southern France in late April with a notional target date in May. The timetable, however, underwent multiple revisions as SHAEF reassessed how much the Germans actually knew of the Allies' genuine invasion preparations based on their reconnaissance efforts. Originally, Allied leaders anticipated that the Germans would observe the buildup of invasion forces in the UK during the spring, requiring "A" Force to play up the diversionary threat to southern France as early as Stage 2 of Zeppelin. After noting the lack of German aerial reconnaissance over the British Isles, SHAEF postponed the initiation of the notional threat into late May, coinciding with Stage 4 of Zeppelin, with a notional D-day identified as June 19. As the plan took shape, the main objective was to keep the Germans pinned down in southern France with the threat of a second invasion of France after the Normandy operation commenced.[42]

Stage 2 began on March 10, having been approved by General Wilson one week prior. The deception story stated that Allied plans remained unaltered, but the lack of progress in Italy, on which the Balkans operation depended, had forced the Allies to delay the invasion timetable. Because the strategic plans were unchanged in spite of the postponement, the preinvasion preparations continued unaltered across the Mediterranean.[43] The deception story meticulously built on the work accomplished during Stage 1. The primary objective in Stage 2 was to keep the Germans from making corrections to their faulty dispositions. To that end, it was paramount to maintain an active threat to the Balkans and provide sufficient visual evidence of invasion preparations for the enemy's benefit.

As before, "A" Force sent out requests for assistance from AFHQ. G-3 was asked to continue its operations around the Dalmatian coast and Aegean and Ionian islands, conduct beach reconnaissance at Pola, and arrange for the commander in chief to visit Cairo by early April at the latest. "A" Force hoped that a visit by the commander in chief would cause concern and speculation among the Germans. SOE and OSS were asked to overtly increase their support to the resistance movements in Albania, Crete, and the Peloponnese. Additionally, "A" Force again asked the chief engineer to create a visible display of one hundred dummy LCTs at Bizerte after efforts to erect the display were delayed from February 25 until March 10 due to unforeseen circumstances. Further orders were to construct hides at ports across the Adriatic, while at the same time concealing any Anvil preparations that might be visible in Corsica. G-2, meanwhile, was asked to continue its activities outlined under Stage 1. The only addition was to ensure that all preparations for Anvil were to remain hidden until May 21.[44]

"A" Force called on GHQ Middle East to continue the administrative and visual efforts initiated in Stage 1, specifically at Tobruk. In Cyrenaica as a whole, "A" Force requested any action that would show an escalation in activity, to include increasing the number of LCTs from 75 to 100 and continuing work on the displays so that the total strength displayed would appear to consist of one armored division, 100 Waco gliders (in Tobruk specifically), 150 Mosquitos, 60 Lightnings, and 200 single-engine fighters. "A" Force additionally required an increase in both land and air forces in Cyprus and Syria, as well as an enlarged display of camps, dumps, and motor transport in Cyprus specifically. Finally, GHQ Middle East was asked to coordinate additional visits between the Middle East and Soviet authorities to emphasize the spirit of Anglo-Soviet cooperation as it related to the Balkans.[45]

The Mediterranean commander in chief was asked to order naval operations targeting shipping in the Aegean and Ionian Seas, with specific focus on the shipping lanes serving Crete. Furthermore, he was to ensure that naval wireless deception was increased to indicate significant activity at Tobruk. "A" Force remained responsible for conveying the deception through its secret channels and coordinating the spread of rumors and propaganda in conjunction with its partner organizations in the theater.[46]

Clarke placed tremendous value on the role of the air force. He believed that air support was crucial to lend legitimacy to the deception. To that end, MAAF was asked to play a vigorous role in support of Zeppelin. It was to continue air attacks against the Balkans, to include periodic strikes against Istria, continue its photographic reconnaissance efforts with the addition of Pola, increase the number of aircraft in Cyprus and Syria, and use wireless deception to indicate a notable increase in airpower at Cyrenaica. Finally, Clarke asked that MAAF delay as long as possible the transfer of gliders and troop carrier command aircraft from Sicily—where they were needed for deception—to Sardinia—where they would be needed for Anvil.[47]

All of the efforts assigned to Stage 2 were designed to create a very specific threat to Germany's vulnerable periphery. With the dates postponed due, allegedly, to Allied "failure to make any headway in ITALY during February," the new invasion dates were as follows: British forces were preparing an assault against Crete and the Peloponnese, while Polish forces were poised to attack Albania, on April 21. Meanwhile, the US Seventh Army was preparing to land at Pola and the Soviets were set to land at Varna on May 21. In addition, the story maintained that the British had secured the Soviet Union's consent for a British advance through Turkey. Details of Britain's plans for its two armored divisions of Saturn Force positioned in Syria to advance through Thrace and into Salonika in July were added in Stage 2.[48]

In order to pass the deception story's new timetable, "A" Force had to find a foolproof way to convey the postponement to the enemy. "A" Force eventually concocted a relatively simple, but effective, solution code-named Dungloe. The goal of Dungloe was to send a preprepared message to Yugoslav resistance forces ahead of the "invasion," appearing to be an alert to be on the ready. The instructions, which identified the code-greeting written in Serbo-Croat, explained the procedure:

> Warning to be ready for the Allied invasion of the BALKANS will be passed to you by means of a code word in the Yugoslav broadcasts from London.
>
> The code word will be the introduction of the greeting "DRAGI SLUSATELI" ("Dear Listeners").
>
> This greeting will be introduced by the announcer precisely thirty days before the date fixed for the invasion to start. It will be used on this one day only.

If for any reason it is necessary to postpone the invasion the special greeting will be repeated again for *two consecutive days*. It will then be introduced for a third time *for one day only* precisely thirty days before the new date.[49]

British agents based in London passed the code and instructions, allegedly emanating from Yugoslav circles in London, to German intelligence on March 13. From that point forward, "A" Force could easily relay the notional assault dates and postponements directly to German intelligence by way of the BBC. After "A" Force received confirmation that the message was successfully planted on German authorities in Belgrade, the first code message was sent on March 22, indicating that the invasion of the Balkans would begin on April 21. Major-General R. A. D. Brooks, a member of the Foreign Office's Political Intelligence Department, was responsible for arranging the BBC transmissions.[50]

One of the most important and pressing tasks of Stage 2 was to provide ample visual evidence of the buildup in the Mediterranean that the enemy would expect to see if the threat to the Balkans was genuine. As a result, Jones's massive display in Cyrenaica was prominently featured in the deception plan. From the time work began in Cyrenaica, efforts continued on an escalated scale intended to demonstrate to the enemy that the invasion of Crete was imminent. The rapid buildup continued unabated until March 14. Beginning on March 15, the display entered a three-week period of calculated inactivity in an effort to help pass along the first notional postponement. In order to do so, several specific actions were taken:

> All "coastal movement" landing-craft eased and most of the L.C.T.'s in TOBRUK were brought ashore and hidden. On the aerodrome aircraft were dispersed and simulation of flying activity was reduced. The 8th Armoured Division moved their dummy tanks well inland from TOBRUK, and set up an apparent training camp some miles away in the desert.

The display buildup and notional invasion preparations did not resume until April 8. In that way, the Cyrenaica display was an important piece of the deception puzzle in conveying the first postponement.[51]

On April 8, the Cyrenaica display was reactivated in full force to simulate preparations for the April 21 assault on Crete. The 8th Armoured Division returned to Tobruk, and the number of LCTs at Tobruk was finally increased to one hundred. Between Bu Amud and Derna, Jones displayed two additional dummy squadrons, along with sixty dummy Lightnings at Matruh. All total, the dummy air display was increased to represent fourteen squadrons. Moreover, Jones was able to bring in dummy gliders, which were considered invaluable in order to simulate the approach of an airborne assault. Ninety WACO gliders were placed in Gambut and El Adem. The display in Cyrenaica saw increased activity until April 20 when the second postponement went into effect.[52]

Throughout each phase of the display, the dummy formations had to be continually supplemented by genuine movements in and around Tobruk, along with antiaircraft to defend the harbor, airfield, and display areas. Between March 1 and 10, supporting units of troops moved into the area, traveling during the daylight hours when they could be observed. AA units concentrated, along with their camps and transport, near the airfield and divisional displays. To further the ruse, they carried out activity drills when alerted to incoming enemy reconnaissance. AA units also activated a smoke screen, which proved particularly useful to provide security for defective LCTs. In order to ensure that the displays appeared genuine from the air, 24th Armoured Brigade requested aerial photography and interpretation reports to assess the quality of the displays and to determine if additional measures were required in order to obtain the maximum realism.[53]

While Jones and his team went to great lengths to ensure that the displays were convincing, safeguarding their security continued to be just as vital to the success of the plan. Patrols were organized along the coastline and around Tobruk to prevent the enemy from landing agents in the area. The 24th Armoured Brigade enacted several additional measures as well:

a. That all leave outside CYRENAICA would be suspended.
b. That all officers mail would be censored at base and censorship of green envelopes would be 100%.
c. That wherever possible, hospital cases would be dealt with in CYRENAICA and not evacuated to the DELTA.
d. That all units in transit through CYRENAICA would not be passed through TOBRUK, but, arrangements made for units to be passed around TOBRUK.
e. That arrangements would be made to ensure that all personnel entering TOBRUK were on official business.

The 24th Armoured Brigade deemed the security measures a success.[54]

Efforts were also underway in Bizerte in the western Mediterranean. There, the director of works at AFHQ was called on to construct the one hundred requested dummy LCTs. The US 84th Engineer Battalion, under the command of AFHQ, was responsible for assembly, launch, maintenance, and recovery. The Royal Navy handled the moorings and was responsible for the movement of the craft once they were afloat.[55]

Clarke was generally pleased with Stage 2, which drew to a close on April 14, but he also referred to it as the most difficult of the stages. Certainly the sheer scale of the administrative and physical measures, to include the camouflage efforts and extensive displays, was monumental, but implementation generally ran smoothly. The challenge came as Clarke faced multiple hurdles that threatened to undermine the deception efforts.[56]

The first concern was connected to the role played by MAAF. Clarke lamented that the scale of air support was unsatisfactory and not in keeping with what the air staff had promised A" Force when Zeppelin was approved. Clarke concluded that "it seemed to emphasise the lesson of past plans that the success of a large-scale Strategic Deception Plan hung very largely upon the factual support that could be given to it by air operations." He had identified a "noticeable and regular increase" in the air campaign against the Balkans as crucial to the success of the deception efforts during Stages 1 and 2. Without those efforts, the Germans might not consider the threat real. Clarke eventually called attention to MAAF's lackluster efforts. After that, MAAF made great strides to increase its air support. The deceptive air campaign was noticeably increased by early April.[57]

The second complication came from the weakening of Middle East forces in order to bolster Alexander's armies in Italy. Clarke was concerned that the threat to the Balkans, on which the entire success of Zeppelin rested, would diminish due to the "sheer lack of apparent forces to sustain it." The notional Twelfth Army, for example, comprised five real divisions, four bogus divisions, and three brigades "masquerading" as three additional divisions, bringing the total strength to twelve divisions. After three divisions were transferred to Italy, the Twelfth Army had lost three of its five genuine divisions and was at risk of losing two of the brigades masquerading as divisions. If the Germans noticed the significant weakening, they were likely to conclude that the Allies were no longer capable of assaulting the Balkans. The concern became so acute that Clarke considered warning the Combined Chiefs of Staff that it was becoming impossible to simultaneously maintain the war effort in Italy and the threat to the Balkans with the resources at hand. Because both the genuine war effort and the deception campaign across the Mediterranean were considered crucial to keeping the Germans pinned down outside of France, the shortage was quickly becoming dangerous. General Wilson intervened to salvage the situation and made it abundantly clear that the diversionary threat to the Balkans remained a top priority, insisting that resources be allocated to maintain the threat. In the end, a compromise was struck. The two brigades in question remained in Egypt, and the number of bogus units was increased bringing the Twelfth Army to two real divisions, seven bogus divisions, and three brigades posing as divisions—maintaining a total of twelve divisions. This amounted to a 250 percent exaggeration of strength, which greatly exceeded anything "A" Force had ever attempted in the past.[58]

Connected to the weakening of Middle East forces in support of the Italian campaign was an overall decline in support for the deception efforts by those in charge of the campaign in Italy. The commanders felt that they were constantly competing with Zeppelin for resources, yet the deception campaign offered no benefit to those in Italy. The commanders had vigorously supported past campaigns that sought to aid their own military campaigns, but had little enthusiasm for Zeppelin as its objectives were singularly focused on western Europe. Clarke acknowledged that Zeppelin had become a "very considerable nuisance" to the commanders focused on conquering Rome. He added that "with it the unfortunate officers at "A" Force soon missed the spirit in which they had been welcomed while they were working to ensure Surprise on the beaches of SICILY or ANZIO." Again, Wilson's personal intervention and direct support of the Balkans diversion proved instrumental in securing the support that "A" Force needed to make Zeppelin a success.[59]

With the concerns addressed, "A" Force could safely proceed with its efforts. Stage 2 drew to a close on April 14. As D-day approached, the intensity of the deception efforts would only increase.

While the deceptionists worked tirelessly to bring Zeppelin to life across the Mediterranean, the war continued in Italy. The landing at Anzio had failed in its objectives to dislodge the Germans from the Gustav Line and facilitate an Allied drive to Rome. As a result, the US Fifth Army and the Germans remained deadlocked along the Gustav Line, leading Alexander to eventually call off his failed winter campaign in March. Disappointed but undeterred, Alexander began making plans for a spring offensive that would combine the US Fifth and British Eighth Armies along the western portion of the well-defended line. The objective was to relocate the bulk of the Eighth Army and its headquarters west of the Apennines, which had served as the divider between the two armies. To do so without alerting the Germans, Tac HQ "A" Force was called in to implement a security plan to provide cover for the Eighth Army's move west—Plan Northways. Northways was implemented exclusively through the dissemination of false information and extensive use of wireless deception.[60] So while "A" Force was putting the first two stages of Zeppelin into operation, Alexander was positioning his armies in Italy to finally break through the Gustav Line and begin the drive on Rome. The last stages of Zeppelin, along with the powerful Allied advance in Italy, played a decisive role in keeping the Germans pinned down across the Mediterranean in the tense days leading up to D-day. In that regard, the Mediterranean proved exceedingly effective in its role as a diversionary theater of operations.

7 THE CLIMAX OF PLAN ZEPPELIN
VENDETTA AND TURPITUDE

By April 1944, the Allies were in the crucial final months of preparation for D-day. While the Allies focused on mobilizing and training the invasion forces, and the military planners concentrated on ensuring the troops would be properly equipped, resupplied, and reinforced once the operation began, the entire effort was supported by a series of deception campaigns coordinated by the London Controlling Section and "A" Force. In many respects, the success of the Normandy invasion depended on the success of deception. If the enemy were prepared and able to concentrate his full weight at the point of attack, D-day very likely would fail. The fact that the Germans were spread thin protecting every point of vulnerability along Fortress Europe—to include Norway and the Mediterranean from southern France to the Balkans—created the conditions Allied leadership knew were essential in order to achieve victory. Of course, the threats were manufactured as part of the Bodyguard deception campaign, which included Fortitude North, Fortitude South, Zeppelin, and various subsidiary plans and diplomatic efforts. The deception campaigns successfully diverted the Germans' attention to areas the Allies had no intention of invading, yet it forced Germany to reinforce those threatened regions in order to defend its empire. Without the diversionary threats, the Germans would have been considerably better prepared to defend the northwestern French coast on D-day.

"A" Force was singularly responsible for the threats to Germany's southern periphery, stretching across the Mediterranean. It likewise played a decisive role in diplomatic efforts targeting neutral countries, which caused the Germans considerable anxiety, and continually worked to play up the threat of Turkey entering the war or otherwise cooperating militarily with the British. Specifically, however, it was through the Zeppelin deception campaign that "A" Force manufactured continual threats to Germany's European possessions and forced the diversion of manpower and extensive resources to defend against mostly notional threats.

On April 14, Stage 2 of Zeppelin drew to a close. It was replaced the same day with the third stage on the direct orders of the Supreme Allied Commander. Stage 3 did not see any major revisions or additions. Instead, its purpose was to the stay the course already laid out during the previous months. It did, however, enact the second postponement. The new target date for the landings in Crete, the Dodecanese, and Albania was identified as May 21. That coincided with the previous date assigned to the American assault at Pola and Soviet landing at Varna. Thus, all five landings were now alleged to occur on the same day in May. The reasoning provided for that alignment was that the Soviets requested the attacks occur simultaneously in order to "bring about the maximum distraction of the Germans at the critical moment." The postponement was passed to the enemy in the usual manner, largely relying on agent reports and physical efforts carefully designed to convey a reduction in activity and overall readiness. Specific measures, which mirrored the first postponement, entailed ceasing coastal activity, bringing the LCTs ashore, dispersing aircraft on the airstrips, and transferring the 8th Armoured Division inland. In that way, the second postponement went into effect on April 21.[1]

The fourth stage of Zeppelin, which Brigadier Dudley Clarke described as the most important stage, began on May 10. Stage 4 was approved by General Henry Maitland Wilson on April 29. Clarke then flew to London to meet with SHAEF to work out the details before implementation could begin.

Stage 4 represented a major shift in Plan Zeppelin. For months Supreme Allied Commander Dwight D. Eisenhower and the Allied leadership had wavered on when, or even if, the Allies should attempt Operation Anvil—the invasion of southern France. Much of the uncertainty revolved around the availability of landing craft and determining when the Germans were most likely to be aware of the impending assault on northwestern France. The options were to either mount a genuine invasion, in which the question of timing was yet another concern, or manufacture the threat utilizing deception alone. During that period of indecisiveness corresponding with the first three stages of Zeppelin, the leadership decided to conceal all signs of preparations in order to avoid enemy reinforcement of any region of France. After multiple meetings, back-and-forth correspondence, and considerable frustration, the leadership finally gained clarity on the invasion of southern France.[2]

As April opened, Eisenhower made the decisive call on France. He ruled out the possibility of coordinating Anvil to coincide with Overlord and called on "A" Force to mount a deceptive threat to southern France during the crucial period of D −5 to D +20/25. After much consideration, Clarke decided to begin fabricating the threat of invasion on May 10, providing a notional invasion date of June 19th. Given that the notional invasion was set to commence after D-day, its chief objective was to keep the German reserves then located in southern France pinned down during and after D-day in anticipation of an imminent follow-on invasion. The deceptive threat fell exclusively to "A" Force. It became known as Plan Vendetta, one of two major subsidiary plans under Zeppelin.[3]

One of the most immediate concerns was that of manpower and resources, not an unfamiliar problem. From the very beginning of Zeppelin, the Allies struggled to provide adequate resources and manpower to meet the dual demands of the genuine campaign in Italy and the deceptive threats across the Mediterranean. Adding an additional component to Zeppelin put further pressure on an already overstretched system. While the US Seventh Army, along with a French corps, was designated as the assault force for the invasion of southern France, the army was largely notional. Clarke hoped that the force would comprise seven genuine and four bogus divisions, but the reality proved the exact opposite. To make matters worse, as the plan developed, additional forces were transferred from North Africa to Italy, namely the 91st US Infantry Division, which Clarke lamented threw "an almost intolerable strain upon the resources of Order of Battle Deception."[4]

The lack of manpower did more than cause great stress for "A" Force regarding its ability to support the threat to southern France; it also forced Clarke to scale down the threat to the Balkans. The deception story, as modified, claimed that the Allies had abandoned their plans to carry out a large-scale attack on the Balkans for the time being in favor of mounting an assault against southern France. It continued that the Allies still planned to attack Pola and Durazzo, but had decided to push the assault date back from May 21 to June 19 to coincide with the operation against southern France. Turkey maintained its place in the story, which purported that the Allies still intended to travel through Turkey in order to reach Salonika by land, but had postponed the operation until July or August. Finally, "A" Force added a new component to the threat to the eastern Mediterranean: the claim that an infantry division from the Middle East was slated to invade Rhodes in August.[5]

Even though "A" Force was able to modify the deception story in order to accommodate the new focus on France, it had to find a way to justify the changes to the Germans. At that exact time, the Greek forces in North Africa began to rise up. While the situation itself was quite chaotic, the timing was rather fortuitous and provided the justification for the Allies' change of plan. In order to build up the threat to Greece during the early stages of Zeppelin, "A" Force had incorporated Greek formations into the deception. The Greeks, however, proved to be a constant source of frustration for the officers at "A" Force. In April, a Greek brigade, which "A" Force identified in exaggerated form under the Wantage Order of Battle Plan as the 1st Greek Division, mutinied. In addition, Greek crews stationed on warships in Alexandria mutinied as well.[6] General Harold Alexander, writing later as SACMED, blamed the Communist forces within the National Liberation Front (EAM, Εθνικό Απελευθερωτικό Μέτωπο) in Greece for instigating the uprisings, stating that they "stirred up mutiny among Communist supporters in the Greek Navy and Army in Egypt which led to fratricidal strife."[7] The disturbance became so dire that it was impossible to conceal. While the situation was unfortunate, it gave Clarke the excuse he needed to put the alleged invasion of Greece on hold, given the extent of civil strife and instability the country was facing.

"A" Force passed the story primarily through its secret channels, each of whom conveniently added components that helped reinforce other aspects of Vendetta. They claimed: (1) The Greeks could not agree on the type of government the Allies should set up after the invasion, and their disagreements were only exacerbated by rumors (spread by the British for security reasons) that claimed they were being sent to fight in Italy instead of Greece. (2) After the mutiny, the Greek forces were in "no condition to undertake operations for some time," resulting in the 1st Greek Division being demobilized. The British intended to reconstitute the division under the British Ninth Army in Syria to participate in the drive to Salonika though Turkey during the summer. (3) With the 1st Greek Division demobilized, it became impossible to continue plans to invade Crete and the Peloponnese in May. Meanwhile, the British were under considerable pressure from the French to mount an assault against the Germans in southern France, and the Soviets, then advancing toward the Balkans, insisted that the British stage a landing in Istria in June. (4) General Wilson flew to London on April 30, where he proposed that all Mediterranean operations should occur simultaneously on June 19. This was allegedly agreed upon by the British Chiefs of Staff, the Americans, and the Soviets.[8]

The final story, which "A" Force secret channels and other sources dutifully relayed to the enemy, stated: "The cancellation of the attacks on GREECE and the diversion of the British Twelfth Army to ISTRIA set free the American Seventh Army and a substantial amount of assault shipping. As a result, a large-scale landing in SOUTHERN FRANCE became possible for the first time."[9] Furthermore, it specifically called for the US Seventh Army, along with a French corps, to stage a landing at Sète–Narbonne in southern France. From there they were to seize the Carcassonne Gap and proceed on to Bordeaux and Toulouse. The British Twelfth Army was set to lead the attack on Pola, while the Polish forces of the Twelfth Army were slated for Durazzo.[10]

The Supreme Allied Commander gave the order to the Joint Planning Staff at AFHQ to begin working on Plan Vendetta on April 20. The planning for Vendetta went forward as if the plan was genuine. After consulting with "A" Force, it was decided that "A" Force, in the place of the commander in chief, would provide the Joint Planning Staff with the objectives, target dates, and list of available forces. Clarke described "A" Force's position during Vendetta as "a novel one":

> In the first place "A" Force regulated the tempo and the direction of the "physical implementation" by the Seventh Army by guiding the hand of the Joint Planning Staff at A.F.H.Q. in regard to all the notional aspects of the "story" as it was gradually unfolded. At their instigation the J.P.S. would then arrange for orders to be sent to General PATCH, as though issuing from the Supreme Allied Commander, to regulate the action he was required to take in preparing for the "assault" at SETE-NARBONNE.[11]

On April 20, "A" Force submitted the "Outline Plan," which appeared to be issued by the Supreme Allied Commander himself. The plan was approved on May 10 and delivered to Gen. Alexander "Sandy" Patch, Patton's successor as the commander of the US Seventh Army, the following day. Everything about the plan appeared genuine, and the training exercises, concentration of manpower and assault shipping, and other preparations were to proceed as if the operation was real.[12] That fell in line with the lesson deception planners learned early in the war: "A deception plan must be carried out on the same basis as the real plan. That is to say, the resources must be there either in reality or by simulation."[13] Moreover, only a handful of officers knew that Vendetta was a ruse.

General Patch moved his headquarters to Algeria from Palermo on May 23, and was joined by Maj. E. J. Sweeney as the "A" Force representative attached to his staff. Sweeney's role was to advise Patch regarding "how far he should go in carrying out literally the instructions he received from A.F.H.Q. This was needed in order to avoid a great deal of wasted effort, which would have been needed if the assault were really to be mounted, but which was unnecessary for the purposes of Deception alone."[14]

The timing of the plan, which called for a full dress rehearsal on June 10–11 and invasion date of June 19, held until June 10. At that point, the notional operation was postponed by five days. In contrast to other postponements, this one was not the result of a calculated deceptive move, but a practical decision based on genuine circumstances that could adversely impact the plan. An issue arose regarding the 91st US Infantry Division. Despite "A" Force's pleas for the 91st Division to remain in Oran to form part of the Vendetta force, the demands of the Italian campaign necessitated its transfer to Italy. The plan was to transfer the division on June 16. Besides the loss of one genuine division, the problem was that those convoys would be sailing east to Italy when the Germans would expect them to be sailing north toward France. To accommodate the move, the deception story stated that the 91st Division intended to sail to Naples in order to rendezvous with other forces departing from the peninsula, before joining up with the assault forces sailing from Corsica. The timetable, however, did not support a June 19 invasion. As a result, it was delayed by five days to June 24.[15]

"A" Force channels were particularly useful in explaining the movement and intentions of the 91st Division. Primo reported from Italy on June 20: "Warned by SIGMA yesterday of imminent arrival by sea of 91st U.S. Div. (Inf.) we noted on the morning of the 19th 7 large transports of a new type in the Bay BAGNOLI. 3 of these were landing with their own LCP [landing craft personnel] large numbers of U.S. infantrymen." He ended with his own observation that "the transports in question may well be 'landing ship infantry.'" On June 23, Primo reported that the 91st Division was leaving by sea, and while he could not report accurately on its destination, a contact of his informed him that personnel of the 45th US Division were boasting that they were "about to embark for operation in FRANCE." The following day, Primo alerted the Germans that an American aircraft carrier had arrived in the Naples harbor on June 22.[16]

Another reason for the delay, which played well into the revised June 24 notional assault date, was the sailing of two fleet carriers, *Victorious* and *Indomitable*, through the Strait of Gibraltar toward the Far East on June 17—a move the Germans were certain to observe. Moreover, the ships were set to arrive at Algiers on June 18, where they were scheduled to remain for twenty-four hours. The arrival of two fleet carriers was most advantageous, and "A" Force seized the opportunity to capitalize on their presence, just as it had previously with Plan Dundee in the leadup to the Anzio operation. "A" Force explained that the carriers were intended to provide fighter cover for the landings.[17] Given their date of arrival, however, the carriers could not have feasibly participated in an operation on June 19, making the new date of June 24 more plausible.

Implementation of Vendetta was a complicated affair involving fifty-three different items and multiple entities. Of the fifty-three tasks,

> 32 involved genuine troop, ship or aircraft movements and real admin-
> istrative preparations as though for an actual amphibious operation. 7
> involved real operations by the Air Forces, Navies, Raiding Parties and
> Resistance Groups. 5 concerned special W/T [wireless transmission]
> schemes; and 3 visits and inspections by various high-ranking officers.
> Out of these 47 special measures, the responsibility for 28 rested with
> the Seventh Army and 10 with A.F.H.Q.; while the French Army,
> M.A.A.F. and the Allied Navies each accepted executive action for
> three. . . . The remaining 6 items were allotted to "A" Force.

Full-scale physical implementation began on May 24.[18]

One of the most painstaking aspects of the physical implementation was acti-
vating the dummy displays. The invasion force was alleged to consist of three corps headquarters—one British, one American, and one French—comprising twelve divisions total. In fact, two of the corps headquarters and four divisions were entirely notional, while an additional four divisions were only partial and thus not up to division strength. The genuine divisions were the 91st US Infantry Division (North Africa), before its transfer to Italy, the 1st and 2nd French Armoured Divisions (North Africa), and the 9th French Colonial Division (Corsica).[19]

The lack of genuine divisions was compounded by another familiar problem—insufficient numbers of landing craft to support the threatened invasion. In order to provide adequate visual evidence, two displays were erected at the Bone (Algeria) and Ferryville (Tunisia) harbors. The American 84th Engineer Battalion erected ninety-three dummy LCTs, otherwise referred to as Bigbobs, for placement at the two sites. At Bone, for example, the 84th Engineer Battalion erected thirty-six Bigbob Mark Vs, which were dummy replicas of the LCT V. On average they were able to produce one Bigbob a day under the cover of the hangar, launching it just after midnight, which earned them praise from the British. A report from June 17, 1944, stated that the "speed and efficiency of the work done by the 84th Engineers was outstanding." Once completed, the Bigbobs were moored in the outer harbor where they were fully visible to aerial reconnaissance. While they looked realistic from the air, they were easily exposed as dummies from "close range horizontal observation." As a result, extreme security measures were needed in order to keep potential observers on land or at sea away from the display. The port was closed to local fishermen, nearby roads were shut down, and a wire fence was erected to establish a perimeter around the harbor.[20]

The physical implementation contained many of the tactics used in previous deceptions: the Allies issued maps and pamphlets, recruited guides and interpreters, ordered English-French and English-Spanish dictionaries, carried out aerial reconnaissance and PR missions, simulated wireless activity, sought out partisan support, organized genuine troop movements and bombing raids, canceled leave, and even ordered medical evaluations. Detailed lists were drawn up detailing the exact activity desired on a daily basis for each organization involved.[21]

In addition to the usual methods, two new "tricks" were used. The first was to stage large coastal and landing exercises. Accordingly, two French armored units moved up the coast at Oran to hold coastal exercises in early June. Those exercises were observed by the American theater commander, Gen. Jacob L. Devers. Immediately thereafter, a large-scale amphibious landing exercise took place at Oran from June 9 to 11. All told, 13,000 men participated, supported by 2,000 vehicles, 14 transport ships, 2 aircraft carriers, and escorts. In addition, there were 25 destroyers and 30 cargo ships already at Oran, making for a significant display of force. The exercise was witnessed by Adm. Henry Kent Hewitt, the US naval commander, and General Jean de Lattre de Tassigny, the French commander in chief.[22] On June 8, "A" Force agent Jewel alerted the Germans to the significant increase in activity in Oran, including the presence of vehicles with their exhaust pipes removed "to enable them to travel in water." The following day, Jewel reported: "Forgot to tell you that the Deputy Commander-in-Chief of the MEDITERRANEAN was among those who were present at the exercises and reviewing of the troops in ORANIE," while also noting "hundreds of trucks and jeeps" at the port. On June 10, Jewel contributed another piece to the Vendetta puzzle: "American Army is requesting all sections to supply lists of personnel knowing French and Spanish well."[23] In this way the agents reinforced any information the Germans may have gleaned from their own reconnaissance or other sources.

Another unique method employed for Vendetta was a French-led effort, beginning on June 11, to block the borders of Spanish Morocco to everyone except Allied diplomats "as though to prevent a possible leakage of information as to momentous preparations going on behind the curtain." They also removed from French territory "all cipher and diplomatic bag facilities from the neutral consulates." The move was considered rather unusual and caused much speculation among the Spanish and Germans.[24]

"A" Force was responsible for implementing six of the fifty-three items associated with Vendetta. Those included coordinating efforts with the PWB to highlight the threat to southern France and organizing the extensive display of dummies in North Africa. "A" Force "undertook all responsibilities" for passing the story to the Germans piece by piece through its secret agent reports. Finally, "A" Force assisted in the diplomatic effort to influence neutral countries spearheaded by the LCS diplomatic deception plan, Royal Flush. On March 13, Clarke submitted a report to Colonel John Bevan showing how Zeppelin could be aided by diplomatic efforts. To assist the subplan Vendetta, the deceptionists organized for the American ambassador in Madrid to request on June 3 that Spain allow the Allies to use port facilities at Barcelona in order to evacuate the wounded from southern France, as well as to bring in food supplies for the civilian population. Clarke concluded that the "measures undoubtedly had a prompt effect in directing the already sensitive attentions of the German Diplomatic and Intelligence agents in SPAIN towards the neighboring coast of SOUTHERN FRANCE."[25]

Vendetta was without doubt a success. During May the Germans began strengthening their existing panzer divisions in southern France and transferred an additional reserve division to Toulouse. On June 6, when the Allies landed at Normandy, the Germans had ten divisions in southern France: "2 Panzer Divisions, 3 Field Infantry Divisions, and 5 Low-Establishment Reserve Divisions." Only one of the divisions, an SS panzer division, moved north in mid-June, albeit *after* D-day; the rest remained in southern France until July. The Germans had also greatly overestimated Allied strength. A captured map revealed that they believed the Allies had "8 Infantry Divisions, 2 Parachute Divisions and 5 Armoured Divisions" in North Africa, when in reality there was only one genuine infantry division and 3 armored divisions. They also credited Corsica with a parachute brigade and 2 infantry divisions.[26]

Beyond the reinforcement of southern France, there were other indicators that the Germans expected an Allied attack. Karl Praeger, a radio commentator broadcasting from Berlin, reported that

15 enemy divisions are stationed at present in FRENCH NORTH AFRICA ready for an attack on EUROPE's Southern flank. It is most likely that the Island of CORSICA has been converted during the past few months into a large-scale springboard against the French and perhaps also Italian RIVIERA. . . . Concentrations of landing vessels in North African ports have also been observed.[27]

Rumors were abundant and seemed to intensify with the amphibious exercises at Oran and the closing of the Spanish Moroccan frontier. On June 13, a German plane was shot down off the coast of Corsica, and its crew reported that multiple planes of the Luftwaffe Sixth Staffel were sent out specifically to search for "invasion shipping" off the coast of France. On June 17, Red Cross ships were prohibited from sailing to Marseille by the Portuguese Office of the International Red Cross. Lisbon's Ministry of Marine followed suit and forbade all Portuguese ships from sailing to southern France. Finally, almost one year later, Colonel General Alfred Jodl, Adolf Hitler's close associate and chief of the Operations Staff for the Wehrmacht, was interviewed by the British. During the interview, he stated that the Germans expected an attack on southern France to precede that of northern France due to the buildup they observed in Corsica during the spring of 1944.[28] All indicators suggest that the Germans were at a heightened state of readiness and fully expected the Allies to invade southern France in late June.

Vendetta reached its climax in mid-June and, having achieved its objectives, began to wind down after June 19. However, the enemy still expected an Allied attack in southern France on June 24—that never came. Moreover, the 91st US Infantry Division was in Italy, the French 9th Colonial Division from Corsica had invaded Elba on June 18, and *Victorious* and *Indomitable* left Algiers for Port Said on June 19—all of which the enemy was, or was likely to be, aware of. "A" Force had to provide an explanation to the enemy for the apparent change in plans. The explanation, which was sent out by cipher to key regional leaders on June 24, claimed that the invasion had been postponed:

One. Assault on Southern FRANCE has been postponed and convoys recalled to ITALIAN ports.

Two. Postponement caused by suspicion that element of surprise has been lost. Enemy broadcasts confirm this.

Three. Air reconnaissance June 22 revealed that troops have not moved to Northern FRANCE as expected but are concentrating in neighbourhood of South coast assault areas.

Four. No new D-Day has yet been selected.

Five. Intention is to delay assault by Seventh Army until substantial movement of GERMAN reserves starts towards North.[29]

On July 7, "A" Force brought Vendetta to a close. It was replaced by Plan Ferdinand. All focus shifted as the Allies began preparing for the real invasion of southern France—Operation Anvil (later known as Dragoon). Anvil was planned for mid-August, so the Allies reversed course and initiated steps to conceal all signs of the genuine invasion preparations.[30]

Dudley Clarke was a movie buff. While visiting Caserta, he had taken the opportunity to watch *Three Graves to Cairo*, a popular film of the day being shown by the Americans. While watching the movie, he was struck by the likeness of one of the actors to General Bernard Law Montgomery. British actor Miles Mander, who played a tank corps commander, even sported a black beret so reminiscent of Montgomery. The image gave Clarke the idea that the actor could be employed to impersonate Montgomery at some point in the future.[31]

While Vendetta was underway, the London Controlling Section, SHAEF Ops B, MI6, and "A" Force came together to implement a minor subsidiary plan designed to "lower German vigilance" in northern France and reinforce the Vendetta story, all at the same time. Plan Copperhead aspired to convince the Germans in late May that General Montgomery was in Gibraltar and then Algiers for a leaders' conference—giving Clarke the opportunity to put his impersonation plan into action. If Montgomery, the recently named commander in chief of the British invasion armies, was visiting North Africa in late May, then it was highly unlikely that a cross-Channel invasion was imminent at that time. At least that is what the deceptionists hoped the Germans would conclude.[32]

Copperhead (originally referred to as Telescope) was written by Clarke back in February, with the original intent of directing German attention away from Normandy immediately before the landings were to take place. By the time Copperhead came to fruition, it was obvious that it could be used to support the Vendetta story as well. Generals Eisenhower and Montgomery gave their approval on April 19, and the COS formally approved Copperhead on May 9. Montgomery offered his full support, including providing clothing and personal items to the man chosen to impersonate him. He even provided details of his habits so they could be replicated with accuracy.[33]

The deception story, dutifully passed by secret channels at SHAEF and "A" Force, and by way of diplomatic means, was written as follows:

> It has been decided that a triangular meeting is essential between General WILSON, General MONTGOMERY and Major-General PATCH (U.S. Seventh Army) in order to co-ordinate, with the FRENCH High Command, the operations against Southern FRANCE which are to precede the launching of "OVERLORD." Generals MONTGOMERY and PATCH will, therefore, meet General WILSON in ALGIERS about 29th May, 1944.
>
> This date has been chosen to enable General MONTGOMERY to arrive back in the UNITED KINGDOM immediately after the second large scale exercise. This exercise is due to take place about 3rd June and, being primarily a naval concern, does not necessarily require his presence.
>
> The General will travel via GIBRALTAR in his own aircraft and will be accompanied by a senior staff officer and one A.D.C.[34]

With the story written, the next task was to choose a man who closely resembled Montgomery. Clarke originally hoped the actor Miles Mander could play the part, but he turned out to be too tall. While it may seem like a minor detail, it was enough to expose the entire charade. In the end, the British settled on Lieutenant Clifton James of the Royal Army Pay Corps to impersonate the general. In addition to his physical qualifications, Noël Wild, the head of SHAEF Ops B, noted in a letter to Clarke that James worked as a "second rate actor" in peacetime.[35]

At 8:00 A.M. on May 27, Montgomery's double arrived in Gibraltar. Major Harry Gummer, the "A" Force outstation officer responsible for all arrangements once the crew reached Gibraltar, had planned the day's events down to the smallest detail, even down to the minute. "Montgomery" flew in a "York," one of Britain's newest planes and one that was reserved for high-profile guests. The impersonator disembarked dressed in full battle dress and the distinctive beret, accompanied by a fake brigadier and aide-de-camp. He was greeted by the governor of Gibraltar, General Ralph "Rusty" Eastwood, who was fully aware of the scheme at hand and played his part with skill. "Montgomery" and Eastwood cordially greeted each other on the tarmac before heading to the Government House, where "Montgomery" stayed for two hours. At 10:00 A.M., "Montgomery" and ten others accompanying him returned to the refueled airplane. By 10:30, they were in the air and headed for their final destination: Algiers.[36]

The short visit to Gibraltar went according to plan. Major Gummer made sure that news of "Montgomery's" visit made its way to the enemy. In fact, Gibraltar was an ideal choice as it was bordered by Spanish territory and the Germans occupied neighboring territory where they could observe with a telescope all activity at the Gibraltar airstrip. There was one German agent in particular who was well known to the British. Clarke noted that he was "known to watch and report all aircraft arriving and departing from GIBRALTAR aerodrome. He does this with the aid of field glasses only just beyond the borders of the aerodrome. All his reports, which are extremely detailed, are intercepted and read by us." The British considered that airstrip to be the "one place in the world where the comings and goings of Allied personalities took place under the direct eyes of the enemy," making it the perfect location for General Montgomery's double to make an appearance.[37]

Major Gummer was meticulous in his planning and ensured that "Montgomery's" visit would not go unnoticed in the unlikely event that the Germans failed to observe the airstrip activity on May 27. He asked the colonial secretary to invite a Spanish agent, identified only as Molinar, to his office that morning. Molinar was an intelligence officer to the Spanish military governor but, more importantly, was known to the British as an agent working for the GIS. The morning meeting was timed perfectly so that the colonial secretary and Molinar walked outside at the exact moment that "Montgomery" was getting in his car to return to the plane. Gummer reported that "Molinar recognized General MONTGOMERY and was obviously excited. Immediately after leaving the Colonial Secretary he motored very fast to LA LINEA where he put through an urgent trunk call. I imagine, therefore, that by now the good tidings are on their way to BERLIN."[38]

Three hours after their departure from Gibraltar, the Copperhead crew arrived in Algiers. Again, James's impersonation passed the test as unsuspecting British and American officers cheered when they recognized "Montgomery" at the Maison Blanche airstrip. Shortly thereafter, General Wilson arrived at the supreme commander's house, accompanied by two American motorcycle escorts. All of this activity was relayed to the Germans by way of the "A" Force channel Gaol. On May 28, Gaol reported: "Aviator friends saw Gen. MONTGOMERY and another British General alight this afternoon from a 4 engined YORK at MAISON BLANCHE. General Wilson's own personal car and another were there to meet them." He also announced that General Patch and his staff had returned from London on May 27. With that, the charade came to an end. James was quietly transferred to Cairo, where he remained until after D-day. Clarke recorded that James, a lieutenant by rank, earned the pay of a full general during the course of Copperhead![39]

The Germans were obviously interested in the activity and keen to find out more. After learning of "Montgomery's" visit to Gibraltar and receiving Goal's report on the general's arrival in Algiers, the Germans sent information requests to their agents, who, unbeknownst to them, were "A" Force agents. Specifically, they wanted to know if Montgomery was in fact in Algiers and if he had met with Wilson. Jewel and Gilbert responded on June 2 that there were rumors circulating that Montgomery was in Algiers, but neither could provide additional information or confirmation. On the same day, Gaol reported that Montgomery had fallen ill upon his arrival in Algiers. He further reported that on the morning of June 2, Generals Montgomery and Patch flew out of Maison Blanche heading west. The plane returned in the evening with only Montgomery on board.[40] Collectively, the agents' messages not only provided "evidence" that Montgomery was in Algiers, but also placed him there only days before D-day.

As was typical of British deception, every possible detail was considered and "nothing was left to chance." The British were meticulous in their planning and painstakingly assessed every detail of the plan. In that way, if the Germans made contact with agents outside of "A" Force's control, the deception would not have been exposed as a fraud because the impersonation scheme was so thorough. The LCS handled the preoperation planning and selection of the impersonator, while "A" Force took the lead with planning the details of "Montgomery's" visit to Gibraltar and Algiers. The agents' messages were all sent from "A" Force's secret channels, who were in position to observe the activity, as opposed to those under the control of MI5 in London.[41]

Copperhead was one piece of a very large puzzle. If nothing else, it served to reinforce other elements of the Fortitude and Zeppelin (Vendetta) deception campaigns. Given the Germans' acute interest in Montgomery's whereabouts and activities, as well as their decreased vigilance in Normandy on June 6, one might wonder if the Germans concluded that Montgomery's absence from Britain negated an immediate threat to France.

In addition to Vendetta, "A" Force implemented a deception plan in the eastern Mediterranean that remained operational throughout the month of June.[42] Plan Turpitude, another subsidiary Zeppelin plan, was a physical deception effort that centered largely on Turkey. Interestingly, it contained two separate deception stories. With the enemy in mind, the first deception story claimed that "operations against GREECE are to be centred entirely upon the seizure of SALONIKA and a subsequent advance up the STRUMA VALLEY to join with the Russians. For this operational facilities in TURKEY and the reduction of RHODES is essential." The story purported that the Allies selected one "reorganized" Greek division to join the two existing armored divisions preparing to move into Thrace, while another infantry division was assigned to the Rhodes operation scheduled for August. Moreover, both ground and air forces were to concentrate in northern Syria for a drive through Turkey. Even though the Turks were not prepared to enter the war on the Allied side, a reality the Germans were well aware of, the story alleged that the Allies intended to issue an ultimatum to Turkey—after the Soviets entered Bulgaria on June 19—requesting air and transit facilities within Turkey.[43]

Similar to other deception plans, "A" Force intended to employ notional forces in Syria for Turpitude. However, the flat terrain, large number of civilians in the region, and the local population's ability to observe the military buildup meant that "A" Force could not use dummies on the scale that it had previously. Instead, Turpitude required an extensive concentration of genuine forces and equipment. That also meant that large numbers of Allied personnel were involved, yet security prevented them from knowing that they were involved in deceptive activities. For that reason, a second deception story was devised to mislead the Allied troops, officers, and administrative personnel who were not privy to the true nature of the operation. That story, which was disseminated in official orders, read:

> The Allies' success in ITALY and the imminence of the Second Front has brought about a favourable change in TURKEY's relations with us.
> In order to take advantage of any further development in Turkish policy and at the same time to encourage her to take a strong line with the Germans, we propose to build up Army and Air Forces in NORTHERN SYRIA and to create a situation which can be rapidly reinforced from other theatres.

The forces in northern Syria trained and prepared for what they believed to be a genuine operation. Unbeknownst to them, their activity was solely intended to mislead the local civilian population, among whom "pilfering, rumours, and uncontrolled movement were rife," and the Turks stationed at nearby Turkish observation posts. In this particular case, the displays were not intended to mislead enemy reconnaissance.[44]

The timeline for the alleged operations in the eastern Mediterranean was carefully coordinated with the western Mediterranean component of Zeppelin. On June 19, the Soviets were allegedly supposed to land at Varna, the British Twelfth Army was to capture Pola, the Polish 3rd Corps was to take Durazzo, and the US Seventh

Army and French forces were slated to invade southern France—although the threat to southern France was later postponed to June 24. Immediately thereafter, according to the story, the Allies intended to issue an ultimatum to Turkey. In July, British forces planned to enter Turkey from their staging area in northern Syria in order to "occupy airfields in ANATOLIA and concentrate a mobile offensive Corps in THRACE." The British forces planned to move out of Thrace in August to seize their true objective: Salonika. The British also intended to seize Rhodes in August, according to Zeppelin.[45]

Plan Turpitude was prepared by Colonel Michael Crichton at Advanced Head-quarters "A" Force and approved on May 12. Clarke, who had been in Algiers working on Plan Vendetta, arrived in Cairo on May 15 to assist with the early implementation. Major David Mure, the "A" Force outstation officer in Beirut, aided the local implementation of the plan from his position in Lebanon.[46]

Turpitude benefited from extensive cooperation between the British services, as well as saw the greatest commitment to a deception campaign from the RAF in the Mediterranean. On May 17, a joint committee comprising the three armed services and GHQ branches G (Ops), G(CAM), and "A" Force met to discuss the implementation of Turpitude. At that meeting, the RAF representative determined the RAF's role to be so crucial to Turpitude's success that he composed a com-prehensive report detailing the specific tasks required of the RAF and submitted it to the Air Officer C-in-C "with strong recommendations for their fulfilment." His recommendations found favor with the result that "airfields round ALEPPO should be made operative and all aircraft and R.A.F. personnel, who could be made available, should be utilised to implement the Plan." The RAF force, designated COL FORCE, was headquartered in Aleppo. COL FORCE activated airfields and supplied at least eighteen units, among which were four fighter squadrons, one heavy bomber squadron that included ten Liberators, three field squadrons, one antiaircraft squadron, one armored car company, four maintenance and supply units, and three signal units. The RAF also implemented extensive radio and wireless deception schemes in order to provide authenticity and make it appear as if the air concentration was larger than it was. In a creative use of resources, many of the aircraft used were "condemned" aircraft, those considered to be outdated or otherwise "awaiting disposal." The full air force display became operational between June 4 and June 10.[47]

Altogether, the RAF activated airfields, assisted G(CAM) in creating what appeared to be fuel dumps near the airfields, simulated air activity, put security measures into place, and conducted training exercises in the display area. Moreover,

Plan Turpitude. Map by Erin Greb Cartography.

RAF training units located in southern Syria were called on to fly near the frontier in order to increase the visibility of British airpower.[48]

In addition to its efforts in Syria, the RAF also assisted in "A" Force's endeavor to play up the threat of militarizing Cyprus. Cyprus was used as a notional base for air operations against Rhodes and Thrace. As an added value, Cyprus conveniently offered the shortest and most plausible route to Thrace, although the planes would have to fly over Turkey. Because the bombers would have to enter Turkish airspace, arrangements were made to discuss with Turkish authorities the possibility of British operational overflights. The RAF provided support on Cyprus, while "A" Force was able to supplement the force with three squadrons of dummy Spitfires operated by the 85th South African Engineering Corps. The display was largely designed to fool enemy air reconnaissance over the island, but could not discount the casual ground observer. The display was activated through a staged process to clearly represent the preparation of airfields, the arrival of aircraft, and finally an increase in air activity consistent with preinvasion preparations.[49]

The RAF contribution was extraordinary. Clarke may have complained about the RAF's lackluster enthusiasm and failure to commit fully to deception efforts many times in the past, but he had nothing but praise for the RAF's contribution to Turpitude. He acknowledged that the greatest burden of implementation fell squarely on the RAF, and the RAF exceeded all expectations. He wrote that the RAF contribution to the deception "was as thorough as the most exacting could have wished, while the 'activation' of all these units was continued in the most realistic fashion for the full three weeks in which it was required." The display remained active until June 26, when Turpitude came to an end.[50]

The army's contribution was also extensive. The task of building up northern Syria as a base for advanced operations, at least insofar as the enemy was concerned, fell to General William Holmes, commander of the Ninth Army, in coordination with GHQ Middle East. The concentration of genuine forces in northern Syria, which was coordinated by the Ninth Army, was referred to as Scheme Revivor. As the deceptionists intended, it was meant to mislead both the British forces involved and the local civilians. The concentration of notional forces was the responsibility of GHQ Middle East.[51]

The deceptionists hoped to convince the Germans that the buildup in northern Syria represented Allied "Advanced Elements" only, and that the remainder of the assault force was being held back until two to three days prior to the advance into Turkey. The "Advanced Elements" were to ensure the safe passage of the main force from the Nile Delta and Palestine when the order to advance came. The invasion force was alleged to consist of the Ninth Army's 31st Indian Armoured Division, 20th Armoured Division (notional), and 6th Indian Infantry Division. The three divisions were to be joined in Turkey by a reorganized Greek division.[52]

On June 5, the Ninth Army moved its headquarters from Beirut to Aleppo. Prior to that, it issued orders on May 22 for the transfer of the 31st Indian Armoured Division from Damascus to Aleppo. The move began on May 26 and was completed by June 5. Likewise, the 87th Armoured Brigade, originating from the Delta, had established itself in its assembly positions by June 8. By mid-June a brigade of the 6th Indian Division had arrived from Iraq. The men and matériel were transferred by road and rail into Aleppo, giving ample opportunity for local observation. The arrival of the forces was actively reinforced by additional measures to provide evidence of the concentration of troops and British intentions. The Ninth Army, for example, surveyed campsites, reviewed accommodations, made preparations for the transport of all supplies and equipment, repaired roads, prepared two L of C headquarters, issued maps with topographical information, supplied soldiers in northern Syria with printed guidebooks on Turkey, increased patrols of the Syrian-Turkish border, and enhanced security measures in and around Aleppo. From what Clarke once referred to as a "virtual backwater," northern Syria had been transformed into a "hive of military activity" by mid-June.[53]

The concentration of genuine forces in northern Syria was quite notable and somewhat unusual for "A" Force considering that most of its deception efforts in North Africa relied heavily on bogus forces represented by dummy tanks, planes, water craft, guns, and equipment. Although the assembly area in northern Syria was not deemed suitable for large-scale use of dummies, there were still opportunities to enhance the genuine display with dummies. The 20th Armoured Division, for example, was entirely notional. Colonel Jones's 24th Armoured Brigade was transferred from Egypt to masquerade as the 20th Armoured Division north of Aleppo. It was reinforced by one squadron of real tanks, transport vehicles, a Pioneer Company, and a signals unit to simulate wireless activities. All of these efforts were used to bring the division to life.[54]

The Royal Navy also played an important role in Turpitude, specifically in simulating naval activity at the ports of Latakia, Syria, and Tripoli, Lebanon. It began with a visit from British naval authorities to the two ports. They inquired about the berthing facilities and asked questions that gave the appearance that the ports would be brought to full use in the very near future. In addition to the inquiries, the navy commandeered local sea craft as well as contributed two LCTs, built two additional loading ramps, and conducted soundings for additional berths at Latakia. The RAF participated by providing antiaircraft cover, which attracted a significant amount of local curiosity, while the Ninth Army provided a smoke screen. To furnish additional evidence of an impending military operation, the navy brought in tanks and practiced loading them onto the LCTs. The navy conducted reconnaissance and carried out similar observable activities in order to bring Tripoli to life. These measures continued until June 26, when Turpitude was brought to a close. It should be noted that similar measures were employed in Cyprus to make it appear as though the port there would be fully operational by August.[55]

Throughout the deception, it was important that the local population take notice of the buildup of forces. It was possible, therefore, for the local population to observe the concentration of forces on the ground and at the ports. Had that been unintentional, it would have constituted a deplorable lapse in security and concealment. With genuine concealment in mind, a Ninth Army camouflage team recommended setting up the concentration of forces in the wooded areas surrounding Aleppo, to move forces and conduct necessary activity only at night, and to prohibit military vehicles from traveling on the main roads in and out of Aleppo. In this case, however, concealment was not the objective as the display was specifically designed to mislead the civilian population. Thus, the deception called for "poor implementation" of the concealment plan using the following methods:

i.   Badly sited concealment positions in woods visible from the TURKISH frontier (use of appropriate, but badly garnished, nets).

ii.   A number of vehs [vehicles] and tents not concealed in unit areas and visible from the TURKISH frontier.

iii. Vehs and convoys passing through ALEPPO, and along the main roads north during daylight hours.

iv.   Movements and activity by vehs, (on a limited scale) in their Harbour areas, along tracks to main roads and along main roads during hours of daylight.

v.   Extensive use of lights—vehs, torches, tents, fires, etc., at night in Harbour areas.

vi.   Smoke from kitchens during the day.

vii. Washing visible during the day.

viii. Appearance of significant eqpt [equipment] (such as bridging or road repair eqpt) which may be required in early stages of an entry into TURKEY.[56]

In this way, it could be safely assumed that the local population and Turkish forces at observation points spotted the concentration and took note of the preinvasion activity.

In addition to the genuine military and dummy display efforts surrounding northern Syria and Cyprus, the deceptionists utilized multiple other means to convey the deception. SIME helped to pass the deception story through its controlled channels, as did "A" Force's secret channels. The deceptionists readily employed diplomatic measures as well. For example, the British had repeatedly requested that the Turks allow the British to retrieve radar equipment previously set up in Turkey. Up until that point, the negotiations proved fruitless in spite of British persistence. The British viewed the Turks' attitude as "obstructive," but the deceptionists realized they could use that to their advantage. They advised British authorities to suddenly cease all requests for the return of the radar equipment. The deceptionists hoped it would be one more piece of evidence to reinforce the idea that the British intended to move into Turkey and therefore no longer wanted the radar removed. In yet another example, SIME and "A" Force worked together to stage the Booth affair, whereby Major R. B. Booth "accidentally" declared British administration currency for Greece and Bulgaria when passing by train into Turkey. His lapse in judgment, supposedly the result of exhaustion and drunkenness, was followed by a full-on diplomatic effort to have the record of that currency destroyed. While the entire affair was a ruse, the hope was that the Turks would duly inform the Germans that the British had already issued currency and made advanced administrative preparations for the Allied seizure of both Greece and Bulgaria.[57]

Turpitude was brought to a close on June 26, twenty days after the Allies successfully landed at Normandy. There is ample evidence that Turpitude was a success and achieved its objectives of keeping the Germans guessing regarding Allied intentions and committed in the Balkans in anticipation of an attack there. Rumors abounded in military and civilian circles as both sought to determine British intentions. A report from British sources in Ankara revealed that some German sources saw the British concentration in northern Syria as clear evidence that the British were prepared to assist the Turks in "combined action" against the Germans. The presence of British armored units was the decisive piece of evidence because the Turks lacked armor, thus they had to be supplemented by the British. Others believed the Turks would simply allow the British to pass through Turkey, but did not expect the Turks to join the war as a combatant. Revealing that the deception story made its way into the desired circles, rumors circulated in Hungary and Romania that the British had delivered an ultimatum to Turkey on June 25 demanding that the Turks enter the war to coincide with a British assault on the Balkans. With regard to Cyprus, the Germans were increasingly concerned over the militarization of Cyprus, which led them to conclude that the British intended to resume operations in the Aegean.[58]

Rumors were rife among civilians in Syria and neighboring countries, many of whom expressed anxiety that the British would grant Turkey territory in northern Syria in exchange for Turkey's cooperation in the war. Others, notably both Christian and Muslim religious sources, voiced relief that the British presence would prevent an invasion from Turkey. Many sources believed that Britain was planning to invade Turkey itself, some claimed with Soviet help, as opposed to passing through or working with Turkey. Regardless of the conclusion the various sources and observers arrived at, they all had observed the military buildup in northern Syria. Sources estimated that British strength ranged from 20,000 to 2 million troops in the region. One wild report even claimed there were 20,000 newly arrived aircraft in Syria and Egypt, while another stated that the British carried out air raid alarms so they could bring in war materials to the port at Latakia without being noticed.[59] Clarke, who noted that the civilian rumors became so numerous as to force the Ninth Army to begin issuing a daily rumor report, stated that "there was no vestige of doubt that the MEDITERRANEAN countries were swallowing the story of 'TURPITUDE' with something like avidity."[60]

While the circulation of rumors proved that the deception story had been effectively disseminated and the British had provided ample physical evidence of invasion preparations, the most important evidence of Turpitude's success came from the German military itself. Throughout April and May, the Germans reinforced Crete and Rhodes. R. G. Moore, a British wing commander and senior signals and cipher security officer, concluded that the reinforcement indicated that the Germans were preparing "to meet a heavy attack." Moore pointed out that British airpower had been reduced by 53 percent in the eastern Mediterranean between February and June, further underscoring the extent to which the Germans were duped by "A" Force's order of battle deception efforts. Moore also noted an increase in enemy air reconnaissance over the eastern Mediterranean. From March to April, the British observed 13 enemy reconnaissance flights a week; that number increased to 20 per week in May and June. The number of known enemy sorties was even more telling. Moore recorded 19 flights in February, 66 in March, 110 in April, and 70 in both May and June. Interestingly, the number dropped to only 5 in July after Turpitude had run its course.[61]

Of all of the evidence of Turpitude's success, the most important pertained to German strength in the Balkans. Not a single German division left the Balkans during the operation of Turpitude, which coincided with the Allied landing at Normandy on June 6, 1944. At the time of D-day, there were twenty-five German divisions scattered among Greece, the Balkans, Crete, and the Dodecanese. They were held there in anticipation of an imminent invasion, as well as to contain the partisan efforts, which the British had actively supported. This unquestionably demonstrated the deceptionists' success at maintaining the impression of a threat against the Germans in the Balkans.[62]

In addition to the success of Turpitude, Germany had an additional twenty-five divisions committed in Italy due to the ongoing war on the peninsula. When the number of German divisions in Italy and the Balkans is combined with those held in southern France owing to Plan Vendetta, another ten divisions must be added to the total, bringing the full number of German divisions committed against

Anglo-American forces outside of northwestern France to sixty.[63] If there was ever proof of the value of the Mediterranean theater to the overall Allied war effort, those sixty divisions were it.

While the Allies were able to distract the Germans with contrived threats across the Mediterranean in the months and days leading up to D-day, they also accomplished their goal of demanding the Germans' attention through genuine operations in Italy. After the lackluster Anzio operation and failed winter campaign, General Alexander began planning for a spring offensive to break the Gustav Line: Operation Diadem. While the immediate target was Rome, the overall strategic objective was to keep the Germans engaged in Italy to prevent them from reinforcing France in the crucial days preceding D-day. Alexander's plan was fairly simple: he intended to secretly concentrate the British Eighth Army and US Fifth Army along the western sector of the line to deliver an overwhelming blow to the Germans along the Liri Valley sector. The British were to attack Cassino, while the Americans would simultaneously attack along the Garigliano front. Plan Northways had gone into effect in early March 1944, which saw the Eighth Army move west of the Apennines. The plan for the spring offensive was for the Eighth Army and US Fifth Army to work together to crush their way through the formidable German defenses. While the plan was simple and straightforward, the challenge was to ensure that the Germans were unprepared at the time of the attack. As such, the Allies had to give the Germans the impression that they were going on the defensive, while they were in reality amassing a tremendous offensive force just south of the Gustav Line, directly under the enemy's nose. In typical deception fashion, the Allies used the threat of an invasion to the north of Rome as a distraction to render the Germans vulnerable. The deception plan was approved on April 10 and given the name Nunton. It was put into operation by Tac HQ "A" Force.[64]

The object of Nunton, as defined by Tac HQ, was to convince the Germans to reduce their vigilance on the Liri front near Cassino by lulling them into a false sense of security. They sought to convey that the Allied armies were going on the defensive and would thin out their line by borrowing divisions from both the Fifth and Eighth Armies in order to form an amphibious assault force. The story claimed that the Allies planned to land north of Rome at Civitavecchia, allowing them to descend on Rome from the north and sever the Germans' supply lines. They hoped the Germans would let their guard down along the Gustav Line, while simultaneously holding their reserves in the north to defend against the threatened amphibious landing, positioning them far away from the planned offensive.[65]

The need to mislead the Germans was great. Previous attempts to breech the Gustav Line failed due to the Germans' formidable defenses, sheer determination to hold the line, and Field Marshal Kesselring's uncanny ability to appreciate Allied intentions once they gave battle and make adjustments accordingly. During the winter, the Germans received roughly 15,000 reinforcements a month. Moreover, they had no fewer than twenty-three divisions to hold Cassino, prevent a breakout from Anzio, and defend Rome. Adolf Hitler was adamant that the Germans hold their positions in Italy. Yet, the Germans were not without vulnerabilities. In the face of Allied land, air, and sea superiority, their defensive line(s) could only hold for so long. For his part, Kesselring was aware of the Allies' strengthening and expressed concern that the Allies had adopted new "operational principles," thus replacing their "method of cautious and calculated advance according to plan with limited objectives" with an "inspirational strategy" that he clearly viewed as more threatening to his ability to defend the Gustav Line indefinitely. Moreover, the demands of the German war effort on the eastern front and need to fortify western Europe meant that the Italian campaign was required to be relatively self-sufficient. To make matters even worse for the Germans, Kesselring was largely unaware of Allied plans. He made assumptions regarding the Allies' strength, positions, and likely objectives, but readily admitted that the location and potential thrust of the French Expeditionary Corps, for example, "remained an important and dangerous unknown factor."[66] In fact, events would prove that the Germans were greatly misled by the deception campaign and possessed horribly flawed intelligence on Allied positions and intentions.

Kesselring feared that the Allies might try to "force a decision" by way of landings in the area of Civitavecchia or Leghorn. Of particular interest, he blamed Germany's propaganda machine for unnecessarily provoking the Allies, which he deemed "a cardinal error of our German propaganda, which could not do enough to taunt the enemy for their lack of initiative."[67] What he did not realize was that the timing and objective of the spring offensive had nothing to do with German taunting, but was carefully calculated to assist Operation Overlord by maintaining the maximum pressure on Germany's armies in Italy. The overriding objective of the Mediterranean Strategy in the first half of 1944 was to prevent the Germans, by any and all means possible, from reinforcing northwestern France, and Italy provided the best opportunity to engage the Germans.

The Allies intended to open Operation Diadem, which would be the fourth battle for Monte Cassino, on May 11. Alexander's plan was to concentrate both of his armies directly along the Cassino front. The Eighth Army's 10th and 13th Corps, supported by Polish and Canadian forces, were positioned on the right side of the line along the road to Cassino. Accordingly, the right flank comprised ten divisions and seven brigades. On the left side of the line that met up with the coast was the US II Corps of the Fifth Army and the French Expeditionary Corps, a total of six divisions. The French 2nd Moroccan Infantry Division and 6th South African Armoured Division were held in reserve. The assault forces, therefore, carried a strength of at least twenty divisions. All that remained on the Adriatic coast was the 10th Indian Division with the 23rd British Armoured Brigade in reserve.[68]

As military preparations for Operation Diadem began, the deception planning began in earnest as well. Unlike countless other deceptions where competing interests and demands proved a handicap to deception planning, Nunton received an unprecedented level of support from the military services. Colonel S. B. D. Hood, head of Tac HQ, met with Allied leaders in Algiers in April and from there secured the complete support of both the Eighth and Fifth Army commands. Records state that Nunton "received the fullest measure of practical support which the most exacting of Deception Staffs might have wished." Due to that active support, the report concluded that it met every one of its objectives and "remains both in its planning and execution as a model of perhaps the most successful Tactical Deception Plan ever executed in the MEDITERRANEAN Theatre." Nunton was further well served by the fact that Tac HQ had more than a month to put the plan into operation, and it was allotted both facilities and troops to support the idea of assault forces training for an amphibious landing. All told, Tac HQ was provided with a corps headquarters and four genuine divisions to represent the assault force. The Royal Navy supplied ships, while Admiral Hewitt of the United States Navy provided an American naval task force to represent the plan at sea. The notional target date for the assault against Civitavecchia was May 15, timed to occur after the genuine attack and designed to keep Germany's reserves committed in the north.[69]

One additional element played into Allied hands—history. Across time, Rome's conquerors had all approached Rome from the north. The deception story played on that very fact and emphasized that Alexander thought it best to follow historical precedent instead of trying to challenge it. Thus, the landing at Civitavecchia would enable the Allies to descend on Rome from the north, just as its past conquerors had.[70]

Considering that Alexander intended to concentrate two entire armies along the southernmost sector of the Gustav Line, and the Eighth Army had to complete its move southwest to Cassino (the southernmost point along the Gustav Line), Hood had to devise a story to explain the movement. The story claimed that four of its divisions were moving south to Salerno to take part in the Civitavecchia invasion; they would come under the command of the 1st Canadian Corps Headquarters once in Salerno. Thus, the greatest care was given to focus the enemy's attention on Salerno and Naples and provide ample evidence of amphibious assault training and preparations.[71]

Naples was brought to life by the Fifth Army. The Fifth Army, and notably the US II Corps, stationed its reserves at Naples, where they were joined by units of the French Expeditionary Corps. Hood requested that those forces remain in Naples and conduct training exercises there until the last possible moment when they had to be brought up to the front. The Inter-Service Training Centre carried out amphibious exercises, while the British and American navies transferred landing craft to the Bay of Naples. All of the physical activity was supplemented by wireless efforts to simulate a notable increase in wireless traffic, including naval wireless traffic.[72]

The Eighth Army was responsible for conducting similar activity at Salerno. In addition to the concentration of reserves and the standard training measures, the 20th Beach Group was transferred to Salerno, and the British carried out combined operations exercises at sea. Since Salerno was designated as the headquarters for the Canadian corps, accommodations were dutifully commandeered and signage erected. On April 22, the 1st Canadian Corps, 1st Canadian Division, and 5th Canadian Armoured Division established their headquarters at Salerno, complete with wireless activity. Finally, the 36th US Division was placed under the command of the 1st Canadian Corps as well.[73]

While the Allies were able to provide an abundance of evidence of preinvasion amphibious training and concentration in both Naples and Salerno, it was paramount to draw the enemy's attention to the notional target—Civitavecchia. To that end, the MAAF carried out daily photographic reconnaissance sorties and aerial bombardment that intensified from D −4 forward. "A" Force contributed directly by organizing a beach reconnaissance mission. Corsica similarly played an important role in the ruse. It was occupied at that time by the 9th Division of the French Colonial Infantry. The 9th Division was in reality preparing for an assault on Elba, but the training and preparations were relayed to the enemy as Civitavecchia assault exercises. Ten days after the offensive began along the Gustav Line, the Allies amassed landing craft at Corsica, giving the impression that the Civitavecchia campaign was imminent.[74] "A" Force agent Gilbert, who had wireless contact with the GIS in France, provided further evidence of the looming threat to the Germans. On May 15, he reported: "Liaison officer on return from CORSICA reports: many troops of 9th D.I.C. [*Division d'Infanterie*

Coloniale] at present in CORSICA, may be entire division which received full quota amphibious training awaiting orders to take part soon in a landing to support the present offensive."[75]

As the message from Gilbert demonstrates, "A" Force secret channels played a central role in disseminating the deception story to the enemy. Operating from Italy and across North Africa, they were able to provide a continuous flow of information regarding troop arrivals, disembarkations, and training and occasionally offered their "own" opinions regarding the intended destinations of individual units. Of particular interest, many of the reports centered around the activities of Polish and French forces, as well as the arrival and training of airborne units. The Germans showed obvious interest in the reports and frequently requested additional information. As an example, the Germans reached out to Primo, an Italian double agent working from Naples, with the request: "Please let us know as quickly as possible what transfers of troops and material have been made in the last few weeks from NAPLES in the direction CORSICA and SARDINIA." Primo responded on May 16, one day after the threatened invasion of Civitavecchia, with somewhat vague information regarding the transfer of Allied air force personnel northeast of Rome.[76] The information relayed by numerous agents in varied locations provided additional evidence in support of the deception story.

When it was time to move the invasion forces forward, the Allies did so with extreme care. The units were under orders to remain in the training areas until the last possible moment. When they did advance, they were to travel only at night and without the use of lights. The units were also only allowed to use specified roads. When it was necessary to construct new roads, they were instructed to make use of the landscape and natural camouflage, such as olive groves, even if that meant taking a more circuitous path. If they had to use stones in the road construction, they were instructed never to use light colored stones and were ordered to cover the stones with dirt so the roads would not be obvious from aerial reconnaissance. When on the move, they were to drive slowly to avoid creating visible dust clouds in the wake of the moving vehicles. The deceptionists likewise used elaborate camouflage measures in order to hide the arrival of the invasion forces to avoid alerting the Germans to the upcoming offensive.[77] Every little detail was taken into consideration when implementing Plan Nunton.

After weeks of preparing for the offensive and carefully feeding the deception story to the enemy, the Allies were ready to advance. If Operation Diadem went as planned, the combined weight of the British Eighth and US Fifth Armies, joined by Maj. Gen. Lucian Truscott's VI Corps at Anzio, would be sufficient to push the German Tenth Army (stationed along the Gustav Line) and Fourteenth Army (holding the VI Corps at Anzio) north of Rome. The Allies hoped to possess Rome before Operation Overlord began. While the Civitavecchia diversion was designed to keep Kesselring's reserves tied down far north of the action, additional measures were implemented to ensure that the Germans would be unable to mount a timely defense. In particular, tactical air support was used to target the Germans' lines of supply for weeks prior to the offensive. It is estimated that the Germans saw a deficit in their daily supply requirements of approximately 1,500 tons, and their petrol supply was greatly disrupted, to their detriment, once the offensive began.[78]

At 11:00 P.M. on May 11, Diadem commenced with a 2,000-gun artillery barrage. The Germans were caught completely unprepared. In fact, only hours before the attack began, the Germans had announced over wireless that the "best British troops" had been redeployed and were no longer positioned along the Cassino front. As clear evidence of their lack of readiness, the German forces stationed along the Liri Valley were reorganizing when the assault began and were literally caught in the middle of a post transfer. Moreover, Kesselring's key generals—Fridolin von Senger und Etterlin and Heinrich von Vietinghoff—were on leave, and his best-known and most battle-hardened divisions—the Hermann Goering Division, 26th Panzer Division, and 29th Panzer Division, among multiple others—were positioned to the north of the Gustav Line in order to defend against an amphibious attack. As for Kesselring, he expected the attack at the Gustav Line to come later in the month, around May 24.[79]

After the offensive began, Kesselring identified four lingering questions that inhibited his armies' response:

> When would the Allies start operations from the beachhead?
> Where and in what strength would the French Expeditionary Corps attack?
> Would the offensive be supported by an airborne landing in the Liri Valley?
> Would there be a fresh invasion in the region of Rome or further north?[80]

These questions reveal the unknowns Kesselring faced and that crippled Germany's response to the Allied offensive. The devastation dealt to the Germans was swift and severe. Kesselring noted that the artillery barrage and bombing succeeded in softening the German positions, and by the morning of May 12 the Tenth Army and 14th Corps headquarters were in complete disarray. The situation was made worse by the fact that the Germans still had very little intelligence on the US Fifth Army and the French Expeditionary Corps. After correctly guessing that the threat of an Allied amphibious attack to the north was not imminent, Kesselring ordered the 26th and 29th Panzer Grenadier Divisions forward. However, the order came too late and the divisions encountered great difficulty in reaching their positions.[81] Neither of the veteran divisions was able to influence the battle as they had on previous occasions.

Kesselring also faced opposition from some of his commanders who did not dismiss the idea of an Allied attack north of Rome as quickly as Kesselring did. The most notable example came from the Fourteenth Army commander, General Eberhard von Mackensen. Kesselring ordered the Fourteenth Army to release the 29th Panzer Grenadiers to the Tenth Army on May 19, but Mackensen initially refused to let go of his reserves—reserves positioned in the north to defend against the threatened amphibious landing. That delay prevented the 29th Panzer Grenadiers from reaching their destination in time to thwart the Allied advance. The Fourteenth Army also failed to make the adjustments Kesselring insisted on in order to prevent an Allied breakout from Anzio. Kesselring blamed the Fourteenth Army's failings for his inability to defend the Gustav Line and hold Rome.[82] It is interesting to note that captured documents from the Fourteenth Army reveal that its assessment of Allied intentions and strength was based on the information fed to them through Plan Nunton. That could certainly explain the commander's hesitancy to weaken his coastal defenses and his decision to defy Kesselring's orders.

In spite of Kesselring's determined efforts to rally his defensive forces, the Gustav Line faltered. On May 18, the Eighth Army took Cassino. After months of deadlock, British troops had finally breached the Gustav Line forcing the Germans to fall back. On May 25, the Fifth Army linked up with the US VI Corps from Anzio. The combined Allied forces continued their drive north until they reached the outskirts of Rome. The battle for Rome began on May 31, and by June 4 the Italian capital was in Allied hands.[83] By a slim margin of only two days, the Allies had achieved their objective of capturing Rome prior to D-day.

There was no doubt whatsoever that Plan Nunton had succeeded in deceiving the Germans. It is considered to be one of "A" Force's greatest deception successes. Dudley Clarke wrote that it "succeeded in attaining all the objects it set out to accomplish" and praised it as the "most successful Tactical Deception Plan ever executed" by "A" Force in the Mediterranean.[84] In a postwar letter to Maj. Gen. Clayton Bissell, Lt. Gen. Mark Clark referenced Nunton as an "outstanding example" of an effective cover plan. He added: "The enemy had disposed just prior to the Allied offensive, 4 divisions on coast defense north of the ANZIO beach-head. If those 4 divisions, including some of his best, had been disposed initially in opposition to the offensive the success of the Allied offensive would have been seriously jeopardized."[85]

The greatest evidence of Nunton's success came directly from the Germans. In addition to their faulty force dispositions and failure to quickly redirect their reserves to the front for fear of leaving themselves vulnerable to an amphibious attack, captured maps and documents provide further proof of Nunton's success. When the Allies captured the German Fourteenth Army's maps revealing their assessment of Allied positions at the time of the offensive, they aligned perfectly with the deception story. The Germans had underestimated Allied strength by a minimum of seven divisions along the Gustav Line, and listed eight divisions as "unlocated." The Germans were left guessing about the strength and location of the 1st Canadian Corps, as well as both the Polish and French forces, and had failed altogether to take notice of two newly arrived reinforcement divisions. They believed that any attack along the Gustav Line would be diversionary in character to draw focus away from an amphibious assault in the north.[86] The Wantage Order of Battle Plan records affirm that the enemy saw the frontal attack as a diversion as "his dispositions on 11 May were clearly based on this belief; he had the minimum number of troops in the line and his reserve divisions disposed along the West coast to meet the landing he confidently expected."[87] That assessment was supported by a captured map that showed three Allied divisions and one Guards Brigade conducting landing exercises in Salerno and Naples as part of their training for an amphibious assault. Clarke was elated to find that the 1st Canadian and 36th US Divisions were both specifically identified as part of the Civitavecchia invasion forces. Finally, the Germans believed that the Allies maintained two corps headquarters and four divisions along the Adriatic coast, when in fact only the 10th Indian Division and one armored brigade remained on the eastern portion of the line.[88]

Having reviewed the Fourteenth Army's captured intelligence files and maps, General Alexander's staff concluded that the German's dispositions on May 11 were based exclusively off of the erroneous assessment of Allied strength, positions, and intentions meticulously fed to them by way of the Nunton deception plan:

> He had the minimum number of troops in the line and his reserve divisions were disposed along the west coast to meet the landing which he confidently expected. As a result our attack was made in much greater strength than he expected (in the French sector, for instance, in more than four times the strength he expected) which greatly assisted

our initial success. All German divisions in reserve were either grouped round the ANZIO Beachhead or strung out along the Western coast, and by the time the enemy had decided his fears of a landing were groundless, these reserves were so slow in reaching the scene of battle that they were drawn in and destroyed piecemeal.

The report concluded that the German assessment was "faulty and corresponded exactly to what the Allied Command wanted him to believe." Alexander congratulated Hood and Tac HQ "A" Force for their success with Nunton, stating that their contribution to the victory was "enormous."[89]

With sixty German divisions dispersed across the Mediterranean theater on June 6, 1944, there can be little doubt that the Mediterranean Strategy succeeded in drawing the Germans' attention to diversionary threats across the theater. Likewise, Plan Zeppelin and its subsidiary plans were largely responsible for the thirty-five divisions held in southern France and the Balkans as those military threats were not genuine, but were instead manufactured through deception.[90] "A" Force used every trick it had and put everything on the line to ensure Overlord's success. It created threats that the Germans simply could not afford to ignore, forcing the enemy to commit his manpower and precious resources to defend the southern periphery of Fortress Europe.

It should also be mentioned that the Soviets played an important role in their portion of Zeppelin—namely the threat to Bulgaria by way of a bogus invasion of Varna. After securing Stalin's support for the deception, Clarke requested that the Soviets apply diplomatic pressure and utilize propaganda in order to convince Bulgaria to join the Allies, concentrate shipping at Soviet ports in the Black Sea so it would appear as though the Soviets were preparing for an invasion, and collect information pertaining to landing facilities and transportation within Bulgaria. While the Soviets never carried out the latter two tasks, their diplomatic and propaganda efforts were particularly successful and caused the Germans considerable anxiety. The USSR's contribution culminated on May 20 when it formally demanded that Bulgaria sever its ties with Germany and allow Soviet consuls into the cities of Burgas, Ruschuk (Ruse), and Varna.[91] The threat to Bulgaria was an important piece of the Zeppelin puzzle, and one that Clarke could include only with Stalin's express support.

When assessing Zeppelin's objectives, General Wilson declared the deception a success on each point. In a report to the Combined Chiefs of Staff dated June 28, 1944, Wilson wrote:

a. The number of German divisions in the MEDITERRANEAN Theatre at the end of June is substantially the same as in early February.

b. No divisions moved from the MEDITERRANEAN Theatre to N.W. Europe during the preparatory period of "OVERLORD."

c. So far as is known to date, only one division has moved from the MEDITER- RANEAN Theatre towards the "OVERLORD" area; and none arrived in time to influence the battle during the "critical period" defined by SHAEF.

d. Captured documents prove that immediately before "OVERLORD" the German High Command estimated some thirty offensive divisions to be still uncommitted in the MEDITERRANEAN Theatre.[92]

Wilson's last point demonstrates the overwhelming success of Clarke's order of battle deception. The Allies most certainly did not have thirty divisions sitting idle in the Mediterranean, so the thirty divisions referenced could only be the product of the Wantage Order of Battle Plan and the Germans' chronic tendency to overestimate Allied strength.

After D-day, the Mediterranean Strategy changed to accommodate the new Allied situation. There was no longer any need to maintain the diversionary threat to the Balkans, and Turkey similarly lost much of its strategic importance—though both threats were kept alive in lesser form. The new situation called for continued operations in Italy, as well as a genuine assault on southern France to assist in the country's liberation. As a result, the deception efforts were to focus on providing cover for Operation Anvil and continue to assist the Allied Armies in Italy (AAI).[93]

Given the changed strategic situation, "A" Force began what turned out to be a series of reorganizations. Most importantly at that time, Main HQ "A" Force moved to Algiers from Cairo. Since 1943, Clarke had spent most of his time in Algiers and conducted "A" Force's deception activities from there, so it was both logical and practical to move the main headquarters to reflect that reality. Main HQ opened in Algiers on June 12. Advanced HQ (West) remained in Algiers under Lieutenant Colonel Train. Both Advanced HQ (East) and Rear HQ were based in Cairo. Tac HQ also saw changes as Colonel Hood was transferred to England, where he continued to participate in tactical deception efforts. Lieutenant-Colonel R. A. Bromley-Davenport replaced Hood as the new head of Tac HQ "A" Force. At the same time, on June 16, Tac HQ left its old headquarters at Caserta to join Alexander just outside of Rome at Frascati. Clarke's official move to Algiers proved to be short-lived. On July 20, Main HQ "A" Force relocated to Italy, and only days later Tac HQ moved north of Rome to Lake Bolsena.[94]

It is perhaps worth noting that Clarke initially expected "A" Force to be compromised after Overlord. On May 15, the Mediterranean commanders in chief instructed "A" Force to assume all risks and utilize its every resource without regard for the future. Clarke took that order to heart and was willing to run his well-oiled machine to a "standstill" in order to see the Allies successful in France. Accordingly, Clarke sent a directive to his secret agent handlers saying: "Once we have entered the month of June all considerations regarding the safety of our channels (outside ITALY) are to be subordinated to the demands of the plans on which we are now working and every risk accepted which can further the success of these plans." Considering that the "A" Force secret channels sent a total of 577 messages to the Germans conveying the Zeppelin story, Clarke's willingness to sacrifice them for the sake of Overlord speaks volumes. Ironically, not even one "A" Force agent's cover was blown during Zeppelin![95]

With Operation Overlord a success and Zeppelin officially concluded on July 6, "A" Force was ready and able to move on to its next challenge. Incidentally, that would see the introduction of a new deception plan, Plan Ferdinand, in order to provide cover for the real invasion of southern France. Fortunately for "A" Force, its entire deception machinery remained intact and its channels continued to enjoy the enemy's confidence.

8 "A" FORCE'S LAST ACT

On June 6, 1944, the Allies carried out the largest amphibious landing in history. After years of contemplating the invasion, multiple leadership conferences, and many months of concerted planning, the Allies were finally ready to launch the much anticipated invasion. However, there was never a guarantee that D-day would be successful. In fact, Allied planners were doubtful and recognized that the odds were not in their favor. Carrying out an invasion by sea, against an entrenched, battle-hardened, and formidable enemy posed a daunting challenge. Yet, the Normandy invasion succeeded. In addition to the tremendous effort to prepare and equip the Allied forces for the cross-Channel invasion, there can be little doubt that deception made a significant contribution to the Allied success. Of the sixty German divisions spread across the Mediterranean theater, thirty-five divisions in southern France and the Balkans were held in check almost exclusively by deceptive threats and twenty-five divisions were positioned in Italy to defend against the Allied drive up the peninsula. But even in Italy the threat to the Germans was augmented by deception efforts, forcing the enemy to maintain adequate reinforcements in order to defend against notional threats. If it was not for Plan Zeppelin and the Mediterranean Strategy as a whole, those sixty enemy divisions would have been divided between the eastern front and northwest France. It is anyone's guess how that may have impacted the progress of the war, but it certainly could have resulted in very different outcome for D-day.

Plan Zeppelin was initially expected to draw to a conclusion in the weeks immediately following D-day. However, at SHAEF's request the decision was made to extend the Zeppelin threats into July in order to prevent the Germans from transferring divisions currently stationed across the Mediterranean to France. On July 6, Zeppelin officially closed down. It was immediately replaced by Plan Ferdinand, which began the following day. While Plan Vendetta, one of Zeppelin's subsidiary campaigns, manufactured a deceptive threat to southern France prior to D-day, Allied leaders intended to launch a genuine invasion of southern France after D-day in order to assist the liberation of France. Thus, Plan Ferdinand was developed in order to provide cover for the genuine campaign against southern France—Operation Anvil. Interestingly, there was considerable continuity between Zeppelin and Ferdinand as Ferdinand kept many of the Zeppelin threats alive, yet Ferdinand had the difficult task of reversing course on some of those threats in order to shift the enemy's focus away from the French Riviera after months of threatening the southern French coast.

Considering that the Allies had devoted so much effort into building up the notional threat against southern France prior to D-day, one of the immediate challenges was to explain why that attack had not occurred. The deception story held that the Allies had fully expected the Germans to withdraw forces from southern France (and the Balkans) after the Normandy landings, thus weakening their defenses. Because they did not do that, the Allies no longer believed an amphibious assault on southern France would meet with success. On July 25, "A" Force agent Jewel relayed the story to the Germans:

> The 2nd. Lt. from DE LATTRE's HQ. went to a lecture recently given by General BETHOUART to officers of the HQ. in which he said among other things that: The Allies are satisfied with the progress of operations in NORMANDY, but hoped that they would provoke the retreat of a greater number of divs. from South of FRANCE and the BALKANS. Faced with this situation the Allied High Command has renounced the landing in the South of France as its resources were too limited.[1]

With the invasion allegedly canceled, Allied leaders met in Italy to discuss future operations. The meeting was factual, but the results as presented to the Germans by way of secret channels were entirely false.[2]

The fictional report, relayed to the Germans through multiple sources including a message from "A" Force agent Gilbert on July 18, stated that American generals George C. Marshall (US Army Chief of Staff) and Henry H. "Hap" Arnold (commanding general of USAAF) met with British generals Henry Maitland Wilson (SACMED) and Harold Alexander (commanding general of the Allied Armies in Italy). The story claimed that the British generals argued the best use of Allied resources in the Mediterranean would be to focus exclusively on winning the war in Italy. They did not support further efforts to attack southern France. Allegedly, the CCS gave their formal consent on July 2. The result, notionally ordered by Wilson, called for the Allies to concentrate their strength in Italy. As such, the British and American forces in North Africa, as well as a French corps, were to be transferred to Alexander's command in Italy. In reality, the exact opposite was the case. Multiple American and French formations were separated from Alexander's command to form the Anvil invasion forces. Nonetheless, according to the deception story, Alexander was granted approval to launch an "encircling" attack against the Germans' new defensive line, the Gothic Line—which ran from Pisa in the west to Rimini in the east. The idea was that Alexander would seek to encircle the Germans by way of a landing via the Gulf of Genoa and a coordinated attack in the east along the Adriatic coast. Finally, the conference supposedly determined that the British Ninth and Twelfth Armies were to be held in reserve to exploit any changes in Turkey's wartime position or a weakening of German strength in the Balkans, respectively. In actuality, the Allies no longer sought to maintain an active threat with respect to the Balkans or Turkey, yet hoped that the "presence" of reserves would encourage the Germans to maintain their strength and vigilance in the region, as opposed to reassigning those divisions to the western front.[3]

It is notable that the deception story also claimed that Gen. Alexander "Sandy" Patch's Seventh Army and the French forces under its command were being transferred to Italy to assist Alexander's advance. The story asserted that both the Seventh Army and French forces were to be stationed in southern Italy as a reserve army until Alexander was ready to advance across the Po River. Secret agent Armour reported on July 17 that "HQ 7th. Army in NAPLES, it would seem to constitute a reserve for ITALIAN front." Jewel reinforced the ruse with the report that "DE LATTRE's HQ. is in the process of moving to ITALY where certain divisions which are already there will come under its command. It is still part of the Seventh Army whose HQ. is already in ITALY."⁴ The Germans would have known that the US Seventh Army, accompanied by French forces, was the force tasked to lead the invasion of southern France, as provided under Plan Vendetta. It was hoped that news of its transfer to Italy would signal an end to that threat. In truth, however, the Seventh Army remained the lead force for Operation Anvil.

In a rather unusual turn of events, the needs of the military planners for both the Italian campaign and the invasion of southern France aligned. The result was two mutually reinforcing deceptions plans. The strategic plan, Ferdinand, sought to reduce German vigilance in southern France while offering alternative targets for future Allied operations. The tactical plan, Ottrington, was carried out by Tac HQ "A" Force in Italy with the goal of convincing the Germans that the Allies intended to attack the Gothic Line from the eastern and western flanks as opposed to the center. In the east the British 5th Corps would attack north along the Adriatic coast toward Ravenna, while the Fifth Army's VI Corps in the west was slated to launch an amphibious force from Naples to Genoa on July 28 in order to outflank the German Gothic Line from the sea. In reality, Alexander intended to strike the center of the line, between Florence and Bologna. The strategic and tactical deception plans coalesced to emphasize Genoa as the main target of future operations. The designation of Naples as the concentration area served the purposes of both plans as well. It was a logical port from which to launch an amphibious operation against Genoa, while at the same time it was where the Anvil forces were factually concentrated and undergoing training.⁵

The deception story, which also saw a continuation of certain elements of the Zeppelin plan, is broken down in the "A" Force Narrative War Diary as follows:

a. U.S. 6th Corps (the real "ANVIL" force) to assault GENOA from NAPLES about 28th July.
b. U.S. Seventh Army, with the U.S. 31 Corps (Bogus) and the French 2nd Corps (again part of the real "ANVIL" forces) to form a Reserve Army at NAPLES to exploit across the River PO after the A.A.I. had broken through the GOTHIC LINE.
c. British 5th Corps to advance up the East coast of ITALY towards RAVENNA at the same time as the GENOA landing.
d. 3 Polish Corps (mostly bogus) to attack across the ADRIATIC from S.E. ITALY, with 5 Br. Airborne Div. (Bogus), with a target and a date to be decided later.

e. British Twelfth Army (mostly bogus) to be ready to land in the BALKANS from the MIDDLE EAST.

f. British Ninth Army (half bogus) to be ready to enter TURKEY to operate against EASTERN GREECE and the AEGEAN from Turkish bases.

g. Russian forces "being assembled" to enter VARNA.

h. TURKEY preparing to come into the war when RUSSIA occupied BULGARIA.[6]

The real plan was for the US VI Corps, composed of the 3rd, 36th, and 45th Divisions and now under the Seventh Army, to land just to the east of Toulon, France, at St. Tropez on August 15. Over the course of the next few days, they would be assisted by the 1st French Corps, which included the 1st Motorized and 3rd Algerian Divisions, and US airborne forces. The invasion forces remained in Naples until it was time to embark. On August 1, the code name for Operation Anvil was changed to Dragoon (from here on referred to as such).[7] The name was changed for security purposes. Because the code name Anvil was in usage for many months, planners were concerned that it may be compromised.

Plan Ferdinand went into operation on July 7. Like most plans, however, it did undergo multiple revisions so that the final approved version was not confirmed until July 28. One of the early obstacles encountered was the difficulty in reconciling General Patch's desires to achieve surprise and induce the Germans to reduce their defenses in the target zone between Toulon and Nice with Gen. Dwight D. Eisenhower's order to maintain pressure on southern France in order to keep the German divisions in the south contained there and away from the fighting in northwestern France. After a back-and-forth, General Wilson decided that the interests of Dragoon had to take precedence and ordered "A" Force on July 5 to move forward with developing a deception plan designed to alleviate German concerns of an attack on southern France. Eisenhower ultimately accepted Ferdinand.[8]

Ferdinand was implemented largely by way of disseminating the story through traditional and secret channels, diversionary bombing, and diversionary naval activity. With regard to the secret channels, between July 8 and August 16 "A" Force agents sent no fewer than seventy-three messages to the Germans relaying the deception story. Collectively, they created a clear picture: the American, British, and French forces had left North Africa for Italy, where most were located in the Naples area. The agents carefully reported on troop arrivals and/or departures, insignia, rumors pertaining to likely destinations, and more. They also passed on information to provide cover for General Alexander's upcoming offensive against the

Gothic Line and specifically directed the Germans' attention toward the invasion of Genoa. Gilbert, for example, reported:

> Confirm GENOA is goal for present preparations in NAPLES–SALERNO area, where three divisions are concentrated under 6th. American Corps.
> Operation is to begin towards end repeat end of August.
> An important Angol-American [sic] airborne force will take part.
> Source: American officer arrived yesterday.

The Germans routinely requested clarification or additional information on certain formations, underscoring their interest in the agents' reports.[9]

As for the bombing campaign, it was important but also rather delicate. The challenge came as it was difficult to reconcile the conflicting requirements of achieving surprise and softening the target beaches prior to landing. The site of the landing was unique. Dudley Clarke noted that past landings encountered field defenses, such as in Sicily and Italy, or wartime installations, such as in Normandy, but the Dragoon forces would face the "full strength of static defences built in peace and brought to their highest possible efficiency by the French in anticipation of the War with ITALY." He added that there were at least forty coastal defense batteries along the targeted beaches, many in concrete encasements, and the navy insisted that they be "silenced" in order to prevent heavy losses.[10] The problem was that silencing those batteries via aerial bombardment was likely to alert the Germans to the coming offensive, thus negating the possibility of surprise. Even worse, a report by Major-General T. S. Airey, assistant chief of staff, AFHQ, suggested that if the element of surprise was lost, the Germans could increase their coastal defenses by as many as ninety mobile assault guns.[11]

Other concerns related to the distribution of resources and the morale of the air crews. In terms of the former, preassault bombing called for extensive resources, which were always scarce. The Air Staff logged their concerns stating that to "knock out emplaced guns with certainty would require systematic and heavy attack extending over a period. The use of heavy or medium bombers for this purpose would require tremendous expenditure of effort, over 90% of which would be wasted. Experience in ITALY has shown that approximately 70 sorties are necessary to ensure the silencing of one open battery." The Air Staff was clearly not enthusiastic about the plan, especially when diversionary bombing was added to the requirements. Moreover, the morale of the airmen, who were not privy to the deception, had to be taken into consideration as they had trouble understanding the value of the diversionary bombing operations given that they appeared to lack a clear objective.[12]

After extensive deliberations hashed out in a leadership conference beginning July 28, Allied leaders finally reached a compromise on August 1. The plan was to carry out a four-day bombing campaign, from D −5 to D −1 against the Dragoon coastline, Genoa, Marseille, and Sète. While many of the raids were diversionary in character, others had genuine military objectives. The targets at Marseille were in fact naval targets, while one hundred fighters targeted German radar stations on Sète. The others were diversionary and were purposefully carried out with the intent of misleading the Germans as to the direction of the attack.[13]

The navy bore the brunt of the diversionary activity developed as part of a tactical cover plan. The goal was to draw the Germans' attention away from the St. Tropez–Hyères area where the landings were to take place. Instead, the navy sought to direct the enemy's attention to the Gulf of Genoa as well as demonstrated off the beaches between Cannes and Nice and off the coast of Ciotat, just east of Marseille (see map 5). A Special Operations Group was formed and provided with a "Headquarters Ship, two Gunboats, two Fighter Direction Ships, and forty-one Motor Launches or similar small craft." The ships were equipped with "every form of mechanical deception device available," and came under the command of Capt. Henry C. Johnson of the United States Navy.[14] The day before the invasion, the Special Operations Group split into two parties and left Corsica to begin their diversionary journey. The larger of the two sailed north toward Genoa. It continued on that course until 9:30 P.M., when it changed direction and headed west to Nice. Arriving off the coast of Nice at 11:00 P.M., it proceeded to bombard the coastline and made a simulated landing using Special Service Troops. This was carefully timed with the genuine invasion, which began at 3:30 A.M. on August 15. At that time, the Special Operations Group left Nice and headed fifty miles west to St. Tropez, where it linked up with the naval forces assisting Dragoon.[15]

The smaller of the two parties also left Corsica on August 14 and sailed throughout the day on a path that took it past Marseille toward Sète. At 1:00 A.M. on August 15, it altered course toward Ciotat, where it demonstrated off the coast. It joined the Dragoon forces by 9:00 A.M. The naval diversion also included the "dropping of dummy parachutists near the FRANCO-ITALIAN frontier and by special MAQUIS activities in the same neighbourhood."[16] In that way, the navy helped play up the diversionary threat to multiple possible targets leaving the Germans guessing as to the genuine target location when the attack began.

Responsibility for the tactical operations carried out under Ferdinand fell to a newly formed force: No. 2 Tac HQ "A" Force. The formation of "No. 2 Tac HQ" came as a result of yet another reorganization of "A" Force. Back in July, AFHQ had moved from North Africa to Caserta, Italy. It was followed by Main HQ "A" Force, which was finally and permanently relieved of its MI9 duties. From there Tac HQ "A" Force was divided into two units. "No. 1 Tac HQ," which was headquartered in Bolsena under the leadership of Lieutenant-Colonel R. A. Bromley-Davenport, remained with the Allied Armies in Italy. It was restructured as an all-British unit. The Americans were separated out to form "No. 2 Tac HQ." Lt. Col. E. J. Sweeney took charge of the all-American tactical deception unit that was transferred to General Patch's Seventh Army. Henceforth, it was responsible for tactical deception operations carried out by the Seventh Army, and later the US 6th Army Group in Europe.[17]

In addition to the methods of implementation provided directly by Ferdinand, the deception was also assisted from Italy by Plan Ottrington. The two plans were so deeply interconnected that the "A" Force Narrative War Diary refers to Ottrington as "the part of 'FERDINAND' which concerned ITALY." It was originally Alexander's plan to attack the center of the Gothic Line with both the British Eighth and US Fifth Armies. As a result, the primary aim of Ottrington in Italy was to weaken Field Marshal Albrecht Kesselring's defenses in the center of the line by manufacturing threats to the periphery. The Gulf of Genoa proved to be the perfect diversionary target for both Alexander's offensive and Dragoon. Accordingly, the deceptionists intended to make it appear as though the US VI Corps, which the Germans still believed to be part of the US Fifth Army, was headed to Naples to train for an amphibious assault, or "left hook," against Genoa. In reality, of course, the VI Corps was transferred to the US Seventh Army and formed the main Dragoon assault force. On the eastern flank, the story claimed the Eighth Army's 5th Corps was preparing to attack near Rimini. The offensive was said to begin on August 15, which was consistent with Dragoon but one week prior to the actual planned offensive in Italy.[18]

Ottrington was implemented through various methods. Wireless deception was used to support the story and inflate the perception of Allied strength along the threatened points of the Gothic Line. To provide visual evidence of the latter, the 101 RTR was assigned to the British 5th Corps beginning July 6. The 101 RTR assembled a display of more than a hundred dummy tanks and transport vehicles to simulate the presence of an armored division. The display was situated in Pescara from July 16 to 24. After that it was moved forward to Macerata until August 11, signaling the imminence of an attack. "A" Force employed its secret channels as well. Addict, in particular, was an especially useful source for "A" Force. Once a radio operator working for the Germans, he turned himself in to an American officer the day after Rome was captured. He was turned into a double agent and was able to provide very "useful" information to the Germans from his base in Rome. He allegedly ate routinely at the Hotel Diana, which served as a mess for French officers. It was there that he was able to "overhear" talk of upcoming plans and gain much intelligence after befriending a French military truck driver who made regular trips to the French consulate in Florence. "A" Force was able to pass many pieces of the Ottrington story to the Germans through the Addict channel.[19]

Ottrington came to an end on August 10 after Alexander changed his battle plan, necessitating a new deception plan. Where Ferdinand was concerned, Ottrington served its purpose and did much to advance the threat to Genoa. Ottrington's successor plan, Ulster, continued to play up the threat to Genoa as well, furthering the assistance to Ferdinand.[20]

In the meantime, the diversionary naval activity, combined with the diversionary aerial bombings and efforts employed as part of Ferdinand, all served to keep the Germans guessing regarding the Allies' intended target in France. On August 21, the AFHQ Weekly Report, No. 103, stated:

> Though the Germans were not taken by surprise by the actual fact of an Allied landing, their intelligence was much at fault both as to its exact timing and as to the target area; and reliable reports, supported by troop dispositions at the time of the invasion, indicate that GENOA was regarded as the most probable objective with the SETE-NARBONNE Coast as a favoured alternative. The full force of the Allied assault was accordingly met by a single low established Division supported by coast defence and static forces in the assault area.[21]

General Wilson echoed the AFHQ assessment in his memoirs where he stated that the "enemy had evidently expected an attack but its point of impact surprised him as he expected Genoa to be the objective."[22]

During the entire operation of Ferdinand, the Germans did not make any appreciable changes to their force dispositions in southern France. As evidence that they were not overly concerned about an impending invasion, they transferred the 9th Panzer Division, which had been stationed in Avignon as a mobile reserve and was the one division Allied commanders feared, to the German Seventh Army in northwest France in the beginning of August. It was replaced by the 11th Panzer Division, but that division was sent to Sète-Narbonne and thus was not an immediate threat during the invasion.[23]

It was quite fortunate that the Germans were not aware of more given the egregious lack of security among the French forces. On June 21, Lieutenant-General

J. A. H. Gammel, Wilson's chief of staff, circulated an extensive security plan for Operation Dragoon. In it he stated that preparations for the invasion should be "implemented in such a way that these factors will not be revealed to, and cannot be deduced by, either the enemy, the civilian population or our own forces apart from those whose duty requires such knowledge." He continued that the "exact dates of our fresh assaults, exactly where they are to be made, and preparations at the loading and mounting points must all be guarded with the closest secrecy."[24] Many French soldiers, however, were unable to contain their excitement at the prospect of the upcoming operation and spoke openly about it. Even the Deuxième Bureau, the French military intelligence organization, became alarmed when it learned that the "coming landings were being widely talked about both in NORTH AFRICA and ITALY." Wilson finally had to reach out to the French commanders directly to ask them to put a gag order on their men. "A" Force stepped in and used its secret channels to try to counter the loose talk as well.[25] On August 8, Jewel sent a message discounting the so-called rumors:

> According to 2nd. Lt. there is no truth in the rumours which continue to circulate with persistence regarding a landing in S. FRANCE. He has just learned from the HQ. of the Staff of the National Defense that General De GUALLE [sic] himself, in order to keep up the Army's morale and for reasons of prestige, has insisted on continuing these rumours ever since the plan was abandoned at the end of June.[26]

In that way, "A" Force hoped the Germans would discount any information they received about the landings.

Considering Ferdinand's primary object—to provide cover for the genuine landings in southern France—it was considered a success. Operation Dragoon, which began on August 15, "greatly exceeded expectations." The invasion forces were opposed by only one division and thus met with minimal resistance. They were followed by the eager French, led by General Jean de Lattre de Tassigny, and assisted on the ground by the French Resistance. In less than one week, the Allied troops were positioned just outside the Rhône Valley ready to continue their drive north. On September 12, 1944, the Dragoon forces met up with General Patton's Third Army outside of Dijon. The offensive also opened the Port of Marseille for Allied shipping, which received more supplies than any other port in the five months following Dragoon.[27]

Meanwhile, Ferdinand was extended until September 8 in order to provide explanation for the landings in southern France (as opposed to Genoa), to offer support for Alexander's offensive in Italy, and to assist in keeping the Germans in northwest Italy occupied to deter them from interfering with General Patch's advance in France. The solution to the latter two objectives was to maintain the threat to Genoa. While the secret channels continued playing up the threat to Genoa, an explanation was nonetheless needed to give account for the operation in France. For that, the deceptionists again blamed General Charles de Gaulle. The new story purported that de Gaulle was increasingly anxious to have French forces in France before the liberation of Paris. Thus, Allied leaders gave in to his insistence and decided to send the US Seventh Army, accompanied by a French corps, into southern France without delay. However, the story continued, the Allies still intended to launch the invasion of Genoa. For that, they claimed, the US XXXI Corps was still in Naples and preparing to lead the assault.[28]

The extension of Ferdinand also served to assist Alexander in Italy, although Alexander's plans for Italy had become complicated. He originally had hoped to follow up on the success of Operation Diadem with a quick attack against the Germans' next line of defense—the Gothic Line. The British saw the advance as a way to capitalize on their recent success in Italy. The Americans, on the other hand, had been adamant that the invasion of southern France proceed and take precedence over further advances in Italy. The Combined Chiefs of Staff ultimately sided with the American argument. That meant a weakening of Alexander's strength as the US VI Corps and a French corps, a total of seven divisions, were withdrawn from the US Fifth Army to form the Dragoon assault force. The weakening thus resulted in a delay and gave the Germans time to fortify the Gothic Line.[29]

The Germans initially envisioned the Gothic Line as an impenetrable line that would prevent the Allies from clearing the Apennines and taking Italy. After Kesselring convinced Hitler in the fall of 1943 that he could mount a protracted defense of southern Italy and significantly delay the Allied advance, most of the work on the Gothic Line came to a halt in favor of reinforcing the Gustav Line. After Diadem, the Germans retreated to the Gothic Line, where they renewed their efforts to strengthen it. The line was defended by the German Tenth Army, under General Heinrich von Vietinghoff's capable command, and the severely weakened Fourteenth Army, led by General Joachim Lemelsen. Lemelsen had only recently taken command of the army following General Eberhard von Mackensen's dismissal. Though the Fourteenth Army was in disarray and the Gothic Line was not the formidable defense once intended, every day gave the Germans time to strengthen the line, reinforce, and prepare for the Allies' next advance.[30]

Alexander's initial plan, to carry out a concentrated attack against the center of the Gothic Line, proved unfeasible after Dragoon was given the go-ahead and the seven divisions were withdrawn from the AAI. More importantly, the 1st French Corps consisted of mountain divisions, and they were necessary for the central punch into mountainous terrain. With the Fifth Army weakened and the mountain divisions gone, the British Eighth Army commander, General Sir Oliver Leese, challenged the wisdom of the plan in a meeting with Alexander, Wilson, and General John Harding on August 4. Leese's concerns were well founded. The British Eighth Army was expected to lead the offensive, but it lacked troops trained for or experienced in mountain warfare. Leese argued that the Eighth Army should lead the offensive up the Adriatic coast instead. Even though Alexander disliked the idea of changing his plan, he did finally accept Leese's argument. The new battle plan became known as "Olive" after the Eighth Army commander.[31]

The major challenge for "A" Force was that Plan Ottrington had spent weeks, from June 30 to August 10, telling the Germans that the Eighth Army intended to attack north along the Adriatic. Moreover, Ottrington was paying dividends evidenced by the transfer of the German 1st Parachute Division to the Adriatic coast. With the introduction of the new "Olive" battle plan, the arrival of the 1st Parachute Division was anything but advantageous. Now that the deceptive plan became the genuine plan, the deceptionists had to figure out how to reverse course, and do so quickly enough to make a difference. Ottrington was thus replaced with Plan Ulster, and Ferdinand was extended to lend support.[32]

Ulster, in conjunction with Ferdinand, continued to play up the threat to Genoa, though no new assault date was ever provided to the enemy. The primary objective of the new deception plan called for "A" Force to keep Kesselring's forces contained along the center of the line by convincing him that the Fifth Army would lead the new offensive. In that way, they sought to direct the Germans' attention away from the Adriatic by downplaying any intentions on the part of the Allies to attack in the east. They hoped the Germans would concentrate their defenses along the center long enough for the Eighth Army to strike, and then send them east as reinforcements in time for the Fifth Army—reinforced with the British 13th Corps, two armored divisions, and two infantry divisions from the Eighth Army—to attack up the middle toward Bologna.[33]

Given the amount of effort "A" Force had already put into building up the threat of the Eighth Army in the east, the only way to reverse it was to present it as a fake. That called for "A" Force to resort to a double bluff. The double bluff was not something "A" Force had ever attempted on the strategic level. It was tricky at best and risked exposing "A" Force's methods of implementation to the enemy. For that very reason, "A" Force had avoided it in the past. Yet, the situation was very different in August 1944. D-day was past, Dragoon went forward on August 15, "A" Force was scaling down, and there were no future strategic deception plans in the making. For that reason, Clarke decided that "A" Force could assume the risk, though he still was not a fan of the double bluff method.[34]

The idea was to present the previous activities on the eastern coast as a feint designed to mislead the Germans and draw their reserves away from the point of the main attack—the center. To that end, they had to expose their previous efforts as deceptive. The wireless channels, for example, were deliberately exposed. The operators were instructed to handle them in such a way that the Germans would realize they were bogus. The dummy displays were allowed to "decay," repairs were carried out in areas where they could be observed by civilians, and the dummies themselves were "allowed to become more obvious, tks [tanks] were sited in the open where no tracks existed, and security precautions with regard to the civilian population were relaxed."[35] "A" Force double agent Addict reported the presence of dummies in his August 10 message: "Pole angry because has discovered that concentration of armour already reported in ADRIATIC sector was only cardboard theatre props placed there by British which might bring about German action against Polish forces."[36]

In addition to exposing the previous methods as fakes, No. 1 Tac HQ worked diligently on a plan to conceal the move of the Eighth Army to the coast, as well as the arrival of reinforcements to the Eighth Army sector. The opposite was the case for the Fifth Army, where efforts were made to ensure that the Germans learned of the preparations underway for the upcoming "large-scale attack." A September 9 report from G(Cam) AAI explained that Company "D" 84th Engineer Battalion created false ammunition dumps, with a parenthetical side note boasting "(these were excellent)." In addition, the report states that "false gun positions with flash were used and operated by a party from Co[mpan]y 'D' in conjunction with the gunners," and makes clear that the activity was under "distant ground observation."[37] Furthermore, intelligence channels passed information regarding the preparations for mountain warfare and arrival of trained mountain forces, a factor that could only pertain to an attack up the center.[38]

Overall, Clarke counted Ulster as a success. A captured German POW revealed that the Germans knew there was a "concentration of dummy tanks on the Eighth Army's front." More importantly, the Germans did not reinforce the Adriatic front

The Italian Campaign, 1944–1945. Map by Erin Greb Cartography.

during the operation of Ulster. There was nothing the deceptionists could do about the 1st Parachute Division that had already arrived, but it could be counted as a victory that no additional reinforcements were sent east until three days after the offensive began.[39]

The Eighth Army offensive began on August 25. By the end of August it had breached the Gothic Line, and by September 22 Rimini was in Allied hands. The Fifth Army launched its attack three weeks after the Eighth Army on September 12. Although the Allies achieved tactical surprise, the Germans mounted a stiff defense.

By the end of 1944, the Allies had broken the Gothic Line, but they made few gains beyond it. Due to German resistance and the onset of another harsh Italian winter, the Allies' objective—Bologna—remained in German hands until the spring of 1945.[40]

While the cover plan could be considered a success in helping the Allies achieve tactical surprise, Dudley Clarke did not like the idea of using the double bluff and did not recommend that it be used in the future. He wrote:

> It was found, for technical reasons, extremely difficult to produce the required effect in the progress of the wireless deception. For one thing—and this applied too to the Camouflage and Dummy displays— it meant that the soldiers had to behave in a way which was directly contrary to all their previous training in procedure and security. Not only this, but they found it almost impossible deliberately to make a Deception appear false, without in the course of it disclosing that that was exactly what they were intending.

He concluded that the original objections—that a double bluff ran the risk of exposing the deception organization's methods of implementation—remained valid. So even though Ulster met with positive results, Clarke would not have taken the risk of a double bluff a second time.[41]

After Operations Dragoon and Olive commenced, "A" Force found itself in a unique position: the need for strategic deception in the Mediterranean had passed. As it turned out, Plan Ferdinand was "A" Force's last strategic deception of the war. The London Controlling Section did not see the need for additional strategic deception plans in the region as the Germans had retreated from southern France and were retreating in the Balkans. Moreover, the CCS judged Germany's situation to be fragile, its resources stretched thin, and a lack of reserves greatly limited its offensive options. While there remained opportunities for tactical deception to assist the Allies in Italy, the "increasing collapse of the German Intelligence system, and the enemy's consequent inability to react in a logical manner to much of the operational information which reached him" meant that strategic deception efforts were unlikely to make any notable impact in the future.[42]

Although "A" Force was not called on to implement another strategic deception plan, it did deliver two additional plans—Undercut and Second Undercut. Interestingly, Dudley Clarke did not approve of the original Undercut. He called it a "good example of a Bad Plan, based on a wrong object, which was quite ineffectual and illustrates the misuse of a Deception Staff."[43] Nevertheless, it was likely a consequence of "A" Force's many successes in the past. During its early years in North Africa, "A" Force struggled to convince the military commanders of the usefulness of deception. Many leaders held traditional military views and thus initially failed to see the value and benefit of deception. However, the North African campaign and the subsequent deception coup with Operation Husky in Sicily convinced the military that deception was a powerful weapon and vital component to any operation. After that, the Allies incorporated deception into their operational planning for every major military campaign. The problem with that came in September 1944 when "A" Force was asked to develop a cover plan for Operation Manna directed at the Balkans. Clarke commented that "deception in the MEDITERRANEAN moved from the sublime to the almost ridiculous" with Undercut.[44]

Operation Manna came about as the Germans began to withdraw from the Balkans. The British no longer had offensive plans, real or deceptive, toward the Balkans, but they had long intended to exploit any opportunity that presented itself in the region. As the Germans began to pull out, the British formed Force 140 under Lieutenant-General Ronald MacKenzie Scobie to enter Athens. The purpose, according to Alexander, was to "maintain law and order, establish the Government in Athens, and arrange for food and supplies." Force 140 comprised only two brigades, although the plan was to follow it later with the 4th Indian Division and Greek Mountain Brigade.[45] Because Force 140 was so small, the main concern was that it was not in a position to fend off German resistance, and the Germans might be tempted to give fight if they became aware of its weakness. The initial plan with Undercut was to simulate greater strength by way of an order of battle deception. However, the plan had to be changed in response to concerns over Greece's fragile political state. The British decided that it would be better if neither the Germans nor the Greeks knew about Britain's plans for Force 140, thus changing the plan from one of force maximization to secrecy. Furthermore, there was no indication that the Germans had any intention of remaining in Greece as their rapid retreat evidenced. Given the circumstances, there was no "object," and Clarke did not see any justification for a deception plan.[46]

To his chagrin, Clarke was overruled. Wilson decided at the Supreme Allied Commander's conference on September 5 that a cover plan, dubbed Undercut, was needed in order to conceal the true purpose of Force 140. Ironically, by that time the goal was not to conceal that information from the Germans, but from the Greeks instead. Clarke was adamant that the plan should not be implemented and argued that "A" Force was not in the business of deceiving the Greeks. Moreover, he was concerned that any such attempt would be "useless" and "harmful." Nonetheless, "A" Force was given a direct order on September 9 to begin work on the plan. Clarke recorded: "A great deal of misunderstanding arose unfortunately among the staff of A.F.H.Q., which by that time had come to look upon a Deception Plan as such an established accompaniment to any operation of war that they found it difficult to appreciate the difference of the altered circumstances."[47]

In order to furnish an alternative explanation for Force 140, the plan was to circulate rumors identifying false destinations for its formations. The units then based in southeast Italy were said to be heading to Istria, while it was proposed that those in Egypt were going to Rhodes; in essence, then, the plan was to hide from the Greeks that Force 140 was headed to Athens. The plan was farcical at best and met with immediate resistance. On September 14, naval authorities lodged their opposition. They disapproved of any measures to try to convince their forces that they were not going to Greece on the grounds that "most of the ships involved were Greek, that the Greek Naval Staff had been planning the Operation themsleves [sic], and that all were fully aware of the real purpose of 'MANNA.'" The situation became even worse after Greek resistance leaders arrived in Italy to meet with General Scobie and were briefed on the plans for Operation Manna. After learning of the meeting, Clarke sent a letter on September 16 to Colonel John Bevan that began: "This is daily becoming more and more stupid."[48] If the object of Undercut was to achieve secrecy, it was an utter failure. On September 30, the commanders in chief of the Middle East advised Wilson to abandon Undercut as it had become "impracticable and unnecessary." To everyone's relief, Wilson agreed and the plan was called off on October 2.[49]

Clarke was not surprised that Undercut failed to achieve its purpose, but he was at least relieved that the failure came at a time when strategic deception had reached its natural end; otherwise it could have resulted in serious damage to "A" Force and its credibility. He argued that deception should never be used as an alternative to secrecy. He stated that Undercut was a good example of the "consequences of demanding a Deception Plan with no apparent object largely because a Deception Staff was at hand with little else to do." Clarke clearly did not appreciate what he saw as the blatant misuse of "A" Force. He continually referred back to the lesson that the organization learned the hard way in 1941 with Plan Camilla: the most important aspect of a deception was to have a clearly defined object. With his frustration on full display, he wrote in bold: "UNLESS A DECEPTION PLAN STARTS WITH A PROPER OBJECT (i.e. to make the enemy act in an advantageous manner to ourselves) <u>IT WILL NOT ONLY BE USELESS BUT MAY WELL BE POSITIVELY DANGEROUS.</u>"[50]

Even though Undercut was abandoned, the original idea of misleading the Germans as to the strength of Force 140 was revived and formulated into a reboot of the original plan. Second Undercut, as it was, had a defined object: to convince the Germans that Force 140 was larger than it truly was in order to discourage any temptation to attack the meager force. It was implemented after Force 140 landed in Greece. Second Undercut fell into the category of "A" Force's order of battle deceptions. In this case, the goal was straightforward and utilized deception to exaggerate Force 140's strength. Clarke was concerned that the name itself—Force 140—revealed that it was nothing more than a task force. To that end, Force 140 became the 3rd Corps, indicating it was a force comprised of multiple divisions as opposed to two brigades. As part of the Wantage Order of Battle Plan, a new bogus division was created, the 34th Infantry Division, as part of the 3rd Corps. Moreover, the 5th Airborne Division, also bogus, was allegedly on standby in Sicily.[51]

The usual administrative measures were implemented to bring the bogus divisions to life and ensure that there was ample visual evidence of their existence. The divisional sign of the bogus 34th Infantry Division—a checkerboard with sixteen 4 × 4 black and white squares—was displayed on the vehicles of five different units. The personnel of those units were also misled, as they were informed that their units were to come under the command of the 34th Infantry Division once it was fully established in Greece. Secret channels reported sightings of the bogus divisions to German intelligence.[52]

Second Undercut began when the Manna forces entered Athens on October 14. The stated object of Second Undercut was twofold: to make Force 140 appear stronger, and to deter German resistance. As for the first part of the object, it can be judged a success. Captured documents showed that the Germans believed the bogus 34th Infantry Division and 3rd Corps to be real. They had both listed in their order of battle assessment of the strength of the British garrison in Greece. With regard to the second part, it is unclear whether Second Undercut made any impact or not. The Germans did not offer any resistance as the British entered Athens, but there was no evidence to suggest that they ever intended to do anything other than retreat. As such, it is impossible to say whether or not Second Undercut had an appreciable impact.[53]

Whereas Ferdinand was "A" Force's last strategic deception, Second Undercut was the last plan carried out by "A" Force while it remained a complete organization.

After Second Undercut, "A" Force began a series of reorganizations as it began to shut down in stages. What remained intact was No. 1 Tac HQ in Italy. It continued to operate and provide tactical deception plans to assist the Allied Armies in Italy. Thus, from here forward, the history of "A" Force is in effect the history of No. 1 Tac HQ in Italy.

In the fall of 1944, "A" Force began the first of three planned stages of reduction. The CCS determined that there was no need for another "Overall Deception Plan for the War against Germany." From there on, any deception efforts would be carried out on the local level at the discretion of theater commanders. After meeting with Alexander and consulting with the Mediterranean, Middle East, and Persia and Iraq Command theater headquarters, as well as with the London Controlling Section, Clarke presented Wilson with a plan to reduce "A" Force. Wilson approved it on October 5.[54]

When discussions began in early October, all that remained of "A" Force was Rear HQ in Cairo, Main HQ in Italy, and No. 1 Tac HQ with the AAI. On October 15, Main HQ closed down. That left No 1. Tac HQ in charge of all deception in Italy. It moved its headquarters to Siena and assumed control of the three "A" Force outstations still in operation in Italy: at Bari, Florence, and Rome. No. 1 Tac HQ also saw a change in leadership as Lieutenant-Colonel Crichton relieved Lieutenant-Colonel Bromley-Davenport. Bromley-Davenport returned to the UK after five years of service. As Cairo had always served as the base of "A" Force operations, Rear HQ remained there, under Clarke's direct command, and retained administrative control of "A" Force. Once the reduction was complete, "A" Force numbered only sixteen officers and thirty-three other ranks.[55]

"A" Force was not the only organization to undergo a reorganization. In December 1944, Wilson left for the United States to head the British staff mission in Washington, D.C., following the sudden death of General Sir John Dill. On December 12, Alexander was promoted to field marshal and took Wilson's position as SACMED.[56] He held the dual position of SACMED and head of AFHQ until the war's end. The AAI, which went back to its original title of 15th Army Group, came under the command of Lt. Gen. Mark Clark.[57]

After assuming the position of SACMED, Alexander moved to Caserta, where AFHQ was located. Before leaving Siena, however, he requested that part of "A" Force accompany him. The supreme commander's request required Clarke to make adjustments to the previous reorganization, thus prompting the second stage in

"A" Force's reorganization/reduction. Clarke traveled from Cairo to Caserta on December 10 to assess Alexander's needs and oversee the changes. The result was that No. 1 Tac HQ split into two entities. Main HQ "A" Force was revived and set up in Caserta as Alexander requested. Crichton, who had only recently left Caserta, now returned to head Main HQ. Tac HQ "A" Force relocated to Florence to assist the 15th Army Group. It was reduced in size and came under the leadership of Lt. Col. J. D. R. "David" Elkington.[58]

Further changes pertained to "A" Force in Cairo. Rear HQ "A" Force was repurposed to handle the remaining intelligence channels operating in the region. At the time, it was thought that the channels may be able to assist South-East Asia Command in the war against Japan, but the need never materialized. In the meantime, Rear HQ was reduced to only one officer. The Cairo Rear Party was formed under Dudley Clarke. With the war nearing its end and "A" Force's duties confined to minor operations in Italy to assist the 15th Army Group, Clarke began to prepare the "A" Force records for transfer to the UK. He was also responsible for the administrative task of closing down the Cairo office, which included making arrangements for the equipment, property, and personnel who served there.[59]

As 1945 dawned, Alexander and the armies comprising the 15th Army Group found themselves in an eerily familiar position: bogged down in severe winter conditions and short of their objective. The Allies' total strength in Italy amounted to twenty divisions, along with three Italian Gruppi, a Jewish Palestinian Brigade, two brigades of Commandos and Special Forces comprising the "Land Forces, Adriatic," and one additional British division that was in the Middle East to rest and reequip. Opposing the 15th Army Group, German strength amounted to thirty-two divisions—twenty-seven German and five Italian Fascist divisions.

The 15th Army Group was not in a position to launch a major offensive until the spring, but Alexander initiated what he termed the "offensive defense" in an effort to improve his armies' positions over the winter.[60] When they were not engaged in limited offensives, the Allied armies assumed a defensive posture and were able to rest and regroup. Alexander pointed out that a full-scale offensive was not practical at the time due to the harsh winter conditions, in addition to the "greatly increased development and strength of the enemy's defences covering BOLOGNA, the formation by the enemy of a reserve of some four divisions, the fact that 15 Army Group had available only fifteen days artillery ammunition on a full offensive scale, and the pressing need for major reorganisation in certain British, Dominion and

Indian divisions and in the Polish Corps."[61] For that reason, the Allies maintained the "offensive defense" in Italy until spring.

The only deception plan in operation at the opening of 1945 was the Wantage Order of Battle Plan. Consistent with the reorganization and downscaling of the deception apparatus as a whole, Wantage was also being scaled down. Wantage had reached its height throughout the first half of 1944 when "A" Force was operating Plan Zeppelin, which included Plans Vendetta and Turpitude. The object was to exaggerate the Allies' strength in the Mediterranean by 40 percent and convince the Germans that the Allies possessed sufficient strength to carry out operations across the expanse of the Mediterranean theater. In fact, captured German documents showing their assessment of the Allies' order of battle revealed that the enemy overestimated Allied strength by 50 percent and believed twenty-four notional divisions to be genuine. By the end of 1944, however, such exaggeration in strength was no longer necessary. Considering that it required tremendous administrative efforts to maintain the bogus formations, it was most practical for "A" Force to downscale Wantage in 1945.[62]

The challenge to eliminating notional divisions was that it had to be conducted in a manner that would not expose the deception to the enemy. In most cases, it was gradually conveyed to the enemy that the formations were either disbanded, broken up to provide other essential services, reduced in size, or transferred. In that way, their sudden absence did not appear suspicious. "A" Force did maintain numerous notional divisions to supplement the 15th Army Group as needed.[63]

The US Fifth and British Eighth Armies, making up the 15th Army Group, were the only active armies in the Mediterranean in 1945. Beyond their goal of driving the Germans out of Italy, they were also expected to assist the European theater, just as they did in 1944. On December 18, 1944, SACMED clarified the Mediterranean deception policy for 1945:

> I consider that the object of deception plans should be to compel the enemy to keep committed the maximum forces dispersed along the whole front from SOUTH WEST HUNGARY to the FRENCH ALPS for as long as possible. This we can best achieve on the ITALIAN part of the line by tactical deception combined with the real operations of the 15th Army Group.[64]

Thus the goal was to keep the Germans committed in Italy, rendering them unable to transfer their battle-hardened divisions to the western front. This coincided with the period of Alexander's "offensive defense."

It was during that time that Lieutenant-Colonel Elkington's Tac HQ "A" Force was called on to develop a deception plan designed to "create in the minds of the enemy a nervousness as to our offensive intentions along the entire front" and to prevent him from forming a "large central reserve." In that vein, Plan Oakleaf was born. The hope was that the Germans would not realize Alexander had halted the Allies' winter offensive, but would instead fear that an attack was imminent and thus maintain their strength along the front. Tac HQ "A" Force intended for Oakleaf to be in operation for the duration of the 15th Army Group's rest and regrouping period from January until March. Oakleaf was approved on January 18.[65]

To pass Oakleaf to the enemy and keep the Germans anxious, numerous methods were employed. The divisions that were granted periods of rest and regrouping were asked to remain close to the front line. The deception claimed that Alexander wanted them close so that they would be available when he decided to resume the offensive. The two armies were to mimic offensive action by way of patrolling and conducting small-scale raids. The Allied troops were told that the offensive was only temporarily halted; thus, they could expect it to resume soon. The 15th Army Group contributed by conducting a signal scheme whereby either increased wireless activity or silence was coordinated with the movement of formations, signs were displayed, and support to the partisans maintained. The MAAF was asked to continue active support of the 15th Army Group from the air, and the PWB continued its radio propaganda and leaflet campaign. Tac HQ was responsible for coordinating the transmission of the story to the enemy by way of its secret channels.[66]

While Oakleaf was designed to keep the Germans alert, the plan did not attempt to provide a target date or specific point of attack to the enemy. The reason for the ambiguity was that Alexander had yet to formalize his plans for the spring offensive. As such, the deception team did not feel it could maintain the threat to a specific target over a period of many months. Naming a target location also ran the risk of limiting Alexander's options. Moreover, because Alexander had not chosen the exact date for the spring offensive, there was no logical reason to offer a deceptive target date at that stage.[67]

On February 3, with Oakleaf underway, a directive arrived from the Combined Chiefs of Staff that changed the general situation in the Mediterranean. Coming on the heels of the Germans' surprise December 1944 offensive in the Ardennes, commonly known as the Battle of the Bulge, the CCS decided to amass the "maximum possible strength" in western Europe with the goal of bringing about Germany's collapse. As a result, they intended to transfer up to five divisions from Italy and two fighter groups to the western front. They also advocated for the end of British obligations in Greece in order to free those forces for redeployment. They therefore redefined the object of the Mediterranean theater: "You should do your utmost, by means of such limited offensive action as may be possible and by the skilful use of cover and deception plans, to contain the German forces now in ITALY and prevent their withdrawal to other fronts." The object was largely consistent with the previous policy; it was simply made more challenging since it would have to be accomplished with fewer genuine forces at AFHQ's disposal.[68]

The existing deception plan, Oakleaf, was designed to keep the Germans committed in Italy with the threat of potential Allied offensive action. Everyone involved, however, quickly realized that it would be difficult to maintain the existing threat level if the Germans realized the Allies were transferring multiple divisions to the western front. That reality resulted in a new plan in order to provide cover for the transfer of the outgoing forces. Crichton, who was promoted to colonel in January, received orders to report to 15th Army Group Headquarters, along with the chief security officer of AFHQ, to develop a supporting cover plan. The resulting plan, code-named Penknife, was composed, approved, and put into action within only forty-eight hours—which Clarke noted as an example of just how "'cover plan minded' 15 Army Group had become." From there forward, Plans Oakleaf and Penknife ran concurrently as mutually supporting plans.[69]

Penknife addressed the Allies' urgent need to conceal the transfer of the 1st Canadian Corps, which was headed to the western front to join the First Canadian Army (the code name Goldflake was used in official documents to refer to these forces while in transit). The corps consisted of its headquarters, 1st Canadian Infantry Division, 5th Canadian Armoured Division, and 1st Canadian Armoured Brigade. The story transmitted to the enemy was that the corps was being withdrawn for rest. It added that during that process some of the men were being returned to Canada and would be replaced by new draftees. And, the story continued, after nearly two years of active overseas service, the corps would become part of the 15th Army Group Reserve. In reality, the formations were embarking for France from the ports of Naples and Leghorn beginning February 15. The story about the troop rotations was designed to provide cover for the embarkations should they be observed, as they would be nearly impossible to conceal in their entirety.[70]

Penknife was a complex cover plan, and its implementation was rather involved. Security measures were used to try to conceal the transfer of the corps to Naples and Leghorn. As the Canadian forces withdrew from the front, for example, they were under orders to remove all identifying signs from personnel and vehicles. As for the ports, they were isolated and cut off from civilian traffic. The troops were not allowed to exchange money while in Italy, nor were they issued maps of France. All existing signage for Canadian installations remained in place, and the Canadian clubs, hotels, and hostels remained fully operational. In the event that any Canadian facility had to be closed, the story issued was that it was temporary to allow for spring cleaning.[71]

Wireless deception, which had become a staple of any deception/cover plan, was readily utilized. By 1945, those efforts were greatly enhanced by the arrival in late 1944 of "A" Detachment of 5 Wireless Group, which was on loan to the 15th Army Group from General Bernard Law Montgomery's 21st Army Group. "A" Detachment revolutionized wireless deception. The Germans were highly adept at intercepting Allied signals, and were quite familiar with their wireless operators. The characteristics unique to each operator were both known and readily recognizable to the enemy. Prior to the arrival of "A" Detachment, operators had to remain behind to represent a formation after its departure in order to prevent the enemy from detecting the change. The nine officers and seventy-six other ranks of "A" Detachment brought special equipment that allowed them to simulate the continued presence of formations "by the recording and monitoring of their W/T [wireless transmission] operators and R/T [radio transmission] users," thereby allowing them to reproduce communications with accuracy.[72]

When the 1st Canadian Corps departed from the Fifth and Eighth Armies, it initially left personnel and wireless sets behind to continue representing the corps headquarters, divisions, and brigade. "A" Detachment then made recordings in order to simulate the Canadians' transmissions. As the Canadians withdrew from the line, supposedly for rest, they went on wireless silence. A notional headquarters was subsequently established at Macerata, complete with a dummy wireless network to simulate the headquarters, which was connected to 15th Army Group headquarters. The extensive wireless operation was carried out by signal officers of the Eighth Army, Fifth Army, and "A" Detachment of 5 Wireless Group.[73]

Camouflage was another important component of Penknife. It was employed to provide visual evidence for German reconnaissance that ships leaving Leghorn were not returning empty, as well as to create the appearance of an armored division in Pisa and an infantry division and armored brigade at Macerata in the event those areas were observed by enemy agents. The former was important because the deception story held that the Canadians leaving Italy were returning to Canada, but that they were being replaced by newly drafted soldiers. The Royal Navy was asked to help camouflage the cargo of departing ships and create the appearance of cargo on retuning ships. The 101 RTR provided their "rigid aluminum frame special vehicles" for the ruse so that the LSTs never returned empty. 101 RTR helped load ten special 2.5-ton trucks on each LST and kept additional special vehicles in Leghorn for use if needed. In a Plan Penknife progress report dated February 27, Colonel Crichton reported: "An "A" Force officer sailed on first convoy from LEGHORN and reports that Dummy Vehicles were successfully erected on return journey and the display appeared effective." Another report, from Captain E. G. J. Dawes, stated: "From the eye, and through binoculars, the dummy vehicles gave the impression of being real, when looked at from the bridge of a ship. The Naval officers also confirm this opinion." That was significant for Dawes because the ships passed "within visual distance" of the northern tip of Corsica, from which their cargo could be observed. The Allies were also fortunate to experience good weather for all of the convoys carrying the dummy vehicles on the return trip from Marseille.[74]

Also on site at Pisa and Macerata was 101 RTR. At Pisa, the team set up a "tank park" consisting of fifty armored vehicles. Company "D" 84th Engineer Battalion painted signs on the vehicles so that they appeared to belong to the 5th Canadian Armoured Division. Macerata was supplemented by actual troops and transport in order to enhance the amount of activity present in the region. AFHQ took on the responsibility of ensuring that the "maximum possible concentration" of Canadian personnel, those who still remained in Italy, were posted at Macerata. Like at Pisa, a "tank park" was established and signs were painted on the vehicles to represent the 1st Canadian Armoured Brigade. Given the lack of security and likelihood that the vehicles would be observed, 101 RTR did not use dummies in either location, lest they be exposed as fakes.[75]

While the Royal Navy was called on to assist with camouflage efforts, MAAF was asked to "take all possible steps" to deny enemy reconnaissance of Naples and Leghorn. Beyond the ports themselves, they were to provide similar assistance as the ships sailed from Naples and Leghorn to Marseille.[76] While it was hoped that the Germans would not observe any of the activity, the camouflage measures were in place just in case.

The "A" Force secret channels actively fed the deception story to the enemy. Clarke recorded that the Germans demonstrated considerable interest in the Allies' plans and force dispositions. They frequently sent detailed questionnaires to the agents requesting additional information. Clarke remarked that the German military intelligence organization, the Abwehr, "reacted well throughout, and not only gave us valuable help in the shape of provoking our spurious answers but also provided good indications as to their own state of mind."[77]

The final piece of the puzzle was to ensure that the enemy could not glean any factual information on the 1st Canadian Corps from open source intelligence (OSINT). Thus, there was no disruption in the coverage of the Canadian forces by the press. For the duration of Plan Penknife, the press continued publishing articles and photographs of the Canadians and their activities in Italy. Moreover, publication of *The Maple Leaf*, a newspaper for Canadian troops serving overseas, continued unabated. Finally, strict censorship measures were imposed that forbade the press from mentioning the transfer of the 1st Canadian Corps until those restrictions were lifted.[78]

All throughout Penknife, "A" Force coordinated closely with SHAEF and Ops B. While Penknife worked to conceal the transfer of the Canadian forces from Italy, there had to be coordination with SHAEF to conceal their arrival in France. On February 12, Colonel Nöel Wild of Ops B arrived in Italy to meet with Crichton. Wild reassured Crichton that the "utmost security precautions have been taken with regard to the arrival of the GOLDFLAKE forces at MARSEILLES." The 1st Canadian Corps remained on wireless silence, and no signs were erected to identify the corps. SHAEF also arranged for the Canadian forces to take their leave in the UK, where greater security could be maintained.[79]

Wild and Crichton met again, this time in London, from March 1 to 5. AFHQ needed to move forward with its spring offensive planning, so it was agreed Penknife would end on April 15. The plan was to begin closing it down on March 25 and then notionally sail the 1st Canadian Corps to France with an arrival date of April 15. The timing corresponded with when the Germans were expected to take note of the Canadians on the western front. Penknife was rather delicate because it was always understood that the Germans would eventually discover the Canadians were in western Europe. Crichton and Wild agreed that the secret channels should eventually provide information on the Canadians' departure from Italy, albeit after the fact, to avoid exposing the deception or discrediting the channels.[80]

Wild did not anticipate that the 1st Canadian Corps would be committed to battle under the 21st Army Group until May 1, although he did not have the authority to make those decisions and readily acknowledged that fact. "A" Force experienced a major setback on March 11 when Wild informed Crichton that the 21st Army Group had called the Canadian forces up to the front line—they were expected to take their positions by March 15. The news came while Penknife was still fully operational, and it would be very difficult to explain how the 1st Canadian Corps was in Italy and France at the same time. With little else they could do to mitigate the situation, "A" Force decided to maintain its security measures but cease all intelligence efforts. While it created quite the panic at the time, it turned out that no harm was done. In fact, the Germans seemed rather confused regarding the Canadians' location until April 18. Penknife officially concluded on March 13.[81]

Even though the Canadians were put into action sooner than planned, resulting in a premature end to Plan Penknife, the deception was nonetheless deemed a success. The Germans somehow failed to identify the Canadian forces in France for more than a month after they were transferred to the front line. A captured German document from March 16, notably compiled one day *after* the Canadian forces joined the 21st Army Group at the front, detailed the "enemy situation" in Italy and placed the "1 Cdn Div vic MAZERATTA. 5 Cdn Armd Div in LUCCA area." Interrogation of captured German officers revealed that the Germans were concerned about the 1st Canadian Corps, and perhaps even suspicious about its location, but they were unable to disprove the deception story fed to them and still assumed it to be in Italy until April. Thus, Penknife achieved its objective of concealing the transfer of the 1st Canadian Corps to France.[82]

Similar to Penknife, "A" Force viewed Oakleaf as a success as well. Admittedly, the Germans did withdraw three divisions from Italy over the three months of Oakleaf's operation. What was remarkable, however, was that they did not transfer more than those three divisions when there was nothing stopping them from doing so. Elkington noted that over the course of three months, the Allies mounted only one minor offensive action and often maintained the line with "second grade troops." In Elkington's appraisal, Oakleaf was a success as it "operated over a time when one disaster after another were falling on the enemy on other fronts, and when it appeared logical that he should withdraw divs from ITALY for employment elsewhere even if it had meant shortening his front or withdrawing to another line." Because the Germans did not withdraw more than the three divisions, it can be assumed that Oakleaf achieved its object of creating a "nervousness" regarding Allied intentions and kept them firmly committed in Italy.[83]

As Oakleaf and Penknife were drawing to a close, the 15th Army Group was preparing for its final spring offensive. Working on the assumption that the Germans realized the Canadian forces had left, "A" Force replaced them with notional forces developed under the Wantage Order of Battle Plan. Accordingly, the bogus 14th Corps and 34th British Infantry Division were transferred to the command of 15th Army Group to bolster its appearance of strength.[84]

The 15th Army Group spent months training, reequipping, and preparing for the spring offensive. In Alexander's words, the "object was to destroy the enemy south of the Po. The method was first to envelop the enemy's left flank, drawing off thereby his reserves, and then to deliver a sudden blow at his centre."[85] The Fifth Army was opposed by the German Fourteenth Army, while the Eighth Army sat opposite the German Tenth Army. Interestingly, there was new leadership on both sides of the line. After Clark was named head of 15th Army Group, Gen. L. K. Truscott replaced him as commander of the Fifth Army. Leese left the Eighth Army for Burma in October 1944. He was replaced by General R. L. McCreery. On the German side, Hitler appointed Kesselring Oberbefehlshaber (commander in chief) West and transferred him to the western front in March, leaving Vietinghoff to step into his place as commander of Army Group C. D-day for the spring offensive was April 9.[86]

Unfortunately for "A" Force, it had very little time to develop and implement a deception plan. Plan Playmate was conceived on March 7, but at that time Penknife was still in operation. Playmate, therefore, was not put into action until the end of March, allowing it only a couple of weeks to reach and impact the enemy. Elkington later blamed the time limitations for its underwhelming achievements.[87]

There could be no doubt that the Germans anticipated an offensive in the spring, so the object of Playmate, like so many previous deception plans, was to mislead the enemy as to the exact time and location of the attack. According to the deception story, the Allies intended to wait until spring was more advanced so they would enjoy favorable weather conducive to air support.[88] In regard to location, the idea was to convince the Germans that the Allies had decided to bypass Bologna and instead launch their attack along the eastern coast of Italy. Playmate sought to achieve two specific goals within its objectives: (1) to make the enemy believe that the Eighth Army was going to lead the offensive in the east along Route 9, combined with an amphibious "hook attack" near Porto Garibaldi north of the Po; and (2) to convince him that the US II Corps was transferred to the Eighth Army sector to assist with that offensive. In reality, the US II Corps remained with the Fifth Army, which was the main strike force for the coming offensive. Truscott's plan was for the Fifth Army to attack just west of Route 64 and Bologna to isolate Bologna, as opposed to a direct engagement against its formidable defenses. The plan called for the Eighth Army to attack first in order to draw off Germany's reserves before the Fifth Army went on the offensive in the center.[89]

Since the Allies hoped to achieve surprise, they worked to conceal signs of offensive preparations. The Fifth Army was to utilize camouflage to hide its dumps and, in particular, prevent the enemy from observing the increase in artillery. Even though the deception story claimed that the attack would be spearheaded by the Eighth Army, the same order to utilize camouflage and concealment applied to the Eighth Army so the Germans would not suspect that the attack was imminent. Leave for soldiers continued as normal in both sectors.[90]

In the effort to convince the Germans that the US II Corps had transferred to the Eighth Army sector, the deception story held that "the fact that General McCreery successfully commanded US formations in the Spring of 1944 has decided him to place the US II Corps consisting of the 85 Div and 88 Div under command Eighth Army with a view to exploiting forward after the initial assault has gone in."[91] The two armies employed wireless schemes whereby the US II Corps practiced wireless silence in the Fifth Army sector and utilized phantom networks in the Eighth Army sector. A US Sonic Warfare Unit assisted by playing soundtracks to simulate the sounds of the US II Corps moving east. To provide additional evidence of the transfer, US reconnaissance parties were sent out to the Forli area, and US officers, representing the 85th and 88th Divisions, reconnoitered areas held by the Italian Gruppi.[92]

In spite of these efforts, the Germans did not seem to accept that the US II Corps was no longer with the Fifth Army. The main evidence for that is that the 90th Panzer Grenadier Division, minus two of its battalions, remained firmly rooted outside of Modena—even after the Eighth Army launched its attack in the east. The Allies had hoped to see it shift east prior to the Fifth Army's offensive. It is possible, however, that the division remained in place due to the presence of the 10th US Mountain Division in the Fifth Army sector. Elkington explained that a "factor which is possibly the reason for failure to draw the 90 PG into the battle prior to the Fifth Army attack, was the fact that the enemy was known to have been very nervous of the sector WEST of BOLOGNA ever since the attack by 10 US Mtn Div in Feb." Regardless, because the enemy did not act as the Allies wanted him to act, Clarke viewed that part of the deception as a failure.[93]

Playmate was most successful in creating the amphibious threat in the Eighth Army sector. The 101 RTR was called in to assist the Royal Navy and help to create the impression that Porto Corsini, on the Adriatic coast, was to be the embarkation port for the amphibious attack. The navy provided ships, including four LCTs, which were then equipped with dummy equipment, empty ammunition boxes, and Bofors guns. The guns were all pointed toward the bows and "made to resemble the turret of a light tank, with the barrel partly concealed. Hessian and canvas was used to conceal the hull positions." Three Sherman tanks arrived and were used to create life by their constant movement in and out of the port. The passengers were regularly rotated so it gave the appearance of a larger number of tanks. The 101 RTR erected dummy Sherman and Churchill tanks on the quay side—they arrived during the night of April 6–7. Every night the men moved the display of twenty-six tanks and forty-three vehicles around to simulate genuine activity.[94]

Major R. C. Gifford of 101 RTR viewed their efforts (referred to as Operation "Impact Eton") as successful. The original plan called for the LCTs to sail up the eastern Italian coast as a diversion, but that had to be canceled owing to the presence of German E-boats, or surface vessels. The E-boats, which were spotted on at least five nights during April, patrolled the waters between Ancona and Porto Corsini. German planes were spotted on eight different nights flying over the port, and on April 16 they sprayed the road leading from Ravenna to the port with machine-gun fire.[95] Moreover, prior to the offensive Vietinghoff transferred the 29th Panzer Grenadier Division to the Venice–Treviso region, north of the Po River. That was not only highly advantageous to the Allied armies, but also solid evidence that the Germans believed the amphibious threat to be genuine.[96]

In Clarke's assessment, the Germans were unsure of the exact time and location of the offensive, but they clearly knew it was coming. In matters completely beyond their control, "various high ranking officers made speeches announcing that an offensive was about to take place." Even though specifics were never revealed, it was enough to heighten the Germans' level of alert.[97]

While Plan Playmate met with only marginal success, the spring offensive was a resounding success. The prelude to the offensive began on April 5 with a diversionary attack in the west toward Spezia by the 92nd US Division (the "Buffalo Soldiers"). The Eighth Army opened the spring offensive with an artillery barrage from 1,500 guns on April 9. Five days later, in the early hours of April 14, the Fifth Army attacked. The armies were assisted by an impressive display of airpower—the greatest show of airpower seen in the entire Mediterranean conflict. As 825 heavy bombers dropped 175,000 bombs on enemy positions, 1,000 fighters and fighter-bombers targeted "gun sites, mortar positions and headquarters and also everything seen moving on roads approaching the battle area"—all before the Eighth Army infantry began to advance. The air forces then headed west to provide tactical air support for the Fifth Army's attack, which opened with a forty-minute aerial assault from 500 aircraft.[98] The Germans put up stiff resistance, but this time proved unable to withstand the combined weight of the Fifth and Eighth Armies and Allied airpower. On April 17, Hitler ordered Vietinghoff to stand firm and "defend every inch of the north Italian areas entrusted to your command."[99] In a move highly reminiscent of General Erwin Rommel at the Second Battle of El Alamein, Vietinghoff allowed his armies to retreat three days later. In yet another parallel, that delay proved costly. The Allies entered Bologna the very next day, on April 21. On April 22, the Fifth Army's 6th

South African Armoured Division and the Eighth Army's 6th British Armoured Division met at the Po, and on April 24 the Allies began crossing the river.[100]

Unable to sustain the defense, Army Group C surrendered on May 2, 1945. By that time Adolf Hitler was dead by his own hand and Kesselring, who was the longest-serving German commander in chief and highest-ranking military authority in the south, reluctantly permitted his former armies to surrender.[101] The war in Italy was over. Clarke noted that "it was a source of satisfaction to "A" Force, as an old-established section of the MEDITERRANEAN Forces, that it was the German Army in ITALY which was the first one to make its surrender."[102] On May 7, 1945, Germany signed an unconditional surrender, officially ending World War II in Europe.

EPILOGUE

Brigadier Dudley Clarke left Cairo to return home on April 23, 1945. The "A" Force records, amassed over a period of more than four years, were loaded on a ship and followed him home.[1] Clarke had served in Cairo since December 1940. What remained of "A" Force began to shut down after Army Group C's surrender. On May 2, Colonel Michael Crichton asked AFHQ to disband "A" Force. Crichton was eager to ensure that "A" Force was not conscripted into a "totally inappropriate role" after the war in Italy ended. He stated in a letter to Colonel Nöel Wild at Ops B on March 31, 1945: "I am going to make preliminary dispositions in order not to be caught up in post war occupational schemes and I will try to withdraw "A" Force intact to U.K. as soon as possible." True to his word, he made his request the very day the German armies surrendered.[2] Field Marshal Harold Alexander agreed to the request and made provisions for "A" Force to be disbanded and the men dispatched to England together at the end of May. On June 18, they paraded one last time before being dismissed by Clarke.[3] "A" Force was created to meet the special circumstances of World War II, not to be a permanent deception body. Once the war was over, so too was "A" Force.

On June 12, 1945, Clarke was appointed to the London Controlling Section's Historical Records of Deception section to write the history of "A" Force and produce a "top secret manual" on deception.[4] In 1947, after completing that task, he retired from the British Army. After that he joined the Conservative Central Office to found and run a public opinion research department. That work lasted until the Conservative Party was voted back into office in 1951. From there he took a job as director at a private security firm, Securicor, Ltd.[5]

For the most part, those who knew or worked with Clarke seemed to think highly of him. He was hardworking, good-humored, slow to anger, and not known to hold grudges. His friends recalled that he was a "mild mannered man, who never boasted of his achievements nor ever received the credit due to him for playing such an important part in the creation of the Commandos and his work in deception."[6] This observation raises an interesting point. While Clarke is known today for his exceptional command of "A" Force, and he was regarded as the foremost practitioner of deception by his peers during the war, most people, including those in the military, never knew who he was or what he did. Because deception was such secretive work, and Clarke took his responsibility seriously, he never advertised his accomplishments, even after the war.

Similarly, due to the secretive nature of his work, Clarke was not lavished with awards and national recognition like other military commanders were. The British government did bestow upon him the designations of Companion of the Order of Bath and Commander of the Order of the British Empire. The greatest official recognition, however, came from the United States. In 1944, President Franklin D. Roosevelt honored Clarke with the Legion of Merit Award, which reads:

> Brigadier Dudley W. Clarke, Royal Artillery, British Army. For exceptionally meritorious conduct in the performance of outstanding services during the period 15 September 1942 to 9 May 1944. During this period he planned and directed the execution of certain important strategic and technical aspects of the Allied operations during the landings in North Africa, the Tunisian campaign, the Sicilian campaign and the Italian campaign. By his outstanding intelligence, professional skill, energy and grasp of the many complex problems he has dealt with he has contributed in an unusual degree to the success of the Allied campaigns and to the welfare of the Allied personnel in the Mediterranean Theater.[7]

Roosevelt clearly could not divulge what those "certain important strategic and technical aspects of the Allied operations" were, nor could he expound upon the "complex problems" Clarke faced. Later Field Marshal Alexander paid Clarke and his "A" Force organization one of its highest compliments. He stated simply: "We would not have won our battles without it."[8]

Repeatedly throughout the war, Allied leaders—from field commanders, to theater commanders, all the way up to President Roosevelt and Prime Minister Churchill—acknowledged that Clarke's deceptions helped win battles and save lives. Clarke demonstrated that deception was an immensely powerful weapon that could achieve astounding results at the lowest cost. For all it accomplished and as important as it was to Allied victory in World War II, most of the Allied soldiers never had any idea that deception was being practiced all around them. Many even participated unknowingly—just consider all of the supplemental troop movements, training exercises on land and at sea, bombing of diversionary targets, land and air reconnaissance of cover locations, and so on. Yet, for deception to succeed, it had to be shrouded in a thick cloud of secrecy.

While the role of "A" Force was cloaked in secrecy and few knew much about it until the "A" Force files were declassified in the 1990s, Clarke had fully expected that "A" Force's secrets would come to light shortly after the war ended. In fact, he apparently hoped that they would. In the fall of 1944, when the Wantage Order of Battle Plan was being scaled down, Clarke wrote a letter to Colonel John Bevan at the LCS in which he expressed his desire that "as few restrictions as possible should be placed on Historians, either Allied or enemy, for it is important for the world to get a true picture of all aspects as far as this is practicable." What seemed to bother Clarke was that the British public held the Germans in such high esteem for their "bright ideas," yet regarded the British General Staff as "a collection of 'blimps.'" He said: "I have always thought it something of a tragedy that the man in the street has always regarded the German Intelligence as the best in the world."[9] Of course, Clarke had just spent years fooling the GIS, so he was acutely aware of Germany's intelligence shortcomings.

Clarke also relished the idea of making a movie based on "A" Force. He was an avid movie buff and acquired much of his inspiration from movies, so it is not at all surprising that he could envision "A" Force's exploits on the big screen. In a letter to a friend in 1957, Clarke wrote, "We have got a fine story to tell, and to tell in the grand manner, if and when the day ever comes when there might be good national value in the telling." What he feared, however, was Hollywood getting hold of that story. "Is it not," he asked, "rather a pity to whittle away bits of the story—piece by piece—in some irresponsible Yankee movie?"[10] Unfortunately for Clarke, he never was able to watch his story on the big screen, and his legacy has not produced that movie to date.

An important part of Clarke's legacy was his relationship with the Americans who worked with "A" Force, were incorporated directly into "A" Force, or were otherwise exposed to Britain's deception machinery. "A" Force was always a British organization at its core, and it retained its unique British character, yet many Americans worked under Clarke in "A" Force and learned the art of deception from its most skilled practitioner. American military leaders did not tend to view deception and cover the same as their British counterparts, nor did they immediately see its value or even have the structure to implement it. Colonel Newman Smith of Joint Security Control explained that "the plethora of resources available to the United States, and the stupendous task of mobilizing them, undoubtedly minimized the value of efforts diverted to the luxury of long-range strategic cover and deception. The natural consequence was to overlook or discount this weapon."[11] American general Jacob L. Devers compared the British and American systems and found that the United States lacked the structure to implement deception on the level the British did. He noted that in Britain deception was closely coordinated between the War Cabinet, most governmental departments, and the Foreign Office. The centralized foundation allowed the British to coordinate global deception and maintain its continuity throughout the process. He noted that the Americans had experience with tactical deception, but were "wholly ignorant" when it came to strategic cover plans. Devers concluded that "this method of developing a broad strategic plan of deception at the very highest level, following it down the subordinate channels to a very low tactical level, giving the whole pattern a common theme, and maintaining logical continuity therein throughout a war, is an art wholly unknown to our service at the outbreak of the war and is known to all too few now."[12]

US involvement in World War II exposed the Americans to both the British way of war and the use of both tactical and strategic deception. That exposure clearly made an impact. Gen. Dwight D. Eisenhower came to readily support the use of deception, and by the end of 1943 he recommended that due to the proven success of strategic deception throughout the war, "no major operation be undertaken without planning and executing appropriate deception measures."[13]

After the war, American commanders were asked to submit their opinions on deception to Maj. Gen. Clayton Bissell. The question at that time was whether the United States should develop an American deception organization. Those who served in the European and Mediterranean theaters saw how impactful deception was, and they overwhelming supported the idea. General Devers and Maj. Gen. Daniel Noce were enthusiastic supporters. Devers recommended it be organized along lines very similar to "A" Force, while Noce emphasized the overarching importance of security and suggested that deception should not be taught at the war colleges or General Staff School, and that the history of World War II deception should remain secret. General Patton also supported the creation of an American deception organization. Writing only two months before his untimely death, he stated: "I am of the opinion that without the effect of these strategic cover plans the landing in Normandy and the securing of the initial lodgment area would not have been accomplished without terrific losses which might have jeopardized the entire campaign."[14] For a proud man who was put in charge of a fake army prior to D-day, the First United States Army Group, that was a strong endorsement.

Organized British deception did more than just impact the war; it also influenced American military opinion. The Americans learned a great deal from Britain's creativity and its system of command and administration that permitted such flexibility—which General Noce credited to Britain's "European and Insular psychology."[15]

When all is said and done, Dudley Clarke's greatest legacy can be measured by the number of lives saved and the number of days the war was shortened. Of course, it is impossible to put an actual number to either. But every time deception gave the Allies the advantage, and that advantage translated into a swifter battle victory, lives were saved—on *both* sides of the line. And with each battle victory, the Allies were one step closer to securing Germany's surrender. It may have been days or weeks, or perhaps months to years, but deception definitely helped shorten the war by giving the Allies the advantage on the battlefield. And that was Clarke's overarching objective. He wanted to avoid a repeat of World War I, with its deadlocked offensives and horrific carnage. Just after World War II began, Clarke recorded in his diary: "Therein, in my mind, lies the one way of winning the war against Germany without the mass slaughter of 1914–18. And I feel more and more convinced each day that it *can* be won by subterranean methods so much better than by formal military ones, which must at least take a long time and a crippling number of lives."[16] This one statement reveals so much about Clarke: his desire was to save lives, to shorten the war, and to do so using unconventional means.

Clarke was not the only deceptionist with an aversion to the carnage of war. Less than two weeks before the 15th Army Group's spring offensive that ended the war in

Italy, Michael Crichton wrote a letter to Nöel Wild. He stated: "Would to God that the end comes before 15 Army Group launches it's [sic] offensive which to my way of thinking will entail a criminal loss of Allied lives for the doubtful glorification of a few high ranking generals. The whole idea of it makes me feel physically sick."[17]

Saving lives by way of brilliant, yet painstaking deception was ultimately Clarke's greatest accomplishment. It all occurred during his eighth wartime assignment, the one that he was never allowed to talk or write about. Regardless, it was the assignment he referred to as "infinitely the most gratifying assignment of them all."[18]

Dudley Clarke died on May 7, 1974, in virtual anonymity. Clarke had hoped to write the story of "A" Force himself. He titled his work *The Secret War*. Ironically, General Archibald Wavell had once remarked that "if he is ever able to tell the story of his work in the last five years of the war, the book will be, as Kipling once said of another story, well worth buying but even more worth suppressing."[19] The British government followed suit with the latter and denied its publication, citing the Official Secrets Act.

It has been my distinct honor to write Clarke's story, but it is only fitting to give him the last word:

> The Secret War of which these pages tell was a war of wits—of fantasy and imagination—fought out on an almost private basis between the supreme heads of Hitler's Intelligence (and Mussolini's) and a small band of men and women—British, American and French—operating from the opposite shores of the Mediterranean Sea. The author had the honour of leading that team through five crowded, urgent years—years which brought, moreover, a rare privilege to a professional soldier.
>
> For the secret war was waged rather to conserve than to destroy: the stakes were the lives of front-line troops, and the organisation which fought it was able to count its gains from the number of casualties it could avert. If this account of its strivings and achievements to that end should ever again help others to work for the same aim, however different may be the methods they devise—it will have served its purpose.
>
> *The Secret War*, First Outline Draft
> Dudley Clarke, July 18, 1953[20]

NOTES

INTRODUCTION

1. "Report by Major R. B. Booth on His Visit to Turkey Covering Period 12–21 June 1944" and Michael Crichton, letter dated June 15, 1944—both in Strategic Plans 1944 (Jan.–June), Plan "Zeppelin" (V), Plan "Turpitude," WO 169/24921, "A" Force Collection, National Archives, Kew, UK (hereafter cited as NA).

2. Historical Record of Deception in the War against Germany and Italy, CAB 154/101, 179, NA.

3. Ibid.

4. Dudley Clarke Papers, Box 99/2/1, Imperial War Museum, London, UK.

5. Hy Rothstein and Barton Whaley, eds., *The Art and Science of Military Deception* (Artech House, 2013), xix.

6. For information on the origins of British deception, see Whitney T. Bendeck, *"A" Force: The Origins of British Deception during the Second World War* (Annapolis, Md.: Naval Institute Press, 2013).

7. Winston Churchill, *Memoirs of the Second World War* (Boston: Houghton Mifflin, 1959), 295.

8. Prior to the formation of "A" Force, ISSB (Inter-Services Security Board) had carried out efforts in Europe to deceive the enemy through the development of strategic cover plans. Its purpose, organization, and responsibilities were rather limited in comparison to "A" Force.

9. Appendix "A"—"Some Notes on the Organization of Deception in the United States Forces" by Dudley Clarke, 40, in "Informal Memorandum on the Origin, Development and Activities of the Special (Deception) Section, Joint Security Control, 1942–1945," Joint Security Control.

10. Field Marshal The Earl Archibald P. Wavell, introduction to Dudley Clarke, *Seven Assignments* (London: Jonathan Cape, 1948), 7.

11. Ibid.

12. Appendix "A," 42–43. A copy of this letter can also be found in Theory and Practice of Deception, WO 169/24874, NA.

13. Ibid., 43.

14. Ibid., 43–44.

15. Ibid., 40, 45–47.

16. "A" Force, Narrative War Diary, Jan. 1–Dec. 31, 1944, WO 169/24850, 42, NA.

17. "A" Force, Narrative War Diary, Nov. 13, 1940–Dec. 31, 1941, WO 169/24847, 45, NA. I use the term Palestine throughout, although at that time it was officially known as the British Mandate of Palestine.

18. Middle East Channels in General, WO 169/24891, NA.

19. For the various letters written back and forth, see Miscellaneous Activities 1943–1944, WO 169/24878, NA.

20. David Strangeways Oral History, 16755/6, reel 4, Imperial War Museum, London, UK. Strangeways had specific praise for Col. Billy Harris and Lt. Col. Ralph Ingersoll.

21. "A" Force, Narrative War Diary, Nov. 13, 1940–Dec. 31, 1941, WO 169/24847, 92, NA.

22. Michael Howard, *British Intelligence in the Second World War*, vol. 5: *Strategic Deception* (London: HMSO, 1990), 152; June 14th Report, "A" Force, Narrative War Diary, Jan. 1–Dec. 31, 1944, WO 169/24850, 96–97, NA.

CHAPTER 1

1. Dudley Clarke Papers, Box 99/2/2.

2. David Mure, *Practise to Deceive* (London: William Kimber, 1977), 249.

3. Dudley Clarke Papers; Thaddeus Holt, *The Deceivers: Allied Military Deception in the Second World War* (New York: Scribner, 2004), 9–10.

4. Clarke, *Seven Assignments*, 187.

5. Wavell, introduction to Clarke, *Seven Assignments*, 7.

6. Clarke, *Seven Assignments*.

7. Ibid.

8. Dudley Clarke Papers, Box 99/2/1.

9. Clarke, *Seven Assignments*, 218–19.

10. Ibid., 220–21.

11. Ibid., 221–38.

12. Dudley Clarke Papers, Box 99/2/1.

13. Clarke, *Seven Assignments*, 262.

14. Papers Concerning the Theory and Practice of Deception in General, WO 169/24874 (hereafter cited as Theory and Practice of Deception).

15. Holt, *Deceivers*, 13–14.

16. Terry Crowdy, *Deceiving Hitler: Double Cross and Deception in World War II* (Oxford: Osprey, 2008), 142–43.

17. "A" Force was formed under the British army and was thus uniquely positioned to carry out both strategic and tactical deceptions. Other organizations (such as the London Controlling Section, ISSB, the Twenty Committee [XX], etc.) focused mainly on strategic efforts. Those bodies were often composed of representatives from the various services, but they were not under direct military authority. Some armies contained deception units, the British Eighth Army being an example, but those units only carried out tactical deceptions and did so as directed by the chief deception officer (in the Middle East and Mediterranean theaters, that was Dudley Clarke). They were not in a position to implement strategic measures. Thus "A" Force alone was tasked with organizing both strategic and tactical deception.

18. Appendix "A," 40.

19. Clarke's relationship with the commanding generals was rather unique. By contrast, Nöel Wild, the head of Ops B under SHAEF in London, never had that kind of access to the military leadership, nor input in the planning of operations.

20. Howard, *Strategic Deception*, 22.

21. Ibid.

22. F. H. Hinsley and C. A. G. Simkins, *British Intelligence in the Second World War*, vol. 4: *Security and Counter-Intelligence* (London: HMSO, 1990), 247.

23. Historical Record of Deception, CAB 154/100, 64, NA.

24. "A" Force's developed deception policy for the Middle East and Mediterranean remained in place until the London Controlling Section began providing centralized coordination of deception in 1942. As a point of clarity, either theater title—Middle East or Mediterranean—was used at given times in the war, and the theater commands often overlapped. The high degree of ambiguity forced Allied leaders to clarify the responsibility of the two theaters at the end of 1943. One way to distinguish is by the following: until May 1943, the land campaign fell under the direction of the Middle East theater, while naval operations fell under the Mediterranean. When the ground war expanded beyond North Africa to Sicily and the Italian Peninsula, the land campaign then largely fell under the Mediterranean theater. The Middle East theater continued to operate, but its focus was

primarily on the eastern Mediterranean, including the Balkans, and the land spanning from Egypt to Iran/Iraq in the east and Syria in the north.

25. For a comprehensive history of "A" Force, see Bendeck, *"A" Force.*

26. "A" Force, Narrative War Diary, Jan. 1–Dec. 31, 1942, WO 169/24848, 107, NA.

27. Howard, *Strategic Deception*, 22. Italy declared war on Britain in June 1940, effectively beginning the North African campaign. The use of the terms "Western Desert Campaign" or "desert war/campaign" refer to the battle for North Africa. Likewise, the desert campaign can be considered part of both the Middle East and Mediterranean theaters of operations. Finally, the use of the term "British forces" is understood to include both British and non-British colonial forces.

28. Clarke's extensive record of "A" Force's wartime activities, and especially his Papers Concerning the Theory and Practice of Deception in General, provide a thorough record of deception in modern warfare, as well as an authoritative manual for its practice.

29. "A" Force, Narrative War Diary, Nov. 13, 1940–Dec. 31, 1941, WO 169/24847, 7, NA.

30. Howard, *Strategic Deception*, 22.

31. Historical Record of Deception, CAB 154/100, 52.

32. Ibid.

33. Howard, *Strategic Deception*, 23.

34. Historical Record of Deception, CAB 154/100, 57–58.

35. In May 1942, a frustrated Stanley requested that he be released of his responsibilities so he could return to politics. The request was granted. For more information see Howard, *Strategic Deception*, 25.

36. Ibid., 25–27.

37. Historical Record of Deception, CAB 154/100, 49. The American counterpart to the London Controlling Section was Joint Security Control.

38. Theory and Practice of Deception, WO 169/24874.

39. "A" Force, Narrative War Diary, Jan. 1–Dec. 31, 1944, WO 169/24850, 10.

40. Historical Record of Deception, CAB 154/100, 1.

41. Ibid.

CHAPTER 2

1. Michael Howard, *Grand Strategy*, vol. 4: *August 1942–September 1943* (London: HMSO, 1972), 268.

2. Alexander's 18th Army Group headquarters consisted of the British First and Eighth Armies.

3. Feb. 9th Report, "A" Force, Narrative War Diary, Jan. 1–Dec. 31, 1943, WO 169/24849, NA.

4. Ibid. Since its formation, "A" Force was also responsible for coordinating escape and evasion—MI9 efforts—in the Middle East and Mediterranean as part of its cover. With the formation of a tactical headquarters, Strangeways had to coordinate both

deception (designated as "G" Section) and MI9 (designated as "N" Section) activities from Algiers. Two of the five officers allotted to Tactical HQ were assigned to MI9.

5. Feb. 25th Report, "A" Force, Narrative War Diary, Jan. 1–Dec. 31, 1943, WO 169/24849. The "triangle" was established in December 1942.

6. Goldbranson was part of Joint Security Control, though he did not head the organization itself. In 1942, he was appointed by Brigadier E. E. Mockler-Ferryman, a British intelligence officer, as the American "cover officer" and liaison with the London Controlling Section. For that reason, the "A" Force files identify him as the head of American deception. Goldbranson was one of four prominent American deceptionists. The others were Newman Smith, Bill Baumer, and Harold "Baron" Kelm. For more specific information on each individual, see Holt, *Deceivers*, 252–53.

7. "A" Force, Narrative War Diary, Jan. 1–Dec. 31, 1942, WO 169/24848, 126–27.

8. Ibid., 126.

9. Ibid., 127.

10. Feb. 25th Report, "A" Force, Narrative War Diary, Jan. 1–Dec. 31, 1943, WO 169/24849.

11. Ibid. See also "A" Force, Detailed War Diary (Controlling Headquarters), WO 169/24856, NA.

12. "A" Force, Strategic Plans 1943, Jan.–Mar., WO 169/24910, NA; Developments in Strategic Deception, WO 169/24871, NA.

13. Feb. 27th Report, "A" Force, Narrative War Diary, Jan. 1–Dec. 31, 1943, WO 169/24849.

14. The Germans joined their Italian ally in February 1941; the Americans joined the British with Operation Torch in November 1942.

15. For more information see David M. Glantz and Jonathan House, *The Stalingrad Trilogy* (Lawrence: University Press of Kansas); Antony Beevor, *Stalingrad: The Fateful Siege: 1942–1943* (New York: Penguin, 1998); William Craig, *Enemy at the Gates: The Battle for Stalingrad* (New York: Penguin, 1973).

16. Churchill, *Memoirs*, 683.

17. Michael J. Lyons, *World War II: A Short History*, 3rd ed. (Upper Saddle River, N.J.: Prentice Hall, 1999), 204–15. For more information on the Atlantic campaign, see Marc Milner, *Battle of the Atlantic* (Stroud, UK: Tempus, 2005); Andrew Williams, *Battle of the Atlantic: Hitler's Grey Wolves of the Sea and the Allies' Desperate Struggle to Defeat Them* (New York: Basic Books, 2003). For more information on the code-breaking work at Bletchley Park, to include the account of the capture of U-110, see Hugh Sebag-Montefiore, *Enigma: The Battle for Code* (London: Cassell Military Paperbacks, 2004).

18. Brigadier C. J. C. Molony, *The Mediterranean and Middle East*, vol. 5: *The Campaign in Sicily 1943 and the Campaign in Italy 3rd September 1943 to 31st March 1944* (London: HMSO, 1973), 1.

19. For more information on the battle for North Africa, see *The Mediterranean and Middle East*, vols. 1–4 (London: HMSO); Barrie Pitt, *The Crucible of War* series; Jon Latimer, *Alamein* (Cambridge, Mass.: Harvard University Press, 2002).

20. Churchill, *Memoirs*, 687.

21. Ibid.

22. See Howard, *Grand Strategy*, 226–27, for discussion of the various Allied military options in 1943.

23. Maurice Matloff, *Strategic Planning for Coalition Warfare, 1943–1944* (Washington, D.C.: Office of the Chief of Military History, Department of the Army, 1959), 18.

24. Anthony Eden, *The Reckoning: The Memoirs of Anthony Eden, Earl of Avon* (Boston: Houghton Mifflin, 1965), 319.

25. Howard, *Grand Strategy*, 207–8.

26. Ibid., 197.

27. In late 1942, British planners were not yet committed to a ground campaign against Italy.

28. Howard, *Grand Strategy*, 232; Churchill, *Memoirs*, 676. The strength of this plan was that it would force Germany to choose between Russia or the Balkans. If Germany reinforced the Balkans, it would have to be at the expense of the eastern front. Otherwise, Germany would have to abandon the Balkans. Either scenario worked to the Allies' advantage.

29. Howard, *Grand Strategy*, 198.

30. Ibid., 215.

31. Mark A. Stoler, *Allies and Adversaries: The Joint Chiefs of Staff, the Grand Alliance, and U.S. Strategy in World War II* (Chapel Hill: University of North Carolina Press, 2000), 100, 103.

32. Howard, *Grand Strategy*, 7.

33. Ibid., 111. The American concern surrounding Britain's imperial ambitions was based off of suspicions that the British had used the United States and manipulated its entry into World War I solely to preserve the floundering British Empire.

34. Stoler, *Allies and Adversaries*, 46, 68.

35. Ibid., 77.

36. Quoted in ibid., 88.

37. Ibid., 84–86.

38. Matloff, *Strategic Planning for Coalition Warfare*, 14, 15.

39. Howard, *Grand Strategy*, 219.

40. Ibid., 240. The Russians were not in attendance on account of the ongoing Battle of Stalingrad.

41. "Cover Plans for Operation Symbol," London Controlling Section, L.C.S. (43) & (44) Series, CAB 81/77, NA.

42. Ibid.

43. Howard, *Grand Strategy*, 241–42.

44. Ibid., 251, 254.

45. Ibid., 252, 253.

46. Ibid., 245.

47. Ibid., 252–54. See also Major-General I.S.O. Playfair and Brigadier C. J. C. Molony, *The Mediterranean and Middle East*, vol. 4: *The Destruction of the Axis Forces in Africa* (London: HMSO, 1966), 262.

48. Field Marshal Lord Alanbrooke, *War Diaries, 1939–1945*, ed. Alex Danchev and Daniel Todman (Berkeley: University of California Press, 2001), 364, January 20, 1943.

49. Howard, *Grand Strategy*, 266; Churchill, *Memoirs*, 668.

50. Playfair and Molony, *Mediterranean and Middle East*, 4:262–63.

51. Molony, *Mediterranean and Middle East*, 5:6.

52. Ian Gooderson, *A Hard Way to Make a War: The Italian Campaign in the Second World War* (London: Conway, 2008), 21.

53. Molony, *Mediterranean and Middle East*, 5:24.

54. Eden, *Reckoning*, 421. Eden also recounts that Churchill was furious with him for obstructing his "Turkish plans" and enlisting the support of the War Cabinet.

55. While most American leaders saw little value in pursuing Turkey, Roosevelt seemed supportive of Churchill's efforts with regard to Turkey.

56. Robin Denniston, *Churchill's Secret War: Diplomatic Decrypts, the Foreign Office and Turkey 1942–44* (Stroud, UK: Sutton, 1997), xii, 7.

57. Adana Conference, "A" Force, Strategic Plans 1943, Jan.–Mar., WO 169/24910, NA.

58. Churchill, *Memoirs*, 677–78.

59. Playfair and Molony, *Mediterranean and Middle East*, 4:267.

60. Ibid.

61. Frank G. Weber, *The Evasive Neutral: Germany, Britain and the Quest for a Turkish Alliance in the Second World War* (Columbia: University of Missouri Press, 1979), 165.

62. Selim Deringil, *Turkish Foreign Policy during the Second World War: An 'Active' Neutrality* (Cambridge: Cambridge University Press, 1989), 5.

63. "A" Force, Narrative War Diary, Jan. 1–Dec. 31, 1942, WO 169/24848, 124–25.

64. Jan. 15th Report, "A" Force, Narrative War Diary, Jan. 1–Dec. 31, 1943, WO 169/24849.

65. Defence Committee, Plan Withstand, "A" Force, Strategic Plans 1943, Jan.–Mar., WO 169/24910.

66. Jan. 15th Report, "A" Force, Narrative War Diary, Jan. 1–Dec. 31, 1943, WO 169/24849.

67. Second Draft for Plan "WITHSTAND." "A" Force, Strategic Plans 1943, Jan.–Mar., WO 169/24910.

68. Jan. 15th Report, "A" Force, Narrative War Diary, Jan. 1–Dec. 31, 1943, WO 169/24849.

69. Second Draft for Plan "WITHSTAND," "A" Force, Strategic Plans 1943, Jan.–Mar., WO 169/24910.

70. Ibid.

71. Ibid.

72. Jan. 15th Report, "A" Force, Narrative War Diary, Jan. 1–Dec. 31, 1943, WO 169/24849.

73. The story also provided British support for a Turkish attack on Bulgaria. The Turks regarded Bulgaria with much suspicion and insecurity, just as they did the Soviet Union.

74. "Warehouse (1943)" Plan (Second Draft), "A" Force, Strategic Plans 1943, Jan.–Mar., WO 169/24910.

75. March 1st Report, "A" Force, Narrative War Diary, Jan. 1–Dec. 31, 1943, WO 169/24849. See also "Cascade" Order of Battle Plan 1942–1943, WO 169/24926, NA.

76. "Warehouse (1943)" Plan (Second Draft), "A" Force, Strategic Plans 1943, Jan.–Mar., WO 169/24910.

77. March 1st Report, "A" Force, Narrative War Diary, Jan. 1–Dec. 31, 1943, WO 169/24849.

78. Jan. 15th Report, "A" Force, Narrative War Diary, Jan. 1–Dec. 31, 1943, WO 169/24849.

79. Theory and Practice of Deception , WO 169/24874.

CHAPTER 3

1. Quoted in Martin Blumenson, *Sicily: Whose Victory?* (New York: Ballantine, 1968), 17.

2. Ibid., 27.

3. As became standard practice, the London Controlling Section provided all high-ranking officials with credible cover stories to explain their absence from London, while concealing their departure from the country. For specific details on the cover plan for Trident, see "Plan 'Trident' Cover Plan," London Controlling Section, L.C.S. (43) & (44) Series, CAB 81/77.

4. Churchill, *Memoirs*, 688, 691.

5. Blumenson, *Sicily*, 19–20.

6. Molony, *Mediterranean and Middle East*, 5:7–8.

7. Blumenson, *Sicily*, 21. As an aside, the designation of 141 came from the room number at the St. George's Hotel in Algiers, where initial Allied planning for the invasion of Sicily took place.

8. Molony, *Mediterranean and Middle East*, 5:12–15. The port at Messina was not included in this plan, as the Allies knew it would be the most heavily defended and easiest to reinforce from the Italian Peninsula.

9. Quoted in Molony, *Mediterranean and Middle East*, 5:18. The exact date of the telegram is not specified.

10. Field Marshal the Viscount Montgomery of Alamein, *The Memoirs of Field-Marshal Montgomery of Alamein* (Cleveland: World Publishing, 1958), 158.

11. Gooderson, *Hard Way*, 47–56.

12. Blumenson, *Sicily*, 25.

13. For more information on the Dieppe Raid, see UK War Office, *The Dieppe Raid: The Combined Operations Assault on Hitler's European Fortress, August 1942: An Official History* (S. Yorkshire, UK: Frontline, 2019); Mark Zuehlke, *Tragedy at Dieppe: Operation Jubilee, August 19, 1942* (Vancouver: Douglas & McIntyre, 2013).

14. March 21st Report, "A" Force, Narrative War Diary, Jan. 1–Dec. 31, 1943, WO 169/24849.

15. Ibid.

16. Ibid.

17. Ibid.

18. "Plan 'Barclay' (Approved Version)," "A" Force, Strategic Plans 1943, Apr.–July—Plan Barclay (I), WO 169/24911, NA.

19. Ibid.

20. Ibid.

21. Quoted in ibid.

22. Ibid.

23. March 21st Report, "A" Force, Narrative War Diary, Jan. 1–Dec. 31, 1943, WO 169/24849.

24. March 28th Report, "A" Force, Narrative War Diary, Jan. 1–Dec. 31, 1943, WO 169/24849. The "40" Committee was established on March 28, 1943, and was chaired by Michael Crichton of "A" Force. An SIS officer and French officer were the other members.

25. "Recapitulation of Messages Put Over to the Enemy Under the Control of Advance H.Q. "A" Force to Aid Plan 'Barclay,'" "A" Force, Strategic Plans 1943, Apr.–July—Plan Barclay (I), WO 169/24911.

26. March 21st Report, "A" Force, Narrative War Diary, Jan. 1–Dec. 31, 1943, WO 169/24849. It is interesting that the Allies faced the exact difficulties in fighting the war in Italy that were outlined in the deception story as reasons provided for *not* invading Italy.

27. March 21st Report, "A" Force, Narrative War Diary, Jan. 1–Dec. 31, 1943, WO 169/24849; "Precis of Plan 'Barclay,'" London Controlling Section, L.C.S. (43) & (44) Series, CAB 81/77.

28. March 21st Report, "A" Force, Narrative War Diary, Jan. 1–Dec. 31, 1943, WO 169/24849.

29. Ibid. It should be noted that within the "A" Force, Narrative War Diary, there is a slight discrepancy with the dates. The discrepancy likely reflects a flexible timeline in terms of when the enemy intelligence was expected to receive word of the postponements and the "official" initiation of the subsequent stage.

30. Ibid.

31. Ibid.

32. Ibid.

33. Ibid. At each stage, "A" Force received confirmation of success from captured enemy documents, Ultra intercepts, and the news press. For a detailed list of intelligence reports, see ibid.

34. "Recapitulation of Messages Put Over to the Enemy Under the Control of Advance H.Q. "A" Force to Aid Plan 'Barclay,'" "A" Force, Strategic Plans 1943, Apr.–July—Plan Barclay (I), WO 169/24911.

35. March 21st Report, "A" Force, Narrative War Diary, Jan. 1–Dec. 31, 1943, WO 169/24849.

36. "Plan 'Barclay' (Approved Version)," L.C.S. (43) & (44) Series, CAB 81/77.

37. March 21st Report, "A" Force, Narrative War Diary, Jan. 1–Dec. 31, 1943, WO 169/24849. The file does not identify the specific press.

38. Ibid.

39. Ibid.

40. Ibid.

41. Ibid.

42. Western Desert Plans for 1942, WO 169/24906, NA. See also Bendeck, *"A" Force*, 181–82.

43. For more information on "A" Force's use of wireless deception, see Signals Deception, CAB 154/7, NA. This file is listed as No. 30 in the "A" Force War Diary collection, but it is located with the Cabinet files instead of in the War Office/"A" Force Collection.

44. "Plan 'Barclay' (Approved Version)," L.C.S. (43) & (44) Series, CAB 81/77.

45. March 21st Report, "A" Force, Narrative War Diary, Jan. 1–Dec. 31, 1943, WO 169/24849.

46. Ibid.

47. "CSO 15 Army Group Memorandum NO 84, Wireless Deception," Signals Deception, CAB 154/7.

48. March 21st Report, "A" Force, Narrative War Diary, Jan. 1–Dec. 31, 1943, WO 169/24849.

49. Progress Report on Plan "Barclay" As of Midnight June 6th 1943, "A" Force, Strategic Plans 1943, Apr.–July—Plan Barclay (I), WO 169/24911.

50. March 21st Report, "A" Force, Narrative War Diary, Jan. 1–Dec. 31, 1943, WO 169/24849.

51. Ibid.

52. "Cipher Message Out," "A" Force, Strategic Plans 1943, Apr.–July—Plan Barclay (II), WO 169/24912, NA.

53. March 21st Report, "A" Force, Narrative War Diary, Jan. 1–Dec. 31, 1943, WO 169/24849.

54. Ibid.

55. "Plan 'Barclay' (Approved Version)," L.C.S. (43) & (44) Series, CAB 81/77; March 21st Report, "A" Force, Narrative War Diary, Jan. 1–Dec. 31, 1943, WO 169/24849.

56. March 21st Report, "A" Force, Narrative War Diary, Jan. 1–Dec. 31, 1943, WO 169/24849.

57. Ibid.

58. Ibid.

59. "A" Force, Strategic Plans 1943, Apr.–July—Plan Barclay (II), WO 169/24912.

60. "Propaganda Plan," "A" Force, Strategic Plans 1943, Apr.–July—Plan Barclay (II), WO 169/24912.

61. "Plan 'Barclay' (Approved Version)," "A" Force, Strategic Plans 1943, Apr.–July—Plan Barclay (I), WO 169/24911.

62. March 21st Report, "A" Force, Narrative War Diary, Jan. 1–Dec. 31, 1943, WO 169/24849.

63. Ibid.

64. This deception is one of the most thoroughly covered in deception histories due to its bizarre and somewhat morbid nature. For published accounts of Operation Mincemeat, see Ewen Montagu, *The Man Who Never Was: World War II's Boldest Counterintelligence*

Operation (Annapolis, Md.: Naval Institute Press, 2001); Ben Macintyre, *Operation Mincemeat: How a Dead Man and a Bizarre Plan Fooled the Nazis and Assured an Allied Victory* (New York: Broadway Books 2011).

65. March 21st Report, "A" Force, Narrative War Diary, Jan. 1–Dec. 31, 1943, WO 169/24849.

66. Mincemeat: Report by Col. Montagu, 1, CAB 154/112, NA.

67. Macintyre, *Operation Mincemeat*, 14–15.

68. Mincemeat, 1, CAB 154/112.

69. Ibid.

70. Ibid., 6–8.

71. Ibid., 7–8.

72. Montagu, *Man Who Never Was*, 64–65.

73. Mincemeat, 2–3, CAB 154/112.

74. Ibid., 11. Montagu provides May 3 as the date the British were notified.

75. Mincemeat, 10–11, CAB 154/112.

76. Montagu, *Man Who Never Was*, 118.

77. Ibid., 17. While Montagu states that the subject died in late 1942, the Cabinet files list his date of death as January 28, 1943 (see CAB 154/112).

78. "Extract from Documents in Kriegstagebuch," Plan Mincemeat, CAB 154/67, NA.

79. Mincemeat, 12, 15–20, CAB 154/112.

80. "Extract from Documents in Kriegstagebuch," Plan Mincemeat, CAB 154/67.

81. March 21st Report, "A" Force, Narrative War Diary, Jan. 1–Dec. 31, 1943, WO 169/24849.

82. "Extract from Documents in Kriegstagebuch," Plan Mincemeat, CAB 154/67.

83. Montagu, *Man Who Never Was*, 142–43.

84. Dudley Clarke Papers, Box 99/2/1.

85. Ibid.

86. March 21st Report, "A" Force, Narrative War Diary, Jan. 1–Dec. 31, 1943, WO 169/24849.

87. Montagu, *Man Who Never Was*, 125–26.

88. March 21st Report, "A" Force, Narrative War Diary, Jan. 1–Dec. 31, 1943, WO 169/24849.

89. Ibid.

90. Ibid.

91. Ibid.

92. "Deception Operations in Cyrenaica," "A" Force, Strategic Plans 1943, Apr.–July, Plan Barclay (II), WO 169/24912.

93. March 21st Report, "A" Force, Narrative War Diary, Jan. 1–Dec. 31, 1943, WO 169/24849.

94. Ibid.

95. Ibid.

96. Ibid.

97. "Report on Display of Dummies," "A" Force, Strategic Plans 1943, Apr.–July, Plan Barclay (II), WO 169/24912.

98. March 21st Report, "A" Force, Narrative War Diary, Jan. 1–Dec. 31, 1943, WO 169/24849.

99. "Plan 'Derrick,'" Plans Conducted by Tac HQ "A" Force at General Alexander's Army Group HQs during 1943, WO 169/24908, NA.

100. March 21st Report, "A" Force, Narrative War Diary, Jan. 1–Dec. 31, 1943, WO 169/24849.

101. "Plan 'Derrick,'" Plans Conducted by Tac HQ "A" Force at General Alexander's Army Group HQs during 1943, WO 169/24908.

102. March 21st Report, "A" Force, Narrative War Diary, Jan. 1–Dec. 31, 1943, WO 169/24849. The Tac HQ files provide that all diversionary activities were planned for D+2 and into D+3, but the Narrative War Diary explains that the date was subsequently moved up by one day.

103. March 21st Report, "A" Force, Narrative War Diary, Jan. 1–Dec. 31, 1943, WO 169/24849.

104. Ibid.

105. For background on the Technical Unit, see "A" Force Technical Unit, WO 169/24869, NA.

106. March 21st Report, "A" Force, Narrative War Diary, Jan. 1–Dec. 31, 1943, WO 169/24849.

107. Ibid.

108. Ibid.

109. Montagu, *Man Who Never Was*, 143; emphasis in original.

110. March 21st Report, "A" Force, Narrative War Diary, Jan. 1–Dec. 31, 1943, WO 169/24849. The file does not provide any further information on the reinforcement of southern France.

111. Douglas Porch, *The Path to Victory: The Mediterranean Theater in World War II* (New York: Farrar, Straus, and Giroux, 2004), 423–24.

112. March 21st Report, "A" Force, Narrative War Diary, Jan. 1–Dec. 31, 1943, WO 169/24849.

113. Ibid.

114. Ibid.

CHAPTER 4

1. Robert M. Citino, *The Wehrmacht Retreats: Fighting a Lost War, 1943* (Lawrence: University Press of Kansas, 2012), 170; John Ellis, *Brute Force: Allied Strategy and Tactics in the Second World War* (New York: Viking, 1990), 308–9; Porch, *Path to Victory*, 423–24. The two Allied armies fell under the overall command of General Alexander's 15th Army Group.

2. Albrecht Kesselring, *The Memoirs of Field-Marshal Kesselring* (Novato, Calif.: Presidio, 1989), 161.

3. March 21st Report, "A" Force, Narrative War Diary, Jan. 1–Dec. 31, 1943, WO 169/24849.

4. Kesselring, *Memoirs*, 158, 161.

5. Field Marshal the Viscount Montgomery of Alamein, *El Alamein to the River Sangro* (London: Hutchinson, 1948), 79.

6. It is interesting to note that Guzzoni expected the Allies to land on the southeastern tip of the island. That view was not held by Kesselring, who positioned the 15th Panzer

Grenadier Division in the west and the Hermann Goering Division in the east, rendering neither capable of responding to the Allied landings. See Carlo D'Este, *Bitter Victory: The Battle for Sicily, July–August 1943* (London: William Collins, Sons, 1988), 208–9.

7. Porch, *Path to Victory*, 425; Gooderson, *Hard Way*, 78; 82–85. On a more ominous note, Allied airborne operations suffered many setbacks during the Sicily campaign. These ranged from scattered landings of airborne forces, friendly fire, and horrific casualties as glider pilots became disoriented in poor weather and crash-landed their craft in the sea. Gooderson points out that while the Crete campaign nearly resulted in the end of German airborne operations, future Allied operations nearly met the same fate as a result of Sicily.

8. Kesselring, *Memoirs*, 163.

9. D'Este, *Bitter Victory*, 321.

10. For more information on the ill-fated battle, see Martin Blumenson, *Kasserine Pass: Rommel's Bloody, Climactic Battle for Tunisia* (New York: Cooper Square, 2000).

11. D'Este, *Bitter Victory*, 323.

12. Quoted in Molony, *Mediterranean and Middle East*, 5:88–89.

13. Martin Blumenson, ed., *The Patton Papers, 1940–1945* (Boston: Houghton Mifflin, 1974), 325. Clearly unimpressed with Montgomery, Patton states that he could have taken Messina in ten days had it not been for Montgomery's interference.

14. D'Este, *Bitter Victory*, 322–29. The American forces that were positioned just off the Vizzini road made much quicker progress than the Eighth Army, using four-wheel-drive vehicles better suited to the terrain. It was a costly mistake to hand the northern thrust over to the Eighth Army (322).

15. Gooderson, *Hard Way*, 94.

16. Kesselring, *Memoirs*, 165.

17. Gooderson, *Hard Way*, 92–99.

18. Ibid., 100; Ellis, *Brute Force*, 318. Gooderson and Ellis report slightly different figures for the numbers of men and vehicles evacuated. Porch cites the numbers as 55,000 Germans, 70,000 Italians, 10,000 vehicles, 51 tanks, and 163 guns. See Porch, *Path to Victory*, 444.

19. Kesselring, *Memoirs*, 165.

20. Omar N. Bradley and Clay Blair, *A General's Life* (New York: Simon & Schuster, 1983), 186.

21. Gooderson, *Hard Way*, 160.

22. The plan, ultimately dubbed "Axis," called for the Germans to transfer seven divisions from the eastern front and six from France in order to defend Italy and, in the event of Italy's capitulation, to replace the Italian divisions at that time positioned in the Balkans. For more information see Gooderson, *Hard Way*, 153–59.

23. Gooderson, *Hard Way*, 151.

24. Molony, *Mediterranean and Middle East*, 5:67.

25. Historical Record of Deception, CAB 154/101, 168.

26. For background on this pattern, see Bendeck: *"A" Force.*

27. Dwight D. Eisenhower, *Crusade in Europe* (Baltimore: Johns Hopkins University Press, 1997), 168.

28. For more information on the Trident conference, see Howard, *Grand Strategy,* 4:409–57; and Matloff, *Strategic Planning for Coalition Warfare,* 126–45.

29. For full details of the Quadrant conference, to include decisions on the Pacific theater, see John Ehrman, *Grand Strategy,* vol. 5: *August 1943–September 1944* (London: HMSO, 1956), 1–15; and Matloff, *Strategic Planning for Coalition Warfare,* 211–43.

30. Ellis, *Brute Force,* 292.

31. Matloff, *Strategic Planning for Coalition Warfare,* 245–46; Eisenhower, *Crusade in Europe,* 187.

32. July 22nd Report, "A" Force, Narrative War Diary, Jan. 1–Dec. 31, 1943, WO 169/24849, NA.

33. Ibid.

34. Ibid. Clarke's concerns proved accurate. After the Italian surrender, the Germans did in fact evacuate Sardinia, as well as Corsica.

35. Ibid.; "Plan Boothby," Plans Conducted by Tac HQ "A" Force at General Alexander's Army Group HQs during 1943, WO 169/24908, NA.

36. July 22nd Report, "A" Force, Narrative War Diary, Jan. 1–Dec. 31, 1943, WO 169/24849; emphasis in original.

37. Ibid.

38. Ibid.

39. "Basic Leaflet Directive," Strategic Plans 1943, Aug.–Dec., WO 169/24913, NA.

40. July 22nd Report, "A" Force, Narrative War Diary, Jan. 1–Dec. 31, 1943, WO 169/24849.

41. Ibid.

42. Ibid. Sergeant-Major Silvestri's first name was not provided in the document.

43. "Plan Boothby, Part II," 1943 War Diary of Tac HQ "A" Force, WO 169/24853, NA. The III Corps was supposed to land on the heel while the remainder of the Twelfth Army was slated for the Balkans by way of the Peloponnese.

44. "Plan Boothby," Plans Conducted by Tac HQ "A" Force at General Alexander's Army Group HQs during 1943, WO 169/24908.

45. July 22nd Report, "A" Force, Narrative War Diary, Jan. 1–Dec. 31, 1943, WO 169/24849.

46. Ibid.

47. The "A" Force file does not identify the specific parachute division. Kesselring, however, puts the 1st Parachute Division in Apulia, or the southeastern region of Italy, on the day that the Salerno invasion began. See Kesselring, *Memoirs,* 182.

48. July 22nd Report, "A" Force, Narrative War Diary, Jan. 1–Dec. 31, 1943, WO 169/24849.

49. Jones had already renamed his dummy formations so the enemy would not realize that tank regiments with numbers over 100 were in fact dummy units. As such, the

101 and 102 RTRs were renamed 62 and 65 RTR, respectively. His headquarters was named the "24th Armoured Brigade." See August 25th Report, "A" Force, Narrative War Diary, Jan. 1–Dec. 31, 1943, WO 169/24849.

50. Sadly, Major Baxter died in a plane crash while assisting the Sicily invasion. He was overseeing the dropping of pintails, which was part of the tactical plan, Plan Derrick. His plane caught fire shortly after takeoff killing everyone on board.

51. Historical Record of Deception, CAB 154/100, 77.

52. August 25th Report, "A" Force, Narrative War Diary, Jan. 1–Dec. 31, 1943, WO 169/24849.

53. Kesselring, *Memoirs*, 165.

54. Gooderson, *Hard Way*, 153–60.

55. Citino, *Wehrmacht Retreats*, 244.

56. Gooderson, *Hard Way*, 160–62.

57. Eisenhower, *Crusade in Europe*, 183.

58. Citino, *Wehrmacht Retreats*, 246–47; Gooderson, *Hard Way*, 165–66, 179–83.

59. Eisenhower, *Crusade in Europe*, 185–86.

60. Kesselring, *Memoirs*, 184.

61. Gooderson, *Hard Way*, 186–87.

62. Kesselring, *Memoirs*, 183–84.

63. Appendix "D"—Letters from Senior U.S. Commanders, Mark Clark, in "Informal Memorandum on the Origin, Development and Activities of the Special (Deception) Section, Joint Security Control, 1942–1945," 101a, Joint Security Control.

64. Gooderson, *Hard Way*, 194.

65. Ibid., 191, 194–95, 201. Of note, the Salerno landing was the only large-scale opposed landing of the entire Italian campaign.

66. Citino, *Wehrmacht Retreats*, 265.

67. Dominik Graham and Shelford Bidwell, *Tug of War: The Battle for Italy, 1943–1945* (London: Hodder and Stoughton, 1986), 80; 89.

68. Gooderson, *Hard Way*, 215–16.

69. For more information on Operation Slapstick, see Citino, *Wehrmacht Retreats*, 249–52.

70. "Plan 'Carnegie,'" Plans Conducted by Tac HQ "A" Force at General Alexander's Army Group HQs during 1943, WO 169/24908.

71. Ibid.; August 9th Report, "A" Force, Narrative War Diary, Jan. 1–Dec. 31, 1943, WO 169/24849.

72. For detailed information on this channel, see "A" Force, Case History (V), "Gilbert" (Tunis, 1943–44), WO 169/24898, NA.

73. "Plan 'Carnegie,'" Plans Conducted by Tac HQ "A" Force at General Alexander's Army Group HQs during 1943, WO 169/24908.

74. August 9th Report, "A" Force, Narrative War Diary, Jan. 1–Dec. 31, 1943, WO 169/24849.

75. Gooderson, *Hard Way*, 213–17.

76. Citino, *Wehrmacht Retreats*, 265.

77. Kesselring, *Memoirs*, 183–84, 187.

78. Ibid., 187.

79. September 18th Report, "A" Force, Narrative War Diary, Jan. 1–Dec. 31, 1943, WO 169/24849.

80. The significance of Kos, Leros, Rhodes, and Samos should not be overlooked. Churchill never gave up hope of luring Turkey into the war. One of Turkey's conditions was that Kos, Leros, Rhodes, and Samos be in Allied hands. That would in effect clear the sea route between Istanbul and Smyrna. See Michael Woodbine Parish, *Aegean Adventures 1940–43 and the End of Churchill's Dream* (Sussex, UK: Book Guild, 1993), 194. For a more comprehensive study of the Aegean campaigns, see Peter C. Smith and Edwin R. Walker, *War in the Aegean: The Campaign for the Eastern Mediterranean in World War II* (Mechanicsburg, Pa: Stackpole, 2008).

81. For more information on Italy's contribution to the Allied war effort, see Charles T. O'Reilly, *Forgotten Battles: Italy's War of Liberation, 1943–1945* (Lanham, Md.: Lexington, 2001). After Italy declared war on Germany on October 13, 1943, Italy formed the Italian Co-Belligerent Army. It provided approximately 50,000 troops to assist the Allies. The Italian partisans, who also supported the Allied war effort, numbered close to 350,000.

82. September 18th Report, "A" Force, Narrative War Diary, Jan. 1–Dec. 31, 1943, WO 169/24849.

83. Ibid.

84. Ibid., "Plan Fairlands," Strategic Plans 1943, Aug.–Dec., WO 169/24913.

85. Ibid.

86. September 18th Report, "A" Force, Narrative War Diary, Jan. 1–Dec. 31, 1943, WO 169/24849.

87. "Informal Memorandum on the Origin, Development and Activities of the Special (Deception) Section, Joint Security Control, 1942–1945," 1–10, 11.

88. Ibid.,14.

89. The Seventh Army was effectively sidelined after Patton was censured for slapping two American soldiers.

90. September 18th Report, "A" Force, Narrative War Diary, Jan. 1–Dec. 31, 1943, WO 169/24849.

91. Historical Record of Deception, CAB 154/101, 34. Leros fell on November 16.

92. September 18th Report, "A" Force, Narrative War Diary, Jan. 1–Dec. 31, 1943, WO 169/24849.

93. Ibid.

94. Excepts found in "Plan Fairlands," Strategic Plans 1943, Aug.–Dec., WO 169/24913.

95. September 18th Report, "A" Force, Narrative War Diary, Jan. 1–Dec. 31, 1943, WO 169/24849.

96. For a detailed discussion of these battles, see Molony, *Mediterranean and Middle East*, 5:429–528.

97. Eisenhower, *Crusade in Europe*, 207. Interestingly, only weeks prior, President Roosevelt had planned to appoint General Marshall and recall Eisenhower to Washington.

98. Molony, *Mediterranean and Middle East*, 5:510. Molony provides an insightful assessment of Montgomery's leadership of the Eighth Army, including both his strengths and weaknesses (510–13).

99. Ibid., 371, 576.

100. December 19th Report, "A" Force, Narrative War Diary, Jan. 1–Dec. 31, 1943, WO 169/24849.

101. Historical Record of Deception, CAB 154/100, 75; December 19th Report, "A" Force, Narrative War Diary, Jan. 1–Dec. 31, 1943, WO 169/24849.

102. Clarke did play a crucial role in advising the London planners and contributing to the development of Plan Bodyguard, in addition to coordinating the Mediterranean diversions and deceptions tasked to "A" Force.

103. Noël Wild, foreword to David Mure, *Master of Deception: Tangled Webs in London and the Middle East* (London: William Kimber, 1980), 10.

104. December 19th Report, "A" Force, Narrative War Diary, Jan. 1–Dec. 31, 1943, WO 169/24849. Before transferring to London in the early part of 1944, Lieutenant-Colonel S. B. D. Hood temporarily replaced Strangeways as the head of Tac HQ in Italy.

105. Historical Record of Deception, CAB 154/100, 75.

106. "A" Force, Developments in Strategic Deception, WO 169/24871; Appendix "G," in "Informal Memorandum on the Origin, Development and Activities of the Special (Deception) Section, Joint Security Control, 1942–1945," Joint Security Control.

107. December 19th Report, "A" Force, Narrative War Diary, Jan. 1–Dec. 31, 1943, WO 169/24849.

108. Citino, *Wehrmacht Retreats*, 269. The line of defense became known as the Gustav Line.

109. Kesselring, *Memoirs*, 190–91.

CHAPTER 5

1. Although much of the decision making during Sextant focused on operations in the CBI and Pacific Theaters, those decisions fall outside the scope of this study. For a comprehensive review of the Cairo Conference and its discussions pertaining to the war against Japan, see Ehrman, *Grand Strategy*, 5:570–84.

2. Matthew Jones, *Britain, the United States and the Mediterranean War, 1942–44* (London: Macmillan, 1996), 101, 105.

3. In *The Mediterranean Strategy in the Second World War* (New York: Frederick A. Praeger, 1968), Michael Howard makes an intriguing argument that the British would have been better off pursuing operations in the Aegean and Balkans as the focal point of the

Mediterranean Strategy from the beginning, as opposed to launching the campaign in Italy. He argues that the war in Italy became a war of attrition that hurt the Allies just as much as it did the Germans, while an Aegean/Balkans campaign would have posed a more direct threat to Germany's flank in southern Russia and proved more taxing on German resources, at less cost to the Allies. Churchill recognized the strategic advantage of exploiting German vulnerabilities in the eastern Mediterranean. However, by the end of 1943, he was in the minority in calling for an expansion of the war to the east. Howard points out that the prime minister did not see such a campaign as an alternative to Italy, but wanted to carry out both. That simply was no longer within the realm of possibility, especially given the need to prioritize resources, particularly landing craft, for Overlord (50–51, 70).

4. Matloff, *Strategic Planning for Coalition Warfare*, 353–54.

5. Ehrman, *Grand Strategy*, 5:155–83; Matloff, *Strategic Planning for Coalition Warfare*, 358–66; Historical Record of Deception, CAB 154/101, 34–36.

6. Ehrman, *Grand Strategy*, 5:173.

7. Historical Record of Deception, CAB 154/101, 8.

8. Molony, *Mediterranean and Middle East*, 5:510, 572–74.

9. Historical Record of Deception, CAB 154/101, 35.

10. Ibid., 98.

11. Jones, *Britain, the United States*, 103, 107.

12. Ibid., 104–5; Howard, *Mediterranean Strategy*, 49.

13. An example of this complexity can be found in the objective to capture Rhodes. After Italy surrendered, the British hoped to gain control over Rhodes, and that responsibility fell to the all-British Middle East Command. Middle East Command made plans to capture Rhodes, but AFHQ controlled the resources and could not spare them for a further campaign in the Aegean. Thus, Middle East Command was hamstrung and had no ability to see its objectives to fruition.

14. Jones, *Britain, the United States*, 97–98, 106–10.

15. Lieutenant-General Sir Frederick Morgan, *Overture to Overlord* (Garden City, N.Y.: Doubleday, 1950), 6–7.

16. Dwight D. Eisenhower, foreword to Morgan, *Overture to Overlord*, vi.

17. Morgan, *Overture to Overlord*, x.

18. "Informal Memorandum on the Origin, Development and Activities of the Special (Deception) Section, Joint Security Control, 1942–1945," 14–15.

19. Historical Record of Deception, CAB 154/101, 35–36.

20. Historical Record of Deception, CAB 154/100, 75.

21. Ibid., 73; Historical Record of Deception, CAB 154/101, 56.

22. Historical Record of Deception, CAB 154/101, 39.

23. Churchill, *Memoirs*, 767.

24. Historical Record of Deception, CAB 154/101, 37.

25. The transfer of Erwin Rommel in 1943 from Italy to western France to attend to the construction of the Atlantic Wall clearly indicates that the Germans anticipated an Allied attack in that region.

26. Historical Record of Deception, CAB 154/101, 3–4.

27. Ibid., 4.

28. Ibid., 55, 49.

29. Roger Hesketh, *Fortitude: The D-Day Deception Campaign* (Woodstock, N.Y.: Overlook Press, 2000), 8–9, 168. Interestingly, David Strangeways read the initial draft of Fortitude South and then rewrote it. He stated that the people who wrote the plan had no actual experience with deception and had made it too complicated. Based on his three years of experience implementing deception under "A" Force, he revised the plan, and Montgomery approved it. See David Strangeways Oral History, 16755/6, reel 4.

30. Historical Record of Deception, CAB 154/101, 7.

31. Ibid., 46, 49–53.

32. Ibid., 46–48.

33. Ibid., 48–49, 52; Crowdy, *Deceiving Hitler*, 290.

34. The sources do not confirm if the deceptive information from Royal Flush was, in fact, passed on the Germans.

35. Historical Record of Deception, CAB 154/101, 70.

36. January 1st Report, "A" Force, Narrative War Diary, Jan. 1–Dec. 31, 1944, WO 169/24850, 1.

37. The original plan was to remove seven divisions, but in the end eight left the Mediterranean. They were, in chronological order, the 1st American Infantry Division and 50th British Infantry Division (October), the British 51st and 1st Airborne Divisions along with the American 2nd Armored and 9th Infantry Divisions (November), and lastly the British 7th Armoured Division and American 82nd Airborne (December). See "A" Force, Narrative War Diary, Jan. 1–Dec. 31, 1944, WO 169/24850, 1.

38. Plan "Foynes," Strategic Plans 1943, Aug.–Dec., WO 169/24913; "Plan Foynes," London Controlling Section, L.C.S. (43) & (44) Series, CAB 81/77; "Implementation Sheet, Plan Foynes," Cover and Deception Policy, December 1943 to March 1945, WO 219/2246, NA.

39. "Implementation of Plan 'Oakfield' by Agents," Implementation by Most Secret Intelligence Methods in General, WO 169/24884, NA.

40. Case History (V) "Gilbert" (Tunis, 1943–44), WO 169/24898, double punctuation in original.

41. January 1st Report, "A" Force, Narrative War Diary, Jan. 1–Dec. 31, 1944, WO 169/24850, 1–2.

42. Ibid., 4.

43. Plan "Foynes," Strategic Plans 1943, Aug.–Dec., WO 169/24913; "Plan Foynes," London Controlling Section, L.C.S. (43) & (44) Series, CAB 81/77.

44. January 1st Report, "A" Force, Narrative War Diary, Jan. 1–Dec. 31, 1944, WO 169/24850, 4–5.

45. "Plan 'Oakfield' (Approved Version)," London Controlling Section, L.C.S. (43) & (44) Series, CAB 81/77.

46. "Plan 'Oakfield,'" 7–8, Strategic Plans 1943, Aug.–Dec., WO 169/24913.

47. "Implementation of Plan 'Oakfield' by Agents," Implementation by Most Secret Intelligence Methods in General, WO 169/24884.

48. January 4th Report, "A" Force, Narrative War Diary, Jan. 1–Dec. 31, 1944, WO 169/24850, 6.

49. Ibid., 8.

50. Ibid., 7; Gooderson, *Hard Way*, 253.

51. Kesselring, *Memoirs*, 191–93.

52. Gooderson, *Hard Way*, 251–71.

53. January 4th Report, "A" Force, Narrative War Diary, Jan. 1–Dec. 31, 1944, WO 169/24850, 8; "Plan 'Oakfield,'" 7, Strategic Plans 1943, Aug.–Dec., WO 169/24913.

54. "Plan 'Oakfield,'" 7, Strategic Plans 1943, Aug.–Dec., WO 169/24913; "Outline Plan 'Dundee," Strategic Plans 1943, Aug.–Dec., WO 169/24913.

55. January 4th Report, "A" Force, Narrative War Diary, Jan. 1–Dec. 31, 1944, WO 169/24850, 9–10.

56. Ibid., 9; "Plan 'Oakfield,'" 6, Strategic Plans 1943, Aug.–Dec., WO 169/24913.

57. January 4th Report, "A" Force, Narrative War Diary, Jan. 1–Dec. 31, 1944, WO 169/24850, 10.

58. "Implementation of Plan 'Oakfield' by Agents," Implementation by Most Secret Intelligence Methods in General, WO 169/24884.

59. "Plan 'Oakfield' (Approved Version)," London Controlling Section, L.C.S. (43) & (44) Series, CAB 81/77.

60. Ibid.; January 4th Report, "A" Force, Narrative War Diary, Jan. 1–Dec. 31, 1944, WO 169/24850, 12.

61. "Implementation of Plan 'Oakfield' by Agents," Implementation by Most Secret Intelligence Methods in General, WO 169/24884.

62. January 4th Report, "A" Force, Narrative War Diary, Jan. 1–Dec. 31, 1944, WO 169/24850, 11.

63. "Implementation of Plan 'Oakfield' by Agents," Implementation by Most Secret Intelligence Methods in General, WO 169/24884.

64. "Plan 'Chettyford,'" Plans Conducted by Tac HQ "A" Force for General Alexander's Allied Armies in Italy during 1944, WO 169/24914.

65. January 4th Report, "A" Force, Narrative War Diary, Jan. 1–Dec. 31, 1944, WO 169/24850, 11–12.

66. "Plan 'Oakfield,'" 12, Strategic Plans 1943, Aug.–Dec., WO 169/24913; "Plan 'Oakfield' (Approved Version)," London Controlling Section, L.C.S. (43) & (44) Series, CAB 81/77.

67. January 4th and 22nd Reports, "A" Force, Narrative War Diary, Jan. 1–Dec. 31, 1944, WO 169/24850, 13, 19–21.

68. Ibid., 20–21.

69. "Chapter IX, Signal Deception," Signals Deception, CAB 154/7.

70. David Strangeways Oral History, 16755/6, reel 4; italics added to represent vocal emphasis.

71. January 22nd Report, "A" Force, Narrative War Diary, Jan. 1–Dec. 31, 1944, WO 169/24850, 20; "Plan 'Chettyford,'" Plans Conducted by Tac HQ "A" Force for General Alexander's Allied Armies in Italy during 1944, WO 169/24914.

72. "Plan 'Chettyford,'" Plans Conducted by Tac HQ "A" Force for General Alexander's Allied Armies in Italy during 1944, WO 169/24914.

73. Ibid.

74. Gooderson, *Hard Way*, 262–63, 268; Martin Blumenson, *Anzio: The Gamble That Failed* (Philadelphia: J. B. Lippincott, 1963), 75–76.

75. Quoted in Blumenson, *Anzio*, 74.

76. "Anzio," Developments in Strategic Deception, WO 169/24871.

77. January 4th Report, "A" Force, Narrative War Diary, Jan. 1–Dec. 31, 1944, WO 169/24850, 14–15.

78. January 22nd Report, "A" Force, Narrative War Diary, Jan. 1–Dec. 31, 1944, WO 169/24850, 21–23.

79. Blumenson, *Anzio*, 84.

80. Gooderson, *Hard Way*, 268–70.

81. Kesselring, *Memoirs*, 194.

82. January 22nd Report, "A" Force, Narrative War Diary, Jan. 1–Dec. 31, 1944, WO 169/24850, 22.

83. "Plan 'Clairvale,'" Plans Conducted by Tac HQ "A" Force for General Alexander's Allied Armies in Italy during 1944, WO 169/24914.

84. Theory and Practice of Deception , WO 169/24874.

85. "Implementation of Plan 'Oakfield' by Agents," Implementation by Most Secret Intelligence Methods in General, WO 169/24884. Gilbert, like Garbo—the well-known double agent who played such an important role in the leadup to and aftermath of D-day—had agents under his authority, although Gilbert's were real while Garbo's were a figment of his imagination. Gilbert credited most of the information on Termoli to his agent Le Duc.

86. January 22nd Report, "A" Force, Narrative War Diary, Jan. 1–Dec. 31, 1944, WO 169/24850, 22–23; "Plan 'Clairvale,'" Plans Conducted by Tac HQ "A" Force for General Alexander's Allied Armies in Italy during 1944, WO 169/24914.

87. January 22nd Report, "A" Force, Narrative War Diary, Jan. 1–Dec. 31, 1944, WO 169/24850, 23.

88. January 4th Report, "A" Force, Narrative War Diary, Jan. 1–Dec. 31, 1944, WO 169/24850, 15.

89. Robert M. Citino, for example, refers to Shingle as "one of the most controversial Allied operations of the war." See Citino, *Wehrmacht Retreats*, 278. See also John S. D. Eisenhower, *They Fought at Anzio* (Columbia: University of Missouri Press, 2007).

90. Peter Verney, *Anzio 1944: An Unexpected Fury* (London: B. T. Batsford, 1978), 247.

91. Blumenson, *Anzio*, 85–92; Gooderson, *Hard Way*, 270–73.

92. Alan F. Wilt, *The Atlantic Wall: Hitler's Defenses in the West, 1941–1944* (Ames: Iowa State University Press, 1975), 3 (quotation), 103–7.

CHAPTER 6

Epigraph: February 4th Report, "A" Force, Narrative War Diary, Jan. 1–Dec. 31, 1944, WO 169/24850, 29.

1. Strategic Plans 1944 (Jan.–June), Plan "Zeppelin" (II), WO 169/24916, NA.

2. February 4th Report, "A" Force, Narrative War Diary, Jan. 1–Dec. 31, 1944, WO 169/24850, 29–30. The "A" Force, Narrative War Diary provides the date as January 21, but the London Controlling Section lists it as January 19 (see Historical Record of Deception, CAB 154/101, 37).

3. "Plan 'Bodyguard,'" Strategic Plans 1944 (Jan.–June), Plan "Zeppelin" (I), WO 169/24915, NA.

4. Ibid. The Allied armies were named Central Mediterranean Forces in January 1944, then became the Allied Armies in Italy (AAI) in March.

5. An additional limiting factor regarding landing craft in the European theater of operations was the extensive need for landing craft in the Pacific Theater. The American island-hopping campaign against the Japanese was carried out by way of amphibious landings, thus American deployment of landing craft had to be methodically divided between the two theaters.

6. February 4th Report, "A" Force, Narrative War Diary, Jan. 1–Dec. 31, 1944, WO 169/24850, 30–31.

7. "Plan 'Zeppelin,' Fourth Approved Version," Strategic Plans 1944 (Jan.–June), Plan "Zeppelin" (I), WO 169/24915.

8. February 4th Report, "A" Force, Narrative War Diary, Jan. 1–Dec. 31, 1944, WO 169/24850, 31; Historical Record of Deception, CAB 154/101, 37.

9. "Explanatory Note," Strategic Plans 1944 (Jan.–June), Plan "Zeppelin" (I), WO 169/24915.

10. February 4th Report and March 10th Report, "A" Force, Narrative War Diary, Jan. 1–Dec. 31, 1944, WO 169/24850, 30, 46–47.

11. February 4th Report, "A" Force, Narrative War Diary, Jan. 1–Dec. 31, 1944, WO 169/24850, 31.

12. Ibid., 32.

13. "Plan 'Zeppelin,' Fourth Approved Version," Strategic Plans 1944 (Jan.–June), Plan "Zeppelin" (I), WO 169/24915.

14. February 4th Report, "A" Force, Narrative War Diary, Jan. 1–Dec. 31, 1944, WO 169/24850, 33.

15. Ibid.

16. Strategic Plans 1944 (Jan.–June), Plan "Zeppelin" (II), WO 169/24916.

17. Ibid.

18. Ibid.

19. Ibid. The order simply states "For action by C-in-C Med." It is unclear if it was referring to General Wilson, the commander-in-chief of the Mediterranean Theater, or, more likely, to Admiral John Cunningham, commander-in-chief of the Mediterranean Fleet.

20. Strategic Plans 1944 (Jan.–June), Plan "Zeppelin" (II), WO 169/24916.

21. Ibid.

22. February 4th Report, "A" Force, Narrative War Diary, Jan. 1–Dec. 31, 1944, WO 169/24850, 32–35.

23. For more information on the Cascade Order of Battle deception efforts, see "Cascade" Order of Battle Plan 1942–1943, WO 169/24926.

24. See The Wantage Order of Battle Plan 1944–1945, WO 169/24927, NA.

25. February 6th Report, "A" Force, Narrative War Diary, Jan. 1–Dec. 31, 1944, WO 169/24850, 32.

26. Of the forty-four divisions, ten were American and eleven French. Of those in Italy specifically, seven were American and two French. For more-specific unit designations, see "'Wantage' Order of Battle Plan," The Wantage Order of Battle Plan 1944–1945, WO 169/24927.

27. February 6th Report, "A" Force, Narrative War Diary, Jan. 1–Dec. 31, 1944, WO 169/24850, 38–39.

28. The Twelfth Army had five real and seven notional divisions, while the US Seventh Army had nine real and three bogus, adding up to a total of twenty-four. With reference to the garrison forces, those amounted to seven real and eight notional divisions.

29. "'Wantage' Order of Battle Plan," The Wantage Order of Battle Plan 1944–1945, WO 169/24927; February 6th Report, "A" Force, Narrative War Diary, Jan. 1–Dec. 31, 1944, WO 169/24850, 39–40. This was Operation Dragoon, formerly code-named Operation Anvil.

30. The Wantage Order of Battle Plan 1944–1945, WO 169/24927.

31. For a comprehensive list of communications between the Germans and "A" Force agents, see "Implementation of the Wantage Plan by Secret Intelligence Methods," The Wantage Order of Battle Plan 1944–1945, WO 169/24927.

32. "Displays of Plan Zeppelin Implemented in the Eastern Mediterranean Over the Period Feb 44 to May 44," Zeppelin, WO 169/24918, NA. For more information on orders given to the army, navy, and air commands, see In Cyrenaica, Strategic Plans 1944 (Jan.–June), Plan "Zeppelin" (III), WO 169/24917, NA.

33. Historical Record of Deception, CAB 154/101, 82.

34. Ibid., 82–83.

35. Ibid., 83; "Part I: Preliminaries," Special Landing Craft (Nov. 1943–Aug. 1944), WO 169/24920, NA.

36. Historical Record of Deception, CAB 154/101, 82.

37. "Plan 'Zeppelin"—Progress Report NO. 1," Michael Crichton letter to Clarke dated 24th February, and George Train letter to Clarke dated 20th March—all in Strategic Plans 1944 (Jan.–June), Plan "Zeppelin" (II), WO 169/24916.

38. Michael Crichton letter to Clarke dated 24th February, Strategic Plans 1944 (Jan.–June), WO 169/24916.

39. Appendix E—Note on Reactions to Zeppelin, Strategic Plans 1944 (Jan.–June), Plan "Zeppelin" (II), WO 169/24916.

40. March 10th Report, "A" Force, Narrative War Diary, Jan. 1–Dec. 31, 1944, WO 169/24850, 43, 45.

41. Ibid., 43.

42. Ibid., 44; Historical Record of Deception, CAB 154/101, 78–79; "Notes on Operation 'Vendetta,'" Strategic Plans 1944 (Jan.–June), Plan "Zeppelin" (VI), Plan "Vendetta," WO 169/24922, NA.

43. "Plan 'Zeppelin,' Fourth Approved Version" Strategic Plans 1944 (Jan.–June), Plan "Zeppelin" (I), WO 169/24915.

44. "Stage 2 Plan Zeppelin," Strategic Plans 1944 (Jan.–June), Plan "Zeppelin" (II), WO 169/24916; "Part I: Preliminaries," Special Landing Craft (Nov. 1943–Aug. 1944), WO 169/24920.

45. "Stage 2 Plan Zeppelin," Strategic Plans 1944 (Jan.–June), Plan "Zeppelin" (II), WO 169/24916; Historical Record of Deception, CAB 154/101, 79.

46. "Stage 2 Plan Zeppelin," Strategic Plans 1944 (Jan.–June), Plan "Zeppelin" (II), WO 169/24916.

47. Ibid.

48. "Plan 'Zeppelin,' Fourth Approved Version," Strategic Plans 1944 (Jan.–June), Plan "Zeppelin" (I), WO 169/24915.

49. "Plan 'Dungloe,'" Strategic Plans 1944 (Jan.–June), Plan "Zeppelin" (VII), Plans "Royal Flush," "Dungloe," and "Copperhead," WO 169/24923, NA; emphasis in original.

50. March 10th Report, "A" Force, Narrative War Diary, Jan. 1–Dec. 31, 1944, WO 169/24850, 48–49.

51. Historical Record of Deception, CAB 154/101, 83.

52. April 14th Report, "A" Force, Narrative War Diary, Jan. 1–Dec. 31, 1944, WO 169/24850, 60.

53. "Displays of Plan Zeppelin Implemented in the Eastern Mediterranean over the Period Feb. 44 to May 44," Zeppelin, WO 169/24918.

54. Ibid.

55. Special Landing Craft (Nov. 1943–Aug. 1944), WO 169/24920.

56. March 10th Report, "A" Force, Narrative War Diary, Jan. 1–Dec. 31, 1944, WO 169/24850, 46–47.

57. Ibid., 46; "Plan 'Zeppelin,' Fourth Approved Version," Strategic Plans 1944 (Jan.–June), Plan "Zeppelin" (I), WO 169/24915.

58. March 10th Report, "A" Force, Narrative War Diary, Jan. 1–Dec. 31, 1944, WO 169/24850, 46.

59. Ibid., 46–47.

60. "Plan 'Northways,'" Plans Conducted by Tac HQ "A" Force for General Alexander's Allied Armies in Italy during 1944, WO 169/24914; "Plan 'Northways,'" 1944 War Diary of Tac HQ 'A' Force, WO 169/24857, NA; Historical Record of Deception, CAB 154/101, 111. It is unclear whether Northways had an impact on the enemy or not. After Alexander's mid-March assault against Cassino, the deceptionists assumed that the enemy was aware of the presence of Eighth Army formations in what had been the Fifth Army's sector.

CHAPTER 7

1. April 14th Report, "A" Force, Narrative War Diary, Jan. 1–Dec. 31, 1944, WO 169/24850, 57, 60.

2. May 10th Report, "A" Force, Narrative War Diary, Jan. 1–Dec. 31, 1944, WO 169/24850, 63–64.

3. Ibid., 64.

4. Ibid., 66.

5. Ibid.

6. Ibid., 66–67.

7. Report by the Supreme Allied Commander Mediterranean to the Combined Chiefs of Staff, *Greece 1944–1945* (London: HMSO, 1949), 6. The EAM was a party comprised of the communists and five socialist groups at odds with the Greek government in Cairo.

8. "Plan 'Zeppelin' (Fourth Approved Version)," Strategic Plans 1944 (Jan.–June), Plan "Zeppelin" (VII), Plans "Royal Flush," "Dungloe," and "Copperhead," WO 169/24923.

9. Ibid.

10. "Notes on Operation Vendetta," Strategic Plans 1944 (Jan.–June), Plan "Zeppelin" (VI), Plan "Vendetta," WO 169/24922.

11. May 10th Report, "A" Force, Narrative War Diary, Jan. 1–Dec. 31, 1944, WO 169/24850, 75.

12. Ibid., 71–72.

13. Historical Record on Deception, CAB 154/101, 181.

14. May 10th Report, "A" Force, Narrative War Diary, Jan. 1–Dec. 31, 1944, WO 169/24850, 71–73, 75; "Allied Force Headquarters, G-3 Section, Plans," Strategic Plans 1944 (Jan.–June), Plan "Zeppelin" (VI), Plan "Vendetta," WO 169/24922. The plan was slightly modified after May 10 and was approved in final form on May 25.

15. May 10th Report, "A" Force, Narrative War Diary, Jan. 1–Dec. 31, 1944, WO 169/24850, 73.

16. "Implementation of Plan Zeppelin by Agents," Strategic Plans 1944 (Jan.–June), Plan "Zeppelin" (VI), Plan "Vendetta," WO 169/24922.

17. May 10th Report, "A" Force, Narrative War Diary, Jan. 1–Dec. 31, 1944, WO 169/24850, 73–74.

18. Ibid., 74.

19. Ibid., 74–75.

20. Ibid., 76; "Report on Displays of Bigbobs at Bone, May and June—1944," Strategic Plans 1944 (Jan.–June), Plan "Zeppelin" (VI), Plan "Vendetta," WO 169/24922.

21. "Outline Plan "X,"" Strategic Plans 1944 (Jan.–June), Plan "Zeppelin" (VI), Plan "Vendetta," WO 169/24922; "Plan 'Zeppelin' (Fourth Approved Version)," Strategic Plans 1944 (Jan.–June), Plan "Zeppelin" (VII), Plans "Royal Flush," "Dungloe," and "Copperhead," WO 169/24923.

22. May 10th Report, "A" Force, Narrative War Diary, Jan. 1–Dec. 31, 1944, WO 169/24850, 76.

23. "Implementation of Plan Zeppelin by Agents," Strategic Plans 1944 (Jan.–June), Plan "Zeppelin" (VI), Plan "Vendetta," WO 169/24922.

24. May 10th Report, "A" Force, Narrative War Diary, Jan. 1–Dec. 31, 1944, WO 169/24850, 77. On May 28, General Wilson had requested French assistance from General Charles de Gaulle. Clarke noted that the "French response was excellent" (77).

25. Ibid., 69–70, 74; "Plan 'Royal Flush,'" Strategic Plans 1944 (Jan.–June), Plan "Zeppelin" (VII), Plans "Royal Flush," "Dungloe," and "Copperhead," WO 169/24923.

26. May 10th Report, "A" Force, Narrative War Diary, Jan. 1–Dec. 31, 1944, WO 169/24850, 78.

27. Ibid., 78–79.

28. Ibid., 79–80.

29. "Cipher Message In.," Strategic Plans 1944 (Jan.–June), Plan "Zeppelin" (VI), Plan "Vendetta," WO 169/24922.

30. May 10th Report, "A" Force, Narrative War Diary, Jan. 1–Dec. 31, 1944, WO 169/24850, 77–78.

31. Ibid., 86.

32. Ibid., 85; "Copperhead"—Major Harry Gummer Correspondence, Strategic Plans 1944 (Jan.–June), Plan "Zeppelin" (VII), Plans "Royal Flush," "Dungloe," and "Copperhead," WO 169/24923.

33. May 10th Report, "A" Force, Narrative War Diary, Jan. 1–Dec. 31, 1944, WO 169/24850, 85–86; "Copperhead"—Noël Wild Correspondence, Strategic Plans 1944 (Jan.–June), Plan "Zeppelin" (VII), Plans "Royal Flush," "Dungloe," and "Copperhead," "Plan WO 169/24923.

34. May 10th Report, "A" Force, Narrative War Diary, Jan. 1–Dec. 31, 1944, WO 169/24850, 87.

35. Ibid., 86; "Plan "Copperhead"—Noël Wild Correspondence, Strategic Plans 1944 (Jan.–June), Plan "Zeppelin" (VII), Plans "Royal Flush," "Dungloe," and "Copperhead," WO 169/24923.

36. May 10th Report, "A" Force, Narrative War Diary, Jan. 1–Dec. 31, 1944, WO 169/24850, 87–89; "Plan 'Copperhead,'" Strategic Plans 1944 (Jan.–June), Plan "Zeppelin" (VII), Plans "Royal Flush," "Dungloe," and "Copperhead," WO 169/24923.

37. May 10th Report, "A" Force, Narrative War Diary, Jan. 1–Dec. 31, 1944, WO 169/24850, 85–87; "Plan 'Telescope,'" Strategic Plans 1944 (Jan.–June), Plan "Zeppelin" (VII), Plans "Royal Flush," "Dungloe," and "Copperhead," WO 169/24923.

38. May 10th Report, "A" Force, Narrative War Diary, Jan. 1–Dec. 31, 1944, WO 169/24850, 85–87; Major Gummer Correspondence, Strategic Plans 1944 (Jan.–June), Plan "Zeppelin" (VII), Plans "Royal Flush," "Dungloe," and "Copperhead," WO 169/24923.

39. May 10th Report, "A" Force, Narrative War Diary, Jan. 1–Dec. 31, 1944, WO 169/24850, 89–90; "Implementation of Plan 'Zeppelin' by Agents," Implementation by Most Secret Intelligence Methods in General, WO 169/24884.

40. "Implementation of Plan 'Zeppelin' by Agents," Implementation by Most Secret Intelligence Methods in General, WO 169/24884.

41. Hesketh, Fortitude, 124.

42. Because Plan Turpitude focused on the eastern Mediterranean, it was carried out by the British alone.

43. May 10th Report, "A" Force, Narrative War Diary, Jan. 1–Dec. 31, 1944, WO 169/24850, 80–81; "Plan 'Turpitude'—the Plan Itself," Strategic Plans 1944 (Jan.–June), Plan "Zeppelin" (V), WO 169/24921.

44. Ibid.

45. "Report on Plan Turpitude," Strategic Plans 1944 (Jan.–June), Plan "Zeppelin" (V), WO 169/24921.

46. For more information on Mure's involvement with "A" Force and Plan Turpitude, see Mure, Practise to Deceive.

47. "Report on Plan 'Turpitude' and "Plan 'Turpitude'—the Plan Itself," Strategic Plans 1944 (Jan.–June), Plan "Zeppelin" (V), WO 169/24921; May 10th Report, "A" Force, Narrative War Diary, Jan. 1–Dec. 31, 1944, WO 169/24850, 82.

48. May 10th Report, "A" Force, Narrative War Diary, Jan. 1–Dec. 31, 1944, WO 169/24850, 82; "Plan 'Turpitude'—the Plan Itself," Strategic Plans 1944 (Jan.–June), Plan "Zeppelin" (V), WO 169/24921.

49. "Plan 'Turpitude'—Papers Representing the Implementation of the Plan," Strategic Plans 1944 (Jan.–June), Plan "Zeppelin" (V), WO 169/24921.

50. May 10th Report, "A" Force, Narrative War Diary, Jan. 1–Dec. 31, 1944, WO 169/24850, 82.

51. Ibid.; "Plan 'Turpitude'—Papers Representing the Implementation of the Plan," Strategic Plans 1944 (Jan.–June), Plan "Zeppelin" (V), WO 169/24921.

52. "Plan 'Turpitude'—Papers Representing the Implementation of the Plan" and "Plan 'Turpitude'—the Plan Itself," Strategic Plans 1944 (Jan.–June), Plan "Zeppelin" (V), WO 169/24921.

53. "Plan 'Turpitude'—the Plan Itself," Strategic Plans 1944 (Jan.–June), Plan "Zeppelin" (V), WO 169/24921; May 10th Report, "A" Force, Narrative War Diary, Jan. 1–Dec. 31, 1944, WO 169/24850, 82–83.

54. Ibid. As it turned out, this operation was the last for Colonel Jones; his dummy armored forces were disbanded after Plan Turpitude. Jones had been at work in the Middle East Theater since 1941. With his last task completed, Jones returned to Britain in July 1944.

55. "Plan 'Turpitude'—the Plan Itself," Strategic Plans 1944 (Jan.–June), Plan "Zeppelin" (V), WO 169/24921; May 10th Report, "A" Force, Narrative War Diary, Jan. 1–Dec. 31, 1944, WO 169/24850, 83.

56. "Plan "Turpitude"—Papers Representing the Implementation of the Plan," Strategic Plans 1944 (Jan.–June), Plan "Zeppelin" (V), WO 169/24921.

57. "Plan 'Turpitude'—the Plan Itself," "Report by Major R. B. Booth on His Visit to Turkey Covering Period 12–21 June 1944," and Michael Crichton, letter dated June 15, 1944—all in Strategic Plans 1944 (Jan.–June), Plan "Zeppelin" (V), WO 169/24921. See full discussion of the Booth affair in the Introduction.

58. "Plan "Turpitude"—Papers Representing the Implementation of the Plan," Strategic Plans 1944 (Jan.–June), Plan "Zeppelin" (V), WO 169/24921.

59. Ibid.

60. May 10th Report, "A" Force, Narrative War Diary, Jan. 1–Dec. 31, 1944, WO 169/24850, 84.

61. "Plan "Turpitude"—Papers Representing the Implementation of the Plan," Strategic Plans 1944 (Jan.–June), Plan "Zeppelin" (V), WO 169/24921.

62. June 14th Report, "A" Force, Narrative War Diary, Jan. 1–Dec. 31, 1944, WO 169/24850, 96.

63. Ibid., 96–97.

64. April 10th Report, "A" Force, Narrative War Diary, Jan. 1–Dec. 31, 1944, WO 169/24850, 50.

65. Ibid.; "Plan 'Nunton,'" Plans Conducted by Tac HQ "A" Force for General Alexander's Allied Armies in Italy during 1944, WO 169/24914.

66. G. A. Shepperd, *The Italian Campaign, 1943–45: A Political and Military Reassessment* (New York: Frederick A. Praeger, 1968), 248–50; Kesselring, *Memoirs*, 197–99.

67. Kesselring, *Memoirs*, 198.

68. April 10th Report, "A" Force, Narrative War Diary, Jan. 1–Dec. 31, 1944, WO 169/24850, 51.

69. Ibid., 50–51. The official files refer to Hood alternatingly as both lieutenant-colonel and colonel without either explanation for the discrepancy or information regarding a promotion.

70. Ibid., 50.

71. Ibid., 51.

72. Ibid., 51–52.

73. Ibid., 52.

74. Ibid.; "Plan 'Nunton,'" Plans Conducted by Tac HQ "A" Force for General Alexander's Allied Armies in Italy during 1944, WO 169/24914.

75. "Implementation of Plan 'Zeppelin' by Agents," Implementation by Most Secret Intelligence Methods in General, WO 169/24884.

76. Ibid. The date of the German message was not specified in the report.

77. "Plan 'Nunton,'" Plans Conducted by Tac HQ "A" Force for General Alexander's Allied Armies in Italy during 1944, WO 169/24914. G. A. Shepperd added that the Allies set up vertical screens to prevent German observation from the monastery and placed camouflage netting in the trees above the roads to similarly conceal movement. The "A" Force files do not explicitly cite these measures but do reference camouflage efforts and the need to prevent dust clouds from rising above the camouflaging along the roads, which would be consistent with the information provided by Shepperd. See Shepperd, *Italian Campaign*, 252.

78. Shepperd, *Italian Campaign*, 254–55.

79. Ibid., 257–59; April 10th Report, "A" Force, Narrative War Diary, Jan. 1–Dec. 31, 1944, WO 169/24850, 52.

80. Kesselring, *Memoirs*, 200.

81. Ibid., 200–202.

82. Ibid., 202–3.

83. April 10th Report, "A" Force, Narrative War Diary, Jan. 1–Dec. 31, 1944, WO 169/24850, 53.

84. Ibid.

85. Appendix "D," 101a.

86. April 10th Report, "A" Force, Narrative War Diary, Jan. 1–Dec. 31, 1944, WO 169/24850, 53–54.

87. "Allied Security and Enemy Intelligence," The Wantage Order of Battle Plan 1944–1945, WO 169/24927.

88. April 10th Report, "A" Force, Narrative War Diary, Jan. 1–Dec. 31, 1944, WO 169/24850, 53–54.

89. Ibid.

90. It deserves mention that resistance efforts in the Balkans played a role in occupying the Germans' attention as well, although the Historical Record of Deception referred to the "partisan menace" in Greece as "negligible" and the partisan effort in Yugoslavia as "not beyond the capacity of the security troops originally assigned to the task." Historical Record of Deception, CAB 154/101, 177. In fact, the Germans utilized their police and SS forces to deal with the partisans, not the regular army. On the one hand, the partisans, whom the Germans referred to as terrorists and guerrilla fighters, proved to be a nuisance and sometimes a legitimate challenge, but they did not represent a realistic threat to Germany itself. Allied landings, on the other hand, presented a very real danger to Germany. Thus, it can be inferred that Germany's significant reinforcement of the Balkans was based on its fear of Allied landings as opposed to concern over the partisans (see Bernhard Kroener, Rolf-Dieter Müller, and Hans Umbreit, *Germany and the Second World War*, vol. 5: *Organization and Mobilization in the German Sphere of Power*, pt. 2: *Wartime Administration. Economy, and Manpower Resources 1942–1944/5* (Oxford: Oxford University Press, 2003), 168–98. In any event, the threat of landings *and* the partisan effort were both consistently exaggerated through strategic deception efforts. For more information on the partisan effort in Yugoslavia and SOE operations there, see Heather Williams, *Parachutes, Patriots, and Partisans: The Special Operations Executive and Yugoslavia, 1941–1945* (Madison: University of Wisconsin Press, 2003); and David Stafford, *Britain and European Resistance, 1940–1945: A Survey of the Special Operations Executive, with Documents* (London: Macmillan, 1980).

91. June 14th Report, "A" Force, Narrative War Diary, Jan. 1–Dec. 31, 1944, WO 169/24850, 94–95.

92. Ibid., 96.

93. The AAI was previously known as the Central Mediterranean Forces.

94. June 14th Report, "A" Force, Narrative War Diary, Jan. 1–Dec. 31, 1944, WO 169/24850, 55; June 12th Report, "A" Force, Narrative War Diary, Jan. 1–Dec. 31, 1944, WO 169/24850, 91–92; June 16th Report, "A" Force, Narrative War Diary, Jan. 1–Dec. 31, 1944, WO 169/24850, 103.

95. June 14th Report, "A" Force, Narrative War Diary, Jan. 1–Dec. 31, 1944, WO 169/24850, 94.

CHAPTER 8

1. "Ferdinand," Strategic Plans 1944 (July–Dec.), WO 169/24924, NA.

2. July 7th Report, "A" Force, Narrative War Diary, Jan. 1–Dec. 31, 1944, WO 169/24850, 110.

3. "Ferdinand," Strategic Plans 1944 (July–Dec.), WO 169/24924; July 7th Report, "A" Force, Narrative War Diary, Jan. 1–Dec. 31, 1944, WO 169/24850, 109–11. The deception story also called for General Eisenhower to launch an attack against the Biscay coast, but that proved to be impossible and was later abandoned (112).

4. "Ferdinand," Strategic Plans 1944 (July–Dec.), WO 169/24924.

5. Ibid.; "Plan 'Ottrington,'" Plans Conducted by Tac HQ "A" Force for General Alexander's Allied Armies in Italy during 1944, WO 169/24914.

6. July 7th Report, "A" Force, Narrative War Diary, Jan. 1–Dec. 31, 1944, WO 169/24850, 111–12.

7. Ibid., 113.

8. Ibid., 109, 112.

9. "Ferdinand," Strategic Plans 1944 (July–Dec.), WO 169/24924.

10. July 7th Report, "A" Force, Narrative War Diary, Jan. 1–Dec. 31, 1944, WO 169/24850, 115.

11. "Ferdinand," Strategic Plans 1944 (July–Dec.), "Supreme Allied Commander's Conference," WO 169/24924.

12. Ibid.; July 7th Report, "A" Force, Narrative War Diary, Jan. 1–Dec. 31, 1944, WO 169/24850, 116–17.

13. July 7th Report, "A" Force, Narrative War Diary, Jan. 1–Dec. 31, 1944, WO 169/24850, 116.

14. Ibid., 114.

15. Ibid.

16. Ibid.

17. July 20th Report, "A" Force, Narrative War Diary, Jan. 1–Dec. 31, 1944, WO 169/24850, 121–23.

18. June 16th Report, "A" Force, Narrative War Diary, Jan. 1–Dec. 31, 1944, WO 169/24850, 103–5.

19. Ibid., 104; "Ferdinand," Strategic Plans 1944 (July–Dec.), WO 169/24924; "History of the case ADDICT," Case Histories (VII), Channels in Italy, WO 169/24901, NA.

20. June 16th Report, "A" Force, Narrative War Diary, Jan. 1–Dec. 31, 1944, WO 169/24850, 104–5.

21. July 7th Report, "A" Force, Narrative War Diary, Jan. 1–Dec. 31, 1944, WO 169/24850, 118.

22. Field-Marshal Lord Wilson of Libya, *Eight Years Overseas, 1939–1947* (London: Hutchinson, 1950), 222.

23. July 7th Report, "A" Force, Narrative War Diary, Jan. 1–Dec. 31, 1944, WO 169/24850, 117.

24. "Ferdinand," Strategic Plans 1944 (July–Dec.), WO 169/24924.

25. July 7th Report, "A" Force, Narrative War Diary, Jan. 1–Dec. 31, 1944, WO 169/24850, 118.

26. "Ferdinand," Strategic Plans 1944 (July–Dec.), WO 169/24924.

27. Ibid.; Lyons, *World War II*, 260–61; For more information on the role of the French Resistance in connection to Operation Dragoon, see Arthur Layton Funk, *Hidden Ally: The French Resistance, Special Operations, and the Landings in Southern France, 1944* (New York: Greenwood Press, 1992); M. R. D. Foot, *SOE in France: An Account of the Work of the British Special Operations Executive in France, 1940–1944* (New York: Routledge, 2013). For more information on Operation Dragoon, see William B. Breuer, *Operation Dragoon: The Allied Invasion of the South of France* (Novato, Calif.: Presidio Press, 1987); Robin Cross, *Operation Dragoon: The Allied Liberation of the South of France: 1944* (New York: Pegasus, 2019); Andrew Stewart, ed., *Operation Dragoon: The Invasion of the South of France, 15 August 1944*, Naval Staff Histories of the Second World War (Solihull, UK: Helion, 2015).

28. July 7th Report, "A" Force, Narrative War Diary, Jan. 1–Dec. 31, 1944, WO 169/24850, 119.

29. Gooderson, *Hard Way*, 284–87.

30. Ibid., 281–88.

31. Ibid., 289–90.

32. June 16th Report, "A" Force, Narrative War Diary, Jan. 1–Dec. 31, 1944, WO 169/24850, 105.

33. Ibid., 106.

34. Ibid., 105–6.

35. "Plan 'Ulster,'" Plans Conducted by Tac HQ "A" Force for General Alexander's Allied Armies in Italy during 1944, WO 169/24914.

36. "Ferdinand," Strategic Plans 1944 (July–Dec.), WO 169/24924.

37. "Plan 'Ulster,'" Plans Conducted by Tac HQ "A" Force for General Alexander's Allied Armies in Italy during 1944, WO 169/24914.

38. June 16th Report, "A" Force, Narrative War Diary, Jan. 1–Dec. 31, 1944, WO 169/24850, 106–7.

39. Ibid., 107.

40. Gooderson, *Hard Way*, 291–92.

41. June 16th Report, "A" Force, Narrative War Diary, Jan. 1–Dec. 31, 1944, WO 169/24850, 108.

42. July 7th Report, "A" Force, Narrative War Diary, Jan. 1–Dec. 31, 1944, WO 169/24850, 118–19; Oct. 15th Report, "A" Force, Narrative War Diary, Jan. 1–Dec. 31, 1944, WO 169/24850, 132.

43. "Plan 'Undercut,'" Strategic Plans 1944 (July–Dec.), WO 169/24924.

44. Sept. 8th Report, "A" Force, Narrative War Diary, Jan. 1–Dec. 31, 1944, WO 169/24850, 128.

45. Report by the Supreme Allied Commander Mediterranean to the Combined Chiefs of Staff, *Greece 1944–1945*, 7.

46. Sept. 8th Report, "A" Force, Narrative War Diary, Jan. 1–Dec. 31, 1944, WO 169/24850, 128.

47. Ibid.

48. "Plan 'Undercut,'" Strategic Plans 1944 (July–Dec.), WO 169/24924.

49. Sept. 8th Report, "A" Force, Narrative War Diary, Jan. 1–Dec. 31, 1944, WO 169/24850, 129.

50. Ibid. For more information on Plan Camilla and the lessons learned, see Plan "CAMILLA," WO 169/24903, NA; and Bendeck, *"A" Force*, 65–70.

51. Sept. 8th Report, "A" Force, Narrative War Diary, Jan. 1–Dec. 31, 1944, WO 169/24850, 130.

52. "Plan 'Second Undercut,'" Strategic Plans 1944 (July–Dec.), WO 169/24924.

53. Ibid.; Sept. 8th Report, "A" Force, Narrative War Diary, Jan. 1–Dec. 31, 1944, WO 169/24850, 131.

54. Oct. 15th Report, "A" Force, Narrative War Diary, Jan. 1–Dec. 31, 1944, WO 169/24850, 132.

55. Ibid., 132–33.

56. Gooderson, *Hard Way*, 292.

57. Oct. 16th Report, "A" Force, Narrative War Diary, Jan. 1–Dec. 31, 1944, WO 169/24850, 135.

58. Ibid.; Dec. 9th Report, "A" Force, Narrative War Diary, Jan. 1–Dec. 31, 1944, WO 169/24850, 139.

59. Dec. 9th Report, "A" Force, Narrative War Diary, Jan. 1–Dec. 31, 1944, WO 169/24850, 139.

60. Report by the Supreme Allied Commander Mediterranean, Field-Marshal the Viscount Alexander of Tunis, to the Combined Chiefs of Staff on the Italian Campaign, 12th December 1944 to 2nd May 1945 (London: HMSO, 1951), 24–25. (Hereafter cited as Report by SACMed).

61. Jan. 8th Report, "A" Force, Narrative War Diary, Jan. 1–July 18, 1945, WO 169/24851, 8.

62. "Third (Modified) Edition of the 'Wantage' Order of Battle Plan," The Wantage Order of Battle Plan 1944–1945, WO 169/24927.

63. Ibid.

64. Jan. 8th Report, "A" Force, Narrative War Diary, Jan. 1–July 18, 1945, WO 169/24851, 9.

65. Ibid.; "Plan 'Oakleaf,'" Plans—1945, WO 169/24928, NA.

66. "Plan 'Oakleaf,'" Plans—1945, WO 169/24928.

67. Jan. 8th Report, "A" Force, Narrative War Diary, Jan. 1–July 18, 1945, WO 169/24851, 9.

68. Ibid., 12–13.

69. Ibid., 13.

70. "Plan 'Penknife,'" Plans—1945, WO 169/24928.

71. Ibid.

72. Jan. 1st Report, "A" Force, Narrative War Diary, Jan. 1–July 18, 1945, WO 169/24851, 5.

73. "Plan 'Penknife,'" Plans—1945, WO 169/24928.

74. Ibid.; 1945 Papers, WO 169/24858, NA.

75. "Plan 'Penknife,'" Plans—1945, WO 169/24928.

76. Ibid.

77. Feb. 3rd Report, "A" Force, Narrative War Diary, Jan. 1–July 18, 1945, WO 169/24851, 5.

78. "Plan 'Penknife,'" Plans—1945, WO 169/24928.

79. Ibid.

80. Ibid.; Feb. 3rd Report, "A" Force, Narrative War Diary, Jan. 1–July 18, 1945, WO 169/24851, 15.

81. Feb. 3rd Report, "A" Force, Narrative War Diary, Jan. 1–July 18, 1945, WO 169/24851, 16; "Plan 'Penknife,'" Plans—1945, WO 169/24928.

82. "Plan 'Penknife,'" Plans—1945, WO 169/24928.

83. "Plan 'Oakleaf,'" Plans—1945, WO 169/24928.

84. Feb. 3rd Report, "A" Force, Narrative War Diary, Jan. 1–July 18, 1945, WO 169/24851, 16.

85. Report by SACMed, 34.

86. Ibid., 39; Gooderson, *Hard Way*, 292–94. Vietinghoff at that time was serving in Latvia but was recalled to Italy. He arrived on March 23.

87. "Plan 'Playmate,'" Plans—1945, WO 169/24928.

88. 1945 Papers, WO 169/24858.

89. March 21st Report, "A" Force, Narrative War Diary, Jan. 1–July 18, 1945, WO 169/24851, 17; "Plan 'Playmate,'" Plans—1945, WO 169/24928; Shepperd, *Italian Campaign*, 346–47.

90. "Plan 'Playmate,'" Plans—1945, WO 169/24928.

91. 1945 Papers, WO 169/24858; "Plan 'Playmate,'" Plans—1945, WO 169/24928.

92. Ibid.

93. "Plan 'Playmate,'" Plans—1945, WO 169/24928; March 21st Report, "A" Force, Narrative War Diary, Jan. 1–July 18, 1945, WO 169/24851, 19.

94. "Plan 'Playmate'" and "Report on Operation 'Impact Eton'"—both in Plans—1945, WO 169/24928.

95. Ibid.

96. March 21st Report, "A" Force, Narrative War Diary, Jan. 1–July 18, 1945, WO 169/24851, 19; Shepperd, *Italian Campaign*, 348.

97. March 31st Report, "A" Force, Narrative War Diary, Jan. 1–July 18, 1945, WO 169/24851, 18.

98. Report by SACMed, 41–43.

99. Quoted in Shepperd, *Italian Campaign*, 362.

100. Gooderson, *Hard Way*, 295; Shepperd, *Italian Campaign*, 363–69.

101. Shepperd, *Italian Campaign*, 369; Report by the Supreme Allied Commander Mediterranean, Field-Marshal the Viscount Alexander of Tunis, to the Combined Chiefs of Staff on the Italian Campaign, 12th December 1944 to 2nd May 1945, 39.

102. Dec. 9th Report, "A" Force, Narrative War Diary, Jan. 1–Dec. 31, 1944, WO 169/24850, 140.

EPILOGUE

1. Dec. 9th Report, "A" Force, Narrative War Diary, Jan. 1–Dec. 31, 1944, WO 169/24850, 140.

2. "Plan 'Playmate,'" Plans—1945, WO 169/24928.

3. Dec. 9th Report, "A" Force, Narrative War Diary, Jan. 1–Dec. 31, 1944, WO 169/24850, 140.

4. Security of Deception, WO 169/24875, NA.

5. Dudley Clarke Papers, Box 99/2/1.

6. Ibid.

7. Dudley Clarke Papers, Box 92/2/2.

8. "June 18th Report, A" Force, Narrative War Diary, Jan. 1–July 18, 1945, WO 169/24851, 27.

9. Security of Deception, WO 169/24875.

10. Dudley Clarke Papers, Box 99/2/2.

11. "Informal Memorandum on the Origin, Development and Activities of the Special (Deception) Section, Joint Security Control, 1942–1945," 4.

12. "Appendix 'D': Letters from Senior US. Commanders," in "Informal Memorandum on the Origin, Development and Activities of the Special (Deception) Section, Joint Security Control, 1942–1945," 65.

13. "Informal Memorandum on the Origin, Development and Activities of the Special (Deception) Section, Joint Security Control, 1942–1945," 15.

14. "Appendix 'D,'" "Informal Memorandum on the Origin, Development and Activities of the Special (Deception) Section, Joint Security Control, 1942–1945."

15. Ibid., 80.

16. Dudley Clarke Papers, Box 99/2/1; emphasis in original.

17. "Plan 'Playmate,'" Plans—1945, WO 169/24928.

18. Clarke, *Seven Assignments*, 262.

19. Dudley Clarke Papers, Box 99/2/2.

20. Ibid.

BIBLIOGRAPHY

ARCHIVAL SOURCES

National Archives, Kew, UK

CAB 81/77—London Controlling Section, L.C.S. (43) & (44) Series

CAB 81/78—London Controlling Section, L.C.S. Series 1944, Feb. to Oct.

CAB 154/6—Detailed Particulars of the Various Devices Employed ("A" Force file No. 29)

CAB 154/7—Signals Deception ("A" Force file No. 30)

CAB 154/30—Channels: SOE

CAB 154/32—Channels: Neutral Diplomats and Attachés

CAB 154/67—Plan Mincemeat

CAB 154/100—Historical Record of Deception in the War against Germany and Italy

CAB 154/101—Historical Record of Deception in the War against Germany and Italy

CAB 154/104—Double Crossing and Deception by J. H. Godfrey

CAB 154/112—Mincemeat: Report by Col. Montagu

PREM 3/117—Prime Minister's Office: Operational Papers and Correspondence— Deception

WO 204/1561—Cover Plans (Deception)

WO 204/1562—Cover Plans (Deception—Zeppelin and Ferdinand)

WO 219/2246—Cover and Deception Policy, Dec. 1943 to Mar. 1945

"A" Force Collection

WO 169/24847—"A" Force Narrative War Diary, Nov. 13, 1940–Dec. 31, 1941

WO 169/24848—"A" Force Narrative War Diary, Jan. 1–Dec. 31, 1942

WO 169/24849—"A" Force Narrative War Diary, Jan. 1–Dec. 31, 1943

WO 169/24850—"A" Force Narrative War Diary, Jan. 1–Dec. 31, 1944

WO 169/24851—"A" Force Narrative War Diary, Jan. 1July 18, 1945

WO 169/24853—1943 War Diary of Tac HQ "A" Force

WO 169/24856—"A" Force Detailed War Diary (Controlling Headquarters)

WO 169/24857—1944 War Diary of Tac HQ "A" Force

WO 169/24858—1945 Papers

WO 169/24866—War Establishment and Organisation

WO 169/24868—"A" Force Technical Unit

WO 169/24869—Development of "A" Force Special Units

WO 169/24870—Developments in Tactical Deception

WO 169/24871—Developments in Strategic Deception

WO 169/24872—Liaison with the London Controlling Section (LCS) and Parallel Organisations

WO 169/24873—Development of the Special Inter-Theatre Communications Procedure

WO 169/24874—Papers Concerning the Theory and Practice of Deception in General

WO 169/24875—Security of Deception

WO 169/24878—Miscellaneous Activities 1943–1944

WO 169/24881—Implementation by Physical ("Ops") Methods in General

WO 169/24882—The Employment of Special Deception Units in the Field

WO 169/24884—Implementation by Most Secret Intelligence Methods in General

WO 169/24891—Middle East Channels in General

WO 169/24898—Case History (V), "Gilbert" (Tunis, 1943–44)

WO 169/24901—Case Histories (VII), Channels in Italy

WO 169/24903—Plan "CAMILLA"

WO 169/24906—Western Desert Plans for 1942

WO 169/24908—Plans Conducted by Tac HQ "A" Force at General Alexander's Army Group HQs during 1943

WO 169/24910—Strategic Plans 1943, Jan.–Mar.

WO 169/24911—Strategic Plans 1943, Apr.–July—Plan Barclay (I)

WO 169/24912—Strategic Plans 1943, Apr.–July—Plan Barclay (II)

WO 169/24913—Strategic Plans 1943, Aug.–Dec.

WO 169/24914—Plans Conducted by Tac HQ "A" Force for General Alexander's Allied Armies in Italy during 1944

WO 169/24915—Strategic Plans 1944 (Jan.–June), Plan "Zeppelin" (I)

WO 169/24916—Strategic Plans 1944 (Jan.–June), Plan "Zeppelin" (II)

WO 169/24917—Strategic Plans 1944 (Jan.–June), Plan "Zeppelin" (III)

WO 169/24918—Zeppelin

WO 169/24919—Strategic Plans 1944 (Jan.–June), Plan "Zeppelin" (IV)

WO 169/24920—Special Landing Craft (Nov. 1943–Aug. 1944)

WO 169/24921—Strategic Plans 1944 (Jan.–June), Plan "Zeppelin" (V), Plan "Turpitude"

WO 169/24922—Strategic Plans 1944 (Jan.–June), Plan "Zeppelin" (VI), Plan "Vendetta"

WO 169/24923—Strategic Plans 1944 (Jan. –June), Plan "Zeppelin" (VII), Plans "Royal Flush," "Dungloe," and "Copperhead"

WO 169/24924—Strategic Plans 1944 (July–Dec.)

WO 169/24926—"Cascade" Order of Battle Plan 1942–1943

WO 169/24927—The Wantage Order of Battle Plan 1944–1945

WO 169/24928—Plans—1945

Joint Security Control

"Informal Memorandum on the Origin, Development and Activities of the Special (Deception) Section, Joint Security Control, 1942–1945"

Appendix "A"—Some Notes on the Organization of Deception in the United States Forces (Dudley Clarke)

Appendix "B"—Directive to Controlling Officer (LCS)

Appendix "C"—Joint U.S. Chiefs of Staff Directive

Appendix "D"—Letters from Senior U.S. Commanders

Appendix "E"—Cover and Deception—Task Force Security

Appendix "F"—Special Section of Joint Security Control

Appendix "G"—(provides a list of American deception officers and personnel)

Imperial War Museum, London, UK

Dudley Clarke Papers, Boxes 99/2/1–3

Raymund Maunsell Papers

David Mure Papers

David Strangeways Oral History, 16755/6/1–6

GOVERNMENT PUBLICATIONS

Ehrman, John. *Grand Strategy*. Vol. 5, *August 1943–September 1944*. London: HMSO, 1956.

Hinsley, F. H. *British Intelligence in the Second World War: Its Influence on Strategy and Operations*, vol. 1. London: HMSO, 1979.

———. *British Intelligence in the Second World War: Its Influence on Strategy and Operations*, vol. 2. London: HMSO, 1981.

Hinsley, F. H., and C. A. G. Simkins. *British Intelligence in the Second World War*. Vol. 4, *Security and Counter-Intelligence*. London: HMSO, 1990.

Howard, Michael. *British Intelligence in the Second World War*. Vol. 5, *Strategic Deception*. London: HMSO, 1990.

————. *Grand Strategy.* Vol. 4, *August 1942–September 1943.* London: HMSO, 1972.

Jackson, General Sir William. *The Mediterranean and Middle East.* Vol. 6, *Victory in the Mediterranean Part II—June to October 1944.* London: HMSO, 2009.

————. *The Mediterranean and Middle East.* Vol. 6, *Victory in the Mediterranean Part III—November 1944 to May 1945.* London: HMSO, 2009.

Matloff, Maurice. *Strategic Planning for Coalition Warfare, 1943–1944.* Washington, D.C.: Office of the Chief of Military History, Department of the Army, 1959.

Molony, Brigadier C. J. C. *The Mediterranean and Middle East.* Vol. 5, *The Campaign in Sicily 1943 and the Campaign in Italy 3rd September to 31st March 1944.* London: HMSO, 1973.

————. *The Mediterranean and Middle East.* Vol. 6, *Victory in the Mediterranean Part I—1st April to 4th June 1944.* London: HMSO, 1984.

Playfair, Major-General I. S. O., and Brigadier C. J. C. Molony. *The Mediterranean and Middle East.* Vol. 4, *The Destruction of the Axis Forces in Africa.* London: HMSO, 1966.

Pogue, Forrest C. *The Supreme Command.* Washington, D.C.: Center for Military History, United States Army, 1996.

Report by the Supreme Allied Commander Mediterranean, Field-Marshal the Viscount Alexander of Tunis, to the Combined Chiefs of Staff on the Italian Campaign, 12th December 1944 to 2nd May 1945. London: HMSO, 1951.

Report by the Supreme Allied Commander Mediterranean to the Combined Chiefs of Staff. *Greece 1944–1945.* London: HMSO, 1949.

PUBLISHED PRIMARY SOURCES

Alanbrooke, Field Marshal Lord. *War Diaries, 1939–1945.* Edited by Alex Danchev and Daniel Todman. Berkeley: University of California Press, 2001.

Blumenson, Martin, ed. *The Patton Papers, 1940–1945.* Boston: Houghton Mifflin, 1974.

Bradley, Omar N., and Clay Blair. *A General's Life.* New York: Simon & Schuster, 1983.

Churchill, Winston S. *Memoirs of the Second World War.* Boston: Houghton Mifflin, 1959.

Clarke, Dudley. *Seven Assignments.* London: Jonathan Cape, 1948.

Eden, Anthony. *The Reckoning: The Memoirs of Anthony Eden, Earl of Avon.* Boston: Houghton Mifflin, 1965.

Eisenhower, Dwight D. *Crusade in Europe.* Baltimore: Johns Hopkins University Press, 1997.

Hesketh, Roger. *Fortitude: The D-Day Deception Campaign.* Woodstock, N.Y.: Overlook Press, 2000.

Kesselring, Albrecht. *The Memoirs of Field-Marshal Kesselring.* Novato, Calif.: Presidio, 1989.

Maskelyn, Jasper. *Magic—Top Secret.* London: Stanley Paul, 1950.

Masterman, J. C. *The Double-Cross System in the War of 1939 to 1945.* New Haven, Conn.: Yale University Press, 1972.

Montagu, Ewen. *The Man Who Never Was: World War II's Boldest Counterintelligence Operation.* Annapolis, Md.: Naval Institute Press, 2001.

Montgomery of Alamein, Field Marshal the Viscount. *El Alamein to the River Sangro*. London: Hutchinson, 1948.

———. *The Memoirs of Field-Marshal Montgomery of Alamein*. Cleveland: World Publishing, 1958.

Morgan, Lieutenant-General Sir Frederick. *Overture to Overlord*. Garden City, N.Y.: Doubleday, 1950.

Mure, David. *Practise to Deceive*. London: William Kimber, 1977.

Parish, Michael Woodbine. *Aegean Adventures 1940–43 and the End of Churchill's Dream*. Sussex, UK: Book Guild, 1993.

Wavell, Field Marshal The Earl Archibald P. Introduction to *Seven Assignments* by Dudley Clarke. London: Jonathan Cape, 1948.

Wild, Noël. Foreword to David Mure, *Master of Deception: Tangled Webs in London and the Middle East*. London: William Kimber, 1980.

Wilson of Libya, Field-Marshal Lord. *Eight Years Overseas, 1939–1947*. London: Hutchinson, 1950.

World War II German Military Studies: A Collection of 213 Special Reports on the Second World War Prepared by Former Officers of the Wehrmacht for the United States Army. Vol. 14: *Part VI: The Mediterranean Theater, Continued*. Edited by Donald S. Detwiler. New York: Garland, 1979.

SECONDARY SOURCES

Beevor, Antony. *D-Day: The Battle for Normandy*. New York: Penguin, 2010.

———. *Stalingrad: The Fateful Siege, 1942–1943*. New York: Penguin, 1998.

Bendeck, Whitney T. *"A" Force: The Origins of British Deception during the Second World War*. Annapolis, Md.: Naval Institute Press, 2013.

Blumenson, Martin. *Anzio: The Gamble That Failed*. Philadelphia: J. B. Lippincott, 1963.

———. *Kasserine Pass: Rommel's Bloody, Climactic Battle for Tunisia*. New York: Cooper Square, 2000.

———. *Sicily: Whose Victory?* New York: Ballantine, 1968.

Breuer, William B. *Deceptions of World War II*. New York: John Wiley & Sons, 2001.

———. *Operation Dragoon: The Allied Invasion of the South of France*. Novato, Calif.: Presidio Press, 1987.

Citino, Robert M. *The Wehrmacht Retreats: Fighting a Lost War, 1943*. Lawrence: University Press of Kansas, 2012.

Craig, William. *Enemy at the Gates: The Battle for Stalingrad*. New York: Penguin, 1973.

Cross, Robin. *Operation Dragoon: The Allied Liberation of the South of France: 1944*. New York: Pegasus, 2019.

Crowdy, Terry. *Deceiving Hitler: Double Cross and Deception in World War II*. Oxford, UK: Osprey, 2008.

Cruickshank, Charles. *Deception in World War II*. Oxford: Oxford University Press, 1979.

D'Este, Carlo. *Bitter Victory: The Battle for Sicily, July–August 1943*. London: William Collins, Sons, 1988.

Denniston, Robin. *Churchill's Secret War: Diplomatic Decrypts, the Foreign Office and Turkey 1942–44*. Stroud, UK: Sutton, 1997.

Deringil, Selim. *Turkish Foreign Policy during the Second World War: An 'Active' Neutrality*. Cambridge: Cambridge University Press, 1989.

Dovey, H. O. "The Eighth Assignment, 1941–1942." *Intelligence and National Security* 11, no. 4 (October 1996): 672–95.

———. "The Eighth Assignment, 1943–1945." *Intelligence and National Security* 12, no. 2 (April 1997): 69–90.

Dunnigan, James F., and Albert A. Nofi. *Victory and Deceit: Dirty Tricks at War*. New York: William Morrow, 1995.

Edgerton, David. *Warfare State: Britain, 1920–1970*. Cambridge: Cambridge University Press, 2006.

Eisenhower, John S. D. *They Fought at Anzio*. Columbia: University of Missouri Press, 2007.

Ellis, John. *Brute Force: Allied Strategy and Tactics in the Second World War*. New York: Viking, 1990.

Ferris, John Robert. *Intelligence and Strategy: Selected Essays*. London: Routledge, 2005.

Foot, M. R. D. *SOE in France: An Account of the Work of the British Special Operations Executive in France, 1940–1944*. New York: Routledge, 2013.

Foot, M. R. D., and J. M. Langley. *MI9: The British Secret Service That Fostered Escape and Evasion, 1939–1945, and Its American Counterpart*. London: Bodley Head, 1979.

French, David. *Raising Churchill's Army: The British Army and the War against Germany, 1919–1945*. Oxford: Oxford University Press, 2000.

Funk, Arthur Layton. *Hidden Ally: The French Resistance, Special Operations, and the Landings in Southern France, 1944*. New York: Greenwood Press, 1992.

Germany and the Second World War, Vol. VIII, Organization and Mobilization in the German Sphere of Power: Wartime Administration. Economy, and Manpower Resources 1942–1944/5. Edited by the Research Institute for Military History, Potsdam, Germany. Oxford: Clarendon Press, 2003.

Glantz, David M., and Jonathan House. *The Stalingrad Trilogy*. Lawrence: University Press of Kansas.

Gooch, John. *Military Deception and Strategic Surprise!* London: Routledge, 2007.

Gooderson, Ian. *A Hard Way to Make a War: The Italian Campaign in the Second World War*. London: Conway, 2008.

Graham, Dominik, and Shelford Bidwell. *Tug of War: The Battle for Italy, 1943–1945*. London: Hodder and Stoughton, 1986.

Handel, Michael. *Intelligence and Military Operations*. Edited by Michael Handel. London: Frank Cass, 1990.

Hargreaves, Andrew. *Special Operation in World War II: British and American Irregular Warfare.* Norman: University of Oklahoma Press, 2013.

Hastings, Max. *Overlord: D-Day and the Battle for Normandy.* London: Michael Joseph, 1984.

Holt, Thaddeus. *The Deceivers: Allied Military Deception in the Second World War.* New York: Scribner, 2004.

Howard, Michael. *The Mediterranean Strategy in the Second World War.* New York: Frederick A. Praeger, 1968.

Jones, Matthew. *Britain, the United States and the Mediterranean War, 1942–44.* London: Macmillan, 1996.

Kroener, Bernhard, Rolf-Dieter Müller, and Hans Umbreit. *Germany in the Second World War.* Vol. 5, *Mobilization of the German Sphere of Power,* pt. 2, *Wartime Administration, Economy, and Manpower Resources, 1942–1944/45.* Oxford: Oxford University Press, 2015.

Lamb, Richard. *War in Italy, 1943–1945: A Brutal Story.* New York: St. Martin's Press, 1994.

Latimer, Jon. *Alamein.* Cambridge, Mass.: Harvard University Press, 2002.

———. *Deception in War: The Art of the Bluff, the Value of Deceit, and the Most Thrilling Episodes of Cunning in Military History, from the Trojan Horse to the Gulf War.* New York: Overlook Press, 2013.

Leitz, Christian. *Sympathy for the Devil: Neutral Europe and Nazi Germany in World War II.* New York: New York University Press, 2001.

Lyons, Michael J. *World War II: A Short History.* 3rd ed. Upper Saddle River, N.J.: Prentice Hall, 1999.

Macintyre, Ben. *Operation Mincemeat: How a Dead Man and a Bizarre Plan Fooled the Nazis and Assured an Allied Victory.* New York: Broadway Books, 2011.

Mack Smith, Denis. *Italy: A Modern History.* Ann Arbor: University of Michigan Press, 1969.

Milner, Marc. *Battle of the Atlantic.* Stroud, UK: Tempus, 2005.

Mure, David. *Master of Deception: Tangled Webs in London and the Middle East.* London: William Kimber, 1980.

O'Reilly, Charles T. *Forgotten Battles: Italy's War of Liberation, 1943–1945.* Lanham, Md.: Lexington, 2001.

Overy, Richard. *Why the Allies Won.* New York: W. W. Norton, 1995.

Pitt, Barrie. *The Crucible of War: The Complete Volumes.* New York: Sharpe, 2019.

Porch, Douglas. *The Path to Victory: The Mediterranean Theater in World War II.* New York: Farrar, Straus, and Giroux, 2004.

Rankin, Nicolas. *A Genius for Deception.* Oxford: Oxford University Press, 2008.

Reit, Seymour. *Masquerade: The Amazing Camouflage Deceptions of World War II.* New York: Hawthorn, 1978.

Rothstein, Hy, and Barton Whaley, eds. *The Art and Science of Military Deception.* Artech House, 2013.

Sebag-Montefiore, Hugh. *Enigma: The Battle for Code.* London: Cassell Military Paperbacks, 2004.

Shepperd, G. A. *The Italian Campaign, 1943–45: A Political and Military Reassessment*. New York: Frederick A. Praeger, 1968.

Smith, Peter C., and Edwin R. Walker. *War in the Aegean: The Campaign for the Eastern Mediterranean in World War II*. Mechanicsburg, Pa.: Stackpole, 2008.

Stafford, David. *Britain and European Resistance, 1940–1945: A Survey of the Special Operations Executive, with Documents*. London: Macmillan, 1980.

Stewart, Andrew, ed. *Operation Dragoon: The Invasion of the South of France, 15 August 1944*. Naval Staff Histories of the Second World War. Solihull, UK: Helion, 2015.

Stoler, Mark A. *Allies and Adversaries: The Joint Chiefs of Staff, the Grand Alliance, and U.S. Strategy in World War II*. Chapel Hill: University of North Carolina Press, 2000.

Strawson, John. *The Italian Campaign*. London: Secker & Warburg, 1987.

Sun-Tzu. *The Art of Warfare*. Translated by Roger T. Ames. New York: Ballantine, 1993.

UK War Office. *The Dieppe Raid: The Combined Operations Assault on Hitler's European Fortress, August 1942: An Official History*. S. Yorkshire, UK: Frontline, 2019.

Verney, Peter. *Anzio 1944: An Unexpected Fury*. London: B. T. Batsford, 1978.

Weber, Frank G. *The Evasive Neutral: Germany, Britain and the Quest for a Turkish Alliance in the Second World War*. Columbia: University of Missouri Press, 1979.

Williams, Andrew. *Battle of the Atlantic: Hitler's Grey Wolves of the Sea and the Allies' Desperate Struggle to Defeat Them*. New York: Basic Books, 2003.

Williams, Heather. *Parachutes, Patriots, and Partisans: The Special Operations Executive and Yugoslavia, 1941–1945*. Madison: University of Wisconsin Press, 2003.

Wilt, Alan F. *The Atlantic Wall: Hitler's Defenses in the West, 1941–1944*. Ames: Iowa State University Press, 1975.

Young, Martin, and Robbie Stamp. *Trojan Horses: Deception Operations in the Second World War*. London: Bodley Head, 1989.

Zuehlke, Mark. *Tragedy at Dieppe: Operation Jubilee, August 19, 1942*. Vancouver: Douglas & McIntyre, 2013.

INDEX

Page numbers in *italic* typeface indicate maps or illustrative matter.

Lightning Source UK Ltd.
Milton Keynes UK
UKHW010745181221
395852UK00002B/13